The Cross and the Rising Sun

The Canadian Protestant Missionary Movement in the Japanese Empire, 1872-1931

THE
CROSS
AND THE
RISING
SUN

The
Canadian
Protestant
Missionary
Movement
in the
Japanese
Empire,
1872-1931

A. HAMISH ION

Wilfrid Laurier University Press

Canadian Cataloguing in Publication Data

Ion, A. Hamish.
   The cross and the rising sun

Includes bibliographical references.

ISBN: 978-1-55458-215-0 (v.1) paperback
ISBN: 978-1-55458-216-7 (v.2) paperback

1. Missions, Canadian—Japan—History.
2. Missions, Canadian—Korea—History.
3. Missions, Canadian—Taiwan—History.
4. Protestant churches—Missions—Japan—History.
5. Protestant churches—Missions—Korea—History.
6. Protestant churches—Missions—Taiwan—History.
I. Title.

BV3445.2.I65 1990   266'.02371052   C90-093683-5

WILFRID LAURIER UNIVERSITY PRESS
Waterloo, Ontario, Canada   N2L 3C5

Cover design by Rick McLaughlin

Printed in Canada

To my wife

Contents

Acknowledgements ix

Preface xi

Illustrations xix

Introduction 1
    Early Missions in Japan 3
    Early Missions in Korea and Taiwan 13

CHAPTER ONE

Home Base and Overseas Missions 18
    Church Union 18
    Missionary Societies 23
    Foreign Missions Secretaries 24
    Canadian Methodists and Anglicans 28
    Women's Missionary Work 29
    Canadian Presbyterians in Korea 31
    Mission in North Taiwan 33

CHAPTER TWO

Early Days in Japan 35
    Bunmei—Kaika and Western Teachers 36
    Canadian Methodist Missionaries 38
    The Shizuoka Band 41

CHAPTER THREE

The Koishikawa Band 51
    From Yokohama to Koishikawa 52
    Cochran at the Dōjinsha School 57
    The Ushigome Church 65

CHAPTER FOUR

Contrasts in Japan and Taiwan 71
    Numazu 72
    Yamanashi Prefecture 76
    The Black-Bearded Barbarian in Taiwan 80
    Christianity in Taiwan and Japan 83

CHAPTER FIVE

Christianization in Japan 87

Eby and Immediate Christianization 88
The Self-Support Band 94
The Japan Conference 97
The Central Tabernacle 99

CHAPTER SIX

Missionary Life in the Japanese Empire 102

Lifestyle of the Missionary 102
Intellectual Pursuits 111

CHAPTER SEVEN

Missionaries and Education 116

Schools for Girls 117
Schools for Boys 125
The Kwansei Gakuin 130
Special Schools 133
Mission Schools in Korea 136
The Taiwan Shoestring 140
The Canadian Contribution 144

CHAPTER EIGHT

Evangelism and Social Work 147

Problems and Opportunities 148
Interdenominational Evangelism 155
Local-Level Evangelism 158
Social Work 162
The Korean Contrast 166
Evangelism in Taiwan 173

CHAPTER NINE

Democracy and Imperialism 178

Missionaries and Japanese Immigration to Canada 180
The Movement toward Democracy 183
Canadian Presbyterians and the Beginnings of
Japanese Rule in Korea 186
The March 1, 1919, Movement 188
The Chientao Intervention 196
The Taiwanese Contrast 208

CHAPTER TEN

Toward the Future 215

Notes 222

Select Bibliography 248

Index 262

Acknowledgements

A great many people have encouraged me over the years in the study and research for this book, and it is my pleasure to be able to thank them publicly. Professor Nobuya Bamba introduced me to the delights and hard work of Japanese studies while I was a student at McGill University. Dr. Gordon Daniels of Sheffield University in England painstakingly supervised the doctoral thesis from which this work began. Professor Matsuzawa Hiroaki of Hokkaido University has been a faithful friend and critic of my work over the years. Professor Sugii Mutsuro of Dōshisha University spent long hours helping me with the intricacies of Japanese Christian history. Professor Takahashi Masao and other members of the Nihon Purotesutanto Shi Kenkyūkai in Tokyo have been most helpful. I am indebted to President Sumiya Mikio and to the members and staff of the Hikaku Bunka Kenkyūjo of Tokyo Joshi Daigaku for their kind assistance in facilitating my research. My colleague at the Royal Military College of Canada, Dr. Keith Neilson, took time off his own writing to read the entire manuscript and to offer valuable suggestions for its improvement.

Professors John Howes of the University of British Columbia and Cyril H. Powles of Trinity College, University of Toronto, have been exceptionally kind to me, unstintingly providing encouragement and valuable advice. Professor Ōta Yuzō of McGill has always been an inspiration for hard work. Dr. W. H. H. and Mrs. Gwen Norman have been a constant source of inspiration and assistance. I would like to thank Constance and Mary Chappell, Canon A. C. Hutchinson, Dr. Horace Underwood, and Dr. Samuel Moffett for their help with private papers.

A particular debt is owed to the archivists at the United Church of Canada Archives, Victoria College, University of Toronto and at the General Synod Archives, The Anglican Church of Canada, in Toronto. The Japan Foundation provided financial support for field research in Japan both as a doctoral and post-doctoral fellow. In addition, the Donner Canadian Foundation, by way of its support of the Canadian Missionaries in East Asia study, also helped to subsidize a recent research trip to Japan. A grant from the Arts Division of the Royal Military College of Canada funded most of the final preparation of the manuscript.

I must also thank Olive Koyama of Wilfrid Laurier University Press for her kind help with editorial matters.

This book has been published with the help of a grant from the Canadian Federation for the Humanities, using funds provided by the Social Sciences and Humanities Research Council of Canada.

A. Hamish Ion

Preface

The vast canon of literature about Christian missions, the extensive archival holdings of the various Missionary Societies, and the extraneous materials held in government archives make the records of the Protestant missionary movement one of the richest veins of information about the history of Canadian-Japanese relations. Compared with the missionary movements from Great Britain and the United States, however, the missionary movement from Canada has attracted little attention. This neglect stems partly from the lack of a purpose for investigating missionary activities abroad and from the lack of a suitable methodological approach in analyzing missionary records.

These problems have been circumvented in this study, for its purpose is to stress the importance of Canadian missionaries in the Japanese Empire as agents of informal relations between Canada and Japan. My approach to the problems of the history of the Canadian missionary experience in the Japanese Empire is an amalgam that owes a good deal to different approaches adopted by other authors. A brief and highly selective look at how other authors have regarded missionary endeavour is useful as a means of pointing out the broader context of the Canadian missionary movement in the Japanese Empire.

Much of what has been written about the history of Canadian missions has been undertaken by missionaries, their families, or mission supporters, largely because publicity was necessary to sustain interest in or support for any missionary endeavour. The bulk of this writing was directed toward a church audience, the most likely group to contribute financial support. Much of it has a puerile tone, for many mission stories were aimed at Sunday school children whose pennies could be more easily garnered than the dollars of their parents. Another highly developed and often quite sophisticated form is the hagiographic biography. The continued success of a mission owed much to a sympathetic biography of one of its pioneer missionaries. Indeed, the exploits of the founder of a mission could turn that missionary into a virtual household name.

Notes for the Preface are found on pp. 222-24.

The British were particularly adept at such hagiography. David Livingstone, the most famous of all nineteenth-century missionaries, became not only a household name but also a Scottish national hero.[1] Mary Slessor of the Calabar mission was another who became well known in the late nineteenth and early twentieth centuries.[2] During that time, a particular mission often became largely associated with the name of a single missionary; J. Hudson Taylor of the China Inland Mission is only one example.[3] Families also often became intimately involved in helping to sustain missions in which their relations had served. Such is clear in the case of the Bickersteth family in England after Edward Bickersteth became British Anglican Bishop of South Toyko in the late 1880s.[4]

Although Canadians were much more reticent than the British when it came to missionary biography, the Canadian Presbyterian mission in north Taiwan cultivated the image of George Leslie Mackay, its pioneer missionary, in order to attract funds.[5] Johnathan Goforth, a Canadian who served in northern China and was deeply influenced by Mackay's example, was another Presbyterian subject of a biography.[6] William J. McKenzie, whose tragic death in Korea in 1895 stimulated the Canadian Presbyterians to open their Korean mission three years later, was the subject of a book.[7] The life and work of another Canadian, Dr. W. J. Hall from Glen Buell, Leeds County, Ontario, who also died in Korea during the early 1890s while serving with the Methodist Episcopal (North) mission, was written by his widow.[8]

The existence of hagiographic biographies is one indication not only of familial commitment, but also of church commitment to a particular mission. It is of some interest, therefore, that Mackay, McKenzie, and Hall were the only Canadian missionaries in what became the Japanese Empire to be the subjects of a major contemporaneous biography. Davidson McDonald, one of the two founding missionaries of the Canadian Methodist mission, and Caroline Macdonald, an independent missionary, were the only two missionaries in Japan who came close to having a biography written about them. In Korea, Malcolm C. Fenwick, another independent missionary, solved the problem by writing his own autobiography.[9] It is not too far-fetched to suggest that a major reason why Canadians in the Japanese Empire did not become subjects of more hagiographic biographies was simply because they were Canadians. In the United States, a broader church constituency allowed the fluent pen of W. E. Griffis, an old Japan hand and a supporter of missions, to write a number of biographies of nineteenth-century American missionaries and their Christian converts in Japan.[10] There was another important reason why Canadians were overlooked. The more exotic the locale and the greater the physical sufferings the missionary endured, the more likely it was that he or she would attract the attention of a biographer. With its headhunting aborigines and tropical diseases, the Taiwan where George Leslie Mackay began working in 1872 was far more dangerous and exotic than the Japan where McDonald went in 1873. And compared to life in China, by the 1870s life in Japan involved no great physical hardship for the missionary. The biographies of Bishop White of Honan, Robert McClure, and James Endicott reveal a China going through exciting revolutionary times,[11] but only recently have the equally daring adventures of the pioneer Canadian Presbyterian missionaries in north Korea attracted biographical attention.[12]

Though the missionaries in Japan may not have been as fortunate as missionaries in other locales in attracting Western biographers, they have been much better treated by the Japanese. There are Japanese biographies of Canadian Anglican missionary John Waller and Canadian Methodist Daniel Norman, which attests to the intense loyalty of their Japanese disciples and their impact on local Japanese history.[13] Although the lack of exoticism meant that mission work in Japan did not fire the imagination of the home constituency (it had little of the drama captured by Andrew Fulton's title for his absorbing history of the Irish Presbyterian mission in Manchuria, *Through Earthquake, Wind and Fire*[14]) the work of missionaries in Japan has attracted the attention of numerous Japanese local historians. Davidson McDonald and George Cochran, the two pioneer Canadian Methodist missionaries, are remembered for their contributions to the welfare of the Japanese at the local level. McDonald has been forgotten in Prince Edward County, Ontario, where he was raised, but he has been remembered in histories of Shizuoka.[15] Charles Bates, another Canadian Methodist who worked in Japan during the early twentieth century, seems to have been forgotten by his alma mater, Queen's University, but he is remembered with great affection at Kwansei Gakuin, the university outside Kobe where he was president for many years. The histories of the educational institutions and churches which Canadians helped to establish in Japan pay great tribute to the work of these missionaries.

Another factor that bears on what has been written about Canadian missionary work in the Japanese Empire is that Canadian missions ceased to be independent organizations in the field at a relatively early date. In 1907, the Canadian Methodist missions joined with the two American Methodist Episcopal missions (North and South) to support the union Japan Methodist Church.[16] Similarly, the Canadian Anglicans, from the beginning of their mission work in Japan in 1888, co-operated with the British and American Anglican missions in supporting the Nihon Seikōkai (Japan Holy Catholic Church). From its beginnings in 1898, the Canadian Presbyterian mission in Korea, which was subsumed under the United Church of Canada by the

Canadian union of 1925, closely co-operated with American Presbyterian missions in the union Korean Presbyterian Church. As the Japanese history of the Nihon Seikōkai reveals, the Canadian contribution to that church is viewed as a part of Anglican history; the Canadian Anglican mission receives no separate treatment.[17] The early histories of the Nihon Seikōkai or its Methodist and Presbyterian counterparts were dominated by British or American missionaries, which means that the Canadian component in all cases has not received the attention it deserves. The one major exception is Kuranaga's history of the Japan Methodist Church.[18] Since 1941, the date which saw the Japanese government-inspired amalgamation of orthodox Protestant denominations into the single Nihon Kirisutokyōdan (Japan United Church), the Canadian Methodist contribution has largely been ignored.[19]

The first English-language history of the missionary movement in Japan is credited to Guido Verbeck, an American Dutch Reformed Church missionary, whose initial survey was published in 1883.[20] Although little more than a list of names, it does mention Canadian missionaries. Otis Cary, the American Mission Board missionary who took on Verbeck's mantle as chronicler of the Protestant missionary movement in the early twentieth century, went little further than Verbeck.[21] Winburn T. Thomas, in his history of the missionary movement in Japan from 1859 to 1889, *Protestant Beginnings in Japan*, pays scant attention to the work of Canadians.[22] Similarly, Charles W. Iglehart and Richard H. Drummond, both authors of more recent and broader histories of Christianity in Japan, barely mention the contribution of Canadian missionaries.[23] From English-language general histories of the Protestant missionary movement or of Christianity in Japan, all that can be gathered is only that Canadian missionaries were in Japan from 1873.

The lack of attention given to the Canadian experience has meant that the Protestant missionary movement has been perceived strictly in terms of the American experience, and the examples used to illustrate the nature of the movement and its reception in Japan have been American. The result has been a uniformity of interpretation, which stresses the primacy of New England Puritanism as seen in the Calvinism of the early American missionaries. As Arminians, as opposed to Calvinists, the Canadian Anglicans and Methodists were theologically different from the majority of American Protestant missionaries, and thus represented a theological, as well as a national, diversity. This point is conveniently overlooked by historians of the Protestant missionary movement.

Although most writing about the missionary movement has been directed toward church supporters, interest in missionary history as an aspect both of the social history of the missionary-sponsoring country and of Western overseas expansionism has increasingly attracted secular historians and social scientists. To some extent, this has been due to the broader academic community accepting the credentials of ex-missionaries such as K. S. Latourette,[24] as historians or social scientists. Of greater importance was the connection which ex-missionaries made between Christian missions and the concerns of the academic community in social history and Western overseas expansionism.

Of special note is the work of the late Canon Max Warren, long-time secretary of the London-based Church Missionary Society, and particularly his two books, *The Missionary Movement from Britain in Modern History* and *Social History and Christian Mission*.[25] In the latter book, Warren stresses the importance of studying Christian missions in their political, social, and economic context.[26] In this respect, Bishop Stephen Neill's *Colonialism and Christian Mission* remains a seminal work.[27] It is by no means coincidental that both Warren and Neill were writing in the early 1960s, when British colonies in Africa were gaining their independence. Although Africa was a prime concern for Warren, it would be wrong to see him as an apologist for African missions. The growing interest of academics in the connection between Christianity and African nationalism, as in George Shepperson and Thomas Price's excellent treatment of John Chilembwe,[28] obliged churchmen such as Warren to write about the missionary movement from a church viewpoint. Neill, like Warren, was primarily concerned with British missionaries. He did not investigate, for instance, the Japanese Empire, because his interest was British colonialism.[29] This is a gap which this study fills, for the Japanese Empire offers an example of missionaries working in colonial circumstances in Korea and Taiwan where the colonial government was not European.

If British academic interest in missionary history owes a great debt to the decolonization process in Africa in the late 1950s and early 1960s, American academic interest in China beginning in the late 1960s reflects the changing attitude toward Chinese history which was part of the reappraisal of the role of the United States in Asia after the Vietnam War. While the British African example saw both ex-missionaries and academics participating in the new appraisal of the missionary movement, the American look at China has been taken almost exclusively by academics. Part of the reason for this might be cultural: the ex-missionary from Oxbridge could be considered an equal by a British academic, but the American academic from Harvard brooks no peers.

The new American approach appeared first in Paul A. Varg's *Missionaries, Chinese and Diplomats*,[30] written in 1958, but the dominating influence since the 1960s has been John King Fairbank and his former Harvard students. As Fairbank pointed out in his introduction to *The*

Missionary Enterprise in China and America, "it is high time that the interactions between China and the United States—the American activities in China, their contributions to Chinese life, and the backflow of aggressive as well as humanitarian attitudes in American policy and folklore—be examined more closely and systematically by scholars."[31]

The work of what might be termed the Fairbank School, illustrated in the monographs of Paul A. Cohen, Ellsworth Carlson, and Irwin T. Hyatt, to mention only three, clearly reveals the impact and importance of the American missionary movement in late nineteenth-century China.[32] James Reed has continued this into the twentieth century by analyzing the missionary mind and American East Asia policy in the immediate aftermath of the 1911 Revolution.[33] Balancing the investigation of American missionaries in China, others, like Valentin H. Rabe, have explored in detail the home base of this American overseas endeavour.[34] Others, such as Jesse G. Lutz, have investigated the missionary movement and its influence on the development of institutions of higher learning in China during the early twentieth century.[35] Jane Hunter has produced an excellent study of female missionaries in turn-of-the-century China which underlines the immense importance of women in the missionary endeavour.[36] What these American academics have shown is the complexity and diversity of the American missionary interaction with China. These authors have done much to relate the missionary movement to the broader issues within Chinese societies and, in the process, have enhanced the academic reputation of missionary studies as a legitimate field of study for the historian and social science specialists of China. Although the impression still remains that the missionary movement has had a pernicious impact on Chinese society as a whole, missionary case studies have shown that generalizations about the role of American missionaries in bringing about damaging changes within Chinese society should be avoided.

This new interest in American China missions might have been expected to stimulate a similar concern about the role of missionaries in United States-Japan relations. This has not been the case, at least partly because there has been no perceived need to reappraise American-Japanese relations, at least in terms of the late nineteenth century. Further, although mission work in China can be interpreted as having had an adverse impact upon Chinese society, the same interpretation cannot be substantiated in terms of Japan. Moreover, just as the interest in missionaries in China can be put under the umbrella of missionaries as Americans and the coming of the Chinese Revolution, the concern in Japan with things Christian might be similarly generalized as an interest in Christianity and the modernization of Japan.

It is some thirty years since Robert S. Schwantes published his study of a century of American-Japanese cultural relations, a work which emphasizes the fact that American missionaries were an influential channel of communication between cultures.[37] This concern with broad cultural contact was not destined to continue as the central issue of American-Japanese relations. By the early 1960s, the mainstream concern became the modernization of Japan, which in itself was a manifestation of an ideological desire to show Japan as a model of capitalistic development for the rash of newly independent African and Asian countries. As a result, there is a difference of emphasis between China and Japan specialists when they look at the missionary movements in their respective regions.

In China, the interest focusses on the missionary as an agent of informal American relations with China, but in Japan the emphasis is on the convert, not the missionary. F. G. Notehelfer's excellent biography of Leroy Janes, an American Board-sponsored lay missionary, or Edward Beauchamp's study of W. E. Griffis, another famous lay missionary teacher, are two examples of academic interest in western Christian workers in Japan.[38] Yet these two studies can also be placed within the parameters of *yatoi* (foreign employee) studies, of which Hazel Jones' *Live Machines* is an outstanding example.[39] *The Modernizers* is the title of a collection of papers Ardath W. Burks edited on overseas students, foreign employees, and Meiji Japan.[40] Westerners are important in so far as they performed a utilitarian function and contributed to the modernization of Japan. Leroy Janes, an American teacher at the Yōgakkō School in Kumamoto, owes his fame to the fact that the leading members of the Kumamoto Band, one of the most famous groups of Japanese Christians, were among his students.[41] Griffis' fame stems from his works interpreting Japan to the West, written after he left Japan, rather than from his actions while in Japan. It is not the missionary per se, but rather the converts he made who are important. Irwin Scheiner's *Christian Conversion and Social Protest in Meiji Japan* was in the mainstream of American academic interest in Christianity in Japan.[42]

Canadian studies have not generally looked at the missionary. John Howes, an authority on the noted Japanese Christian Uchimura Kanzō, sees in Uchimura's struggle to come to terms with being both Christian and Japanese a microcosm of the wider struggle between traditionalism and modernism which confronted Japanese intellectuals after 1868.[43] Similarly, for other academics like Ōta Yuzō and Carlo Caldarola, their concern with Uchimura and the non-church movement is a reflection of their overriding concern with the transmission of Western intellectual ideas to Japan.[44] It is this concern with the history of ideas within Meiji Japan that can also be seen in the change of interest in F. G. Notehelfer's early work from Ebina Danjō, one of the Kumamoto Band Christians, to Kōtoku Shūsui, an early Japanese anarchist.[45] To an extent, then, Christianity in Japan is seen by some scholars as a convenient conduit into the realm of Japanese intellectual history. In contrast to China, the relation of the missionary movement in Japan to the broader issues within the country has not been as clearly made.

There are some exceptions. Cyril H. Powles' book on the British Anglican Shiba Sect missionaries comes closest to dealing with such issues, but Powles dealt with a small group of missionaries over a relatively short period.[46] As far as Canadian works are concerned, both the recent church-sponsored study of the first hundred years of the Japan Mission of the United Church of Canada by Gwen and Howard Norman and William Scott's treatment of the Korean Mission of the United Church of Canada provide, especially in the former case, very detailed information about their particular missions drawn from the United Church of Canada Archives and from personal experience.[47] Both books are modern additions to the older tradition of history written by ex-missionaries, which view missionary history as chronicles of missionary activity and make little reference to the surrounding society. As for the Anglican Church of Canada, no recent book has been published about its mission work in Japan.

Despite what has been written about missionary history in Japan, recent academic writing on missionaries in China show that they represented more than Christian workers in a foreign field, for they were also the informal agents of their own country and civilization.

Illustrations

PLATE

1. George Meacham and the first native preachers xxi
2. Canadian Methodist women missionaries xxi
3. George Cochran xxii
4. Davidson McDonald xxii
5. Charles Eby in later life xxii
6. William McKenzie xxii
7. Tokyo street scene, circa 1885 xxiii
8. Martha J. Cartmell with Tōyō Eiwa Jo Gakkō girls,
   circa 1885 xxiii
9. George Leslie Mackay and his family, circa 1885 xxiv
10. Mackay and his dental assistants, A Hoa and Koa Kau,
    in Taiwan xxiv
11. Wayside meeting at Hagiwara town xxv
12. Deaconess A. L. Archer preaching in Ichinimiya on a
    market day, circa 1919 xxv
13. The old Kofu church xxvi
14. The Canadian Anglican St. John's Church, Nagoya,
    circa 1920 xxvi
15. Principal Kosakai and some boys of the Gifu School for
    the Blind on their annual picnic, circa 1913 xxvii
16. After the confirmation services, Takata, during
    Bishop Hamilton's visit, autumn 1929 xxvii
17. D. M. McRae with language teacher, Wonsan, 1899 xxviii
18. Frank Schofield with an unknown Korean, circa 1919 xxviii
19. W. R. Foote ready to go out itinerating from
    Lungchingtsun xxviii

PLATE 1.—George Meacham and the first native preachers. Seated (left to right) Asagawa Koko (Hiromi), Tsuchiya Hikoroku, Meacham, Yamanaka Emi, Hiraiwa Yoshiyasu; standing: Miyagawa Minoru, Yūki Bunisan, Kobayashi Mitsuyasu (Archives of the United Church of Canada)

PLATE 2.—Canadian Methodist women missionaries: (standing) Miss Isabella Blackmore, Miss L. Hart, Miss K. Morgan; (seated) Mrs. T. A. Large, her daughter Kate, Miss N. Hart, Miss I. Hargrave (Archives of the United Church of Canada)

PLATE 3.—George Cochran
(Archives of the United Church of
Canada)

PLATE 4.—Davidson McDonald
(Archives of the United Church of
Canada)

PLATE 5.—Charles Eby in later life
(Archives of the United Church of
Canada)

PLATE 6.—William McKenzie
(Archives of the United Church of
Canada)

PLATE 7.—Tokyo street scene, circa 1885, with the Tōyō Eiwa Jo Gakkō on the hill (Archives of the United Church of Canada)

PLATE 8.—Martha J. Cartmell with Tōyō Eiwa Jo Gakkō girls, circa 1885 (Archives of the United Church of Canada)

PLATE 9.—George Leslie Mackay and
his family, circa 1885 (Archives of the
United Church of Canada)

PLATE 10.—Mackay and his dental assistants, A Hoa and Koa Kau, in Taiwan
(Archives of the United Church of Canada)

PLATE 11.—Wayside meeting at Hagiwara town. Bishop H. J. Hamilton speaking, Mrs. Hamilton at the organ, the banner up and the hymn book spread; circa 1919 (Anglican Church of Canada/General Synod Archives)

PLATE 12.—Deaconess A. L. Archer preaching in Ichinimiya on a market day, circa 1919 (Anglican Church of Canada/General Synod Archives)

PLATE 13.—The old Kofu church (Archives of the United Church of Canada)

PLATE 14.—The Canadian Anglican St. John's Church, Nagoya, circa 1920 (Anglican Church of Canada/General Synod Archives)

PLATE 15.—Principal Kosakai and some boys of the Gifu School for the Blind on their annual picnic, circa 1913 (Anglican Church of Canada/General Synod Archives)

PLATE 16.—After the confirmation services, Takata, during Bishop Hamilton's visit, autumn 1929. To the bishop's right senior members of the Church Committee: the warden, the president of the Young Men's organization, the president of the Women's Association. Behind the bishop, the Rev. P. S. C. Powles, priest-in-charge, and the Rev. K. Tsukada, deacon (Anglican Church of Canada/General Synod Archives)

PLATE 17.—D. M. McRae with language teacher, Wonsan, 1899 (Archives of the United Church of Canada, McRae Collection)

PLATE 18.—Frank Schofield with an unknown Korean, circa 1919 (Archives of the United Church of Canada)

PLATE 19.—W. R. Foote ready to go out itinerating from Lungching-tsun. Dr. and Mrs. S. H. Martin on the doorstep; circa 1920 (Archives of the United Church of Canada)

Introduction

This book is a study of an epic Canadian adventure in the Japanese Empire — the Protestant missionary movement from Canada to Japan, Korea and Taiwan from its beginnings in 1872 until the Manchurian Crisis of 1931. It deals with Canadian men and women who practised international relations of an informal and personal variety, and whose experiences at "the opposite side of the earth" emphasize the human and humanitarian dimensions within the history of the Canadian-Japanese relationship.

As a group, missionaries represented an early example of Canadians who strove to transcend cultural and linguistic barriers in order to bring peoples of different cultures together. As imperfect as the missionaries' understanding of the peoples of the Japanese Empire might have been, the missionary movement maintained the only continuous contact between Canada and East Asians in the Far East between 1872 and the establishment of the Tokyo Embassy in 1928. The minimal amount of trade between Canada and Japan meant that economic and political involvement did not supply a solid basis upon which to build mutual understanding. Similarly, the deliberate policy to restrict Japanese immigration in order to preserve Canada as a "white man's country" prevented the creation of a Japanese immigrant community in Canada which could act as an alternative means of cultural diffusion between the two countries. Missionaries thus provided the chief links between Canadians and East Asians.

The Protestant missionary movement was a large-scale undertaking for Canadians and a major element in the attempt during the late nineteenth and early twentieth centuries to evangelize the people of East Asia. Only the United States and Great Britain made greater contributions in personnel and money. According to the Canadian Legation in Tokyo, however, by the early 1930s, Canada had more missionaries (if French-Canadian Roman Catholic fathers and sisters are included) in the Japanese Empire — Metropolitan Japan, Korea, and Taiwan — than had any other single country.[1] In East Asia by the

Notes for the Introduction are found on pp. 224-25.

1

early 1930s, only in China did the Canadian missionary movement have fewer numbers. Peter Mitchell and Margo Gewurtz have argued: "for sixty years from the mid-1890s, East Asian countries were the setting for the most significant, sustained Canadian overseas endeavour anywhere in the world. Except for the two world wars, this 'missionary enterprise . . . constituted undoubtedly the largest organized and stable Canadian presence abroad.'"[2] At a different level, the Protestant missionary movement represented the first example of an independent and voluntary Canadian endeavour in Japan, one which served as the harbinger for a broader Canadian involvement with East Asia after 1945.

Before 1931, a missionary from Canada living in a Japanese city was the only Canadian with whom the ordinary Japanese had contact. The missionary served as a living microcosm of Canadian society and the sole conduit for information about Canada for Japanese at the local level. For many Japanese, the memory of Canadian missionaries in their home town in central Japan during the pre-Pacific War era remains a very tenacious one,[3] and a legacy of goodwill toward Canada remains one of the products of the spiritual and secular activities these Canadians who lived in their midst. As far as Canadians at home were concerned, missionary publications and the deputation work of missionaries on furlough were the prime avenues through which Canadians, especially those in rural areas, could learn about things Japanese.

The Canadian Protestant missionary experience is exemplified by the activities of missionaries belonging to the United Church of Canada (and its pre-union Methodist and Presbyterian predecessors), the Anglican Church of Canada, and the Presbyterian Church in Canada. This work concentrates on the experiences of Canadian Methodists and Presbyterians because their numbers were larger and their activities more extensive than those of the Anglicans.

The intention is not to provide a detailed history of these missions and their theology, but rather to analyze the phenomenon of the Canadian missionary movement as a story worth telling, as a significant aspect of Canadian-Japanese relations. Although the prime motive of missionaries in Japan, Korea, and Taiwan was a Christian one, their major importance lies in the link they provided between the Anglo-American world and East Asia.

The majority of Canadian missionaries came from a rural background, most from English or Scottish ancestry. A few, like George Cochran, a Canadian Methodist, were Ulstermen or Irish. The majority of them, particularly the Anglicans and Methodists, came from southern Ontario; some, especially the women missionaries, came from the Maritimes, and Canadian Presbyterians in Korea were almost exclusively drawn from Nova Scotia. Like the Stephen Leacocks or the Sir Andrew McPhails who remained in Canada, missionaries who went to Japan, Korea, and Taiwan in the late nineteenth century were part of a group of upwardly mobile Canadians who were proud of their rural backgrounds. They came from a group of Canadians who, through hard work and self-improvement, freed themselves from the restrictions of rural life to make their way in the wider world.

Reflecting an upbringing that emphasized social progress, equality, and the building of a new society, Canadian missionaries as a group tended to be more egalitarian and democratic, more concerned with social justice and more forward-looking than their British colleagues.[4] Compared with their British counterparts, Canadians had a much weaker identification with Imperial political and cultural extension. On the other side, while Americans wanted to see Japan reformed on the American model, Canadians did not seem as pressing or patronizing. In that sense, they stood, as ever, between the British and the Americans.

EARLY MISSIONS IN JAPAN

The pioneer Canadian missionaries who arrived in Japan in 1873 saw that they could best propagate the gospel by teaching in Japanese schools which were located outside the foreign concessions in the treaty ports. The Christian groups which Davidson McDonald and George Cochran, the first two Canadian Methodist missionaries, helped form in Shizuoka and Tokyo made a Canadian contribution to Christian influence on the intellectual and religious life of early Meiji Japan. But there are other points of interest. Their experiences provide a study of a third national missionary group, an alternative to the better-known British and American missionary movements. The activities of the first Canadian missionaries in Japan, and their interaction with a narrow stratum of Japanese society, also lend themselves to analysis within the general theme of Christianity and the modernization of Meiji Japan.

The rapid pace of Japanese modernization after 1868 meant that, in comparison to China or Korea, the time period during which missionaries were the dominant force within the Japanese Christian movement was much shorter. The crucial point, however, is that the purpose of the missionary movement changed from time to time as it accommodated itself to changes both in the Christian movement and in Japanese society. Irwin Scheiner, in looking at the Japanese Christian movement in the 1870s and 1880s, noted:

> as a result of its cultural identification with the West, Christianity was sought or disdained as national feeling toward things Western either rose or fell. When Christianity was identified with Western

governmental policy toward Japan—even some of the more pro-Western ideologues saw it as an instrument of Western policy—it was dealt with at best as useful in encouraging concessions from the West; and when Japan was at odds with the West it was regarded with distaste.[5]

The experience of Canadian missionaries bears this out: the growth of the Christian movement reflected the pendulum swing of changing attitudes toward the West. Fortunately, during the 1870s when the pioneer Canadian missionaries arrived, national feeling in Japan created an atmosphere that was open to the Christian message. Furthermore, as Professor Scheiner has also pointed out: "evangelization for the missionary was not an isolated task but a part of the entire process of modernization. From this assumption emerged the missionaries' concern not only with religious development but with political, economic and social development as well."[6] Missionary concern for development extended only as far as political, economic, and social change was seen to be beneficial to the spread of Christianity. Missionaries were selective in their support of modernization; they welcomed it so long as change broke down the traditional cultural barriers to Christianity. But modernization did introduce into Japan Western ideas that were inimical to Christianity, such as scientific scepticism, Darwinian and Spencerian evolutionary thought, and Marxism.

Because of the early identification of Canadian Methodists with mission work in Shizuoka and Yamanashi Prefectures, which were the home and stronghold of the former Tokugawa Shogun, Canadian missionaries from the beginning have been associated with the politically defeated and underprivileged. Furthermore, their contact with many former Tokugawa officials, who were involved in scholarly and educational activities, provided the Canadians with an opportunity to help join the work of building a new Japan during the 1870s. George Cochran's baptizing of the great Confucian scholar, Nakamura Masanao, served to symbolize the special relationship between Canadians and Tokugawa supporters. The survivors of the Tokugawa government eventually formed a powerful group of liberal opposition to the Meiji oligarchy. It was in this way, as Matsuzawa Hiroaki has pointed out, that Canadian missionaries came to play an important role in the birth of Japanese liberalism.[7]

Despite their connection to a progressive group within Japanese society, the Canadian Methodist missionaries clearly saw their task not as aiding in the modernization of Japan, but as establishing a strong church organization which would serve as a basis for future Christian development. They were largely successful, although Western domination of the ecclesiastical hierarchy posed serious problems for the long term. Unlike the charismatic missionary heroes of the mid-nineteenth century who opened up new territories for other missionaries, the pioneer Canadian missionaries in Japan were confronted with perhaps the more difficult task of founding churches. In this context, it is significant that the 1870s, when the embryonic missions had yet to put down permanent roots, were the most dynamic years. Much of this early vitality was lost when schools were established in the 1880s and church organization clearly emerged. In a sense, the nature of missionary work changed from the nomadic to the sedentary, with definite mission centres and clear areas of missionary endeavour. In the case of Japan, this change was made all the more dramatic because the climax of missionary influence on Japanese intellectual life clearly came in the 1870s, during the first few years of Canadian missionary work. Although Christian ideas still exerted a significant influence on Japanese intellectual thought over the next fifty years, this influence came from outstanding Japanese Christian leaders rather than from missionaries. However, the relative lack of encouragement given to Japanese members to assume positions of authority in the newly established churches reveals that many missionaries were not fully aware of the decline of their own ability to influence Japanese society outside the confines of the Christian community.

The establishment of mission schools marked the beginning of a change in the relationship of the missionary movement to the indigenous Christian movement and to Japanese society at large. It was an endeavour to eliminate dependency on the whims of individuals and to dissipate the impact of temporary currents within society on mission development. As the possessors and protectors of visible physical plant, the continued existence of the missionary movement was, after the 1880s, linked more closely than before to the Japanese acceptance of Westerners within their midst, in the broadest sense. Missionaries could no longer be removed by the cancellation of individual contracts, but only by the wholesale rejection of everything Western. Missionary investment and commitment in the Japanese Empire was a concrete and integral part of Western relations with Japan. And because of its physical investment in Japan, the missionary movement was cushioned against all but the most extreme reaction of the Japanese against the West.

In the fifty years after 1881, Japanese society underwent a very profound transformation. Underlying it was the process of modernization, industrialization, and urbanization which changed the oriental backwater of Japan of 1881 into one of the world's great military and industrial powers of the 1920s. The progress of Japan was not without its zig-zags, especially in the early 1880s and mid-1890s when anti-Western feeling was pronounced. In the main, however, the rapid emergence of a strong industrial society, in which there were marked tendencies toward democracy and cosmopolitanism (at least by the early 1920s), was beneficial to the mission movement and to the continued gradual growth of the Japanese Christian community.

The sheer rate of progress of the modernization of Japan eventually posed very real difficulties for the missionary movement. As Professor Jesse Lutz has shown in his study of Christian colleges in China, the conflict between missionaries, who viewed the "Christian heritage" as the underlying ethos behind the progress and prosperity of the West, and indigenous "modernizers," who had a broad knowledge of secular thought and refuted this assumption, was not restricted solely to Japan.[8] But because of the very rapid ingestion of Western ideas by the educated classes, Japan was the first country in East Asia where secular Western thought created serious problems for those spreading the Christian message. In 1882, one Canadian Methodist missionary believed that anti-Christian ideas posed a greater challenge to Christianity in Japan than traditional religions.[9] Nonetheless, Canadian missionaries and their British counterparts looked on Japan's efforts to modernize itself with considerable sympathy. A British missionary bishop in the 1880s regarded Japan as the "Britain of the Orient," while a Canadian Methodist publicly advocated the revision of the "unequal treaties" and the termination of extraterritoriality.[10] Yet by the end of the nineteenth century, modernization was beginning to cause problems for the missionary movement. One of the most obvious areas of missionary endeavour that was affected by the modernization of Japan was education.

Nowhere else in East Asia during the late nineteenth century were Christian educational institutions forced to comply with curriculum regulations promulgated by a central government. These same schools were confronted with high-quality competition from government and secular private institutions, a difficulty exacerbated by the limitations of missionary work in Japan compared with other Far Eastern mission fields. For example, medical work, which was an important tool in China, could not be fully exploited in Japan because of the high standard of Japanese medicine. Even more important, the high literacy rate in Japan meant that the Christian message could not be propagated in simplistic terms.

This high rate of literacy posed serious problems for Canadian missions. Although the Congregational and Presbyterian churches in Japan possessed a significant group of Japanese leaders, the Anglican and Methodist churches established by British and Canadian missionaries had no comparable depth of local leadership. Due to the shortage of outstanding leaders after the 1880s, the Nihon Seikōkai (NSKK) (Japan Holy Catholic Church), and the Canadian-sponsored Japan Methodist Church were never in the forefront of intellectual activity. This factor was important because much of the effort of Canadian missions was directed toward the evangelization of students in metropolitan areas.

Chance may have played a part in the dearth of outstanding local leaders in Christian missions, for the most prominent Japanese Christians emerged from only two or three bands of converts. But there were other factors as well. Unlike in larger American non-Conformist missions, there was relatively little scope in British and Canadian missions for the emergence of Japanese leaders. There were few positions of authority, such as magazine editorships or school principalships, outside the ecclesiastical structure; the bishops and archdeacons in the NSKK were always Westerners, and in the case of the Methodists, it was only at the turn of the century that a Japanese became president of the Japan Conference. Especially for the British Anglican missions, their close identification with Britain was also a liability. To become an Anglican convert through British missionaries was to become identified as an Anglophile, and pro-British sentiment during this period was not always high. Although Canadian Methodists were not so closely identified with a powerful imperial nation, their mission church was an integral part of a Canadian church which was controlled by non-Japanese.

Despite these problems, Canadian Anglican and Methodist attitudes toward Japanese culture were often more tolerant than those of many other missionaries. In his study of the High Anglican Shiba Sect, which included Canadian Archdeacon A. C. Shaw, Cyril Powles noted that they furnished "an early example of a group which recognized and practised cultural and intellectual pluralism."[11] In a sense, Shaw's cultural tolerance was not only a reflection of denomination but also a result of social background. Rural Ontario provided Canadian missionaries with the springboard for a much more positive and humanitarian approach to Japanese society than British High Anglicans demonstrated.

By the turn of the century, there was a definite change in emphasis in Canadian Methodist approaches to Japan. The first Canadian Methodists came to Japan "to extend the Gospel of the Grace of God to the millions who are so destitute of the knowledge of Salvation."[12] By the 1900s, this narrow emphasis had begun to change into a broader concern which saw conversion of the "heathen" as the means of promoting humanitarianism in an improved society. In part, this change reflected the realization among missionaries in the field that the Christian message alone could make little progress in the alien society of Japan unless the traditional values of that society were transformed.

While Canadian missionaries were moving toward greater accommodation with Japanese culture and traditional religions, their influence on the Christian movement in Japan declined. The number of Japanese Protestants was destined to remain small, as few as 172,627 in 1928, and was confined to urban areas. However, the influence of Protestantism on Japanese society was far greater than the statistics suggest and can be traced largely to the impact of outstanding Japanese Christians rather than to the pervasive appeal of the Christian message.

The Japanese Christian movement was characterized by groups of followers centred around charismatic leaders and represented a largely independent Christian movement. Japanese Christians held varying attitudes toward missionaries. Uchimura Kanzō, one of Japan's most outstanding Christian leaders, criticized Western missionaries who taught not only Christianity but also "Christian civilization."[13] He had the highest regard, however, both for Bishop M. C. Harris of the Methodist Episcopal Church North, who was instrumental in his conversion, and later for the great Anglo-Catholic monk Herbert Kelly. The Japanese admired the first generation of missionaries for their learning and intellectual breadth. The generation of missionaries, who were products of the student volunteer movement and missionaries by vocation, did not seem as wise and learned as their predecessors, at least in the eyes of a mature Uchimura. In contrast, some Japanese Christian leaders like J. S. Motoda, the first Japanese Anglican Bishop of Tokyo, still felt during the 1920s that missionaries were needed.[14] For their part, missionaries continued to regard themselves as important in the development of the Japanese Christian movement.

By 1905, Japanese Christian leaders had already gained a respected position in international Christian circles and were represented at all major missionary conferences, including the Pan-Anglican Conference at Lambeth in 1907 and the World Missionary Conference in Edinburgh in 1910. In 1907, Tokyo was the first Asian venue for a World's Student Christian Federation Conference, during which the Japanese government, by no means an advocate of Christianity, extended its hospitality in order to gain international esteem. In 1913, John R. Mott, the American YMCA statesman, wrote of Christian prospects in Japan that "this field, like China, is dead-ripe unto harvest."[15] In 1920, Tokyo hosted the Conference of the World Sunday School Association, during which every effort was made by Japanese politicians and businessmen to give a favourable impression of Japan to a wide international public. For its part, the international Christian community openly and warmly welcomed the Japanese Christian movement and its leaders, largely because it assumed that, if Japan became Christianized, most of the Far East would follow.[16]

For many Japanese Christian leaders, recognition and respectability in Japan were extremely important. Certainly, they were for Kozaki Hiromichi; his autobiography features all the influential Japanese politicians, businessmen, and intellectuals he knew.[17] Christianity was officially banned until 1889 and was not regarded as respectable by many Japanese during the late nineteenth century.[18] This was partially due to scepticism concerning the loyalty of Christians to Japan and the antipathy of Christianity to Buddhism and Shintō. At a more profound level, Christianity and later Marxism were regarded as heterodox disciplines in conflict with the Japanese intellectual tradition and the new orthodoxy of *Tennō-sei* (the Emperor system) which developed after 1899. In the context of their own society and its values, Japanese Christians were outsiders, representing a heterodox alternative. Many Christian leaders sought to remove this stigma by accommodating themselves to Japanese society, which meant that the Christian movement tended to align itself with the Japanese status quo. During the late nineteenth century, the Christian movement had been identified with opposition to the government; after 1905, it was largely unable to attract those who were opposed to the status quo.

In 1913, Christians, Buddhists, and Shintōists joined together at the invitation of the Home Ministry for the Three Religions Conference in Tokyo. While some Christians, especially the High Anglicans, remained sceptical of this rapprochement with other major religions, the participation of Christian leaders in this conference, which was convened to discuss ways in which religion could improve the "moral climate" of Japan, was a sign of government recognition of Christianity as one of Japan's major religions. More than that, it was a sign of the growing respectability of the Christian leadership.

By the 1920s, the Japanese Christian movement was highly organized on both a denominational and an interdenominational level. The climax of the ecumenical movement in Japan came in 1923 with the formation of the National Christian Council, which included not only most Protestant denominations, but also Christian schools, social institutions, the YMCA, YWCA, and the WCTU (Women's Christian Temperance Union). The Japanese Christian movement, despite its small numbers, reflected both the denominational structure of Christianity in the West and its auxiliary Christian organizations, such as the YMCA and the Red Cross. Though it was almost inevitable that the major Christian organizations and associations would enter Japan along with denominational Christianity, the sophistication of the Japanese Christian movement reflected the highly developed society in which it worked.

Despite its complex infrastructure and the desire of its conservative majority to acquire respectability, the Japanese Christian movement did at times link itself with movements for social change. And its leaders were prepared to suffer the consequences of taking stands on issues. Uchimura Kanzō and Uemura Masahisa, for example, opposed on pacifist grounds the Russo-Japanese War.[19] In 1911, Uemura conducted a memorial service for Ōishi Seinisuke, a member of his congregation in Tokyo and one of the conspirators executed with Kōtoku Shūsui for allegedly plotting the Emperor's assassination. For many of the Japanese Christians influenced by liberal theological views, Christianity represented a set of principles from which they hoped to construct political doctrines and measures; for some, it was the foundation of the political doctrine of democracy and the fundamental principle behind their pursuit of universal manhood suffrage.[20] The most important Japanese Christian theorist of democracy was Yoshino Sakuzō, the Tokyo Imperial University professor who was a member of Ebina Danjō's famous Hongō Church. Located near the Imperial University, the Hongō Church was a major centre of Christian intellectual activity. In 1919, when Yoshino discussed his conception of democracy and Christianity, he noted that Christian humanism based on universal brotherhood was the banner for the creation of a new world.[21] To him, there was an intimate relationship between democracy and Christianity, one that emphasized personalism and individual rights. Yoshino possessed an optimistic view of human nature and a conviction of the perfectability of human beings through evolutionary progress.

One of Yoshino's students, Imanaka Tsugumaro, who later became a professor at Kyūshū Imperial University, was another member of the Hongō Church interested in the formulation of new political theories. In 1920, he advocated combining Christianity, Marxism, and a representative legislature in happy co-existence and co-operation.[22] Yoshino was not capable of making such a synthesis because his Christian idea of universal brotherhood prevented a compromise with Marxism's belief in an inevitable class struggle. The nettle of class struggle would cause problems for Christian reformers both in Japan and in Korea. Ultimately, since Christians refused to condone class struggle, Marxism eventually overshadowed Christianity in movements for social and political reform.

Some Christians were deeply involved in the genesis of the labour and socialist movements in Japan. Suzuki Bunji, who founded the Yūaikai (one of Japan's first labour associations) in 1912, was closely connected to the Hongō Church. The role of Christianity and Christians in social movements was largely one of heightening social awareness of certain problems and providing the initial leadership for new organizations. As Sumiya Mikio has pointed out, in the working-class and socialist movements, the main objectives were individual freedom and social reform, ideals shared with Christianity. Social reform was not as strong an element in Christianity as it was in socialism, however, thus Christianity's influence on the socialist movement declined.[23] By 1920, the Japanese labour movement was being led more by socialist ideals than by Christian ones.

Christian influence was important in rural as well as in urban movements. Kagawa Toyohiko and Sugiyama Motojirō were two Christians who were important in the initial organization of tenant-farmer associations. Kagawa's social Christianity stressed the participation of Christians in social problems, and for him this meant actively helping to improve the conditions of the poor and underprivileged. In 1922, he helped found the Japan Farmers' Union, which became the national organization for the tenant-farmer associations.[24]

A number of the early leaders of the Japanese socialist movement were Christians or were influenced by Christianity. Among them was Katayama Sen, who in 1897 opened Kingsley Hall in Tokyo as an "institutional expression of concern for the problems of labour."[25] In 1901, Japan's first socialist party, the Shakai Minshutō, was formed by six men, five of them active Christian pastors or laymen. One was Abe Isoo, a Congregationalist pastor in Okayama who had studied at the Hartford Theological Seminary in Connecticut where he was introduced to the ideas of Christian socialism. Abe came to believe that only socialism could fully provide the solution to the problems of the needy and the oppressed in Japan.[26] In 1925, Abe Isoo, Suzuki Bunji, Katayama Tetsu, and Kagawa Toyohiko were among the founders of a second Shakai Minshutō, a forerunner of the present Japan Socialist Party.

In the years following the First World War when the socialist movement was revitalized, it was dominated by individuals and groups who expressed increasingly radical views. Christian socialism was too moderate to exert an influence on them. As well as this reforming activity on the part of Christians, the Japanese Christian movement, throughout the first three decades of the twentieth century, strove primarily to gain respectability. The Christian socialists and political activists themselves often confronted the hostility of their fellow Christians who disapproved of upsetting the status quo. In the face of disapproval from the group, it was difficult to be social and political activists and remain Christian.

As it was, the leading Christian reformers belonged to organizations or churches that had little or no contact with Canadian missionaries, largely because the Canadian missionary movement did not contribute many influential figures to the Japanese Christian movement. Those Japanese Christian leaders with whom they did have contact tended to be those like Nitobe Inazō who acted as bridges between Japan and the outside world. During the 1930s, Canadians, as well as other Western missionaries, looked to Kagawa Toyohiko, a very different type of figure from the establishment-linked Christian leader whom the missionary movement normally favoured, to serve as an emblematic figure for the Japan Christian movement. This change was perhaps a result of the findings of the Laymen's Commission on Christian Missions which had investigated the Japan mission field in 1931. The commission had concluded that missionaries lacked understanding and knowledge of the effects of industrialization and urbanization. Kagawa, the social activist who had devoted many years to working among the slum dwellers of Osaka, was an ideal Japanese Christian for the missionary movement to project abroad because he was knowledgeable about the type of social problems that the Laymen's Commission considered relevant.[27]

The main contact between the Canadian missionary movement and the Japan Christian movement centred around evangelical campaigns, of which the three-year campaign organized by the Edinburgh Conference Continuation Committee between 1913 and 1916 is a prime example. In the main, however, the activities of Canadian missionaries were removed from those of the Japan Christian movement; the Canadians normally functioned within the confines of their own mission and its institutions. Missionaries were observers of, rather than participants in, the endeavours of the Japan Christian movement.

This is not to say that the work of missionaries was unimportant. Caroline Macdonald, a YWCA worker, became one of the most famous Western missionaries in Japan because of her prison work.[28] Canadian Methodist work in the slums of Tokyo during the 1920s brought attention to very severe social problems which had been largely ignored by the authorities. Yet Canadian work was limited because of shortage of personnel and funding. The educational institutions that the Canadians had established continued to flourish, but here as well scarcity of money and competition from both government and other private schools meant that Canadians were hard-pressed. The pace of change in modern Japan meant that missions run on a shoestring had a very difficult time maintaining government standards in their educational work.

Fortunately, the missionary movement did not have to justify its existence in terms of success or failure or productivity, for missionary work was undertaken as much for the benefit of the missionaries themselves and the home church as it was for the Japanese. It was all to the good if missionaries were able to report back to Toronto that their mission work was growing by leaps and bounds. In the final analysis, however, that did not matter. What mattered was the link between the Canadian church and the expansion of Christianity in the Japanese Empire. As the years passed, this link between Canada and Japan took on a momentum of its own, a captive of its own history. The missionaries were perpetually optimistic that the Christianization of the Japanese Empire would come about in the near future, but it was a forlorn hope. Yet the missionary movement from Canada was very much about strength of spirit and test of energy as manifested in Christian service overseas. Adversity quickened the spirit.

EARLY MISSIONS IN KOREA AND TAIWAN

American missionary work began in Korea in the early 1880s, following the opening of the "Hermit Kingdom" to Western intrusion. As in Japan, however, it was a number of years—in fact, not until the early 1900s—before there was a sizable flock of converts. It was in northern Korea where the missionary movement made its greatest early gains. While the capital city of Seoul became a major centre for Christian education and church administration, Korean Christianity maintained, until the end of the Pacific War, its strong northern bias, and P'yongyang remained a key Christian stronghold. Unlike Japan, Korean Christianity derived much of its strength from rural constituencies. In sharp contrast to Japan, following the great revival of the mid-1900s, Korea captured the imagination of the world missionary movement as a country that might perhaps be Christianized. Indeed, the missionary movement was more successful in Korea than in any other part of East Asia in converting a significant percentage of the local population to Christianity.

Although independent Canadian missionaries sponsored by student groups at the University of Toronto began to arrive in Korea in the late 1880s, at the same time as the first Canadian Anglican missionaries in Japan, it was not until 1898 that the Canadian Presbyterian Church formally established its mission in Korea. Canadian Presbyterians found themselves responsible for Christian work in the part of northwestern Korea bounded by the Tumen River, an area which was extended in 1911 to include work among Koreans in the Kantō (Chientao) province of Manchuria. From the start, the Canadians worked in close co-operation with the various American and Australian Presbyterian missions within the context of the Korean Presbyterian Church. Starting some twenty years after the work had begun in Japan, and long after missionary endeavour had commenced in China, the missionaries in Korea were able to take advantage of accumulated missionary experience. Thus, from the beginning, missionaries in Korea approached their mission work more scientifically than had the pioneers in either Japan or China. At the same time, however, the educational level of the Koreans was much lower than that of the Japanese, so that the Christian message propagated in Korea was necessarily a much simpler one than that propagated in Japan. In Korea, as in China, the slower pace of modernization meant that the jack-of-all-trades era lasted much longer there than it did in Japan. While the situations were different, as far as the background of missionaries was concerned, the Korea missionaries belonged to the same group of student volunteers who provided the institutional builders in Japan.

There was a definite time lag in what missionaries were doing in Japan and in Korea. It was only in the late 1910s that missionary educators emerged as a recognized specialization in Korea, a function which had already existed in Japan for some twenty-five years. Japan's annexation of Korea in 1910 marked the beginning of a modernization drive by the Japanese authorities; in Korea this created the same sort of pressure for missionaries to improve their educational and medical facilities as they had faced in Japan thirty years before. The position of mission schools and the quality and content of their education, which had been an issue between missionaries and the educational authorities in Japan during the 1890s, became an important issue between missionaries in Korea and the Japanese Government-General of Chōsen (Korea) in the 1910s. Once Korea had been annexed by Japan, the missionary movement confronted the same question it had faced in metropolitan Japan from the 1880s onward: how the impact of modernization would affect their mission work.

Although many of the same problems occurred in Korea as had earlier appeared in Japan, there were also profound differences. Japanese Christian leaders were at the forefront in meeting the challenges posed to the freedom of action of the Christian movement by government edicts. While a Korean Christian leadership did emerge with the same responsibility for evangelization as their counterparts in Japan, Korean Christian leadership (because they were colonial subjects of the Japanese) were at a profound disadvantage when it came to dealing with the Government-General. Missionaries, in their self-appointed role as defenders of Korean rights, found themselves in a much more exposed position politically. This was a role which disappeared for Japan missionaries after the 1880s.

Criticism of the Japanese colonial authorities came to a head with the Japanese atrocities against Korean demonstrators during the nationwide independence demonstrations of March 1919. Of all Western missionaries, Canadian Presbyterians were the most outspoken and critical of Japanese actions. In 1920, Canadian missionaries vigorously condemned the actions of the Japanese military against Koreans during the Kantō (Chientao) Punitive Expedition. Just as Canadian Methodist missionaries in Japan found themselves helping the underprivileged and politically deprived, Canadians in Korea found themselves identifying with the Koreans against the oppressive Japanese colonial authorities. By the 1920s, Canadian missionaries in Japan and Korea, while sharing common values and especially a strong belief in democracy, held dramatically different views of the Japanese. The missionaries in Japan were pro-Japanese and looked with great sympathy on the development of democracy in metropolitan Japan. The Korea missionaries were violently anti-Japanese and looked with anger on the oppressive nature of Japanese rule in Korea.

If Korea posed special problems for missionaries because of their response to Japanese colonialism, Taiwan represented an even more different experience. Canadian Presbyterian missionary work in north Taiwan began in 1872, a year before the Canadian Methodists started their work in Japan. Just as the intellectual tradition in Japan proved an insurmountable barrier to Christian growth, the traditional culture and family organization of the Chinese population in Taiwan meant that few Taiwanese would become Christian. The annexation of Taiwan by the Japanese in 1895 was welcomed by the English and Canadian Presbyterian missionaries working on the island, for it meant the end of the despised Chinese officialdom. Likewise, Japanese rule brought with it the hope that traditional Chinese resistance to Christianity might be weakened. It did not work precisely that way. As in Japan and Korea, the missionary movement in Taiwan confronted the impact of Japanese modernization.

Until the 1930s, there was little sense of a distinct Taiwanese nationalism, and virtually no feeling of mainland Chinese nationalism existed. Indigenous nationalism, so important to the development of the Christian movement in Korea, was not present in Taiwan. Japanese colonialism provoked less resistance among the Taiwanese than among Koreans. The Japanese colonial overlords in Taiwan possessed obvious advantages over their counterparts in the peninsula. Taiwan was an island with a population of only three million, and it was semi-tropical with rich agricultural land, which meant that the population was never in danger of starving no matter how much agricultural tribute Japan exacted. Indeed, Japanese colonialism brought increased material prosperity to Taiwan; by 1941, Taiwan possessed the second highest standard of living in East Asia, after Japan.

The Japanese rulers, both in Korea and in Taiwan, made positive strides in the fields of medicine and public health, but here the similarity ended. In communications, port development, and urban planning, as well as in agriculture, the Koreans, in contrast to the Taiwanese, gained little material benefit from Japanese colonialism. The stimulus of Japanese colonialism served to draw Koreans to Christianity; there was no such stimulation in Taiwan. As the Japanese in Taiwan began to institute primary school education and to develop government hospitals and public health facilities, the few mission schools found themselves faced with very serious competition. Missionaries lacked the finances to improve their facilities and were also confronted with a lack of local demand for their Western-style educational alternatives.

The Canadian Presbyterian mission in Taiwan was very small. For the first twenty years of its existence, it was really the domain of one missionary, George Leslie Mackay. The missionary movement in Taiwan was too small to have the visible impact that it had in Korea or Japan. Yet the challenge of Taiwan, while vividly illustrating the weakness of the missionary movement when faced with a colonial government dedicated to modernization, also revealed a very positive side of the missionary movement: unusual circumstances highlighted the sterling qualities that many missionaries possessed.

What happened in the Japanese Empire differed from what took place in Japan, largely because of cultural, political, economic, and religious differences. Even though the response was different, missionaries in Korea in the late nineteenth century were confronted with many of the problems that had faced missionaries in Japan some twenty years before. After 1895 in Taiwan and 1910 in Korea, missionaries encountered the same challenges as their counterparts in Japan: dealing with the modernizing policies of the Japanese authorities. It is the difference in response to Japanese actions in metropolitan Japan and in the two colonies which is important in determining the Canadian experience in the Japanese Empire. What happened to the missionary movement in Korea and Taiwan cannot be divorced from what occurred in Japan proper. The perception of the Japanese held by the Canadian Missionary Societies was conditioned by events in Korea and Taiwan as much as it was by what was going on in Japan. Unflattering though this perception might be to the Japanese, this overall impression is important in the final assessment of the Canadian missionary experience in the Japanese Empire.

To see a unity in the three different mission fields in the missionary response to Japanese rule emphasizes the important fact that the missionary movement was separate from the indigenous Christian movements in those three regions. A duality existed in the propagation of Christianity in the Japanese Empire; the concerns of the missionary movement directed from Toronto were often different from those of the indigenous Christian movement whose concerns reflected the nationalistic and cultural proclivities of its membership. As the missionary movement developed, its separation from the indigenous Christian movement became increasingly pronounced. What emerges as one of the central issues over the whole period from 1872 to 1931 is the response of the missionary movement to the Japanese Empire as well as missionary influence and impact upon the Japanese, Koreans, and Taiwanese. As an act of Christian service, the missionary movement was directed toward the peoples of the Japanese Empire, but it also proved beneficial to the Canadians who participated in it.

It is clear that, from the beginning, the missionary movement had little chance of achieving its goal of Christianizing the Japanese Empire. This was the result, not of a lack of effort on the part of Canadian missionaries, but of the fact that their movement was captive to broader political and cultural forces. They had to contend with the traditional intellectual forces and the new nationalisms that emerged under the pressures of modernization, pressures that differed in each of the three areas. Ultimately, the challenges would prove too great for a voluntary movement with limited resources. When the movement began in the late nineteenth century, however, there was genuine hope and confidence that the missionaries would be able to Christianize the Japanese Empire.

CHAPTER ONE

Home Base and Overseas Missions

The Protestant churches in Canada underwent profound changes between 1872 and 1931; until the creation of the United Church of Canada in 1925, there was an almost continuous process of union and amalgamation. Although church union, both denominational and interdenominational, had important consequences for mission work in the Japanese Empire, the missionary movement itself maintained a remarkable degree of continuity. The structure of the home bases of the missions remained virtually unchanged, and most of those in charge of the home organizations remained at the helm.

CHURCH UNION

Presbyterians and Wesleyan Methodists from Nova Scotia, New Brunswick, Ontario, and Quebec were already involved in overseas mission work when the process of church union and amalgamation began in the 1870s. Maritimers had the early advantage; their ship-building industry and trading relations gave them a broad knowledge of the world beyond their shores. Maritime Presbyterians began mission work in the New Hebrides as early as 1846; in 1868, they opened a mission in Trinidad. Four years later, in 1872, Presbyterians in Ontario and Quebec entered the field with an overseas mission in north Taiwan. In 1873, the Wesleyan Methodist Church, which was based in Ontario and Quebec, opened its mission in Japan.

Then began the process of union and amalgamation for both the Presbyterians and the Wesleyan Methodists. In 1874, all the Presbyterian churches in the new dominations were incorporated under one general assembly.[1] Missionary work remained under the jurisdiction of the regional assemblies. Thus it was that the Foreign Missions Commit-

---

Notes for Chapter One are found on pp. 225-27.

tee of the Maritimes Division of the Presbyterian Church in Canada set
up its own mission in Korea in 1898, but by 1908, it was requesting help
from the Western Division. Six years later, in 1914, Presbyterian missionary work was amalgamated under one mission committee head-
quartered in Toronto. The year 1874 also saw the creation of the
Methodist Church of Canada which united the Wesleyan Methodist
Church in Canada, the New Connexion Methodist Church, and the
Conference of Wesleyan Methodists of Eastern British America. The
new church took over the responsibility for the missions in Newfoundland and Bermuda which had been established by the Methodists of
Eastern British America.[2] In 1882, the Methodist Episcopal Church of
Canada amalgamated with the Methodist Church of Canada, further
strengthening the church in Ontario.

Canadian Anglicans were quicker to link the Maritimes and the
Canadas together. In 1860, the ecclesiastical province of Canada was
created and included all dioceses in Canada West, Canada East, Nova
Scotia, and Fredericton.[3] It was not until 1893 that the Church of
England in Canada took responsibility for the missionary dioceses in
the North-West, thus creating a church that stretched from the Atlantic
to the Pacific. Like their British colleagues, the Canadian Anglican
missionary clergy reflected the High and Low Church proclivities, in
this case, of Trinity and Wycliffe colleges. In Canada, Anglican missionary activities were joined together in a single Missionary Society in 1901.
But in Japan, High and Low churchmen worked in separate areas
until 1912, when the two branches were joined with the establishment
of a Canadian missionary diocese of Mid-Japan under Bishop Heber
James Hamilton.

If Canadian missionary work in the Japanese Empire was a benefi-
ciary of the gradual rationalization of the home missionary organization, it was not overseas missionary work but the challenges of missionary work in the Canadian west that helped bring about this change.
Confederation in 1867 brought with it the possibility of Canadian
expansion to the Pacific coast. After Confederation, the missionary
challenge of western Canada became the overriding concern of Canadian churches,[4] a challenge created by the influx of many different
nationalities and faiths into the prairies and the Pacific coastal regions
of British Columbia.[5] As Home Mission Boards of the Canadian
churches were tackling this problem, they were simultaneously faced in
eastern Canada with severe problems posed by urbanization, which
was undermining denominations that traditionally had derived their
support from rural constituencies. H. H. Walsh, the church historian,
has noted that "next to Confederation, the opening of the west ranks as
one of Canada's greatest accomplishments, and not the least achievement of the Canadian Churches has been the keeping abreast with

Canada's immigrant population on the western frontier."[6] The union of the Methodist, Presbyterian, and Congregational churches in 1925, forming the United Church of Canada, was in part caused by a desire to facilitate this work in western Canada.

Union brought the Canadian Methodist and Presbyterian missions in Japan and Korea under one central United Church Missionary Society in Toronto. The Presbyterian mission in north Taiwan chose to remain outside church union and retained its connection with the rump of the Presbyterian Church in Canada. In both Japan and Korea, the Canadian missionaries continued to work with the Methodist and Presbyterian churches they had traditionally supported. There was no attempt—indeed, by 1925 it was impracticable—for the missions in Japan and Korea to join together as a single United Church unit. In that sense, missionary activity after 1925 continued the separate denominational streams that had disappeared in Canada.

The process of union in Canada was mirrored by mission union in the Japanese Empire, again along denominational lines, which meant amalgamating the Japanese converts of various different missions into an independent Japanese church. Union meant also that missions would co-operate with each other in support of this united independent church. Union did not mean, however, that individual missions lost either their autonomy or the control of funds sent to them from abroad. It was an age in the mission field, as well as in Canada, that saw strength in numbers achieved through union.

The negative aspect of union, which was especially true for the smaller groups, was the loss of intimate identification between individual missions and the larger united body. Aware of this problem, the Canadian Methodist authorities in Toronto for a long time resisted the idea that their missionaries in Japan should co-operate in supporting a united Japan Methodist Church with the two American Methodist Episcopal missions working there. Despite the desire of both Canadian missionaries and their Japanese converts, who saw nothing but benefit arising from the pooling of Methodist missionary effort to help a single Japanese Methodist Church, for some eighteen years Alexander Sutherland, Secretary of the Methodist Church of Canada Missionary Society in Toronto, and Albert Carman, General Superintendent of the Methodist Church of Canada, were able to thwart a Canadian-American missionary union, a definite sign of their great influence and power within the home-church structure. Sutherland believed that the creation of a church in Japan that was an integral part of the Methodist Church of Canada provided a clear identification between Canadians and Japanese, encouraging those at home to donate money for missionary work in Japan. This incentive would be lost if the Canadian Methodists joined with the American Episcopal Methodists. Carman wished to retain the Canadian Methodist mission in Japan as a part of the home church to avoid the conflicts that American Board (Congregationalist) missionaries had encountered with the Kumiai Church, which was independent and outside of American Board control, over the management of Dōshisha College in Kyoto.[7]

Carman feared that there would be difficulties with the Japanese leaders of an independent Japan Methodist Church over mission property; he also feared that there would be theological difficulties because of differences between the Wesleyan Methodist tradition of the Canadian Methodist Church and the Episcopal system of the American Methodist Churches. As the converts of the American Methodist Churches made up the majority of Japanese Methodists, it was likely that a Japan Methodist Church would adopt an Episcopal system. Although Carman himself had been Bishop of the Methodist Episcopal Church of Canada prior to its incorporation into the Methodist Church of Canada in 1882, he was deeply opposed to any basic change in the Japanese Wesleyan Methodist Church the Canadians had formed.

Of greater importance to the question of union in Japan was the fact that Carman was a fundamentalist in his theological views and was much opposed to modernist liberal theology. Liberal theology was already filtering into Methodist thought in the United States and to a lesser extent in Canada. Carman was quite ruthless in exploiting his position as General Superintendent to dismiss professors of theology and pastors in Canadian Methodist institutions in Canada who espoused liberal theology.[8] It is almost certain that Carman was suspicious of the intellectual attitudes of American missionaries working in Japan.

Eventually, however, Carman and Sutherland gave in. In 1907, the independent Japan Methodist Church was formed through the union of the Japan missions of the Methodist Church of Canada, the Methodist Episcopal Church (North), and the Methodist Episcopal Church (South). The new Japan Methodist Church had a modified Episcopal form of government, with a bishop elected for a term of eight years.[9] The Japanese bishop had the power to determine the stationing of Japanese pastors. The stationing of Western missionaries remained under the control of the various missions.

Although affection for the Canadian mission could be very tenacious, Methodist union in Japan meant that the Canadian Methodist mission lost the intimate connection of having a Japanese constituency that was solely its own. Yet it is doubtful whether union meant any loss of attachment to the cause of Canadian Methodist work in Japan among Canadian supporters at home. By 1907, the mission of the Methodist Church of Canada had developed such a momentum from its pre-union work that its continuation, regardless of changes in

Japan, was taken almost for granted. Once started, Canadian missions continued because they had existed in the past. To withdraw from mission work was an admission of weakness which no Canadian church was prepared to make.

Yet identification with specific work was important. From the start of their mission work in Japan, Canadian Anglicans had always worked under British Anglican bishops. In sharp contrast to the well-known Canadian Methodist mission, the Anglican mission was relatively obscure. As J. G. Waller, the Canadian Anglican missionary in Nagano, noted shortly after the creation of the diocese of Mid-Japan in 1912:

> Until the diocese was formed in 1912, twenty-four years after Mr. Robinson left Canada, every man who came as a Missionary to Japan from the Canadian Church of England was either Trinity College or Wycliffe College, both in the same city—Trinity men usually going to Nagano district, and Wycliffe men to the Nagoya one. If the rest of Canada outside of Toronto heard of the Japanese work at all, they usually had the vaguest ideas about it. A short experience of deputation work in Canada, when we were on furlough, showed us that most of those who even knew our names, and they were few, supposed our sphere of work was somewhere in China. Repeatedly, even clergymen, wishing to introduce the missionary from Japan to their congregations, would ask beforehand in what part of China we had been working.[10]

The new diocese of Mid-Japan, manned by Canadian missionaries under a Canadian bishop, served to stimulate interest in and support for Japan work after 1912. Its very name, Mid-Japan, also helped to prevent confusion with China among clergy and lay supporters of Anglican mission work.

The Canadian Presbyterian mission in Korea, founded in 1898, was, like the Canadian Anglican mission in Japan, from its beginnings associated with the two larger American Presbyterian missions and the small Australian Presbyterian mission in supporting the Korean Presbyterian Church. Like the Anglicans who came from Trinity or Wycliffe colleges, or indeed the Methodist missionaries who were overwhelmingly graduates of Victoria College, the early Canadian Presbyterian missionaries were graduates of Dalhousie University in Halifax. As a mission which was solely the responsibility of the Maritimes Division of the Presbyterian Church of Canada prior to 1909, the Korean mission achieved a regional identification which the Anglicans from Toronto failed to attain.

One reason for this lies in the example of Canadian Presbyterian work in north Taiwan. Canadian Presbyterian work was identified with George Leslie Mackay, its founder and a missionary in the Livingstonian mould.[11] In Taiwan, the Canadian Presbyterian mission cooperated with the English Presbyterian mission in the south. Although

W. E. Yates, an independent missionary with a Canadian Anglican background, worked among the aborigines in western Taiwan during the 1920s and 1930s, these two missions were the only Western missions on the island. Taiwan was strictly a Presbyterian mission field. What Canadian Anglicans working in Japan prior to 1912 lacked was a missionary personality who could draw attention to their work.

Union work with other missions undoubtedly did have some drawbacks, but certainly not to the degree that Carman feared in the 1900s. One obvious legacy of such inter-mission co-operation was that the transition from Methodist and Presbyterian missionaries to missionaries of the United Church of Canada was relatively easy for Canadians in the Japanese Empire.

MISSIONARY SOCIETIES

The central aim of Missionary Societies was to generate support for their missionaries and to handle the administrative tasks necessary to maintain them in the field. Although the organizational structures of Canadian Missionary Societies had different names, in essence they were all the same. The Methodist and Presbyterian Churches in Canada, as well as the Canadian Anglicans, supported Missionary Societies that were an integral part of their churches, which meant that the Missionary Societies were responsible to the highest body of their respective churches. Male and female Missionary Societies were financed and organized independently. Although the desire for sexual separation was one of the reasons why independent societies were formed, the Canadian Methodist Church thought that a female society, organized and administered by women, would increase the missionary donation by female church members in Canada.[12]

The major decision-making body in all the Missionary Societies was the Foreign Missions Committee or Board, normally a large committee of thirty or forty members with both lay and clerical representatives. It was a subcommittee of the churches' General Conference, Assembly, or Synod, the bodies that ultimately determined policy. The Foreign Missions Committee met infrequently, and its prime role was to settle broad policy and pass resolutions on the reports of its various subcommittees.

In the mission field, the Methodists and Presbyterians maintained Mission Councils, composed solely of missionary representatives, which were responsible for overseeing the work in the field. The Mission Council normally controlled the distribution of funds from Canada and the stationing of Canadian missionaries. In organization, this was similar to the home Foreign Missions Committee and, importantly, was completely separate from the Japanese or Korean church. The Secretary of the Mission Council was usually the most senior missionary in the field and spokesman for the mission in its dealings with the Foreign Missions Committee at home. Though the Canadian Anglicans maintained a Mission Council, authority in the dioceses in Japan where the Canadians worked remained with the Bishop and the Diocesan Synod.

FOREIGN MISSIONS SECRETARIES

Usually, the most important single figure in the organization of the home society was the Foreign Missions Secretary, who was elected by the highest church body. Terms of office varied within each church; however, even if the Missions Secretary had to stand for periodic re-election, he was unlikely to be replaced except for health reasons.[13] The Missions Secretary supervised the daily running of the society and was a member of the Foreign Missions Committee and all important subcommittees. The Missions Secretary was in regular correspondence with the Secretary of the Mission Council or the missionary bishop in the field.

In most cases, Missions Secretaries required every missionary in the field to write an annual report; some required semi-annual or even quarterly letters. Missions Secretaries usually toured the field at least once during their career, and most had a deep personal knowledge of the problems that confronted their missionaries.

As well as keeping himself informed about the activities of his own missionaries, the Missions Secretary was normally responsible for representing his society on interdenominational missionary committees. The work of the Canadian Methodist mission in Japan and the Canadian Presbyterian mission in Korea involved close co-operation with American missions of the same denominations. Missions Secretaries of both Canadian churches kept in close contact with their counterparts in American churches, which allowed a denomination with many different missions in a single country (for instance, the Presbyterian Church in Korea) to speak with a single voice on important issues.[14] In the case of Taiwan, where Canadian Presbyterians co-operated with their English counterparts, Missions Secretaries of the two societies carried on a somewhat sporadic correspondence, but always kept each other informed of important developments. Contact between Missionary Societies, either at home or abroad, was generally between missions of the same denomination. There was little official contact, for example, between Canadian Presbyterians in Korea and Canadian Methodists in Japan prior to their union in 1925.

The Missions Secretary could wield a good deal of influence on policy in the mission field, such as in the case of the union between the Canadian Methodist mission in Japan and its American Methodist

Episcopal counterparts. Alexander Sutherland, who was the General Secretary of the Missionary Society of the Methodist Church of Canada from 1878 to his death in 1910, was a man not to be crossed by missionaries who might not share his conservative views on the development of the Japan mission. He always won disputes over policy with missionaries.

Sutherland has been described as a "Missionary Statesman in an imperial, if at times imperious, manner."[15] As the man in charge of all Canadian Methodist mission work both in Canada and abroad, Sutherland was perhaps the best informed of all Canadians about events and trends in East Asia and the Canadian west. Born of Scottish parents in Guelph township, he was ordained as a minister in the Wesleyan Methodist Church of Canada in 1859. He first came to prominence in 1874 when he was elected Secretary-Treasurer of the Missionary Society of the Methodist Church of Canada.

In charge of Methodist mission work for more than thirty years, Sutherland was a man of considerable persuasive powers, a talented administrator, and a skilled fund-raiser. Responsible for the daily running of an organization which was multinational in scope and employed hundreds of people at home and abroad, he shouldered a great responsibility with the ambition and business acumen of a captain of industry. Mission administration was Sutherland's forte. His strength lay in his knowledge of the workings of committees and the support of the redoubtable Albert Carman who, as General Superintendent of the Methodist Church, maintained a similarly long and tenacious hold on power. By 1906, a challenge to Sutherland's leadership of the Missionary Society by N. W. Rowell and Joseph Flavelle, two important political figures who felt that Sutherland's rule was inefficient, resulted in an assistant being appointed to help him.[16] Outside of the church, Sutherland served for some years as president of the Ontario Temperance and Prohibitory League and later as president of the Prohibition Third Party. His activities in the Temperance Movement, an important cause for Methodists, reinforces the impression of him as a dour individual.

If Sutherland appears as a man of flint, the same is not true of his Presbyterian contemporary, R. P. MacKay. He became Foreign Missions Secretary of the Western Division of the Presbyterian Church in Canada—and of its successor, the combined Presbyterian Church—in 1892 and remained in the position until 1926. He presided over the massive expansion of Presbyterian missionary work and remained in charge of foreign missions almost as long as Sutherland. MacKay's biographer remembers him as a man of "good cheer,"[17] which is not a term that comes easily when describing Sutherland. Another difference between MacKay and Sutherland is that, in his later years, Mac-

Kay was prepared to delegate work and responsibility. In the Korea mission after 1910, A. E. Armstrong, MacKay's assistant Foreign Missions Secretary, was fully involved in decision-making. Indeed, Armstrong continued his secretarial responsibilities after the formation of the United Church of Canada and was still at the centre of missionary administration in 1941.

While Armstrong was the obvious successor to MacKay, there was no immediate candidate for Sutherland's mantle. By 1910, the generation of the mid-nineteenth century circuit-riding ministers, which included both Sutherland and his friend Carman, as well as the pioneer missionaries of Japan, had virtually disappeared. A new generation of "specialist" administrators took over. F. C. Stephenson, a medical doctor who had been prevented from going out to the mission field because of physical disability, had begun to take over responsibility for the important youth branch of the Methodist Church in the 1900s. As Secretary of the Young People's Forward Movement, he proved to be a skilled advocate of missionary work as late as the 1920s.

James Endicott, one of the student-volunteer generation of missionaries who had served as a missionary in China, returned to Toronto to become Foreign Missions Secretary (1913-1937). For much of the time, Endicott was assisted by Jesse Arnup, who eventually succeeded him. Endicott's responsibilities, unlike Sutherland's, did not include supervision of work in Canada. He was one of a generation of professional missionaries, and he brought to his work a missionary's perspective. He was a missionary by vocation, a product of the missionary system that had emerged in the late nineteenth century. His son, James Endicott, became a controversial Canadian Methodist missionary in China in the 1930s. What Endicott acquired after he became Foreign Missions Secretary was the connection with the home-church constituency which Sutherland and his generation had acquired through years of working in rural pastorates. Along with Armstrong, Endicott would continue to administer mission work for the United Church of Canada till the end of the period.

The Methodist and Presbyterian Foreign Missions Secretaries were all men who had been involved in administrating missions for many years. They supervised a good number of missions in different countries, and experience told them that, no matter what the particular crisis was, it would be weathered and mission work would continue. It was only in 1941, with the beginning of the Pacific War, that it became clear that mission work in the Japanese Empire had come to an end, but only for the duration of the war. Here, experience with Chinese mission work was felt to be paradigmatic. From the beginning of Canadian Methodist work in China in 1891, the progress of the West China mission had been bedevilled by social and political upheaval. Yet it continued and so too would mission work in Japan. In all crises, with the possible exception of Japanese suppression of the March 1, 1919, movement in Korea, Missions Secretaries always took the broad view.

Another marked characteristic of Missions Secretaries was their scrupulous fairness in the division of funds between missions. This does not mean to say that the amount of money given to each mission was the same, for that depended upon size and number of missionaries at work in the field. But money was never given by Missionary Societies for one mission at the expense of another. This meant that Missions Secretaries would instinctively reject unexpected applications for large amounts of money from the mission field, regardless of how convincing the arguments behind the applications were. What had to be maintained was a balance, not only in annual Missionary Society expenditure, but also in the demands of each mission field. By the early twentieth century, experience had shown Missions Secretaries that Asia would not be Christianized quickly. No matter how enthusiastic an individual missionary might be about Christian prospects, Missions Secretaries knew that there were no short-cuts. They were by instinct cautious men whose parsimony was enough to dampen the grandiose dreams of all save the most enthusiastic of missionaries. The length of Mission Secretaries' tenure reveals that these men were in the business of managing missions and did not gamble in souls.

Missions Secretaries and missions needed money to thrive. Although these Societies were a unique form of big business, the fund-raising operation of the Canadians never reached the gigantic scale of their American counterparts.[18] The current expenses of the Missionary Societies were normally defrayed by membership subscriptions of the society or its auxiliaries and from congregational contributions. Deficits were met by special appeals, which attempted to reach the widest possible number of people in a Society's denomination.

Within an individual church, there were usually numerous auxiliary branches which studied and supported missions, as well as auxiliary groups for people of all ages. All auxiliary organizations of individual churches were linked together in regional divisions, which would come together at the annual meeting of the Missionary Society. In the Canadian Methodist Church, the Epworth League was the auxiliary for Sunday school children. Most Canadian Methodist missionaries were affiliated to and partially supported by the Epworth League branches of one or two individual churches. In return for this support, the missionary would keep the young children of his League regularly informed of his activities in a series of newsletters. For older children, the Canadian Methodist Church Young People's Forward Movement carried out similar activities. Adults in an individual congregation could become members of their church's branch of the Missionary

Society itself. As part of his deputation work during his furlough, the missionary would lecture to all these auxiliaries.

Another source of income was large donations from wealthy individuals or families. Income from this source, however, could not be depended upon, and the amounts of money varied greatly. Building programs in the mission field were often funded from large private donations.[19] In the Canadian Methodist Church, the Massey and Eaton families, who were among the wealthiest in Canada, gave substantial amounts for missions.

But Missionary Societies were nearly always short of money. They were not assured of a stable income from year to year because they were dependent on the whims of individual donors. This uncertainty was not conducive to long-term financial planning. While Missionary Societies had to find ways to balance their budgets, they did not experience the financial restraints and disciplines of a profit-making commercial company. Missions were often founded with very little regard to their future cost; it was assumed that, if a Missionary Society could establish a mission, it could support it indefinitely.[20] At the outset, there was usually little thought about how a mission might develop, and there were normally no prescribed limits on its development. Thus plans for the development of missionary work were rarely projected for more than two or three years. But despite the fluctuating fortunes of the income of the Missionary Societies, no Canadian mission in the Japanese Empire was forced to close its doors before 1941.

CANADIAN METHODISTS AND ANGLICANS

The Wesleyan Methodist Church in Canada first entertained the idea of establishing an overseas mission at the annual meeting of its Missionary Society in October 1871.[21] An overseas mission, Wesleyan Methodists argued, would quicken missionary zeal and deepen the spiritual life of the home church.[22] By the next annual meeting in 1872, Japan had been chosen as the mission field, a choice no doubt influenced by the Iwakura Embassy in North America which had done much to heighten interest in Japan.[23]

It was clear at the second annual meeting that not only Christian concern but also a sense of Canadian nationalism was motivating the delegates. There was the definite feeling among them that "the day of small things, as regards the Dominion, was past and the same was true of our Mission work."[24] The Wesleyan Methodists had missions across the North American continent and now planned to continue this westward expansion across the Pacific. "We have a glorious future before us in this great country," they believed and they hoped that mission work would keep pace with Canadian national and material advancement.[25] Confederation had inspired Methodist churches to embark upon a spiritual union in order to create a truly national Methodist Church in the new Canada. The commencement of overseas missions was an early sign that independent Canadian organizations believed that Canada could also play an international role.

In choosing the pioneer missionaries for the new mission in Japan, the Wesleyan Methodist Missionary Society picked two of the most outstanding pastors in their church. The senior man, George Cochran (1833-1900), born in Ulster and raised in Owen Sound, Ontario, was a man of deep learning and good intellect who had served as the pastor of the newly built Metropolitan Church in Toronto, the largest of Methodist churches. His junior colleague, Davidson McDonald (1837-1905), born and raised in Prince Edward County in eastern Ontario, was ordained in 1864. After holding several pastoral charges, he was given permission in 1870 to attend the medical school at Victoria College and graduated in 1873.[26] Although McDonald and Cochran were sent to Japan by the Missionary Society, and were not volunteers in the strict sense, both heartily supported the idea of a mission in Japan, as did the church congregations which quickly raised $10,000 to outfit them. On June 30, 1873, Cochran and McDonald and their families arrived in Yokohama.

In 1887, the autonomous Nihon Seikōkai (NSKK) was formed in Osaka by one American and two British Anglican missions. It was in response to their appeal for missionary reinforcements that John Cooper Robinson, the first Canadian Anglican missionary, was sent to Japan.[27] A graduate of Wycliffe College, he was initially supported in Japan by the Wycliffe College Missionary Society (WM) and the Canadian Church Missionary Society (CCMS). A Low Church Anglican, Robinson worked for most of his career in Nagoya, which was part of the diocese of South Toyko. The High Anglican wing of the Church of England in Canada sent their first missionary, J. G. Waller, in 1890. A graduate of Trinity College, Waller was supported by the Domestic and Foreign Missionary Society (DFMS),[28] and established himself in Nagano in 1892.

Very quickly women missionaries too proved their worth in the mission field. Indeed, they would eventually become, in terms of the type of work they undertook, the backbone of the Canadian missionary endeavour.

WOMEN'S MISSIONARY WORK

The Woman's Missionary Society of the Canadian Methodist Church of Canada (WMS-CM) owed its genesis to the needs of the mission field in Japan.[29] At the 1880 Annual Conference, Alexander Sutherland, Secretary of the Missionary Society, suggested that a committee of ten women be appointed to draft a constitution and bylaws, and the WMS-CM was formed. Although independent of the male Missionary Society, even to the point of paying it own missionaries, the WMS-CM was to work "in harmony with the authorities of the Missionary Society of the Methodist Church of Canada, and be subject to their approval in the employment and remuneration of missionaries or other agents, the designation of fields of labor, and in the general plans and designs of the work."[30]

In the creation of the WMS-CM, Sutherland obviously saw the possibilities of drawing money from a hitherto neglected group of church members and adding to missionary strength at no cost to the Missions Board. What he did not foresee, however, was that the WMS-CM would put great emphasis on its independent status. The women sent to Japan by the WMS-CM were responsible to the Executive Board of the WMS-CM, not to Sutherland and the Missions Board. In Japan, the WMS-CM had its own Mission Council which operated independently of the Mission Council run by male missionaries. This meant that arbitration was difficult in cases of conflict in policy or personality between the two societies. Tensions did arise, especially when the women found their male colleagues not paying sufficient attention to the autonomy of the WMS-CM. But generally there was successful co-operation between them.

An invitation to the WMS-CM to work in Japan quickly came from McDonald in Tokyo,[31] and in late 1882 Martha J. Cartmell, the WMS-CM's first missionary, arrived in Japan. Born in Thorold, Ontario, in 1845, she had been a teacher and headmistress of the Hamilton Public Girls' School.[32] When she returned home in 1885, she was replaced by Eliza Spencer, a graduate of the Toronto Higher Middle School. It was under Eliza Spencer (who married Canadian Methodist missionary T. A. Large in 1887) that the Tōyō Eiwa Jo Gakkō, the Canadian Methodist school for girls in Azabu, Tokyo, became firmly established.[33] Largely because of the successful work of these two women, Japan swiftly became the main mission field for the WMS-CM.

Female education was clearly seen to be one of the major areas in which women missionaries could play a valuable role. Further, it was felt that they could have an important role in evangelistic work, because Japanese women would perhaps be more at ease with a woman visiting their homes. Both in educational and evangelistic work, the WMS-CM came to play a vital role.

Coming later into mission work than the Methodists, the Canadian Anglicans saw from the start the need for single female missionaries. The WM sponsored Miss E. M. Trent in 1894; this is significant, for the Canadian Anglican societies did not view themselves as exclusively male. A female society, the Women's Auxiliary of the Church of England in Canada (WA), had existed since 1885. The WA saw itself as an auxiliary to male missionary activity and only secondarily ran its own missionary work. The WA sent its first missionary, J. Smith, to Japan in 1892. The other Societies still continued to appoint women missionaries until 1902, when the WA became the auxiliary to the amalgamated Missionary Society of the Church of England in Canada (MSCC). Among the early Canadian Anglican women missionaries were Miss Louise Peterson, who built St. Mary's Church in Matsumoto; Miss Young, who was influential in establishing a kindergarten school in Nagoya; Deaconess Archer, who was a dedicated evangelist among female factory workers; and Loretta Shaw who taught at the British Anglican Poole School in Osaka.[34] The major area of endeavour for the Canadian Anglican women missionaries was also female education and evangelistic work among women.

The Canadian Presbyterians in Korea had no reservations about employing women missionaries. In 1901, the Woman's Missionary Society of the Canadian Presbyterian Church (WMS-CP) sent its first single female missionary, Louise McCully, to Korea. She quickly proved herself to be an indefatigable evangelistic worker and champion of women's place within the church.[35] She and her WMS-CP colleagues in Korea were an invaluable addition to the Canadian Presbyterian effort.

The Canadian Presbyterian mission in north Taiwan was one place where women missionaries were not welcome in the late nineteenth century. George Leslie Mackay believed that Western women were not strong enough to withstand the climate and that they would be ineffective as evangelists because of their perceived inability to master the language and their ignorance of Chinese customs.[36] The English Presbyterian mission in south Taiwan, however, welcomed women missionaries, and they proved eminently capable of valuable work among the Chinese, despite the climate.

CANADIAN PRESBYTERIANS IN KOREA

Canadian missionary work in Korea owed its beginnings to the zeal of student bodies at the University of Toronto. In the late 1880s, the student volunteer movement and the personal appeals of missionaries created considerable enthusiasm. Students at Wycliffe and Trinity colleges sent out J. Cooper Robinson, J. G. Waller, and others to begin Canadian Anglican work in Japan. Victoria College students answered the personal appeals of the dynamic Charles Eby for the formation of a Self-Support Band to supplement the regular Canadian Methodist missionary staff.[37] At the same time, student YMCAs sent four men to begin Presbyterian work in Korea: Robert Harkness, James Scarth Gale, Dr. Robert Hardie, and Dr. Oliver R. Avison. Mission work needed more than the support of impecunious students to sustain it. The Canadian Presbyterian Church was unwilling to continue to finance these four men once their limited YMCA funds had been used up. Harkness returned home in 1895; the other three went on to become very distinguished missionaries with American missions in Korea.

Born on a farm near Alma, Ontario, James Scarth Gale, who gained some renown as a novelist and historian, remained in Korea until 1927 with the American Presbyterian (North) mission, stationed first in Wonsan and from 1899 in Seoul. Dr. Oliver R. Avison, whose ability lay in medical administration, organization, and fund-raising, became superintendent of the Royal Hospital (the first government Western hospital in Korea) in Seoul in late 1893, and in 1904, he became head of the Severance Hospital, which he developed into a major teaching institution. He used his indefatigable organizational efforts to improve public health by attempting to combat epidemics such as the major cholera outbreak in Seoul in 1895. Retiring from the American Presbyterian mission in 1932, Avison remained in Korea until being repatriated after the opening of the Pacific War. While Gale had remained publicly silent on political developments in Korea under Japanese rule,[38] Avison was an open (but tactful, while residing in Korea) advocate of independence.

R. A. Hardie, who had been one of Avison's medical students in Toronto, joined the American Presbyterian Mission (North) in 1890. The Toronto University Medical Students' YMCA had agreed to support Hardie and his wife for at least eight years.[39] Hardie came out to work with Gale because it was obvious that missionaries in Korea needed medical help close at hand. In late 1890, he went to the Royal Hospital in Seoul to work with Avison; in 1892, when Gale went to Wonsan, Hardie followed; in 1898, when Gale left Wonsan for Seoul, and the responsibility for Presbyterian work in the city and the northern provinces bordering the Japan Sea was taken over by the newly arrived Canadian Presbyterians, he remained in Wonsan and joined the Methodist Episcopal (South) Mission. During the 1900s, he gave up medical work to concentrate on evangelistic work in northern Korea. Another Canadian missionary in Wonsan was Malcolm C. Fenwick, a Presbyterian turned Baptist, who established a mission in Korea without anybody's help.[40] Fenwick went to Korea in 1889, inspired by the example of David Livingstone. Though he lacked both the college or theological training normally required by orthodox Missionary Societies, by 1896 the determined Fenwick had established the Korean Itinerant Mission, without any organized financial support.

Conditions in the peninsula during the 1890s were difficult and not everybody succeeded. Dr. William James Hall, who arrived in Korea in 1891 as a missionary of the Methodist Episcopal (North) Church,[41] died of typhus fever in November 1894.[42]

But it was the tragic death of William J. McKenzie, a native of Cape Breton, that had the profoundest impact on Canadian Presbyterians. Failing to convince the Canadian Presbyterian authorities that they should support him, McKenzie went out to Korea in October 1893, with enough money donated by churches in Eastern Canada to maintain himself for a year. In February 1894, he took up residence in the seaside village of Sorai to the north of Seoul. In July 1895, he shot himself as he lay ill from sunstroke and fever. After his death, Gale wrote: "when he had borne witness through the time of trial, and had carried his brethren safely in his arms, his work was done. Disease that is stronger than the giant, fastened upon him. He suffered as a brave martyr, tasting in his death a humiliation, that to my mind, made him more like his Saviour."[43] McKenzie's death became a part of the mythology surrounding missionary work in Korea.

To Presbyterians in the Maritimes, McKenzie had died a martyr's death. The Missionary Society of the Maritimes Division of the Canadian Presbyterian Church decided to undertake missionary work in the "hermit kingdom."[44] In his will, McKenzie had left $2,000 for mission work in Korea, and the Christians in Sorai publicly petitioned the Canadian Presbyterians to send out a Christian teacher.[45] Three years after McKenzie's death, in the fall of 1898, the first three official Canadian Presbyterian missionaries, Dr. Robert Grierson, a medical doctor,[46] William Rufus Foote, and Duncan M. McRae, all Nova Scotians and all Dalhousie graduates, left for Korea. When they arrived in Seoul, the Canadian Presbyterians were asked by the American Presbyterian Societies already in the peninsula to undertake work in northeastern Korea with their base in Wonsan.

MISSION IN NORTH TAIWAN

Canadian Presbyterian work in Taiwan was started and largely carried on by one man. George Leslie Mackay, the first Canadian missionary in East Asia, arrived in Taiwan in 1872. It was the beginning of the second stage of Protestant missionary development in the Chinese Empire. The first stage, which had begun in the 1830s and continued until the end of the 1850s, had been characterized by the endeavours of individual pioneer missionaries, such as Charles Gutzlaff and William Chalmers Burns,[47] whose major achievement was stimulating interest in missions for China within the home churches of Britain and the United States. The second stage followed on the heels of the Treaties of

Tientsin and Peking,[48] and resulted in a tremendous growth in both Christian missions and missionary expansion into the interior of China.

Mackay, a native of Ontario and graduate of the Princeton Theological Seminary, left for China in the fall of 1871. Because the English Presbyterians were working in the south and there were no missionaries in the north, Mackay decided to establish his mission in the north with his headquarters at Tamsui. Although Mackay had gained the support of the Foreign Missions Council before he left Canada, he alone was responsible for the idea of starting a Canadian Presbyterian mission in Taiwan. For the next twenty years, the mission in north Taiwan was essentially George Leslie Mackay.

By one year, George Leslie Mackay won the honour of being the first Canadian missionary in East Asia. It was the two Canadian Methodist missionary pioneers in Japan, George Cochran and Davidson McDonald, however, whose efforts met with success first.

CHAPTER TWO

Early Days in Japan

George Cochran and Davidson McDonald arrived in Japan in mid-1873 to establish a Methodist church patterned on the Canadian model. These pioneer missionaries saw their role as simply one of building a strong church organization which would provide a firm foundation for later expansion. In their concern to emulate Western church organization as well as its theology and discipline, they made few concessions to the sensibilities of Japanese culture and society. It is somewhat surprising, given the exotic nature of their religious message and the foreignness of the church organization, that they were able to make any headway at all. But they indeed did make headway, partly because they responded to an immediate need in early Meiji Japan, the great demand for English-language teachers in schools specializing in Western studies.

Missionaries, Cochran and McDonald among them, saw that they could open Christian work through language instruction. Such was the desire to study English and Western scientific subjects that the Japanese most often took the initiative in seeking out missionaries. As the response of the ex-samurai who became converts indicates, the Christian message in the mid-1870s fitted in with the transformation of Japan then taking place. It is this phenomenon, which contrasts sharply with Chinese attitudes toward Mackay in Taiwan, that greatly facilitated the initial success of Canadian Methodist efforts.

The social and political atmosphere in Japan when the two Canadians arrived in 1873 was receptive to change and open to Western influence. By 1881, the mood of Japan was less open, but in the interim the Canadian missionaries had made great strides in developing their mission. During the halcyon days of the mid-1870s, the Canadians formed two groups of Japanese converts, the Koishikawa Band in

Tokyo and the Shizuoka Band, out of whose number came many of the Japanese workers and pastors who contributed to the success of Canadian work in later years. The network of contacts the two Canadian missionaries made while forming these two Christian groups reveals how Western ideas, Christianity among them, were transmitted into Japanese society in both a metropolitan and a provincial setting, and the example of these two Christian groups further illuminates the intellectual response of the Japanese to the deluge of Western ideas that flooded into Japan during the 1870s.

BUNMEI — KAIKA AND WESTERN TEACHERS

In April 1868, five years before Cochran and McDonald arrived, the new Meiji government took the initiative in opening Japanese society to Western influences in order to develop the country economically, industrially, and militarily, an aim symbolized by the idea of *fukoku-kyōhei*—"a rich country and strong army." The new regime hoped to achieve diplomatic equality between Japan and Western countries.[1] Western science was encouraged as a means of achieving progress and Chinese learning was denounced in favour of the *jitsu gaku*—"practical learning" of the West.[2]

The attitude of the Meiji government toward what they thought was Western civilization (which in this Victorian context means modernization) was opportunistic. Although home-made programs and theories of civilization had not been formed, the government avidly and indiscriminately introduced the material aspects of Western civilization, without concern for their effect on the life of the general population. The material objects of civilization flooded Japanese society very quickly. *Bunmei-kaika*, the Japanese term for civilization, was used to refer to anything from the West.[3] Beyond this, most Japanese had little idea of what civilization was or where the flood of new Western ideas was taking their society. As a result, a sense of disorientation accompanied the beginnings of Meiji modernization.[4]

There was an undercurrent of anxiety beneath the surface of Japanese society, which belied its seemingly robust and flamboyant atmosphere. It was against this background that some Japanese intellectuals began working out theories of civilization, in which they criticized the Meiji government's policy of Westernization, particularly its opportunism and superficiality. At the same time, these intellectuals attempted to show the Japanese people what civilization truly was and how they could attain it in Japan. Yet in constructing their own theories of civilization, they were forced to refer to Western theories.

The initiative to develop Japanese theories of civilization had its nucleus in a learned society, the *Meirokusha* (Society of Meiji Six), which was founded in Tokyo in 1873. All its members, among whom were most of the leading Japanese specialists in things Western, were united in their desire to reform the traditional outlook of the people in order to raise Japan to a Western level of civilization and thus bring about equality between Japan and the Treaty Powers. They did not always agree on what theory of civilization should replace the traditional outlook of the Japanese people. Yet what was clear was their general agreement that the introduction of Western ideas into Japan was essential and that, in lieu of sufficient numbers of Japanese specialists in Western studies, Western helpers were needed to provide practical information. The Meiji government, with the power of its exchequer, was able to hire under contract from abroad the Western advisers it felt it needed.[5] The government also sent students overseas to study. Not all the students who went abroad, however, were officially sponsored by the government; from the 1860s, small numbers of Japanese students left Japan on their own initiative.[6]

The Meiji government was not the only body that wanted to hire Westerners, but private individuals or organizations often did not have the finances to search for appropriate employees abroad and to bring them to Japan. They were forced to look for help among the Westerners already in Japan and living in the treaty ports. This meant a limited choice, for most permanent Western residents in the treaty ports were merchants, who were already gainfully employed, or seamen and adventurers, who were mostly educationally or morally unsuitable as teachers. This left the missionaries, who had obvious attractions as morally upright men. More importantly, they had outside sources of income, which meant that the salary a Japanese employer could offer was not a crucial factor in whether they accepted or rejected a teaching contract.

For a missionary, a contract to teach in a Japanese school was attractive, not only because it brought the missionary into greater contact with the Japanese, but also because it allowed him to live outside the confines of the treaty port. For the Japanese, the grave disadvantage of hiring a missionary was that he might use his position to propagate Christianity, a proscribed religion. Since the beginning of the seventeenth century, Christianity had been banned in Japan. Even thought the 1858 treaties between Japan and the Western powers allowed for missionary residency in the treaty ports, proselytizing the Japanese remained strictly prohibited. But it was for his practical knowledge of the West, and not his religion, that the missionary was normally hired. The danger that a Western employee might exploit his position to propagate his own religious ideas was evident in the case of one or two of those employed directly by the government. W. S. Clark, who aided in the establishment of the Sapporo Agricultural College in the late 1870s and whose influence was crucial in the formation of the Sapporo Band, was a government employee, as were Wheeler and others who continued working at the Sapporo Agricultural College after Clark had returned to the United States.[7]

Even though the government, at least in the early 1870s, included a provision in contracts with Western employees that prohibited them from teaching Christianity, and while some earnest Christians like W. E. Griffis, who taught in a school in Fukui in the early 1870s abided by that clause, others did not.[8] E. W. Clark, a friend of Griffis, refused to sign his contract to teach in Shizuoka unless that provision was removed, and in his case it was.[9] The issue of Christianity was more important for private Japanese employers than it was for the government, because private citizens could be prosecuted for breaking the edict against the propagation of Christianity. Indeed, as late as 1869, the expulsion of the Urakami crypto-Christians from Kyushu showed that the government was still prepared to persecute Christians. The Japanese employer had to balance the disadvantages and advantages of hiring a missionary before approaching him with a contract. It was only after 1873 that private Japanese began openly to approach missionaries, which coincided with a decision of the Meiji government to remove the public display of proscription edicts against Christianity (but still not officially tolerate the Western religion) in an attempt to improve relations with the Western powers.

Cochran and McDonald were exceedingly fortunate that one of the first Japanese with whom they had contact not only wanted to hire a Western teacher but also was openly sympathetic to Christianity. This was Nakamura Keiū (Masanao), a leading Confucian scholar and the translator of J. S. Mill's *On Liberty*.[10] Nakamura, a member of the Meirokusha, believed that the adoption of Christianity by the Japanese would materially aid their country in achieving its goal of equality with the West.[11] It has to be stressed, however, that the appeal of Christianity to Nakamura was more moral than spiritual; as Irwin Scheiner has pointed out, Nakamura considered Christianity to be an extension of Confucianism,[12] and Christian ethics were considered superior to Confucian ethics. In that sense, it was a relatively easy transition to move from Confucianism to Christianity. Nakamura's prestige as a scholar and educator, as well as his personal contacts, did much to ensure the initial success of the mission of the Methodist Church of Canada.

CANADIAN METHODIST MISSIONARIES

Cochran and McDonald were ignorant of Japan and Japanese when they landed in Yokohama in June 1873, but the treaty port was not a completely foreign and unintelligible place to the newcomers.[13] By

1873, the seaport was a major centre for both missionary and western business interests and had a Western population of more than 1,000. American missionaries belonging to the Dutch Reformed, Presbyterian, Episcopalian, and Baptist churches were already working in Yokohama; in 1872, although it was still illegal for Japanese to become Christians, the first Japanese Protestant church had been formed by eleven converts of Dutch Reformed missionaries.[14] The two Canadians, however, were not content to live comfortably in the pleasant Western settlement on Yokohama Bluff. They had come more than 8,000 miles "to preach to the heathen" and felt that it was "poor policy to stay within twenty miles of them, instead of going right in amongst them where they were,"[15] that is, in Tokyo.

Despite their desire to begin evangelistic work in Tokyo, restrictions prevented the Canadians from moving immediately from Yokohama. Under the treaty system, Western residence in Tokyo was restricted to the Tsukiji district on the Tokyo waterfront, where the sale of property was strictly controlled by the government, and the cost was very high. As well, Tsukiji was the foreign concession for Tokyo, and there were no better prospects of gaining contact with the "heathen" there than there were in Yokohama. So for the first few months the Canadians reluctantly remained in their rented house close to the British Legation on Yokohama Bluff.

Their immediate task was learning Japanese. McDonald showed more aptitude than Cochran; by December 1873, he had begun giving short, memorized sermons in his Sunday Bible class to the Japanese. (McDonald was one of the very few Western missionaries who became fluent in Japanese. Because the majority of missionaries failed to master the language, in the 1870s the Japanese needed a knowledge of English before they could be converted.[16]) Despite their rudimentary Japanese, the two Canadian searched for broader contact with the Japanese than could be found in Yokohama.

Thus Cochran left Yokohama in October 1873 on a three-week trip into the interior of Japan with Henry Loomis, an American Presbyterian missionary. One of the places they visited was Shizuoka, where E. W. Clark, a young American layman, was a contract teacher at the Gakumonjo school. The school had been established shortly after the Meiji Restoration by ex-retainers of the Tokugawa shogun.[17] At the time of Cochran's visit to Shizuoka, Clark was about to leave the city to become an assistant professor at the Kaisei Gakkō in Tokyo, the predecessor of Tokyo Imperial University. The Shizuoka authorities asked Cochran to replace Clark as English teacher.[18] Cochran thought he had been invited to teach "chiefly because I am British,"[19] but because of his children he declined the offer. He realized, however, that this was one of the first opportunities for a missionary to reside outside the treaty ports.[20] McDonald, who was a husband but not a father, consented to go in his stead.

There was a considerable delay before McDonald could go to Shizuoka. A teaching contract had to be drawn up and government approval obtained before a Westerner was allowed to reside outside of the treaty ports. In January 1874, having given up hope of obtaining government permission, McDonald moved from Yokohama to a hotel in Tsukiji in order to begin work in Tokyo. There he helped in a hospital established by Dr. Henry Faulds of the Scottish United Presbyterian mission and continued to learn Japanese.[21]

In early April 1874, the Canadians made their first converts— Cochran's language teacher and the porter in his house.[22] These two young ex-samurai had joined Cochran's household to learn English and had been drawn to Christianity because of their close contact with Cochran. It was by no means unusual for servants to become converts. The influence of the family, including the children, was often as important as that of the missionary in drawing the servant or lodger to Christianity. The personal conduct of the missionary and the warmth of his family life were often decisive factors in bringing about the conversion of Japanese who were in close contact with him.[23] As if the first two conversions were a good omen, later in April the authorities finally allowed McDonald to go to Shizuoka. At the same time McDonald left Tokyo, Cochran was able to secure a teaching post in Tokyo (outside of the Tsukiji treaty concession) at the Dōjinsha school established by Nakamura Keiū, one of the best Western-studies private schools in the capital.[24]

By April 1874, the two Canadian missionaries had achieved a primary goal—to get away from the treaty concessions and to be truly among the Japanese. By this time, A. C. Shaw, a Canadian serving with the British Anglican Society for the Propagation of the Gospel in Foreign Parts (SPG) who arrived in Japan a month after the two Methodists, had also been able to get permission to reside outside the treaty concessions by signing a two-year contract with Fukuzawa Yukichi, a leading Japanese intellectual, to teach his children English.[25] As well as living in Fukuzawa's house in Mita, Tokyo, and teaching his three children, Shaw also taught moral science at Keiō Gijuku, Fukuzawa's famous private school.

All three Canadian missionaries in Japan were now teaching outside the treaty concessions. The appointments of Cochran and McDonald to teaching posts in Japanese schools led to the foundation of two Christian bands, the Shizuoka Band and the Koishikawa Band, which to some extent fed and reinforced each other.

THE SHIZUOKA BAND

McDonald arrived in Shizuoka in April 1874. On his journey to the inland city, he was accompanied by a "young prince" of the Tokugawa family who was to live with the McDonalds for a time in Shizuoka in order to learn English.[26] That a son of the Tokugawa ex-shogun was to stay with the McDonalds reveals that the Canadian missionary and his wife were embarking on an unusual adventure. In the early 1870s, Shizuoka was by no means simply a provincial town in a prefecture well known for its mandarin oranges and tea. Shizuoka was the ancestral home of the Tokugawa shoguns, and it was there that Tokugawa Yoshinobu, the last shogun, retired following the Meiji Restoration. Many of his former retainers followed him there into semi-exile, and approximately 6,000 ex-Tokugawa samurai were living in Shizuoka and its vicinity in early 1874.

Even though it had lost political power in the Meiji Restoration, the Tokugawa family initially hoped that it might regain its former control of Japan. For this reason, in the autumn of 1868, the family established the Military Academy at Numazu, some thirty miles from Shizuoka, with the leading Western studies scholar, Nishi Amane, as its first headmaster.[27] With a less overtly militaristic aim, the Tokugawa family also founded in late 1868 the Gakumonjo in Shizuoka. By early 1872, this Shizuoka school was the "higher education" centre of a network of eight or nine junior schools which the Tokugawa family had established in Shizuoka prefecture.[28] Before its overthrow in 1868, the Tokugawa shogunate had been at the forefront of the introduction of Western studies into Japan, thus the continued sponsorship of Western studies in Shizuoka prefecture after 1868.

More important factors were involved as well. The purpose of the Gakumonjo was to help provide education in Western studies for the sons of ex-Tokugawa samurai.[29] The followers of the ex-shogun carried considerable resentment against the new Meiji government, for the majority of declassé samurai were living in conditions of great hardship and suffering.[30] It was felt by Katsu Kaishū and other Tokugawa elders that, by educating the sons of ex-samurai in Western science, at least some of the former Tokugawa influence in Japan could be regained. Furthermore, it was believed that, as the demand for experts in Western studies increased, there would be employment possibilities for these young men. Recognizing the future need for Western studies specialists clearly shows the progressive spirit of the Tokugawa exiles.

Since the founding of the Gakumonjo, the Tokugawa authorities had wanted to hire a Western teacher,[31] since the school had been established to teach Western subjects—English, French, German, and Dutch, mathematics and Western science—as well as traditional Chinese studies. Finally, in late 1871, a Western teacher, E. W. Clark, was hired to teach at the Gakumonjo in Shizuoka. A graduate of Rutgers College, Clark taught a wide range of scientific subjects with the aid of some fifty Japanese "assistants" in a school which had nearly 1,000 students.[32] During his first year there, the Gakumonjo was definitely a thriving institution. Among the leading Japanese intellectuals associated with the Gakumonjo who befriended Clark was Nakamura Keiū,[33] who was in charge of Chinese studies. By early 1873, however, Clark was disillusioned with living in Shizuoka, partially because of loneliness after Nakamura had gone to live in Tokyo in late 1872, and partially because of educational changes at the school. Although the Meiji government had tolerated the creation of the Military Academy in Numazu and the Gakumonjo in Shizuoka in 1868, in 1872 it forced their closure. The Military Academy was moved to Tokyo where it was absorbed into the national military college system. The Gakumonjo was simply closed. These closures were a result of the decision of the Meiji government to centralize advanced education in Tokyo at the expense of provincial centres.[34] In a real sense, the attempt by the Tokugawa family to continue to retain influence through the training of experts in Western studies had been frustrated by the Meiji government.

There still remained a desire among those in Shizuoka to continue to make some provision for Western-style education in the city, even though it would not be on the scale of the Gakumonjo. Thus, the Shizuoka authorities were eager to secure a replacement for Clark when he left in late 1873. Following the closure of the Gakumonjo, a small private school, the Shizuhatasha (Shizuhatanoya) was established by Hitomi Fujitarō, one of the Tokugawa elders involved in the Gakumonjo. It was as a teacher for Hitomi's school that McDonald was hired.[35] Thus, McDonald began to teach in Shizuoka in circumstances that were very different from those that had existed more than two years before when Clark had started to work. By April 1874, any hope that Shizuoka might become a major centre in Japan for Western studies had evaporated.

When McDonald began teaching, there were only ten students, most of them former students of Clark, attending the Shizuhatasha.[36] The school was conducted in McDonald's home, a comfortably Western-style stone house located within the confines of the old Shizuoka Castle. School began at eight in the morning; McDonald taught physics, chemistry, natural history, and language study. For English classes, he made use of Ontario school primers.[37] Although teaching was somewhat hampered by language difficulties, the curriculum had a surprisingly high level of educational sophistication. Three of the students, Yamanaka Emi, Tsuyuki Seiichi, and Tsuchiya Hikoroku, had some elementary knowledge of English and served as interpreters while McDonald was still learning Japanese.[38] McDonald's wife also became involved, teaching English, knitting, and music to classes of women. For the McDonalds, teaching was merely their excuse to gain permission to live outside the treaty ports; their primary aim remained to spread the gospel.

While Clark was living in Shizuoka, he had openly held Bible classes. Even though this contravened the proscription edict against Christianity, the Shizuoka authorities had not stopped him. When McDonald was hired to teach in Shizuoka, it was known that he was a missionary, but he was also not prevented from proselytizing. Soon after his arrival, McDonald held his first Bible class, which consisted of a reading of the Lord's Prayer; it was attended by seventeen people.[39] The majority of those present were McDonald's students at the Shizuhatasha, but most crucial was the presence of Sugiyama Magaroku as interpreter. Sugiyama came from a well-known, high-ranking samurai family. Both he and his father taught at the Gakumonjo. He had also been much involved in the process of getting McDonald to Shizuoka. He was already a Christian, having been converted to Christianity some two years before in Yokohama.[40] His younger brother, Tsuchiya Hikoroku, was one of McDonald's students and became one of the leading figures in the Canadian Methodist Church in Shizuoka. Three others present at this first Bible class, Tsuyuki Seiichi, Yamanaka Emi, and Muramatsu Ichi, all of them students at the Shizuhatasha, had been students of Sugiyama at the Gakumonjo. The former two later became pastors, while Muramatsu taught at the Azabu middle school in Tokyo, which was originally founded as a Canadian Methodist school.[41]

McDonald's Bible class was a continuation of a process Clark had begun during his days in Shizuoka. It was part of the intellectual activity of the Shizuhatasha students and not a peculiar new departure, for Clark had conducted similar extra-curricular classes. It was part and parcel of the heady eclectic desire of Japanese youngsters to learn as much as possible of things Western and to transmit this knowledge to a broader audience. It was not the only out-of-class activity; as well as attending Bible classes, Clark's students had been involved in publishing pamphlets on geometry and other things of scientific interest. Yet behind the interest in Christianity was the view held by Sugiyama and Nakamura, subscribed to by Clark and certainly not discounted by McDonald, that characterized Christianity as "the religion of civilization," that is, the essence of Western civilization.[42] If these young men were to understand Western studies, then they would have to know something of Christianity. It was the acceptance of this idea, the one held by their Japanese mentors, that resulted in the young men being open to Christian influence.

Although it is doubtful whether McDonald was fully aware of the complex and subtle motives behind their conversion to Christianity, he was quickly able to convert his students. On September 27, 1874, McDonald baptized eleven young men, all of them students at the Shizuhatasha.[43] Before their baptism, he had given them special instruction about the nature and obligation of Christian life, the doctrines of Christianity, and the Christian church. He had also discussed with them the condition of their country, the possibility of opposition to their baptism, and even the possibility of persecution. Only one of the eleven had any fears about being baptized.[44] They became Christians entirely of their own free choice; McDonald clearly did not put pressure on any of them to convert. This is not to say that the eleven did not realize that their conversion would please him. As one of them, Henry Satoh (Satō Shigemichi, Kenri), later wrote about McDonald, he was "a gentleman widely admired on account of his high character and of his Christian virtues of doing good for others."[45] McDonald was a hero to them. In terms of their understanding of Christianity, however, it was important that Sugiyama Magaroku acted as McDonald's interpreter in his early Bible classes,[46] for he was already a Christian and could help answer their questions from his own knowledge. Furthermore, most of them had attended the earlier Bible classes held by Clark. The first converts' acquisition of Christianity, therefore, was not solely restricted to their ability to comprehend McDonald's English (although they were all English-language students). There was also perhaps an element of wanting to please Sugiyama, an older and more senior person, by following his example and becoming a Christian.

After the baptismal service, a Christian church was organized in accordance with Canadian Methodist discipline. Tsuyuki Seiichi and Yamanaka Emi, two of the student interpreters, were chosen as class leader and assistant leader.[47] In creating a Methodist class and making these appointments, McDonald realized that the Missionary Society authorities in Canada might feel that he was acting prematurely. He justified his action by pointing out that, if he had to leave Shizuoka unexpectedly, there would at least be some Japanese left behind who were accustomed to holding meetings and even to speaking to the people about the truth of the Bible.[48] McDonald was the only missionary in the Shizuoka area, and his continued presence in the city was by no means secure after the expiration of his two-year contract. He wanted to give the converts an anchor in this Japanese-led class to make then independent of his guidance as quickly as possible. McDonald considered the Christian work he was doing as "underground foundational work," which he hoped would eventually rise about the ground and become visible.[49]

McDonald need not have worried that his work would prove unsuccessful. By March 1875, he had baptized twenty-seven people and had begun to hold regular services on Sunday morning and in the evening. A Bible class presided over by Tsuyuki Seiichi was held on Wednesday evenings.[50] The Methodist class members were also very keen to help in evangelistic work. They were able to assist McDonald as interpreters, as many of them, including Henry Satoh (a Reuters correspondent in later life), had become highly proficient in English; they also went independently into the city and the surrounding villages.[51] This Christian activity was very much in keeping with their general desire to communicate their knowledge of Western things to the broader society.

Although this initial interest in Christianity had been largely restricted to McDonald's students at the Shizuhatasha, by 1876, Christianity had gained a certain popularity in Shizuoka among the townspeople. As McDonald wrote about his Sunday services, "we are obliged to check the geta [wooden clogs]. About four Sabbaths ago, they told me that 380 pairs were checked."[52] Attendance was not always that high, but it does indicate that McDonald's services were attracting local attention, even if part of it was due to just plain curiosity. The number of converts increased quite steadily; by 1877, McDonald had baptized more than 120 people.[53] Of these, some sixty-five maintained a connection with the church in Shizuoka.[54] The number of church members was only just more than half the number baptized simply because that many moved away from Shizuoka to Tokyo in search of employment. Shizuoka was a place where there was little opportunity for ambitious young men to improve themselves.

As early as March 1875, McDonald noted about the students in the Shizuhatasha that "those attending the school are Samurai, since the revolution, they have, to a great extent, been obliged to depend upon their own resources, which, with many, so far as money is concerned, are somewhat limited. Some of them, therefore, will probably avail themselves of the first suitable position which is offered to them."[55] Those students who remained in Shizuoka either could not leave the city for family reasons or lacked ambition. Despite this migration from Shizuoka, by 1877, McDonald found it necessary because of the growth of the church to discontinue using his house as a meeting place and to rent a hall in the city. The average attendance at the regular services was thirty-five.[56]

The notable success that McDonald was achieving in his Christian work provoked opposition. There was no official opposition to his propagation of the gospel, for he mingled socially with the Governor and other leading figures in the prefectural government;[57] indeed, the tolerant attitude of the authorities was one reason why McDonald was able to attract so many people to his service. But there was opposition from the Buddhist and Shintō priests in Shizuoka, who were stimulated by McDonald's activities to take better care of their followers. According to McDonald, Shintō priests made people sign a solemn declaration that they would not go to hear the preaching of the gospel and that they would not become Christian. The Shintō priests reputedly not only described Christianity as a corrupt religion, but also threatened that those who became Christians would no longer be regarded as "citizens."[58] Later, this threat would act as a very potent barrier to the growth of Christian numbers.

The Shintō priests could hardly be blamed for attempting to dissuade the local people from attending Christian meetings. In July 1876, Amenomori Nobushige, a student at the Kaisei Gakkō in Tokyo, wrote to his American professor, W. E. Griffis, about the state of affairs in Shizuoka, pointing out that "about five hundred of the people are gathered together on Sunday evenings to receive the 'Bread of Life' sent down from heaven."[59] At the time, these were the largest Christian meetings taking place anywhere in Japan. According to Amenomori, so many people were attending these services precisely because Buddhist and Shintō priests had spoken so harshly against Christianity. The people were curious to find out for themselves whether Christianity was in fact as bad as the priests said it was.[60]

McDonald was equally capable of religious intolerance. He wrote about Buddhism that there is

> but one power that can remove the encumbrance—take it away root and branch—that is, the Gospel; not the Gospel considered as a code of pure morals only for Buddhism has many excellent precepts, but the Gospel as a Divine power in the salvation of the people, purifying the heart and the conscience, and blessing the people with the joys and hopes of spiritual life.[61]

It is too much to expect that a member of the Protestant church, which in Canada was actively trying to convert Roman Catholics, should be tolerant of the religions of a different culture. McDonald, like all other Protestant missionaries in late nineteenth-century Japan, firmly believed in the superiority of Western civilization. The missionaries often instilled in their Japanese converts a similar sense of the superiority of Western civilization and thus the inferiority of Japanese culture.[62] This inevitably increased the sense of alienation from their own society and culture that the Japanese felt when they became Christian. To the Christians in Shizuoka, however, the most immediately irksome result of Buddhist and Shintō opposition was, not that Christians found themselves no longer regarded as "citizens," but that this opposition made it difficult for them to hire a hall for worship in the city. But as the increasing number of converts suggest, Buddhists and Shintōists were not successful in keeping enquirers away from McDonald.

There were pernicious rumours circulating in Shizuoka about McDonald. McDonald himself related one of them: "I give each person who comes to the service an ichibu (25 cents), but . . . no man is able to keep the money, because, just as he is about to start home, I, by magic art, cause the money to return to my own pocket."[63] Stories such as this were common and perhaps more irritating than anything else to McDonald and to missionaries elsewhere who suffered from Japanese narrow-mindedness and prejudice. Such rumours might well have turned people away from contact with Westerners.

Part of the continuing success in expanding the church in Shizuoka, regardless of unjust rumours and the movement of people away from the city, was due to McDonald undertaking medical work as well as teaching.[64] In 1875, McDonald reported that during the year he had "dispensed medicines freely in season and out of season."[65] Though he admitted that medical work was taking an increasing amount of his time and energy, it was also gaining him friends. This, coupled with his desire to continue both his Japanese-language studies and his Christian work, led him to ask for a reduction in his teaching hours, from five to three hours daily.[66]

Among the first patients McDonald treated in Shizuoka was the former shogun's adopted child, who was suffering from tubercular meningitis. Though the child died, McDonald's attending one of the former shogun's children must have raised his reputation in the eyes of the local people and reinforced his connection with the powers in Shizuoka. But McDonald was not merely interested in catering to the medical needs of the elite. In December 1876, the Shizuoka authorities opened a hospital, and McDonald was appointed a doctor.[67] This was the first Western-style hospital in the prefecture. McDonald's medical practice was not restricted to treating patients at the hospital, however; as his medical work became better known, he was frequently asked to visit sick people outside Shizuoka. He felt obliged to assist people living outside the city, even though this often meant travelling considerable distances. On one occasion, a young child died when he did not respond to a request for help, and the grieving father accused him of causing the child's death.[68] The memory of this incident remained with McDonald for the rest of his life, and his medical work came to take precedence over evangelistic work and even personal convenience. He was often called as far away as Numazu and Shimada and eventually became well known, not only in Shizuoka but also throughout the prefecture. He took the opportunity offered by his medical work to carry on Christian work outside of Shizuoka, and it was partially because of his medical work that the church in Shizuoka developed beyond the students at the Shizuhatasha.

As his reputation increased throughout the prefecture, new opportunities for missionary work appeared. During 1875, McDonald was approached by Ebara Soroku, headmaster of a small private Western-studies school in Numazu, to see if a missionary like McDonald could come to teach in Numazu. Ebara had previously employed Westerners from Yokohama at his school, but these men had proved morally unsuitable. It is clear from the experiences of W. E. Griffis, an American layman who had taught in Fukui in the early 1870s, that sexual temptations were a considerable strain for a single man of Christian principle.[69] A married minister was less likely to succumb.

McDonald stressed to the Mission Board in Toronto that this opportunity in Numazu should be taken up. He firmly believed that, as far as possible, missionaries should bring the schools of Japan under their influence, and he warned the church authorities in Toronto that "you can easily imagine the ruinous effect which a teacher of infidel principles would have upon a school like that of Numazu."[70] The Missionary Society was somewhat tardy in responding to his request; there was some difficulty in finding a suitable man who was willing to go to Japan.[71] This problem might be taken as a sign that the initial enthusiasm for the Japan mission among church members in Canada was waning. This was compounded by another, broader reason: temporarily depressed economic times in Canada had reduced Missionary Society revenues.

The opportunity in Numazu was an excellent one largely because of Ebara Soroku, who was not only a man of real character but also, in Tokugawa eyes, a genuine hero of the Restoration War. He was as well a man of considerable local influence in Numazu.[72] It was not until September 1876 that two new missionaries, George M. Meacham and Charles S. Eby, were sent to Japan. Eby remained in Tokyo to help George Cochran at Nakamura Keiū's Dōjinsha school, while Meacham went to Numazu.

With Meacham in Numazu, McDonald began to think about leaving Shizuoka. After three years of isolation in the interior of Japan, he and his wife were beginning to feel the strain of living in an alien society. McDonald also felt that he was falling behind modern medical practices, particularly in the treatment of the eye diseases common in Japan. In 1877, he applied for leave to attend the Ophthalmical Institution in New York. Although the Mission Board was extremely reluctant to give him permission to leave Japan, it eventually did in early 1878. The major worry of the authorities in Toronto was that McDonald's withdrawal might jeopardize continued financial support for the mission;[73] implicitly, they seemed to believe that he was letting down the Methodist Church by giving up what they considered to be important and successful work. It is probable that McDonald would have achieved much if he had remained in Shizuoka for another year, for it was not until 1879 that a temporary reaction against Christianity in Japan began to set in.

McDonald had realized from the start that he would probably be in Shizuoka for only a limited period of time, thus his decision to establish a Methodist class as soon as the first eleven Japanese had been converted in 1874. McDonald had wanted to ensure that he left behind a church structure. In the absence of numerous converts, the aim of all the pioneer Canadian missionaries was to build a strong church organization which would provide a firm foundation for later expansion. In 1876, the mission in Japan was elevated to a higher organizational level; it became the Japan District of the Toronto Conference of the Methodist Church of Canada. Although Canadian missionaries saw the church in Japan developing as an integral part of the Canadian Methodist Church, at the insistence of the Japanese members, it was known locally as the Japan Methodist Church.[74]

Coinciding with this organizational development, in Tokyo George Cochran began to train three or four Japanese evangelists,[75] including Tsuchiya Hikoroku and Yamanaka Emi from Shizuoka. When McDonald left Shizuoka in 1878, his place was taken by Yamanaka Emi, who already had experience as an evangelist. Later, Yamanaka was helped by Asagawa Hiromi, a convert from Numazu.[76] And the continued presence of Meacham in Numazu meant that there was, at least for a short time, a Canadian missionary relatively close by.

Although McDonald returned to Japan in 1880, he took up permanent residence in Tsukiji where he worked for the next twenty-four years as a doctor, with most of his patients coming from the Western community. After 1880, his missionary work was largely concerned with administration rather than with evangelism or teaching. It was not until 1886 that another Canadian Methodist missionary, F. A. Cassidy, took up permanent residence in Shizuoka.

During the mid-1880s, the Shizuoka Methodist Church was under the charge of Hiraiwa Yoshiyasu.[77] Although some of the older members of the church, including Yamanaka Emi, moved away from Christianity because of disagreements with Hiraiwa, under the care of Hiraiwa the Shizuoka Church steadily grew. Using English-language classes to attract young Japanese to Christianity, Hiraiwa was able to form a second Shizuoka Band, which included Yamaji Aizan.[78] The mid-1880s saw Hiraiwa and other Christians in Shizuoka founding schools and study groups which specialized in teaching the English language. Even for Japanese evangelists, English and the propagation of Christianity went hand in hand. But the foundation of Hiraiwa's later success was laid by Clark and McDonald.

In a real sense, the four years that McDonald spent in Shizuoka were the most dramatic and colourful of his long career as a missionary in Japan. As the first missionary and Western physician in Shizuoka, he left a mark on the history of the city and prefecture that transcends the narrow confines of his Christian work. As a living Western encyclopaedia in Shizuoka, he and his Ontario school primers helped lay the foundations of English-language education; contributed to the development of Western-style medical practice; aided in stimulating interest in female education; and influenced a generation of Christians in the city. He built on the earlier work of Clark, and his initial success was greatly aided by Sugiyama Magaroku, who not only was a Christian already but also came from a prestigious family. Although the authorities in Toronto disapproved of McDonald leaving in 1878, his intention from the start had been to lay the foundations of a church in Shizuoka which could continue without the presence of a Western missionary.

The leading members of the Shizuoka Band proved that they were quite capable of continuing the church after McDonald's departure. The acquisition of Western learning opened new horizons for these men as English teachers, journalists, and pastors. Though very few of them gained national prominence in Japan, in either the Christian or the secular spheres, they did have a significant local impact. They belonged to the losing side in the Restoration struggle, and Western studies provided one means of overcoming the disadvantages of being barred from political power. Their opportunities, however, were limited. And for many of the first converts, acquiring the English language and Western knowledge might well have contributed to ending any secular ambition that they might have had; at the same time as they were learning English from the McDonalds, the first Band members were also obviously developing a very strong sense of loyalty to the Canadians. Out of loyalty to the McDonalds and to their Christian ideas, the early converts became evangelists and some later became pastors, thus consciously choosing to forfeit any chance of secular success. What they created was their own group of disciples who would look up to them as they had looked up to McDonald.

While McDonald had been helping form the Shizuoka Band, the Koishikawa Band had been forming around Nakamura Keiū and George Cochran in Tokyo.

CHAPTER THREE

The Koishikawa Band

When McDonald went to Shizuoka, George Cochran began teaching outside the confines of the treaty ports in Koishikawa ward in Tokyo. His post was at the Dōjinsha school, a private school run by Nakamura Keiū who had previously taught at the Gakumonjo in Shizuoka during E. W. Clark's tenure. Thus the connections between the Dōjinsha and Shizuoka were strong. The Dōjinsha school catered to the needs of the Tokugawa constituency, who had remained in Tokyo after 1868 or, like Nakamura himself, had migrated back to Tokyo from Shizuoka in the early 1870s. Nakamura was one of the leading exponents of the need to accept Christianity in order to underpin Japan's civilization, which placed him and his school in the midst of the intellectual debate about the nature of what Japanese civilization should be.

Just as McDonald brought to Shizuoka medical and teaching skills which facilitated his evangelistic work, Cochran too possessed special capabilities well suited to the intellectual climate in which he found himself in Tokyo. The missionary had to be a composite and rounded figure, for the Christian message alone was not sufficient to convince many Japanese to convert. Cochran's particular strengths were his deep intellectual knowledge of Christianity, his standing within the Western missionary community in Japan, and perhaps the warmth of his personality. He was a man of dignity and wisdom, attributes which might not have been of particular use in the circumstances of provincial Shizuoka but which were of considerable value in the atmosphere of the Dōjinsha school and in dealing with Nakamura, a major intellectual figure in early Meiji Japan.

Through Nakamura's efforts, the Christian influence was already strong at the Dōjinsha school when Cochran arrived. Nakamura's presence, advice, and activity led to an open commitment to Christianity by the Japanese who surrounded him at the school. Because

Cochran stressed spirituality rather than the material benefits of Christianity, the growth of the Koishikawa Band had within it seeds of disappointment for him. The initial attraction of Christianity for Nakamura and the other converts was related to the question of evolving theories of Japanese civilization; they stressed the practical and pragmatic benefits that Christianity could offer society and Japanese civilization. Their Confucian background led them to look at the ethical side of Christianity; becoming Christians, they possibly saw the admixture of Confucianism and Christianity as a uniquely Japanese amalgam. Immediately, however, Christianity offered a panacea for the difficulties that confronted Japanese society.

Between missionary and convert, there was a gap in perception about what was important in Christianity. Whether or not Cochran was aware of this conceptual gap, he made no real effort at the Dōjinsha school to dissuade his converts from believing that Christianity would solve the problems of Japanese civilization. Despite this, his role in the formation of the Koishikawa Band should not be exaggerated. He was an essential participant and performed a role that few other missionaries in Japan could have fulfilled so well. The development of the Band came from the Japanese; Cochran acted only as a catalyst. The crucial factor in the formation of the Koishikawa Band was Nakamura's presence and influence at the Dōjinsha school.

FROM YOKOHAMA TO KOISHIKAWA

Cochran's Christian group at the Dōjinsha school belonged to the same group of individuals who made up the core of the Shizuoka Band. When the Gakumonjo in Shizuoka collapsed they moved on to seek new opportunities in Tokyo. Added to this core were some of E. W. Clark's students at the Kaisei Gakkō, the government college where Clark had begun to teach in 1873. Once his students had expressed an interest in Christianity, Clark directed them to Cochran's Bible class. Clark was an inspiring teacher when it came to science but disappointing when it came to explaining Christianity, at least to the precocious students of the Kaisei Gakkō, the premier Western-studies institution in Japan.[1] Clark may have allowed his youthful fervour for Christianity to get the better of his lecturing technique. The mature, dignified, and erudite Cochran had no such difficulty. Like McDonald, he was an imposing figure and instantly garnered respect.

It was Clark who introduced Cochran to Nakamura Keiū, his personal friend and colleague from Gakumonjo days in Shizuoka. The two friends had travelled down from Tokyo to Yokohama for a visit in January 1874 and had heard Cochran give a sermon at the Union Church. The sermon, "The Person and Work of the Holy Spirit," was part of the founding exercises of the Evangelical Alliance in Japan,[2] for which Cochran was corresponding secretary. Impressed by the sermon, Nakamura invited Cochran to visit him in Tokyo. Nakamura had obviously heard of Cochran before their meeting, from his growing prominence among the missionary group in Yokohama and his official post in the new Evangelical Alliance and also from Sugiyama Magoroku who had wanted him to teach in Shizuoka.[3]

Cochran knew Nakamura as the "Chinese translator" to the Meiji government, the translator of Samuel Smiles' *Self-Help* and J. S. Mill's *On Liberty*, and the writer of a memorial asking the government to tolerate Christianity. Cochran was also told that Nakamura had read the Bible in English as well as in Chinese and was very interested in the Christian religion.[4] Cochran did not know, however, that Nakamura also had a good grasp of Christianity from reading W. A. P. Martin's Chinese explanation of Christianity, *Tendō Sakugen*, a very influential text for Japanese interested in Christianity.[5]

Nakamura's knowledge of Christianity was not simply the product of reading. He had also been exposed to Christianity in England where he had lived between 1866 and early 1868 as one of the supervisors of a group of twelve students sent there by the Tokugawa government. While living in London, Nakamura had been struck by the high moral standards of the English people, which he felt had been fostered by Christianity.[6] Such was his admiration of Christianity that Nakamura had been baptized while in England.[7] The impact of the Christianity he had seen in England is evident in his article, "Keitenaijinsetsu" ("Revere God and Love Man"), which was published in 1868.[8] Likewise, his translation of Samuel Smiles' *Self-Help*, which was published under the title of *Saikokurishihen* (*Stories of Success in the West*), would also appear to attribute the ultimate cause of success to Christianity.[9] The appeal of Christianity, however, was not its spiritual tenets but principally its moral code. This is clear in his 1871 memorial addressed to the Emperor urging tolerance of Christianity; in it, he stated that "the industry, patience and perseverance in their arts, inventions, and machinery, all have their origin in the faith, hope and charity of their religion, and religion is the root and foundation on which their prosperity depends."[10] Nakamura even went as far as advocating that the Emperor himself should be baptized, an act that would help improve relations with the West.[11] Nakamura was so eager to continue studying Christianity that when Clark was originally appointed to teach in Shizuoka, he declined an invitation to join the Iwakura Mission on a trip to the United States in order to study Western religion with Clark in Shizuoka.[12] Nakamura acted as the interpreter for Clark's Bible classes. In February 1872, when W. E. Griffis visited Clark in Shizuoka, he noted that Nakamura was Clark's right-hand man, who was at that

time printing his famous translation of J. S. Mill's *On Liberty*.[13] (Clark
wrote the preface for the translation.) It was clear that Nakamura and
Clark supported each other, Clark helping Nakamura with his translations and in return receiving help for his Bible classes and teaching. It
was this type of relationship that Cochran would come to develop with
Nakamura.

At the time of their first meeting, Cochran did not realize that
Nakamura ran the Dōjinsha school, which Nakamura had started in
1873 to educate the young sons of his friends, the children of ex-
Tokugawa samurai. When Cochran first visited the school in January
1874, it had 100 pupils. In 1874, the Dōjinsha, together with Fukuzawa
Yukichi's Keiō Gijuku and Kondō Makatō's Kōshusha, were regarded
as the best three private schools in Tokyo specializing in Western
studies. Most of the pupils were learning English, and quite a number
could speak it with tolerable fluency.

When Cochran visited the school, Nakamura asked him if he would
occasionally preach on Sunday to the students who could understand
English. Nakamura himself also wanted to receive further instruction
in the doctrines of the gospel.[14] Until this time, Clark and W. E. Griffis,
who were both teaching close by at the Kaisei Gakkō, had been conducting Bible classes at the Dōjinsha (Clark was relatively new, as he had
only begun work at the Kaisei Gakkō in December 1873). Nakamura
obviously hoped that Cochran, as a permanent resident in Japan,
unlike the two contract employees at the government college, might be
convinced to give regular Bible classes. The opportunity to have an
English teacher at the school, which was necessary if the Dōjinsha was
to emerge as an important private school, must also have been at the
back of Nakamura's mind. At the time, Fukuzawa Yukichi was also
looking for an English teacher for his Keiō Gijuku, and A. C. Shaw
accepted the position. Whether it was luck or not, the two Canadians
shared a desire to get away from the confines of the treaty concessions
and both had landed teaching jobs at two of the most prestigious
private schools in Tokyo. In April 1874, Nakamura asked Cochran to
take up residence in the Dōjinsha compound, but he already knew
from Sugiyama Magaroku that Cochran wanted to move out of the
treaty concessions and live among the Japanese.[15] The first step, however, was for Cochran to come to the school to teach the Bible, which he
readily agreed to do.

In mid-January, when Cochran gave his first Bible class at the
Dōjinsha, he was astonished to find more than thirty young men
assembled to hear him. Many of them had Bibles in their hands and
were able to understand an English sermon delivered slowly and dis-
tinctly in simple sentences. At Nakamura's request, Cochran's sermon
was "Man's sinful state, and need of a Saviour," definitely not the

easiest of subjects. The student group listened with apparent attention and at the conclusion asked some intelligent questions. Afterward, Cochran told Nakamura that, as he had no intention of establishing his own congregation in Yokohama, he would be pleased to hold regular Sunday services in Nakamura's house. Nakamura willingly accepted Cochran's offer.[16]

It is clear that the student group at the Dōjinsha already knew something of Christianity. In February 1874, S. R. Brown, an American Dutch Reformed Church missionary,[17] attended one of his friend Clark's Bible classes. Like Cochran, Brown was very much impressed both with the Bible class and with Nakamura, whom he considered, if not already one of Christ's disciples, then someone not far from the "kingdom of heaven."[18] Brown went through a portion of the Epistle to the Romans with eighteen people. Among his audience, he recognized one of his former pupils from the government school in Yokohama who was a Christian and now worked as an assistant teacher at the Dōjinsha (it might well have been Sugiyama), another indication of the interrelationship between the Yokohama Band and the groups in Shizuoka and in Koishikawa at the Dōjinsha school. The room in which Brown gave his lecture was well furnished with English Bibles, and the walls were decorated with numerous large illuminated biblical texts. From what Brown wrote, it is clear that the inspiration for, and indeed knowledge of, Christianity came from the Japanese themselves and specifically from Nakamura. Although there was as yet no Japanese translation of the Bible, the Japanese could use W. A. P. Martin's *Tendō Sakugen* either in Japanese or Chinese translation. Obviously, the Japanese whom Cochran and other missionaries received credit for converting often had a good knowledge of Christianity before coming into contact with missionaries.

Cochran began to come up to the Dōjinsha from Yokohama every Saturday and returned home to his family on Monday. Sometimes he stayed with Nakamura, who provided him with a comfortable Japanese bed and excellent Western-style meals; at other times, he stayed with Clark who lived close by with W. E. Griffis and his sister Margaret Clark Griffis. When he stayed with Clark, Cochran would help with his Bible class of Kaisei Gakkō students on Sunday evenings. At this time, Christian influence at the Kaisei Gakkō was quite strong. Two other professors, E. P. Veeder and, after 1875, E. W. Syles, were also giving Christian instruction outside class to their Kaisei Gakkō students. Furthermore, Hatakeyama Yoshinari, the director of the college and a former student and close friend of Clark from Rutgers days, was, like Nakamura, close to becoming a Christian.[19] For Cochran, the opportunity to have contact with Kaisei Gakkō students offered a new channel for potential converts.

Cochran was also introduced to some of Nakamura's Japanese friends. Shortly after Cochran agreed to come and live at the Dōjinsha, the next step in his relationship with Nakamura developed. The Canadian was a guest at a party given by Nakamura "to meet a large company of his friends—distinguished sinologues, and persons of rank."[20] Among them was "Mr. Okubs [sic], the Lord Mayor of the city of Yedo, and a man who had been in public life many years, first under the Tycoon, and now under the Mikado."[21] This was Ōkubo Ichiō, who had been closely associated with the establishment of the Gakumonjo in Shizuoka and who since 1872 had been Lord Mayor of Tokyo.[22] As a man who was still closely associated with Tokugawa family interests, Ōkubo was obviously well aware and supportive of Nakamura's efforts at the Dōjinsha school and of his interests in Christianity. When Nakamura introduced Cochran to Ōkubo, he told him that Cochran was a missionary and had preached the day before in his house. Even though this was strictly against the letter of the law, Ōkubo did not seem to mind. Indeed, it was at the same party that Cochran learned that "Mr. Katsu, the present Admiral of the Navy in Japan, advised the people of Shidzuoka [sic] to secure, if possible, the services of a Missionary to take charge of their school; and this was the chief reason of their overture to Dr. McDonald."[23] As Katsu Kaishū was so obviously in favour of having McDonald in Shizuoka, it was unlikely that Ōkubo who, like Katsu, was one of the very few high ex-Tokugawa officials to serve in a prominent position in the new Meiji government, would object to Cochran teaching at the Dōjinsha.

What is crucial here is that, in McDonald's and Cochran's cases, their appointments had the blessing of the highest authorities among ex-Tokugawa advisers and that, without this approval, it is unlikely they would have obtained their teaching positions. Regardless of what subsequently happened in Shizuoka or at the Dōjinsha school, the personal influence of Ōkubo and Katsu Kaishū obviously could have cut short any Christian activity, and those who later converted did so realizing that these two senior men did not openly disapprove. Like most other things connected with the beginning of Canadian Methodist evangelistic work, the Canadians owed a debt to E. W. Clark, who was a friend of both Ōkubo Ichiō and Katsu Kaishū. Clark's example had obviously helped in convincing them to approve of hiring missionaries for schools catering to those who had been Tokugawa supporters.

While the two Canadian Methodists had the approval of high advisers, there remained an element of competition for respectable English teachers. Fukuzawa Yukichi was in the process of bringing A. C. Shaw to his Keiō Gijuku school.[24] Leading Japanese intellectuals seem to have felt that Canadians were the best teachers. Or was it that Canadians were more eager to get away from the confines of the treaty concessions than their British or American counterparts? Could it be that Canadians were considered less "imperial" than Britons or Americans? Or were they simply regarded as ersatz English? (The Japanese sources do not provide an answer to the last question.) Disregarding nationality, it is clear that there was a shortage of able teachers, and without a doubt, the Japanese were anxious to get those willing to teach under contract as quickly as possible.

Cochran continued to commute from Yokohama to the Dōjinsha school until August 1874, when the lease on his house on Yokohama Bluff expired. In the interim, Nakamura built him a Western-style house in the Dōjinsha compound. Leaving Yokohama posed a problem; Cochran was leaving behind three of his converts. This was a minor example of what was really a major problem: what happened to converts once the missionary left? In a real sense, a missionary was not dependable, for he moved to a new location or went on furlough when it suited him, which was not always when it suited the Japanese Christians who had become his followers. The fate of Cochran's three converts is instructive. One of them, Makino Ekichirō, for a time followed Cochran to Tokyo but soon returned to Yokohama. He later attached himself to the Methodist Episcopalian North mission; in 1876, Maclay, one of their senior missionaries, mentioned of a "Brother Makino" who was in charge of their mission station at Uraga near Yokohama.[25] Another servant, Yasutomi Kiyohiko, also went to Tokyo where he attended a Japanese school; it was only some five miles from the Dōjinsha and allowed him to keep in touch with Cochran. The third convert from Yokohama, Minagaki, who was one of the Canadian's Japanese-language teachers and whom Cochran baptized just prior to leaving Yokohama, became an elder in one of the Presbyterian churches there. The cases of Makino and Minagaki reveal the phenomenon of denominational changeability, which was a marked feature of early Japanese Christianity. More pertinent, however, is the unusual situation of all three converts remaining Christian after Cochran left Yokohama.

Cochran did not see his move to the Dōjinsha as permanent; he still hoped to secure property in Tsukiji, the treaty concession, where a permanent mission centre could be established. He wanted a roof of his own which was independent of the whims of Japanese employers. For the time being, however, he was content to live in Nakamura's compound until a suitably priced property in Tsukiji could be found.

COCHRAN AT THE DŌJINSHA SCHOOL

At the Dōjinsha, Cochran taught English for one or two hours daily, but his main work was religious. He held a morning and afternoon service every Sunday, with an average attendance of between thirty-five and fifty people. The morning service consisted of a reading of the Psalms in alternate responses, prayer, and a short discourse on some topic of Christian doctrine. The evening service was conducted as a Bible class. Cochran noted: "the interest is remarkably good, considering that I speak only to such as are more or less acquainted with English. Mr. Nakamura assists occasionally by interpreting for me. As soon as I am able to use the native language freely, I shall have a larger audience."[26] As in the initial stage at Shizuoka when Sugiyama interpreted for McDonald, Nakamura's presence at Cochran's services obviously was important in stimulating interest among the students. Unlike McDonald, Cochran never fully mastered spoken Japanese. It is doubtful that he could have dramatically increased his audiences even with fluent Japanese, however, for the youthful audience was attracted to his church services because they offered extra English practice.

Five nights a week, Cochran gave Bible classes, which he obviously enjoyed. In early 1873, he wrote:

> a class of twenty people meets in my study, five evenings of the week, to read the New Testament. We have already gone over the Gospels and the Acts of the Apostles, and are now reading in Romans. I explain every thing, as far as time permits, as we go, giving opportunity for asking questions. This is an exceedingly interesting service, and one from which I expect to see considerable fruit.[27]

Every morning Cochran held family prayers to which six or seven Japanese came. Although the majority of the people who attended the Bible classes and services were Dōjinsha students, a number also came from the Kaisei Gakkō to the Sunday services. Many of them knew Cochran through Clark's Bible classes at the college, and Cochran was not wrong when he noted about them that they were "first class young men, who have studied from five to six years, and read, write and speak it [English] fluently."[28]

Amid this intense Christian activity, it was not long before some decided to become Christians. Nakamura was the first to ask for baptism. After prayers one morning in the middle of November 1874, he asked Cochran, "if you are willing, I would like to be baptized on next Christmas-day, as I wish to begin the public profession of my new life from some important Christian epoch."[29] Nakamura made the request voluntarily and also intimated that his eighteen-year-old adopted son Kazuyoshi would like to be baptized as well. Cochran began giving Nakamura and his adopted son special instruction, stressing the spirituality of Christianity as shown in the doctrines of Grace, the necessity of a change of heart in order to gain a new life, and the moral duties involved in the profession of Christianity. For some time before he was baptized, Nakamura carried a copy of the No. 2 Catechism, which he consulted frequently for the proof-texts and definitions of doctrine. The day before his baptism, he asked Cochran if he could assume a Christian name in addition to his Japanese name. Together Cochran and Nakamura searched through the vocabulary of common English names in Webster's Dictionary and Nakamura chose John because it meant "the gracious gift of God."[30]

The baptism took place on Christmas morning in 1874 in the parlour of Cochran's home and was witnessed by both students and friends. Among those present were General Viscount Saigō's wife and daughter bearing a magnificent floral tribute.[31] Cochran preached a short sermon which was followed by the singing of hymns and finally the baptism of Nakamura and his adopted son.

The presence of members of the intellectual and political elite at this ceremony, such as the wife of Saigō Tsugumichi, is significant. The wives and daughters of distinguished men, rather than the distinguished men themselves, were more usually involved in Christian activities. Though it might well be damaging to a prominent man's reputation to become a Christian, it was less so for his wife or daughters. Among the political elite at this time, only Mori Arinori could be considered, with some stretch of the imagination, a Christian. Among the teaching elite, Fukuzawa Yukichi, although he did not become a Christian himself, allowed his daughter to become one.

The conversion of Nakamura was greeted with joy in Canada. At a meeting of the Mission Board, it was reported:

> Dr. Wood having referred to the conversion of Mr. Nakamura of Yedo, it was proposed to present him with a copy of Wesley's Sermons as a token of our Christian regard, and the Rev. I. Elliot kindly offered to present him with a copy of Watson's Institutes. Mr Dowly of Simcoe wished to have the privilege of giving him a copy of Wesley's Sermons.[32]

There is something slightly ironic about this, for it is doubtful that Canadian Methodists at home really understood that Nakamura was an intellectual of considerable standing in Japan. That gifts were sent to Nakamura from Canada does show that his name was known to Canadian Methodists at home.

Nakamura's conversion to Christianity and his baptism was a signal for others to make a public confession of their faith. In March 1875, four teachers in the school, Tōjō Sezō, Tannō Naonobu, Kozū Sensaburō, and Hosoi Seishō, were baptized. Of these, Hosoi later became an evangelist with the Canadian mission. In this baptismal process, there is an interesting hierarchy of teachers following the principal. In May, Nakamura Tetsu, Nakamura's wife, and other members of the family were baptized. At the same time, Asagawa Hiromi (Asakawa Kokō), who later became a pastor, and Yasutomi Kiyohiko, whom Cochran had baptized in Yokohama, joined the Koishikawa Band in Tokyo. Asagawa, like Yasutomi, had first met Cochran in Yokohama and had lived there with the Cochrans to learn English.[33] The connection with the educational activities of the Tokugawa family in Shizuoka Prefecture is clearly seen in the case of Asagawa Hiromi, who is listed by Ebara Soroku among the graduates and teachers of the Numazu Military Academy and its junior school. Among the major-generals, academicians, and bureaucrats, Asagawa stands out as the first Japan Methodist pastor.[34] In August 1875, two more teachers and members of their families were baptized; the group had filled out along family lines.

In keeping with seniority, the next to be baptized were two students of the Kaisei Gakkō, Kawamura Isami and Hiraiwa Yoshiyasu. Kawamura had studied for two years in Ann Arbor, Michigan, where he had also learned something of Christianity. Shortly after his return to Japan, he began attending Cochran's services and became a candidate for baptism. Because he was an only son and his father had been a high-ranking official in the shogunate, it was feared that his father might oppose his becoming Christian. This was not the case, however. His father gave his full consent and even came to see his son baptized.[35] Within six months, Kawamura's mother and his cousin Ito Yuri had also been converted.[36]

Hiraiwa Yoshiyasu, who was baptized with Kawamura, would later become the leading pastor in the Canadian Methodist mission and an influential Japanese Christian.[37] Hiraiwa was nineteen years old at the time of his baptism in 1875, and for more than fifty years, until his death in 1933, he played a crucial role in the life of the Japan Methodist Church. His father, Hiraiwa Kumei, had held a hereditary position under the Tokugawa shogunate, a position which ironically entailed searching out and bringing to justice all persons charged with belonging to the proscribed Christian sect. The family had descended from Hiraiwa Chikayoshi, who had been a prominent supporter of Tokugawa Ieyasu, the founder of the Tokugawa *bakufu*. The Hiraiwa family had been financially ruined shortly after the Meiji Restoration, but the young Hiraiwa was able to continue his education by writing public examinations for entry into the Kaisei Gakkō in 1873, for which he received a full scholarship. His ambition was eventually to study law and join the Justice Department of the Meiji government; he also had a great desire to travel abroad.[38]

At the Kaisei Gakkō, where Clark was one of his professors, Hiraiwa studied natural science. As a young undergraduate, Hiraiwa was fond of reading such books as Darwin's *Origin of Species*, Huxley's *Revolution*, and Haeckel's *Wonders of the Universe*.[39] His readings and his hereditary prejudice made him dislike Christianity intensely, and he bullied his fellow students who attended the Bible classes Clark gave on Sunday evenings. One Sunday, however, he went to one of Clark's Bible classes where he heard organ music for the first time.[40] Attending another Bible class later on to hear more organ music, he met Cochran, who impressed him greatly and who invited him to the next Sunday service at the Dōjinsha. Hiraiwa went because he wanted an able and authoritative teacher from whom he could find out the errors and evils of the Bible.

Hiraiwa began to attend the services at the Dōjinsha regularly; conveniently, the school was on the way home from his Kaisei Gakkō dormitory, where he lived during the week, to his father's house in Koishikawa, where he spent Sundays. Other Kaisei Gakkō students also joined him, including Ota Kenjirō, who later became a pastor. At the time of Nakamura's baptism, which Hiraiwa witnessed, he still had doubts concerning Christianity. After borrowing some books from Cochran's library, he became convinced that Christianity was not evil and that it was much higher and purer in ethical teaching than was Confucianism.[41] He became a Christian in November 1875 and after Christmas began to preach everywhere he went.

Before his baptism, Hiraiwa held a family consultation concerning the step he was about to take. His family offered no opposition, but they were financially destitute and looked to him for support in the future. In 1876, a year after his conversion and baptism, he was forced to leave the Kaisei Gakkō without graduating to support his family. Thus ended any hope of a law career.

What happened to Hiraiwa's family illustrates the family consequences of an eldest son's conversion. As the eldest son in an impoverished family, Hiraiwa had to provide for the education of his brothers and sisters and the welfare of his parents. His two brothers were adopted into wealthier families; his eldest sister later married Kobayashi Mitsuyasu, one of the leading pastors in the Japan Methodist Church; his younger sister later became a high school teacher and was very active in Christian work.

Dropping out of the Kaisei Gakkō meant that Hiraiwa had to repay his scholarship to the Education Ministry; so initially he was under a double financial burden. His talent had caught the attention of a number of influential people, and through the offices of Mitsukuri Rinshō, a leading official in the Education Ministry, Hiraiwa was made a science teacher at the Government Higher Normal School at Ochanomizu in Tokyo. In 1879, he took on the additional duties of teaching gymnastics, and the following year, he was made the headmaster of the school.[42] During this time, he married Matsui Ginko, the sister of Kanda Naibū, a well-known Christian. His wife had been educated at an American mission school and had been baptized by R. S. Brown, a Dutch Reformed missionary. It was through the good offices of Nakamura that the couple had met and married,[43] which indicates the close-knit nature of the Christian group. Soon after his marriage, despite his new and added responsibilities, Hiraiwa gave up his secular ambitions to become a pastor. Inoue Kaoru, a leading member of the Meiji government, is reported to have said about Hiraiwa that "it was a shame he was not in Government because if he was he would be the top man."[44] Hiraiwa was indeed a talented man with an excellent knowledge of English; he might well have had a brilliant secular career had he not become a pastor. His reputation as a Christian leader suffered somewhat because of the small size of the Canadian Methodist mission. As far as the Koishikawa Band was concerned, there was an almost immediate benefit from Hiraiwa's conversion, for he was able to convince his father, brothers, and sisters, and his uncle and his uncle's family to become Christians. Christianity was very much a family affair.

As the number of converts increased, Cochran formed a Methodist class in December 1875, with Nakamura as class leader and his adopted son as steward. The original class numbered eighteen; three left shortly afterward to go to the United States. According to Cochran, the three were Kozu Sensaburō, a man of "good intellectual ability, a fair scholar, quite unassuming and a person of great moral worth," who went to attend the State Normal School in Albany, New York, "Lawara," and "Asukawa" (Asagawa Hiromi), both of whom went as attachés of the Japanese Commission to the Centennial Exhibition in Philadelphia in 1876.[45] The presence of these latter two at the Centennial Exhibition did not escape a Canadian tourist who asked "a visiting Japanese commissioner . . . if he knew Dr. Cochran. The man grasped the hand of the questioner and said eagerly, 'Dr. Cochran baptized me' and introduced me to a fellow-commissioner, also a convert of our new mission."[46]

Those members of the Methodist class who remained in Tokyo apparently entered into the spirit of their meetings. Importantly, they also began to take up a collection at every meeting, which was to be applied to the contingent expenses of worship and the future support of a Japanese agency. Cochran was pleased with this and noted, "there seems to be a strong disposition amongst all native converts in Japan to cultivate the principle of self-support, so far as the propagation of our gospel by a native agency is concerned. And we feel that it is well to encourage them in this."[47]

Cochran was pleased with developments within the Methodist class, but he was less than pleased with the support he was receiving from the church in Canada. In March 1876, he complained to the home authorities:

> cannot the United Methodist Church of Canada establish one
> strong foreign mission? If not, you may rely on it, to keep two men

here, isolated, working alone, is the nearest thing to waste of funds
that you can come to, after a certain point is reached, and we are
almost touching that point at the present time.[48]

Cochran wanted the Missionary Society to send out more missionaries.
There was indeed only so much two men could do; continued expansion required more missionaries. For its part, the Missionary Society
had been unable to send out more men in 1875 because the Society's
income had dropped during the financial depression in Canada. Further, it encountered difficulties in finding suitable candidates. Finally,
in September 1876, George M. Meacham and Charles S. Eby were sent
out.

Cochran took the opportunity of the arrival of these two new missionaries to form the Japan District of the Toronto Conference in
Canada.[49] The mission was thus incorporated as an integral part of the
Methodist Church of Canada, in the same way that, prior to the
Methodist union of 1874, the Wesleyan Methodists in Ontario had
been part of the British Wesleyan Methodist Church. Cochran was
elected chairman of the District, and Eby, because he was going to stay
in Tokyo to help Cochran, was made secretary. At the insistence of
Nakamura and Hiraiwa, a resolution was passed stating that the official
title of the church would be the Japan Methodist Church; it would not
be named part of the Canadian church, which it was de jure.[50]

To encourage self-reliance within the new district, Cochran began to
give the members of the group in Koishikawa the chance to preach.
Every Sunday he held services in Japanese, and every week a different
member of the class gave a short discourse which had been prepared
under Cochran's supervision. Many of the Japanese showed a strong
desire to preach. Charles Eby noted:

> the work of the brethren thus far has been largely among the
> students and teachers, and a remarkable proportion of the con-
> verts are anxious to preach Christ, whom they have learned to love.
> Nearly a score are already local preachers, and more are coming
> on. Most of them, if the way was open, would become evangelists
> and preachers of the most promising class.[51]

He further added that "they are nearly all graduates or under-
graduates of the Imperial University [Kaisei Gakkō], and some of
them, of eminent scholarly attainments. They are thoroughly versed in
Chinese classics and Confucian philosophy, but they are babes in
Christian theology."[52] This already showed the influence of Hiraiwa on
the Koishikawa Band.

The first candidate Cochran began to train as an evangelist was
Asagawa Hiromi, a very keen local preacher. Others followed him:
Hiraiwa and Hosoi Seishō from the Koishikawa Band and Tsuchiya

Hikoroku and Yamanaka Emi from Shizuoka. Apart from the antipathy of friends toward the Christian religion, the major stumbling block to becoming evangelists was a financial one, as is very clear from the case of Hiraiwa.

Cochran felt that the Canadian Methodist mission should be prepared to support these evangelists.[53] The Mission Board in Toronto was at first apprehensive, because it felt that if "they were accorded the full status of minister they might like those in India demand the same remuneration as the missionaries for their services."[54] Because the cost of the Japan mission had risen dramatically in 1876 from $3,346 to $14,430, mainly owing to the cost of buying property and bringing out the two new missionaries, there was serious alarm in Toronto over the rapidly increasing expenditures of the mission and also over the magnitude of the operations in which the missionaries seemed disposed to engage. The cost of supporting Japanese evangelists could only add to this, and with the expansion of the mission, the number of Japanese evangelists could only increase. It was with some relief that the Mission Board learned from McDonald that the rate of pay for Japanese evangelists should range from $6 per month for students to $10, $12, or $15 per month for men in full connection, with an additional $12 per annum for each child. These rates were in line with those of evangelists belonging to other missions, but nowhere near the $1,893 per annum that it was costing the Mission Board to support Cochran and his family in Japan.[55] The rates for Japanese evangelists were niggardly in the extreme and condemned any man who became an evangelist to live in dire poverty, especially since most had wives, children, and families to support. A great many people who considered becoming evangelists did not because they could not afford it. Indeed, it is a testament to the strength of their conviction that any Japanese, whether in the Canadian Methodist mission or in other missions, did in fact become evangelists.

The Canadian missionaries realized, however, that the training of evangelists could not be taken lightly. As Eby pointed out, "the very fact of their previous culture makes the further thorough training in Christian doctrine absolutely necessary before they can be entrusted with the great work of the ministry; for these men must be, to a great extent, the foundation stones of our future Church in Japan."[56] Eby suggested that the Canadian Methodist mission be allowed to buy property and establish a theological school. Alexander Sutherland, the new Secretary of the Mission Board in Toronto, cautioned Cochran about Eby and his plans: "you will need to move with great caution in the matter of the [theological] Institute." He followed this with a warning:

> Let me say confidentially, if you let Bro. Eby hold the reins he will
> drive you into hopeless burdens and embarassments [sic]. You are

the head of the Mission, and both for your own comfort, and the continued confidence of the Church at home, you must keep the control firmly in your own hands. On not a few occasions Brethren who have read Bro. E's letters have greeted me with the remark "I see Eby is at his wild schemes again."[57]

Eby was indeed a dreamer with an expansive imagination, and Sutherland, with his eye forever on the balance sheets of the Missionary Society, found himself at odds with him. In 1877, Sutherland used the excuse he would use time and time again, that the Mission Board did not have money: "Here we are in hearty sympathy with your work in Japan; but with a prospective debt this year of over $50,000, increased expenditure in any department will be a very grave matter at Central Board."[58] The mission in Japan did not get its theological school. Sympathy was cheap.

Despite the difficulties that the missionaries encountered with the Mission Board in Toronto over funds for a theological school, the work of the missionaries in Japan continued. The year 1876 brought some changes. Mrs. Cochran fell sick—partially, it was believed, because their house in the Dōjinsha compound was unhealthily located near a large pond. In June 1876, the Cochrans moved to a new residence in Surugadai, Tokyo, away from the school but still outside the treaty concessions. Cochran still retained his connection with the Dōjinsha, where he continued to teach English and to hold his English Bible classes. He held his Sunday services in his new Surugadai residence.

THE USHIGOME CHURCH

Among those who attended the services in Surugadai were Yokoi Tokio and Yamazaki Tamenori, both of whom belonged to the famed Kumamoto Band and who were now fellow-students of Hiraiwa at the Kaisei Gakkō.[59] Yokoi, the son of the prominent Yokoi Shōnan, Yamazaki, and Wada Masaka were baptized by Cochran in August 1876. The following month the three of them left Tokyo to join their friends at the Dōshisha school in Kyoto, which had been founded by Niijima Jō in 1875 and was supported by the American Board Mission. Yamazaki died in 1881, but Yokoi went on to become a renowned Congregationalist pastor and later president of Dōshisha College. That Cochran attracted such men to his services while they were in Tokyo and baptized them underlines his influence among the young Christians at the Kaisei Gakkō and the importance of the Koishikawa Band at the time.

The Cochrans' stay in Surugadai was short, Cochran had begun to think that it was time for the mission to buy property in Tsukiji: "no missionary should be subordinate to Japanese, either in the service of the Government, or of private individuals, if he can possibly help it. A man is better prepared to work for Christ, and can judge better as to the effect of his work, if he stands on independent ground."[60] Though he thought that he had been employed by Nakamura under the most favourable circumstances, Cochran now wanted to move back to Tsukiji. McDonald was not so adverse to working under contract to the Japanese; perhaps Cochran was envious of other missionaries who lived very well in Western-style houses in Tsukiji. Another, more important reason was that Eby had been unable to obtain government permission to reside outside the treaty concessions, even though Nakamura wished to employ him at the Dōjinsha. The housing problem was solved with the Mission Board giving Cochran and Eby permission to buy property in Tsukiji, where the two missionaries settled at the end of 1876.

Part of the motivation for moving back to the treaty concessions was simply that Cochran was beginning to feel the psychological strain of living too close to the Japanese. The Satsuma Rebellion of 1877 brought about a temporary reaction against Christianity in Japan.[61] The changed Japanese attitude in 1877 caused Cochran to write acidly:

> the Japanese politeness to foreigners is only a mask, under it there
> is a deep hatred to foreigners and their religion. There is spread
> through England and America a most absurd and false idea of the
> civilization and progress of Japan, which it will take some time to
> correct. The longer a man lives here, and the more closely he
> comes to know the native character, the more thoroughly does he
> learn that they are false at the core, just as might be expected of a
> nation as long bound up in superstition and moral night.[62]

After the Satsuma Rebellion, many schools in which English had been taught were closed down. This prompted Cochran to state: "like children that weary of one toy after another, the Japanese have played with many things in western civilization only to cast them aside as they found them unsuited to their tastes or too costly to keep up."[63] Cochran reveals here a certain intolerance and contempt for the Japanese which was typical of many evangelistic Protestant missionaries in Japan at the time. The sentiments, however, do stand in contrast to the positive view of the Japanese that he had held three years before.

The low spirits of the missionaries caused by the depressing situation in Japan had an adverse effect on some of the mission supporters at home. Sutherland warned from Toronto that several members of the Missionary Society's Committee of Finance and Consultation "expressed the opinion that the tone of letters from the Brethren left it very doubtful whether the brethren there intended to remain in the field."[64] Thus, some were hesitant to approve large expenditures for

Japan because they considered it an unwise investment if the missionaries were not prepared to stay.

The dismal outlook was relieved somewhat when Eby was offered a teaching post in Yamanashi Prefecture, as a result of a trip he had taken into the interior in 1877. Just prior to Eby's departure to take up the post, he received another offer, a professorship at Tokyo Imperial University (the former Kaisei Gakkō). Eby turned it down, despite its salary of $2,400, because of the better prospects for proselytizing in Yamanashi Prefecture. Certainly Eby's appointment in Yamanashi Prefecture did have some influence on defeating a motion in the 1878 General Conference in Canada that called for the amalgamation of the Canadian Methodist mission and the mission of the Methodist Episcopal Church North of the United States. This motion had been tabled by those who were disappointed with the first foreign mission of the Canadian Methodist Church because of its expense and the desire of its missionaries for an early return to Canada.[65]

The removal of the missionaries to Tsukiji had left the Japanese without a convenient place to worship. The number of converts made it awkward to hold services in the living-room of Cochran's home. Cochran began to look about for a suitable preaching place. In 1877, he rented a large house belonging to the Matsudaira family on a crowded street in Kagurasaka. Unfortunately, this house was too large and too opulent; some people were afraid to enter and attendance was poor. The failure to attract many people might well have been one reason for Cochran's pessimism in 1877. In February 1878, this place was abandoned and services were carried on in the home of Hiraiwa's uncle Ota Kijirō in Ushigome, Tokyo. Some months afterward, a vacant lot was bought at no. 17 Tsukudō Mayemachi, where a plain, Western-style church edifice (four ken by seven, a relatively small structure) was built.[66] This Canadian Methodist Church building was dedicated on December 29, 1878. Cochran preached the dedication sermon in English and Hiraiwa acted as interpreter. Nakamura delivered the dedication address, and Dr. Julian Soper of the Methodist Episcopal mission gave a congratulatory speech. The total membership of the Tokyo Church was forty-three; it had risen to forty-nine by March 1879.

In that same month, Cochran, having received the reluctant permission of the Mission Board, returned to Canada. His wife had gone home in late 1877 because of poor health, and continuing anxiety about her condition was behind Cochran's request to be withdrawn from Japan. Back in Canada, Cochran took up pastoral duties. The excellent reputation he had gained in Japan led to his appointment as president of the Toronto Conference for an annual term. In 1882, he was asked by the Mission Board to return to Japan as the principal of the new Canadian Methodist mission school, the Tōyō Eiwa Gakkō. His earlier departure in 1879, however, had marked the end of the beginning of Canadian Methodist work in Tokyo.

During the mid-1870s, while Cochran was at the Dōjinsha, A. C. Shaw, who worked for the British Anglican SPG, was living with Fukuzawa Yukichi in Mita.[67] Like Cochran, Shaw enjoyed early success in making converts. By Christmas 1875, he had baptized a number of his students at the Keiō Gijuku, including Ozaki Yukio who later became an important politician.[68] The student converts formed the nucleus of the congregation of St. Andrew's Church in Shiba, which was opened in the summer of 1876. However, Shaw wrote in late December 1875 that the conversion of the Keiō students was exceptionally difficult because the school was "one in which the most advanced opinions of all subjects are held, and in which Mr. Mill's and Mr. Spencer's writings are used as textbooks."[69] Shaw also spent some of his time writing apologies for his faith in response to the numerous attacks on Christianity appearing in Japanese papers.[70] This is certainly different from Cochran's experience at the Dōjinsha. Nakamura was a Christian and Fukuzawa patently was not, thus Cochran did not have to defend his Christian faith. It was just as well that Shaw did not restrict his evangelistic efforts to students; he also held public meetings which a variety of people attended.

In 1877, Shaw concluded that the evangelization of Japan could not be achieved by foreigners; what was necessary was a trained Japanese ministry.[71] By this time, Cochran also had come to realize the importance of training Japanese evangelists. Shaw and other British Anglican SPG missionaries continued to have a close association with Keiō Gijuku, but by 1877, Shaw was no longer living with Fukuzawa. His efforts were directed toward developing missionary-controlled schools and the training of a Japanese ministry. In the four years following their arrival in 1873, Shaw and his British Anglican SPG colleague, W. B. Wright, had converted some 150 Japanese in Tokyo.[72]

The example of Shaw and the SPG in Tokyo shows that Cochran's decision to concentrate on the development of missionary-controlled institutions, rather than working under Japanese employees, was not unusual. The success of Shaw and Wright in gaining converts also emphasizes that, in the mid-1870s, young people in Tokyo were open to Christian ideas. Although there are parallels between the experiences of Shaw and Cochran, the Anglican missionary effort in Tokyo was much greater than that of the Canadian Methodists. Not only was another SPG missionary working in the city, but there were as well missionaries belonging to the American Church Mission. Until September 1876, Cochran, who was helped by his wife, was alone in Tokyo. His achievements were considerable.

Within the space of five years, from 1874 to 1879, an important Christian group had been formed. The Koishikawa Band, which had its base around Nakamura and the Dōjinsha school, was one of the early groups of Christians in Tokyo. It had in its leader Nakamura a man with a national reputation who was a leading advocate of modernization in Japan. Though initially the Band depended upon Nakamura, the dynamism for the expansion of the Band resided in the young Kaisei Gakkō students who were attracted to Cochran. Kaisei Gakkō students, like Hiraiwa, faced financial difficulties, but it is clear that they could obtain good secular positions after leaving college. The case of the two Band members who became commissioners at the Centennial Exhibition in Philadelphia also shows that, in the mid-1870s at least, conversion did not necessarily affect their ability to obtain government appointments. Certainly, the converts were ex-Tokugawa supporters; however, their educational qualifications were such that, unlike those in Shizuoka, they were insiders when it came to opportunities for employment in government service. The decision of Hiraiwa and Asagawa Hiromi to devote their careers to Christian work was a deliberate rejection of a good secular career. Christian conversion in the Koishikawa Band was very much a family affair. There was little alienation from their immediate families, or it would seem, from Japanese society. In this, their example was similar to that of the Shizuoka Band but different from the case of the famous Kumamoto Band, whose young members were confronted with severe opposition from their families when they announced their conversion to Christianity in 1875.

One of the reasons for this difference was the initial and central role of Nakamura. The Koishikawa Band was made up of his disciples, and, in a real sense, his prestige protected and justified the conversion of others. For the Shizuoka Band, Christian endeavour was only one aspect of the activities of the group. The same is true for the Koishikawa Band. As a group identified with Nakamura, they too played a part in the educational and intellectual endeavours associated with his name from 1874 until 1879. These activities are seen, not only in his writings in the *Meiroku Zasshi* and in the publication of the *Dōjinsha Bungaku Zasshi* but also, and more importantly, in the establishment of the Dōjinsha girls' school in 1875, where Mrs. Cochran taught, and in his interest in kindergartens. Christian conversion, in other words, took place for Nakamura and the others during a period of hectic activity.

Cochran saw his own role within the context of evangelistic effort, but in the overall activity of Nakamura and the Koishikawa Band, he was only a necessary catalyst. For them, Cochran was essential in two ways: first, as a Christian authority who reinforced their Christian ideas and, second, as a living reference book of things Western. Cochran, like McDonald in Shizuoka or Clark before him, acted as a catalyst for Christian ideas and for other intellectual activities. However, the educational interests of Nakamura, as seen in his concern for the education of women and young children, were precisely the fields in which missionaries were also interested. Though Nakamura developed his interest in these areas independently, there was a similarity of interest between him and the missionaries. At this time, the missionaries' perception of Western ideas usually paralleled the Japanese perception of those ideas. It is in this similarity of interest that the influence of Cochran and Clark before him can be seen. It is also clear that Christianity also brought with it a commonality of approach toward issues such as education which resulted in similar efforts being made in Korea, Taiwan, and other mission fields. In all areas, missionaries realized that the Christian message alone was not enough to attract converts and that they had to become involved in secular activities to enhance the appeal of their religion. Yet it would be wrong to suggest that missionaries were only motivated by pragmatic concerns, for it is equally true that most of them sincerely believed that their role was not only to save the souls of East Asian peoples but also to improve the conditions of their lives. Their concern with the welfare of the Japanese was one reason why enquirers were attracted to them. Both Cochran and McDonald manifested such a concern.

CHAPTER FOUR

Contrasts in Japan and Taiwan

In the mid-1870s, the Canadian Methodist mission was able to expand its work away from the two original centres in Shizuoka and Koishikawa. The opportunity to begin evangelistic activity in Numazu and in the hinterland of Yamanashi Prefecture was closely intertwined with the skein of contacts McDonald and Cochran had created. As in Shizuoka, interest in Western studies in Numazu owed its genesis to the Tokugawa educational effort in Shizuoka Prefecture after 1868. Like McDonald, George Meacham taught in a private school which continued to provide Western-studies education after the forced closure of the original Tokugawa institution. On a more modest scale, the case of Numazu provides a further example of the impact of Western ideas and Christianity in Shizuoka Prefecture. Just as Nakamura played a key role in the development of the Koishikawa Band, Ebara Soroku had a profound influence on the emergence of the Numazu Christian group.

The educational activity in Numazu was part of a longstanding concern for Western studies among the *sabakuha* in Shizuoka Prefecture; however, the case of Nambu in Yamanashi Prefecture was somewhat different. Though interest in Western studies had existed there for some time before Eby's arrival, it was an interest among rural villagers in a relatively remote, if not also traditionally backward, region. In that sense, the example of Nambu reveals the relative speed with which Western ideas penetrated at least one part of rural Japan. The beginning of Canadian Methodist work in all four places was conditioned by the intellectual response of the Japanese to the deluge of Western ideas coming into their country. What took place in Taiwan stands in starkest contrast to what occurred in Japan. Almost complete intellectual rejection confronted Mackay's attempts to Christianize the north of the island. Where the response to Christianity of the ex-samurai in early Meiji Japan shows that the Christian message fitted in with the broader concerns of Japanese society, this was definitely not the case in Taiwan. While the overt intransigence of the literati was a major barrier to Christian expansion in Taiwan, it was also a manifestation of the gap between the Christian message and the aspirations of Taiwanese society. Thus, Mackay's example illustrates the work of a jack-of-all-trades under very different and difficult circumstances.

NUMAZU

In September 1876, shortly after he arrived in Japan, George Meacham took a contract-teaching position at the Shihan Gakkō in Numazu,[1] which had been arranged by McDonald following a request from the school's headmaster, Ebara Soroku, for a missionary teacher.[2] The Shihan Gakkō was the Numazu equivalent of the Shizuhatasha in Shizuoka, a private junior school which was an outgrowth and continuation of the Numazu Heigakkō (Fuzoku) Shōgakkō (Numazu Military Academy [Attached] Junior School.) The Shihan Gakkō had its immediate predecessor in the Suseinoya (Shuseisha) and itself would serve as the predecessor to the Numazu Chūgakkō (Numazu Middle School), the changes in name being symptomatic of the difficulties of financing private schools. The intent, however, remained constant: to provide junior school education for the children of ex-Tokugawa samurai and the townspeople of Numazu after the closure of the Numazu Military Academy in 1874. Continuity through all these changes was provided by Ebara Soroku who was associated with all these schools from the beginning in 1872.[3]

Ebara Soroku, the central figure in bringing about the emergence of the Numazu Band and in later life a pillar of the Canadian-sponsored Japan Methodist Church, was born in 1842 in Tokyo, the son of a retainer of the Tokugawa Shogun.[4] His early education had been that of typical samurai; he received a literary education in Chinese, history and mathematics (with abacus), and a military training consisting of sword and rifle exercises and horsemanship. The poverty of his family restricted his formal education and required him to work, but he educated himself as much as possible. In his later life, Ebara mentioned having been so poor as a child that he could not afford to buy a kite and that some of his happiest moments as an adult were helping other young people buy kites and things he had not been able to afford.[5] The financial difficulties of his boyhood proved to be one of the mainsprings in motivating him to assist other people in his later career. At eighteen, Ebara was posted as one of the guards for Westerners in Yokohama and there he began to study Dutch in his leisure time. During the 1860s, he served with the Tokugawa army, first against

Chōshū troops and later against the Imperial forces of Chōshū and Satsuma. He fought at the battle of Fushima-Toba in January 1868 and continued to fight after the Shogun surrendered to the Imperial forces. He commanded troops with valour at the Battle of Kazusa but was badly wounded in this engagement. For three weeks after the battle, he hid without medical attention in a farmer's house near the battlefield until escaping to Tokyo. There he remained in hiding with friends in Ushigome before finally escaping to Numazu, where he was able to resume a normal life when the Meiji government granted him amnesty. In 1871, he was sent by the Meiji government on an educational mission to the United States and England. From the time that he returned to Numazu in early 1872, Ebara was regarded as an expert in educational matters at the secondary school level.

Among the students Ebara taught at the Numazu Military Academy junior school were Asagawa Hiromi, Watase Injirō, who later became a teacher at the Tōyō Eiwa Gakkō in Tokyo, and Yūki Bunisan (Muhimitsu), who later became an evangelist for the Canadian Methodist mission in Yamanashi Prefecture.[6] In his work at the various junior schools during this period, Ebara obviously introduced new ideas. Much later, a Canadian Methodist missionary contended that the Shihan Gakkō where Meacham taught was

> the first school in Japan into which chairs or benches were introduced for the accommodation of the pupils who had all been accustomed to squat upon the floor. Hitherto Chinese literature alone had been taught in the schools; he [Ebara] introduced English, mathematics, gymnastics, horsemanship, and swimming. He also originated the system of charging a small tuition fee. For all these innovations he was severely criticised by the conservatives of the time.[7]

Though the Shihan Gakkō was undoubtedly not the first school in Japan to introduce these innovations, the school did show the progressive spirit of the Tokugawa authorities and that of Ebara in junior school education.

To some extent, therefore, the school had an air of familiarity about it, for George Meacham was a man noted for his scholarship. Like the other pioneer Canadian Methodist missionaries, he came from a rather humble background. He was born in 1833 in Ameliasburg, Ontario, where his father was postmaster. Entering the ministry of the Wesleyan Methodist Church in 1856, he served his probation on the Maitland circuit before graduating from Victoria College in 1860. Following graduation, he settled down to pastoral duties, serving in numerous churches in southern Ontario and Quebec. He received his M.A. from Victoria College in 1872, but this did not take him from pastoral duties. In 1875, when he decided to become a missionary, he was stationed at

Dundas, near Hamilton, Ontario. The example of William Arthur, who had served in Mysore and later had written about his experiences, influenced Meacham to volunteer for overseas mission work.[8] When the original choice of the Mission Board, D. G. Sutherland, was unable to go to Japan, Meacham was sent, taking with him to Numazu his wife and his sister-in-law Martha Moulton.

Meacham's reception in Numazu was extremely friendly, partly because he was one of the first Westerners there and thus an oddity to the students and townspeople. The school was a two-storey house built of cut stone and in a style that Meacham though would have done credit to any Canadian town. The school had a faculty of eight, two of whom—apart from Meacham himself—were engaged as English teachers. Meacham noted that "Mr. Yebara [Ebara], the Principal, is a fine man, deeply interested in the study of Christianity: but his knowledge of the English language is so very limited, that he cannot acquire very rapidly that acquaintance with it which he desires. Two of the teachers are profoundly interested in the study of the Bible, and I believe are seeking Christ with great earnestness."[9]

With one of the teachers from the school as interpreter, Meacham began to hold services in the Buddhist temple which served as his home. Initially, some eighty to ninety people attended these meetings, which prompted Meacham to write home: "I never felt more at home in Canada in preaching than here, and never had I better attention, though the poor creatures, many of them, know not a word I say."[10] The curiosity of a Westerner preaching in a Buddhist temple was a powerful attraction to many people. And despite the ludicrousness of the situation—speaking to an audience that did not understand a word of what he was saying—Meacham was obviously enjoying himself. By the end of January 1877, Meacham had managed to convert six people. Ebara Soroku was the first, and the others were the two English teachers in the school and three of the students.[11]

The crucial conversion was Ebara, who, as headmaster of the school and a well-known figure, played the same role in the Numazu group as Nakamura Keiū did in the Dōjinsha group. Prior to his conversion, Ebara had been strongly influenced by Confucianism and remained so, but he had not been unusually religious. As a young man, he had developed a strong dislike for Christianity because its doctrines seemed to him unworthy of intelligent men. This notion was greatly modified by what he learned during his trip to the West. When first introducing Meacham to his students, Ebara told them that Meacham was a minister of the best religion in the world.[12] Ebara's acceptance of Christianity was in tune with his progressive ideas. His decision to become a Christian was influenced more by Tsuchiya Hikoroku and Hashimoto Mutsushi (Asagawa Hiromi) than by Meacham.[13] The connection between the Numazu group and the Shizuoka Band is clear. Tsuchiya Hikoroku was helping Meacham in Numazu at the time of Ebara's baptism.[14] With Shizuoka Band members helping Meacham, his conversions, in light of his language difficulties, seem reasonable. Again, as in the case of Nakamura and the Koishikawa Band, respect for Ebara's reputation and his ideas also must be taken into account in explaining why a number of Meacham's students became Christians. As far as the church in Canada was concerned, however, it was Meacham who received the credit for the developments in Numazu, which were all the more remarkable because he had only been in Japan a few months. Very possibly, Meacham himself was not aware of the importance of his Japanese helpers in bringing about the conversions.

After these conversions, interest in Christianity in Numazu increased; in late January 1877, Meacham addressed an enthusiastic congregation of more than 200 people. Christian work was expanded into the rural district outside of Numazu, with a preaching place established in Niita village six miles away. Shortly after, a second location was found at Yoshiwari, ten miles outside the city. McDonald sent one of his converts, Henry Satoh, to help Meacham in Yoshiwari,[15] another indication that the Numazu group had strong ties to the Shizuoka Band. At first the turnout at Yoshiwari was very good, but it suddenly dropped off because an officer in the local government had banned the services. This was one of the few instances of opposition to Christianity in the Numazu area. At the school, there was some protest against Meacham's Christian activities from one of the teachers, but the protest was in vain because Ebara was the principal.

After eighteen months in Numazu, Meacham had gathered around him a group of thirty-seven converts, and Ebara and one of the English teachers were conducting Bible classes. By that time, plans had been laid for building a permanent chapel. In the early summer of 1878, the Shihan Gakkō burned down; since this was a time of financial depression following the Satsuma Rebellion of 1877, there was no immediate prospect of the school being rebuilt. Because he could not remain outside the treaty concessions without employment, Meacham was forced to leave Numazu and retire to Tsukiji in Tokyo. In Tokyo, Meacham helped in the formation of the Shitaya Church, the second Canadian Methodist congregation, which was organized in February 1880.[16] Later in the 1880s, he taught theological students at the Canadian Methodist mission school, the Tōyō Eiwa Gakkō, and became the minister to the Western congregation at the Yokohama Union Church, a position he held for many years.[17]

Meacham's departure from Numazu meant that there was no Canadian missionary in Shizuoka Prefecture, for McDonald had already left Shizuoka to go back to Canada on furlough. Meacham was replaced by

Asagawa Hiromi. The church in Numazu, like that in Shizuoka, was developed during the early 1880s through the work of Japanese pastors. In 1881, Miyagawa Minori, then pastor in Numazu, reported having forty-eight people in his congregation, which meant that, though the increase in church members in the three years since Meacham had left was not great, membership had remained constant. Also during this period, Ebara Soroku's interest in Christianity had declined, which removed an important figure from church activities. In 1884, Ebara was stricken with tuberculosis but miraculously survived. His Christian faith was rekindled by this illness, and from then his loyalty to the church never wavered. Unlike Nakamura Keiū, who drifted away from Christianity in the 1880s, Ebara remained a committed Christian and a lay figure in the Japan Methodist Church until his death in 1922.

YAMANASHI PREFECTURE

Charles S. Eby, who had come out to Japan with Meacham and had remained in Tokyo to help Cochran, was offered Yamanashi Prefecture. The offer came in the summer of 1878 and almost coincided with Meacham's departure from Numazu. Eby had been born in Goderich, Ontario, in 1845. In 1866, he decided to enter the ministry and enrolled in Victoria College in Cobourg. In 1868, he took a leave of absence from Victoria College and left on an extended trip to Europe to learn German and French. Returning to Canada, he graduated from college in 1871 and was ordained the same year. Over the next five years, he was engaged in mission work among the German immigrants in Hamilton, Ontario.

Eby was the youngest of the first four Methodist missionaries, and the only one who had previous experience in missionary work. Eby was dynamic, energetic, and linguistically gifted, but essentially he was a dreamer. He left considerable debts behind in Canada, which did not endear him to Alexander Sutherland, Missionary Society Secretary. From the start Sutherland was suspicious that Eby's schemes would result in financial disaster for the Canadian Mission in Japan.[18] In this, Sutherland was not far wrong. The Japanese, who were unaware of his flaws when it came to the management of money, always regarded Eby with great respect, if not affection.

The first sign of an opening for Eby in Yamanashi Prefecture came in 1877, when he received an invitation to visit from a group of students in a small village called Nambu. The originator of the invitation was Kondō Kisoku, "a man of some thirty-five years, of great popularity, and held in honour by all the people, [who] has charge of all the school interests of Nambu and this cluster of villages: has a private school for the study of Chinese of his own, and is the representative of the people in the government of this ken [prefecture]."[19] Kondō had studied Western learning in Nagasaki and had returned to Nambu to establish a school, the Moken Juku (Moken Gakunoya), in 1869. By 1876, the curriculum of the school included the study of Francis Guizot's *History of the United States* and J. S. Mill's *Representative Government*. From reading Guizot, the students became interested in Christianity and formed a Christian study club.[20] The club members pressed Kondō to invite a missionary to visit them, someone who could answer their questions about Christianity. Kondō wrote to Ōmori Shunji (Shunko), a friend of his and of Hiraiwa; Ōmori lived in Tokyo and was a member of Eby's Bible class.[21]

In the summer of 1877, Eby set off to visit Nambu, accompanied by Hitaiwa Yoshiyasu, who acted as interpreter. Eby was warmly welcomed by Kondō and his students and began at once preaching and dispensing copies of the Gospel of Matthew. The only difficulty Eby and Hiraiwa encountered during the three weeks they spent in Nambu came from Nichiren priests, who were not well disposed to seeing Christianity being propagated in their village.[22] Their protests were overriden by the chief of police for Yamanashi Prefecture who condoned Eby's activities.[23] Kondō clearly wanted Eby to take up permanent residence in Nambu, but Eby thought Nambu was too small a village to warrant his living there. He made it plain, however, that he was prepared to life in Kofu, a town of some 40,000 and capital of Yamanashi Prefecture, if this could be arranged. From Kofu, either he or Japanese evangelists could visit Nambu, which would became part of a rural Methodist circuit.[24]

In 1878, Eby was asked by a group of young men in Kofu, who wanted to learn English in order to study Western science, to become their teacher. About this group, Eby wrote: "I saw the persons interested in my coming, they are but little more than boys, and of course have very little money at their disposal. We arranged for a contract which was to give me a minimum of work in teaching, so that my strength could be devoted to the gospel."[25] Eby's wife would handle the bulk of English teaching to leave Eby time to proselytize. Because he had time to propagate the gospel in Kofu, Eby refused the professorial post he was offered at the Kaisei Gakkō.

Among the first converts in the city were Shinkai Eitarō, Komiyama Seisō, Terada Kisaku, and Kobayashi Mitsuyasu. The first three later became influential figures in Kofu; Kobayashi became a leading pastor in the Canadian Methodist mission and Hiraiwa's brother-in-law. Terada was known as a disciple of Ebara Soroku, and the connection between the Kofu group and those in Numazu was further strengthened by Yūki Bunisan, another Ebara disciple. In his Christian work, Eby was helped by Asagawa Hiromi who was sent from Tokyo. Asagawa's example greatly influenced Kobayashi Mitsuyasu. It is said that Kobayashi's conversion was brought about by "the good behaviour of two of Dr. Eby's helpers, Asagawa and Kanei, as different, he [Kobayashi] said, from that of ordinary students as snow from charcoal, made a deep impression on his mind; for he saw it was because of their faith in Christ, and on the 17th of July 1878, he began the study of the Gospels with his friend Kaneko."[26] This again stresses the important role the Japanese evangelists played in bringing about conversions, for which credit was normally given to the missionary.

From Kofu, Eby made frequent trips into the surrounding countryside, travelling by horse, *jinriksha*, or on foot, and preaching wherever he went. On these excursions, Eby was accompanied by Asagawa or Kobayashi. In 1880, Eby began to feel that he had outgrown his usefulness in Kofu. Many years later, in reviewing his career as a missionary in Japan, he wrote: "early in 1878, an opening occurred in the interior. In Kofu we put in two and a half of the happiest years of my life. The soil was virgin and difficult. The climate was right for health. A parish of half a million gave room for action. A Church was planted, seed sown amid the hills."[27] All this was true, but Eby's restless personality left him less than content to stay for a long time in a small quiet inland city. In his memoir, he wrote:

> But as I studied the situation, I felt more and more convinced that Tokyo was the place where our strength should be concentrated if we were ever to take Japan for God. Providence pointed out that as my field, as indeed, Dr. Wood had told me he thought it should be, where the preparation that my previous career had given me would have its widest opportunity.[28]

As with virtually all things that Eby did, his decision to leave Kofu did not please Sutherland back in Toronto. Sutherland wrote to McDonald in 1879:

> Why did he [Eby] propose to return? It seems to us that every effort should be made to secure a reengagement; or if that be impossible an opening should be sought elsewhere. One thing is certain, the Board will not look favourably on a project to locate three of our missionaries in Tokyo.[29]

Despite Sutherland's objections, the Japan District Meeting of 1880 made a firm decision in Eby's favour, asking him to return to Tokyo.[30]

Eby felt that the Japanese congregation in Kofu could carry on the propagation of the gospel without his help. In this he was proven correct, for in the next year, with Tsuchiya Hiroku from Shizuoka as pastor, "the spiritual strength of the little flock was greatly increased as is evidenced by the fact—a remarkable fact in Japan—that the removal of the foreign missionary caused no strain, no weakening on the part of those left behind."³¹ Eby's reputation would have been damaged had the church in Kofu dramatically declined after his withdrawal, but a man like Tsuchiya was experienced enough to minister to the needs of a small congregation. The Kofu group numbered forty-five in 1881. In the early 1880s, the church in Kofu, like those in Shizuoka and Numazu, was solely developed and continued by Japanese pastors. It was not until 1887, when John W. Saunby was sent to Kofu, that the Canadian Methodists had a clerical missionary residing in the city. By the end of 1880, the three Canadian missionaries were all living in Tokyo.

The churches Eby and Meacham left behind in Kofu and Numazu have certain similarities with the first two mission centres. Like the Koishikawa Band, which had Nakamura Keiū as its leader, the Numazu group had Ebara Soroku, a man of local prominence as its leader. Like the Koishikawa Band, the Kofu church expanded as the male members converted their immediate families to Christianity. Before his conversion, Ebara Soroku had come to realize that Christianity was the best religion in the world, and Kobayashi Mitsuyasu of the Kofu group had found that "when reading Wilson's Universal History his mind was much enlightened as he discovered the great power of Christianity in promoting the world's civilization, and he was convinced that such a religion must have a great influence upon the private life of individuals."³² Christianity was seen as a great civilizing power and therefore useful for Japan.

The appeal of Christianity was its moral code. Ebara's and Kobayashi's views of Christianity were very much like those of the converts of the Koishikawa Band, for the converts of the first four Canadian Methodist groups were drawn from the same stock of ex-Tokugawa supporters, who looked to the acquisition of Western learning as a means of improving their own and Japan's future. Moreover, many of the converts had known each other before their conversion. It is clear that Christianity spread through a tangled web of personal connections, as well as through the force of its ideas. In a real sense, the ideas of Christianity were secondary to the relationship between the convert and the group leader. Once the leader had accepted Christianity, it was only a matter of time before his close disciples would become Christians. The Shizuoka and Koishikawa Bands were formed during the mid-1870s, when the intellectual climate in Japan was sympathetic toward Christianity, but by the time the Kofu group was formed this sympathetic climate was fast disappearing. To an extent, the church in Kofu developed at this stage because of its remoteness from the centre of intellectual activity (there was clearly a time lag in the transference of ideas) and, perhaps more importantly, because of the immediate needs of those in Yamanashi Prefecture for Western-style education.

The example of these first four Canadian Methodist centres reveals the need for a favourable atmosphere for Christianity. It points to the vital role that the Japanese evangelists played in expanding the various groups. It also suggests that the missionary was perhaps not always aware of why his Christian work was successful, or unsuccessful. On the other hand, without the missionaries, the four groups of Christians could not have been formed.

Following the return of Eby to Tokyo in late 1880, the nature of the Canadian Methodist missionary work in Japan changed, in the sense that the withdrawal from Kofu marked the end of the period of missionaries being prepared to work in Japanese-owned schools. After that, missionaries would work in circumstances that were largely under their own control. The future lay with the creation of a mission, with its own schools, independent of Japanese control. The pioneer missionaries had achieved their task of founding the Japan mission. After 1880, new missionaries, whose role was different from that of the pioneers, would continue the work.

THE BLACK-BEARDED BARBARIAN IN TAIWAN

While the Canadian Methodists were achieving some success in expanding their Christian work in Japan during the 1870s, in Taiwan George Leslie Mackay worked under different and more difficult conditions. The experience of Mackay in Taiwan under Chinese rule was similar to those of missionaries on the mainland in the late nineteenth century. The Chinese intellectual tradition, marked by dislike and distrust of Westerners and their religion, proved to be a virtually insurmountable barrier to the propagation of Christianity. As well, the man in the street was generally unfriendly to missionaries and unsympathetic to religious beliefs that ran counter to the "highly superstitious and eclectic religious proclivities of the general populace."[33] On their side, missionaries who were able to attract converts from the lowest classes viewed the Chinese literati with suspicion, blaming them for the lack of popular response to the Christian message. Difficulties were inevitable in a situation where missionaries, confident in their own civilization and religious beliefs, were confronted by a society that was equally arrogant. Both sides, the Western "barbarian" and the "heathen" Chinese, had to learn accommodation. The late nineteenth century saw the slow development of missionary knowledge of China and its peoples and of missionary methods; but there was still not that identification of Christianity with popular aspirations that might have overcome the barriers reared by intellectual tradition and cultural conflict. This lack of identification with popular aspirations accounted for major differences between what happened in Taiwan under Chinese rule and what occurred in Japan during the 1870s.

What is striking about Mackay's activities in Taiwan under Chinese rule is that he was able to make any progress in his Christian work at all. The disadvantages of Taiwan as a mission field during the late nineteenth century are patently clear: a largely illiterate Chinese population, poor living conditions, and tropical diseases. Mackay's only advantage was his powerful and determined personality.

Mackay made himself useful to the Chinese by practising as an itinerant dentist. In 1895, he claimed to have made some 21,000 extractions in his first twenty years in Taiwan. Dentistry was the means by which Mackay, who had no formal training, was able to get in touch with the ordinary people. As he pointed out, "the priests and other enemies of the mission may persuade people that fever and other diseases have been cured, not by our medicines, but by the intervention of the gods; but the relief from toothache is too unmistakeable, and because of this tooth-extracting has been more than anything else effective in breaking down prejudice and opposition."[34] Like McDonald in Japan, Mackay realized that converts might be gained through medical work.

What is very clear is that, unlike the Canadians in Japan, Mackay did not have many young people coming to him wanting to become Christians. There was no Shizuoka or Koishikawa Band filled with young students eager to go out and preach the gospel. The first people he converted included a student, a painter, a writer, a carpenter, and a farmer.[35] They were not important figures in Taiwanese society who could draw people to Christianity; Mackay did not have a Taiwanese equivalent to Nakamura Keiū or Ebara Soroku. The Christian beliefs that Mackay propagated were unsophisticated, for his mission catered to the lower classes in society, unlike the missions in Japan which catered to the educated elite.

As well as trying to make converts, another major problem for Mackay was finding suitable missionary colleagues. Between 1875 and 1892, three new clerical missionaries were sent to help him. The first two, J. B. Fraser and K. F. Junor, stayed only three and four years, respectively. The third, John Jamieson, lasted for eight years before succumbing to disease. The relations between Jamieson and his wife and Mackay were very strained. Church papers reported the so-called "Jamieson Affair," which resulted from Mackay taking offense at an inoffensive letter Mrs. Jamieson had written.[36] Mackay was obviously a difficult person to deal with. Alvyn Austin has noted that "the qualities that made his a 'missionary entrepreneur' also touched him with madness, a fact tacitly recognized at home."[37] Whether or not that was the case, Mackay had trouble with Canadian colleagues until the arrival of

William Gauld in Tamsui in 1892. Gauld proved himself to be both physically healthy and mentally tough enough to stay many years in Taiwan.

During the late nineteenth century, Canadian missionaries in north Taiwan were troubled by malaria and other tropical diseases. Mackay himself suffered from malaria and acute meningitis, but he died in 1901 from cancer rather than from an illness directly attributable to his work in Taiwan. Interestingly, the English Presbyterians in south Taiwan do not appear to have been as troubled by disease as their Canadian counterparts in the north, perhaps because of the better climate in Tainan, the headquarters of the English Presbyterian mission. As well, they had the financial resources to build up an educational and medical centre in the midst of their extensive mission compound where the majority of missionaries lived and worked, which may account for their remarkable longevity of service. They created within the compound walls an Anglo-Scottish island amid the surrounding tropicana of Taiwan. Mackay was not able to do this; the Canadian mission was not large enough and lacked finances. While the English Presbyterian mission did possess in Campbell Moody an evangelist as fervent and energetic as Mackay, it also had men like William Campbell and Thomas Barclay, who combined evangelistic and administrative ability with a large amount of plain common sense. They kept their mission on an even keel.

Mackay was too adventurous a spirit to settle down to a sedentary occupation as mission school principal. His strong evangelistic streak took him away on expeditions into the hinterland to search out the headhunters in their mountain fastness and the Taiwanese peasants in their rural hamlets in the valleys. Setting a high standard for himself, perhaps Mackay did not want the responsibility of caring for those who did not have his strength and endurance. Alone, he was responsible only for himself, and perhaps he preferred it that way. The mission would then be his own creation.

Despite this, Mackay did look to the future. In the early 1880s, he founded a mission school in Taiwan, Oxford College, named after the Ontario county whose people raised $6,215 in 1881 for its building costs.[38] To Mackay, the establishment of this school in Tamsui probably meant that he was now a principal and teacher as well as an evangelist. The building of the school, however, does mark the end of the first phase of his missionary career in Taiwan.

Of the pioneer Canadian missionaries in Japan and Taiwan, Mackay stands out, because he alone created the mission in north Taiwan. This is not to denigrate the efforts of those who for a short time helped him, but without Mackay there would very probably have been nothing. Only Charles Eby rivalled Mackay in evangelistic drive. Although

Mackay faced greatly physical difficulties in Taiwan, in a real sense, the missionaries in Japan were faced with a more difficult task. For them, the obstacles were not physical but intellectual.

CHRISTIANITY IN TAIWAN AND JAPAN

The Chinese intellectual tradition stood opposed to the propagation of Christianity in Taiwan, which meant that members of the scholar gentry and the literati would not become Christian. Yet it was not only the overt intransigence of the literati, but also a basic difference in social structure between China and Japan which proved to be a barrier to Christianity. Unlike Japan in the mid-1870s, Christianity simply did not fit into what was going on in China. The example of the Taiping Rebellion suggests that a form of political Christianity (like Liberation Theology) might have worked, but Mackay and his colleagues in China were too pietistic to see such a role for Christianity. In Taiwan, those who did become Christian were mostly impoverished, illiterate peasants and townspeople, thus the Christian message Mackay proselytized was a simple one. In that sense, his belief in the superiority of his own religion and his own civilization was not challenged.

This was not the case with the Japan missionaries; they were dealing with a segment of society, largely ex-samurai, who were highly literate not only in the Confucian classics, but also in Western intellectual thought. The Christian message could not be propagated in an unsophisticated manner, especially when, as became clearer from the 1880s onward, the Japanese knowledge of Western Christian thought was often in advance of that of the missionaries. Strong personality and dynamic presence was one thing, but in Japan this had to be combined with deep knowledge of Christianity on an intellectual plane. As well as remaining true to his own personal convictions in the face of the challenge of Japanese intellectual tradition, the missionary had to be a Christian apologist who could answer the criticism of and scepticism about Christianity which the Japanese had learned from other Western sources. In George Cochran and Davidson McDonald, the Canadian Methodist Church had two exemplary missionaries. They were successful in helping to form the first groups of Canadian Methodist converts in Japan; they rode on the crest of the wave of Western ideas entering Japan.

In 1873, when Christianity was first actively propagated in Japan, the Japanese had already begun to introduce sweeping changes in the structure of their own society. The aim of these changes was implicit in the Meiji Charter Oath and was directed toward gaining an equality in diplomatic and military terms between Japan and the Western powers in east Asia. Although it was understood that equality would be achieved through the acquisition of Western knowledge, the mode in which such equality was to be gained was an issue among Japanese intellectuals. Christianity intersected this debate at one point—the degree to which Japan had to accept Westernization as a symbiotic adjunct to modernization. Fortunately for Christianity, at the time of its initial introduction during the 1870s, it was not seen to pose a challenge to Japanese nationalism or particularism. Just as in Korea between 1904 and 1910, when the most dramatic growth in Korean converts was registered, Christianity in the Japan of the 1870s was considered to be compatible with nationalism. Christianity was understood by the Japanese to be a Western philosophy, and the reaction to it, both positive and negative, was in the context of both the European debate over Christianity and the indigenous Japanese debate.

Because the 1870s was an era that produced a galaxy of outstanding Japanese Christian leaders, it has attracted considerable scholarly attention. One of the first historians of the Protestant movement in Japan, Yamaji Aizan (Yakichi), a convert of the Canadian Methodist mission, is still regarded as an intellectual thinker of some importance. His major essay on Protestantism, "Gendai Nippon Kyōkai shiron" ("Treatise on the Modern Japanese Church"), was written in 1906, and his interpretation of the nature of early Japanese Protestanism has had a profound influence on successive generations of Japanese Christian historians.[39] Yamaji's most significant observations in this essay concerned the conversion of the Yokohama Band in 1872; he saw the Band members being drawn to Christianity because of their loss of status and their suffering following the Meiji Restoration.[40] All the Yokohama Band members had belonged to samurai families loyal to the Tokugawa shogunate, and Yamaji believed they became Christians because of a sense of defeatism. They turned to Christianity, according to him, because they had little hope of finding success in the secular world.[41]

The vast majority of early Protestants were, like Yamaji himself, from families who had supported the losing side in the Meiji Restoration, which meant not only a loss of status but also dire financial straits for most of them. As Irwin Scheiner has pointed out, some declassé samurai chose "to redefine their social and political situation in terms of a new normative synthesis and, eventually, to find in that synthesis an alternative path to power."[42] This is not to say that they became "rice Christians"; rather, through the organized structure of the church, they hoped to regain the leadership role that was their birthright as samurai, which they were barred from holding in the broader secular society because of their familial connection with the Tokugawa cause. Both their connection to the losing side in the Restoration struggle and their frustrated secular ambitions meant that Japanese Christians during this period would stand in opposition to the leadership of the Meiji oligarchy. In becoming Christians and accepting a significant element of Western cultural norms, the samurai went further than most of their contemporaries. The latter sought Western knowledge only for its utilitarian value in obtaining jobs in the changed circumstances of Meiji Japan.

A more positive reason why Protestantism attracted some Japanese in the 1870s can be found in an argument offered by Yokoi Tokio, a member of the famous Kumamoto Band who was baptized by Cochran in 1876. In April of that year, Yokoi wrote to friends that the civilizing of Japan could not be undertaken without encouraging the spread of Christianity.[43] If Japan was to gain equality with the Western powers, it needed to be transformed by the new ideas of civilization and enlightenment, summed up in the slogan "*bunmei-kaika.*" To some, Christianity was considered to be the spiritual basis of the visible power of Western countries, a view that missionaries did nothing to discourage. These Japanese, therefore, became Christians because of their commitment to the new Japan (which transcended their personal hostility to the Meiji oligarchy). Although Yamaji Aizan became a member of the Shizuoka Church in the early 1880s, the reasons for conversion of those associated with the four early Canadian Methodist groups suggest that Yokoi Tokio was more correct in his positive assessment than Yamaji was with his negative view, as far as the first converts of the mission were concerned. Yokoi was in contact with Koishikawa Band members in Tokyo, which lends more credibility to his view.

The most famous Protestant groups in Japan during the 1870s were the Yokohama, Kumamoto, and Sapporo Bands, from which were drawn most of the Japanese Christian leadership for the next fifty years. Many of the general conclusions about the initial conversion of Japanese to Christianity have largely been drawn from the examples of these three Bands and the experiences of the Christian leaders who were among their members. Yamaji Aizan highlighted the Yokohama Band, and a more recent author, Sumiya Mikio, in investigating early Japanese Protestantism in the 1870s, draws heavily on the example of these three groups.[44] One of Sumiya's conclusions is that Japanese Christian conversion, which happened on an individual rather than on a group basis (the pattern of early Christian conversion in Europe), faced opposition from the traditional idea of community which stressed group identification.[45] In other words, Sumiya argues that Christianity was opposed by the particularism of the traditional community as well as by the broader intellectual tradition.

While this may well be correct, the idea is clearly derived from the local persecution of Kumamoto Band members after they had declared their commitment to Christianity in their famous Mount

Hanaoka Oath.[46] Dohi Akio, in the most recent general history of Japanese Protestantism, has continued the tradition of stressing these three Bands and paying only passing attention to other groups which were emerging at the same time.[47] Though the important of the Yokohama, Kumamoto, and Sapporo Bands is clear they would seem to form an unnecessarily narrow base from which to draw general conclusions about the beginnings of Japanese Protestantism.[48] Ōhama Tetsuya's *Meiji Kirisuto Kyōkaishi No Kenkyū*, which investigates the finances and organization of local churches in order to identify the peculiarities of Christian faith in Japan, reveals the value of looking at Christianity at the local level.[49] The point to be made is that local church history tends to suggest that Christian conversion was not simply an individual decision but sometimes a group decision.

A skein of mutual acquaintances wove all the first four groups of converts of the Canadian Methodists together. Christian ideas spread among friends, school chums, and family members. It percolated down in hierarchical order from headmaster to assistant teacher to pupil with the one following his senior's lead in accepting baptism. The role of key figures like Sugiyama Magoroku, Nakamura Keiū, and Ebara Soroku was crucially important in bringing about the conver-sion of their pupils and disciples. The groups expanded along family lines, and ties between the different families were often cemented by marriage ties. There was little evidence of hostility toward Christianity among the families to which the converts belonged. This was possibly the result of conversion in the groups coming from the top down, in that it was the most respected member of the group who first became Christian. Further, it is very clear that their conversion did not happen suddenly but occurred after considerable exposure to Christian ideas. For many of the converts, their acceptance of Christianity came during a period of very hectic study of things Western. They identified them-selves with new ideas from the West, which their role models— Nakamura or Ebara—were intent on introducing into Japan. In accepting the validity of some of these ideas, they understandably would be attracted to Christianity, all the more so because the views of Christianity as espoused by the Japanese seniors were reinforced by Meacham, Eby, and the other Canadian missionaries.

In the 1880s, the intellectual challenge to Christianity in Japan from both Western and Japanese ideas intensified. But it was a new genera-tion of missionaries, arriving in the Japanese Empire during the 1880s, that had to meet this challenge. By 1881, the first and perhaps greatest stage in the history of the Canadian missionary movement was over.

CHAPTER FIVE

Christianization in Japan

The fifty years from 1881 mark a long period of tranquillity before the crises of the 1930s. An epoch of institution building, these years would prove to be the golden age of the missionary movement. It was during this period that the flood-tide of the voluntary endeavour which began in the late nineteenth century reached its crest, at about the time of the World Missionary Conference at Edinburgh in 1910, and then gradually began to recede. The First World War accelerated the decline, for during these four years the missionary movement in the Japanese Empire was isolated from the dramatic changes in Western society produced by the war.

The Canadian Methodist pioneers could only guess at the challenges of the future. Cochran, McDonald, and Eby found themselves back in Tokyo in 1881, and it was clear to them that an anti-Western and anti-Christian mood was running high in Japan. There were a number of causes for this: Japanese irritation at their failure to obtain treaty revision with Great Britain during the late 1870s, and reaction against the flood of Western ideas entering Japan, especially scientific scepticism. In their efforts to develop Japanese theories of civilizations, Japanese intellectuals were becoming more selective of the ideas they accepted from the West. For the moment, this worked against Christianity.

There were differing opinions about how the Canadians should be dealing with this unwelcome change in Japanese society. Cochran and McDonald, with the backing of Alexander Sutherland, the Missionary Society Secretary in Toronto, advocated caution. Not so Charles Eby, the most evangelistic of them all, who looked forward to meeting the anti-Christian challenges head on. By the mid-1880s, throwing all caution to the winds, Eby was calling for an unbridled and massive evangelistic assault on Japan. While the student volunteer movement

Notes for Chapter Five are found on pp. 234-35.

was getting underway in Canada in the mid-1880s, Eby was calling for volunteers to come out to Japan. Although ten years later Alexander Sutherland's active dislike for Eby and Eby's barely controllable enthusiasms led to his forced retirement from the mission field, in the 1880s Eby was the most dynamic Canadian missionary in Japan and, in a real sense, the decade belonged to him. As a missionary on an evangelistic rampage, Eby had a profound impact on the future of the Canadian Methodist mission. His excesses played into the hands of Sutherland and McDonald and their successors, who espoused policies of extreme caution. Such caution came to characterize Canadian Methodist missionary endeavour in Japan, almost unbrokenly in the years after the mid-1890s. In a positive sense, Eby did capture, however fleetingly, the optimistic spirit that pervaded the Japanese Christian movement as a result of the May 1883 evangelistic meetings held in Ueno Park in Tokyo.[1] As well, he was responsible for bringing out to Japan many of the student volunteers, the successors of the old guard whose caution he disparaged.

EBY AND IMMEDIATE CHRISTIANIZATION

On his return to Tokyo from Kofu in 1881, it was the challenge of scientific scepticism that brought out the combativeness in Eby's volatile nature. Darwinian ideas had been known in Japan for some time. Hiraiwa Yoshiyasu admitted that he had read Darwin as a student at the Kaisei Gakkō.[2] During the early 1870s, the conflict between evolutionary ideas and Christianity seemed to pose no difficulties to teachers of science like E. W. Clark and W. E. Griffis. Not all Western teachers in Japan were Christians, however, and the popularity of Darwinian ideas began in October 1877 with three lectures given by Edward S. Morse before large audiences at Tokyo Imperial University. "It was delightful," Morse later recorded, "to explain Darwinian theory without running up against theological prejudice as I often did at home."[3] Japanese enthusiasm for Darwin stemmed partly from the fact that his views provided them with Western ideas they could use to discredit Christianity. In 1877, Tom Paine's arguments had been similarly employed by a Japanese graduate of Cornell.[4] Because they gave hope that Japan's goals could be achieved, evolutionary ideas especially appealed to Japanese intellectuals. Christianity became the immediate target for Japanese intellectuals, for it was now seen as a manifestation of foreign interference which was hindering the progress toward fulfilling national goals.

Among those who showed particular interest in evolutionary ideas were the students at Fukuzawa Yukichi's Keiō Gijuku. Both Morse and Ernest P. Fenellosa, another American professor at Tokyo Imperial

University, lectured to study groups of Keiō students in late 1878. Fenellosa stressed that sophisticated faiths had developed gradually from the animistic beliefs of savages and attacked biblical authority.[5] It was not only the lectures by Western sceptics that created such interest but also the translations into Japanese of articles like Robert Ingersoll's "The Christian Religion," originally published in the *North American Review*, and the appearance in 1880 of a translation of *Descent of Man*.[6]

The new Japanese Christian leadership responded to the challenge of scientific scepticism by studying and then attempting to refute the anti-Christian arguments. Hiraiwa noted in 1882:

> as to private study, I am now digging into philosophical books, so as to acquaint myself with the opposer's position, and to qualify myself for future battle. All my university mates and friends (all graduated now) breathe the spirit of Spencer and also are leaning to materialism. I must be able to say some words to them if they ask me the reason of hope in me.[7]

A vital forum for the discussion of new ideas among the young Japanese Christian leadership was the Tokyo Seinenkai (YMCA), founded in early 1880. Formed on the urging of Kanda Naibū, Hiraiwa's future brother-in-law who had been impressed by the activities of the YMCA while a student in the United States, the group initially met twice monthly. One meeting was devoted to scientific and philosophical lectures for members and the other, to popular lectures for non-members.[8] At twenty-five, Hiraiwa was one of the older founding members of the Seinenkai; at this stage, most of the leading Japanese Christians were still in their early twenties.[9]

The founding of the Seinenkai was shortly followed by the publication of a journal, the *Rikugō Zasshi*, which gave the Japanese Christian leadership an excellent vehicle for refuting the attack on Christianity. It was a magazine designed to improve the morals, customs, and manners of all classes, to promote religion, to clear up erroneous views about the Christian religion, and to show what Christianity really was.[10] Under the enlightened editorship of Kosaki Hiromichi, the *Rikugō Zasshi* went a long way toward meeting these goals and swiftly became an influential intellectual journal in its own right.

The young Japanese Christian leadership saw strength in joining together in the Seinenkai against the tide of scepticism; missionaries also saw the benefit of such co-operative efforts. The Seinenkai began publishing the *Rikugō Zasshi* in November 1880, and concerned missionaries began the *Chrysanthemum* magazine in 1881. Eby was its editor from 1881 until its demise in 1883. Yet during its short life, the magazine provided a forum for the view of the Japanese missionary community.

In October 1881, *Chrysanthemum* pulished Fukuzawa Yukichi's "Christianity: A National Injury." "At present no greater danger [than Christianity] threatens Japan," the author wrote, "and there is no more urgent duty resting upon my countrymen than of resisting its progress."[11] Fukuzawa railed against missionaries and their Japanese converts along all-too-familiar lines. With a vehemence evocative of early seventeenth-century Japanese criticism, Fukuzawa argued that

> if all the Christian missionaries are not spies of their respective governments, and in addition to this the Japanese rascals who become their slaves, and aid them in diffusing this religion, should be called the abettors of these (tai-komochi) mountebanks. Are not these Japanese Christians like the very worst robbers, who would consent to sell their country?[12]

The article was published because such accusations needed to be answered, especially because they criticized Christianity, not in terms of its theology, but on nationalistic and political grounds.

In 1882, Hiraiwa said about Fukuzawa that

> he makes determinate effort to make Buddhism Japanese religion [sic] not because he himself believes in it and thinks it best, but simply as his policy in regard to foreign affairs. He came to dislike foreigners and foreign nations, as they, he thinks, despise the Japanese nation and disregard her rights. He edits *Daily News* and writes the editorial every day. The paper takes every opportunity to ridicule and attack Christianity.[13]

That same year, McDonald sombrely noted,

> if, at the commencement of Mission work in this country, any one entertained the thought, or hope that, owing to the readiness on the part of the Japanese to adopt foreign ideas, the people would come in multitudes to Christ, the hope is not likely to be realized for years to come, . . . it seems that every form of unbelief in the Western world is likely to appear in Japan.[14]

Whether or not McDonald had Nakamura Keiū in mind when he wrote this, the Canadian Methodists really did not have to go further than Nakamura to see the influence of Western ideas on his faith. In the early 1880s, Nakamura drifted away from Canadian influence and toward Unitarianism. He was influenced by Kozū Sensaburō, one of the Dōjinsha teachers Cochran had baptized, who had become interested in Unitarianism while studying in Boston.[15]

The influx of new ideas that were unsympathetic to Christianity did bring about a response from missionaries. Eby, like his friend and predecessor Henry Faulds, the Scottish Presbyterian medical doctor, was not prepared to sit idly by.[16] In the late 1870s, Faulds had given public lectures arguing that the theory of evolution was compatible with Christian faith.[17] According to Kozaki Hiromichi, Faulds was "a Hegelian; and he expounded the philosophy of Comte, Kant and Hegel, as well as Darwin's theory of evolution."[18] Faulds thus provided ammunition for Kozaki, Uemura Masahisa, and other Japanese Christians to fire at their sceptical opponents. Faulds returned to Scotland after the demise of the Japan Mission of the United Presbyterian Church of Scotland in 1883, and his place was taken by Eby. Following Fauld's example, Eby arranged for a series of seven lectures in January 1883 at the Meiji Kuaidō, the largest auditorium in Tokyo. J. A. Ewing, an eminent Scottish engineer who was then on the Faculty of Tokyo Imperial University, was scheduled to deliver one lecture, Walter Dixon of the College of Engineering, another, and Eby, the remaining five.

In his first lecture, "Christianity and Civilization with a Prelude on the Antiquity of Man," Eby stated:

> Christianity is (1) a revelation of the mind of God to the mind of man through Jesus Christ, and of the means by which many may be in eternal harmony with God; and (2) an unfolding to us of the Creator's ideal of a complete man, in the man Jesus Christ, and of the way by which mankind may reach this ideal, the following of which is the progress of the truest civilization, and the attainment of which its grandest culmination.[19]

J. A. Bingham, the United States Minister Plenipotentiary who chaired the lecture, noted in his introduction that "modern civilization is largely the offspring of Christianity. It is physical, intellectual and moral development of individual and collective man, the citizen and the nation. Its beneficent outgoings are to be seen in the science, literature and laws, and in the history, past and present, of our race."[20] Bingham was repeating the old adage that Christianity was the underlying force behind the strength of Western civilization. At the same time, by emphasizing Christianity as revelation, he was blunting the attack from scientific scepticism. By having Judge Bingham chair the lecture and asking Sir Harry Parkes, the British Minister Plenipotentiary to give $300 to cover its publication, Eby was able to marshal the diplomatic weight of the English-speaking community behind his views. The lesson for the Japanese was obvious; Christianity was necessary to achieve their national goals. According to the *Japan Weekly Mail*, whose editor Frank Brinkley was a friend of Eby, the lectures were a "most remarkable success."[21]

In 1884, Eby delivered another major public lecture, entitled "The Eastern Pioneer of Western Civilization and the Recognition Her Efforts Receive." It was a defence of British policy toward Japan and a statement of missionary views on the question of extraterritoriality. It exuded sympathy for the Japanese goal of diplomatic equality. Eby was obviously trying to counter Fukuzawa's criticism of Christianity on political grounds. In his lecture, Eby noted:

> we cannot refrain from earnestly protesting against a policy that would treat Japan as China must be treated while opposed to Western civilization, or Corea [sic], now newly opened to the West. We believe that Japan's spirit and progress and pledges are such as entitle her to some place among civilized nations. She ought not to be condemned to a sort of isolation, rejected from the comity of Oriental nations as having abandoned all that the Orient held dear, rejected from the comity of Western nations as not yet having reached the height—not of the average Western nation—but as not yet equal to the ripest and the best.[22]

Because of his publicly proclaimed opinions on extraterritoriality, Eby gained some recognition from Japanese political leaders and was introduced by Frank Brinkley of the *Japan Weekly Mail* to Ito Hirobumi and Inouye Kaoru.

Whether Eby's speech had any influence on the missionary movement's temporary *bête noire*, Fukuzawa Yukichi, is not known. In 1884, however, Fukuzawa changed his attitude toward Christianity; he advocated "the introduction of the Christianity as the religion of Japan."[23] This change reflected a new pro-Western mood in Japan, stimulated by preparations for the promulgation of a Japanese constitution. It was in the interest of the Meiji government to curry favour among the Great Powers in order to obtain maximum diplomatic benefits from their intention to adopt a Western-style constitution.

Though the Meiji constitution was not proclaimed until 1889, the five preceding years were marked by a strong pro-Western feeling, shown by the emergence of a new generation of Japanese intellectuals, including Tokutomi Sohō. Tokutomi, a man still in his early twenties, had been a member of the Kumamoto Band but had rejected Christianity by the early 1880s. A theorist of civilization, he came to the fore in 1886 with the publication of his *Shorai No Nihon* (*Japan in the Future*). Heavily influenced by Spencerian ideas, Tokutomi argued in this book that all societies in the world, including Japan, were divided into two different types: the military type and the industrial type. He believed that every society would progress from the former to the latter along a unilinear course.[24] Provided Japan followed universal trends through the continued adoption of Western reforms, the country would automatically become the equal of the great Western nations. A second work underlined his points. The publication of *Shin Nihon No Seinen* (*The Youth of New Japan*) in 1887 was directed toward the young rising generation in Japan and stressed the major role it could play in promoting the progress of society and in shaping the destiny of the nation.[25] Although Tokutomi changed his views after the Triple Intervention of 1895 when he realized that world trends were not necessarily leading to international co-operation, during the late 1880s his optimism about the future of Japan helped change the view of the rising generation about the West and about the need for the acceptance of fundamental Westernization.

Because of this changed mood, there was much new interest in Christianity. The mass meetings of Japanese Christians at Ueno Park in Tokyo during May 1883 are usually viewed as the beginning of this Christian boom. During these highly successful meetings, it was even predicted that, through the annual doubling of the number of Japanese Christians (then a mere 10,000), within ten years all 35 million Japanese would be Christian.[26] This was not, at the time, a forlorn hope. Hiraiwa wrote to Mrs. George Cochran in January 1884:

> You heard, I suppose, from Dr. Meacham of the Ecumenical gathering of native Christians in last May, which were very grand meetings. Well, that formed a new epoch in the history of Japanese Christianity, which made since then very rapid progress in the realm. Already there have been added more than two thousand souls, by rough calculation, to the whole community of the Protestant Church in the last year, and there were over seven thousand Christians in the realm by the last December, including children.[27]

The mood of the Japanese Christian movement was very optimistic.

It was against this background that Eby delivered a speech entitled "Immediate Christianization of Japan: Prospects, Plans, Results" at the Tokyo and Yokohama Missionary Conference in 1884. Eby called for a tremendous inter-denominational effort in propagating Christianity. He thought that there should be at least 100 missionaries involved in direct evangelistic work and advocated the establishment of a central Apologetical Institute of Christian Philosophy, complete with lecture hall, library, and publishing house. He also suggested the creation of a national Christian university, which would not only offer better advantages than the Tokyo Imperial University but also rival the best universities in the West .[28] Eby's ideas were enthusiastically approved by the Missionary Conference. They were utopian and impractical, however, and reveal a false sense of optimism about the possibilities of Christianizing Japan. Some of his ideas were nevertheless prescient. A national Christian university eventually was established, the International Christian University in Tokyo, but only after the Pacific War. The problem was, not so much that his ideas were bad, but that they were impractical in the circumstances of the 1880s. Despite this, failing to get more than moral support from other missionaries working in Japan, Eby looked to the Canadian Methodist Church to put his ideas into action.

THE SELF-SUPPORT BAND

On furlough in Canada in 1886, Eby proposed the formation of the Self-Support Band:

> One could not be impressed with the greatness of the opportunity in Japan, and the comparatively small amount that we as a Church were able to do or likely to be able to do on ordinary lines. For years the impression had grown upon my mind that indirectly much might be added to the work of the Board by making use of the opportunity in schools where English teachers were required. The impression grew upon me when at home in 1886, and when I returned in the end of that year it seemed to me that the time had come for action. The Government and Directors of the schools were seeking for teachers and found it difficult to get really suitable men. Why not have these schools supplied by Christian men amongst whom we called to that work might graduate into the Missionary force.[29]

The aim of the Self-Support Band was to supply auxiliary workers to the Canadian Methodist mission, without expense to the Mission Board. In conceiving this idea, Eby was greatly influenced by the marked success of Hudson Taylor's China Inland Mission, which by 1885 had some 640 missionaries working in all but three of the Chinese provinces.[30] In Eby's opinion, the separation of the China Inland Mission from the regular church organization was a fundamental mistake. Thus, he saw the Self-Support Band working in conjunction with the Canadian Methodist mission. The idea of supplying the demand for English teachers in Japanese schools with young Canadian Methodists was an excellent one. Indeed, it was an idea that the YMCA and secular organizations in different Western countries later put into general practice. Like so many of Eby's ideas, however, it was ahead of its time. Eby possessed immense charisma, enthusiasm, and dynamism, but he had not the patience to work out details properly. More than that, he had no sense when it came to money.

These latter considerations worried the Mission Board and especially its Secretary, Alexander Sutherland. Though the Mission Board promised its moral support for the Self-Support Band, there was a difference of opinion about it from the beginning. In 1887, Sutherland wrote to Eby: "True, those who go out are not supposed to be dependent on the funds of the Society but when once they get out there is no telling how many may be 'roped in,' to use your expression, and become part of our regular staff."[31] Sutherland went on to say that a great deal of caution had to be exercised, for "the romance of the thing is likely to attract a good many, and although it may be said they go on their own responsibility, yet if they prove failures something will have to be done with them, for they cannot be left to starve in a strange land."[32] Sutherland had a supporter in McDonald, who was on furlough in 1887 when the idea of the Self-Support Band was in vogue among Canadian Methodists. McDonald later wrote:

> was it a wise movement, a necessary movement? I never regarded it as either wise or necessary. From the very first I saw there could be no permanency about it, and believed that my attitude saved the Band from what would have been a serious embarrassment and many individuals from disaster. When I saw home last [1887] the Band furor was at its height. You would be astonished at the number who were under its influence—young men, men with families, physicians in practice, who appealed to me about going. I put the facts and dangers before them in such a way that not one of these men came.[33]

Eby eventually dissolved the Self-Support Band because he felt it lacked the moral support of the Missionary Society. This excuse was a convenient one, for by 1891 yet another anti-Western mood was beginning in Japan, this time arising from the failure of the promulgation of the Meiji constitution in 1889 to bring immediate diplomatic concessions from the Great Powers. By 1891, the opportunities to place young Canadian teachers in Japanese schools no longer existed.

Between 1886 and 1891, however, twelve volunteers came out to Japan under the Self-Support scheme. They included Miss Cushing and E. Odlum, who brought his family. F. A. Cassidy arrived to teach in Shizuoka, and J. W. Saunby went to Kofu. In 1888, J. G. Dunlop, a graduate of Queen's University in Kingston, took up a teaching post at Hamamatsu, and D. R. McKenzie arrived to teach in Kanazawa. In 1889, William Elliot began to teach in Kofu (and later in Matsumoto), and Harper H. Coates was posted to Kofu. In 1890, Ebenezer Crummy took up a position in Toyama. The Self-Support Band was at least partially successful, for it did increase the number of Canadians working in Japan.

Yet, as if answering Sutherland's worst fears, they were all "roped in" to becoming regular missionaries. That very definitely meant expense for the Mission Board. The Canadian Methodists did get their student volunteers, and some, like Saunby, McKenzie, and Coates, would be pillars of the Canadian Methodist Mission for the next thirty or forty years. Others, like Odlum and S. T. Chown, would remain in Japan only for three or four years. The majority, once ensconced as regular missionaries, were quite prepared to stay as long as health and familial commitments allowed them. Rather than leave them "to starve in a strange land," the Mission Board found itself obliged to make them missionaries. If anything happened to them, it would rebound against the Missionary Society. As McDonald pointed out in 1887, there were large numbers of young men with university educations who were quite prepared to go to Japan without knowing what it was like or what to expect. The enthusiasm generated by the Mount Hermon Conference of 1886 was at it height that year. R. P. Wilder and J. N. Forman from Princeton, who visited the colleges and universities in Canada (including Toronto) and the United States to arouse missionary zeal, persuaded more than 2,200 students to volunteer.[34] It was fervour, not knowledge, that drove them to East Asia.

A typical example of this was D. R. McKenzie who became a missionary after answering Eby's letter in the *Christian Guardian* "appealing to young Canadians who desired to become missionaries, to come to Japan to teach in the Government Colleges about to be opened to earn their living, and to act as an auxiliary missionary force to our regular staff, as the Mission Board was not then sending any more missionaries to Japan."[35] What is striking is the apparent casualness with which McKenzie changed the course of his life. Little wonder Sutherland worried.

McKenzie, and many of the others who joined the Self-Support Band, proved that they had the temperament to become fine missionaries. Some, like William McKenzie in Korea, did not. It was the fear that somebody might come to grief, as William McKenzie did, that drove Missionary Societies to stop attempts by individual church members to work in the mission field outside of official church control.

Unlike McDonald, George Cochran held the view in 1888 that the Self-Support Band were doing a good job and that the mission benefited from their presence. Cochran did not hold, as Sutherland did, the view that the Japanese pastors could carry on the evangelistic work alone. Cochran felt that Canadian missionaries were indispensable in evangelistic work; indeed, at Cochran's request in 1887, Eby had been released from other duties to become Evangelistic Superintendent of the Canadian Methodist mission. Never one to be modest, Eby considered that, as a result of his position as Evangelistic Superintendent, "our membership grew 60 percent, our financial income 100 percent. There was progress and enthusiasm all along the line."[36] McDonald, for one, was not impressed. Returning from his furlough in 1888, he replaced Cochran as chairman of the Japan District and immediately abolished Eby's position. McDonald felt that his authority as chairman of the Japan District would be jeopardized if Eby held a special superintendency. Although Eby was no longer in direct charge of evangelistic work, the Canadian Methodist mission continued to increase the number of converts.[37]

THE JAPAN CONFERENCE

Eby's evangelistic leadership stimulated the Japanese desire for greater local autonomy. This was one subject with which the other Methodist missionaries were in agreement with Eby. Given the widespread Japanese Christian desire for greater independence from missionary control, the Canadian Methodists were quite prepared to meet this problem halfway. Their solution was to elevate the Japan mission to the status of a Missionary Conference within the Methodist Church of Canada, which would give the mission in Japan equal status with the various Canadian Conferences within the Methodist Church. There were two exceptions: it could elect representatives to the General Conference, the Mission Board, and other connexional committees only when authorized by the Mission Board, and it could not interfere in any way with the administration of the Mission Board.[38] It was really only the Canadian missionaries themselves who might chafe under such limitations (of course, it meant that Sutherland's position could not be challenged by the missionaries), for the Japanese were not likely to want to interfere in the running of the Canadian church.

As early as January 1888, correspondence had begun on the possibility of raising the status of the mission from a Methodist district to a Conference.[39] Further impetus came in March 1888 in a letter from the stewards of the Shizuoka Methodist Church, who stated that their church was now in a position to become self-supporting, one prerequisite to acquiring Conference status. For the Japanese Christians in Shizuoka, self-support had a somewhat different implication. In their letter to George Cochran, Yamaji Aizan (Yakichi) and the other four stewards wrote:

> Since the first establishment of our Church, fifteen years ago, we have been favored with pecuniary aid from the Methodist Church of Canada, and by her timely aid, under God's blessing, many souls have been led to Christ. The Christian kindness rendered us by the Canadian Church shall long be remembered, both in the history of our Church and in the minds of our posterity.
>
> And we beg to ask you to report our intention as stated above [that is, becoming self-supporting], and our cherished gratitude to the authorities of the Missionary Society of the Church which you represent in this country. It is our hope that our Church will grow more and more by the help of God, and as long as she shall exist the Canadian brethren's kindness and help shall be remembered by our members.[40]

Clearly, to the Shizuoka Church, self-support meant independence from the Canadian missionary authorities. The church members would find out, however, that missionaries did not give up power that easily.

Self-support was not the only item necessary for gaining Conference status. In order to gain Conference status, according to the Discipline of the Methodist Church of Canada, a mission had to have at least fifteen ordained ministers. In 1889, there were nine Canadian missionaries, six ordained Japanese pastors, and six probationers for the ministry, two of whom were ready for ordination. The total Japanese membership of the mission stood at 1,716.[41] A case could be made that the mission passed all the bare minimum requirements for Conference status. In 1889, Alexander Sutherland arrived in Japan with the commission of the Canadian church to create a Japan Mission Conference, if all the requirements of the Discipline were met.[42] The conditions were met, and the Japan Conference of the Methodist Church of Canada was established.

The Japanese were grateful for the help the Canadians had given their church. In 1889, an address from the Japan Conference to the General Mission Board and the church in Canada stated:

> Although we cannot understand fully your circumstances and surroundings in a land so far away and so different from our own, we still do pray that grace, mercy, and peace may abound upon you all. We thank you for your constant sympathy, shown to us so practically by the sending of missionaries for years, and their constant work of love in preaching Jesus to us who were afar off. Through their earnest work, more than a thousand have become children of God, who were formerly stiff-necked and rebellious against the truth as it is in Jesus. We are like boys and girls who have not yet learned geography, but we have learnt most thoroughly that there is such a place as Canada, and that the people there are rich in love and great in good works.[43]

The statement is highly flattering to Canadian missionaries, but it was indeed a genuine expression of gratitude. Ebara Soroku, Yamanaka Emi, and Toyama Kohei, the authors of the letter, did believe that Canadians were "rich in love and great in good works." Their examples were, after all, George Cochran, Davidson McDonald, George Meacham, and Charles Eby. If nothing else, Japanese Methodists were extremely loyal to the missionaries who helped lead them to Christianity.

The formation of the Japan Conference was as much for the missionaries as it was for the Japanese membership. Davidson McDonald was elected the first president. Until 1899, when he retired from active mission work, he was annually re-elected, except in 1892, when George Cochran had a single term. The Japanese had to wait until 1901 for one of their own, Hiraiwa Yoshiyasu, to be elected president. The missionaries did not sacrifice control over Canadian funds coming into Japan, nor did they allow the Conference to have jurisdiction over where missionaries should be posted in Japan. What they had achieved in the creation of the Conference was to ensure, for the time being at least, that the mission in Japan would continue to develop as an integral part of the Canadian Methodist Church.

Deprived of the opportunity to hold the highest position within the Conference until 1901, Japanese members were nonetheless able to wield some power through the various Conference committees. The Educational Committee, on which Ebara Soroku served, was responsible for the administrative rules and curriculum for the mission schools. The Discipline Committee, of which Yamaji Aizan was a member in the late 1890s, made the Japanese pastors abide by the Methodist Discipline. Further, the Conference was also able to lay down the editorial policy for *Gokyō*, the Methodist magazine, which had Yamaji Aizan as its editor in the mid-1890s. The Conference also had charge of its own Japan Methodist Missionary Society whose activities, needless to say, were very limited.

The creation of the Japan Conference set the organizational structure for the Canadian mission in Japan for the next eighteen years. In 1907, the Canadian mission would join with the two American Methodist Episcopal missions to create a united Japan Methodist Church. In the meantime, the events of the 1880s, culminating in the formation of the Japan Conference, led Eby to propose more expansion for the Canadian mission.

THE CENTRAL TABERNACLE

As well as bringing out more personnel for evangelistic work, Eby felt that there was need for an evangelistic headquarters, an idea much in line with his earlier desire for an Apologetical Institute. In the late 1880s, Eby began pressing for the building of a Central Hall in Tokyo, in the neighbourhood of the Imperial University, for converting students. With the building of a very large church, he thought he would be able to reach "the brain of Japan" in the quickest and most effective way. He wanted this vast church to be an interdenominational endeavour, but he was unable to get financial support from the other missions. While in Canada in 1886, Eby started fund-raising for his church project. In 1887, while he was Evangelistic Superintendent, the Mission Council in Japan appealed for $25,000 to build the church.[44] The money was not forthcoming. Though he expressed some sympathy for the project to George Cochran in 1888, Sutherland noted that there were many demands on the Mission Board's funds and that the sum Eby wanted could not be spared.[45] By 1889, Sutherland was having real doubts about the proposed building:

the conception of "getting his [Eby's] finger on the pulse of Japan,"
as he himself has phrased it, is a grand one, but it is, I fear, illusive.
To get one's finger on the pulse of either man or a nation, only
helps to diagnose a disease, and so indicate a remedy, and if we
were in any doubt on the one point or the other, exceptional
treatment might be justified; but we know already what the malady
is that afflicts Japan, and we know what is the only sufficient remedy.
To a limited extent, and among a certain class of people, lectures
on apologetics may serve a useful purpose; but to spend much time
on this work would be a mistake. Not infrequently such lectures
suggest more doubts than they allay, and it is but seldom they
convince, much less convert. Even the Bishop of the Greek Church
in Japan has cautioned his clergy against the practice, bidding
them preach the Gospel and leave the lecturing to the Protestants.[46]

Sutherland's opinion was echoed in Japan by McDonald.

Despite opposition, Eby, as in the case of the Self-Support Band,
prevailed. In 1890, the Central Tabernacle Church, smaller than Eby
envisaged but still with a seating capacity of 600, was built close to
Tokyo Imperial University. It burned down in 1891 and was rebuilt the
same year. It would remain the largest Canadian Methodist church in
Japan until its destruction in the Tokyo earthquake of 1923. It might be
taken as the crowning achievement of the great growth of the Canadian Methodist mission in the 1880s. It also revealed, however, the
dangerous enthusiasm engendered by the growth of that decade, for
the Central Tabernacle proved to be a mixed blessing. Its evangelistic
programs never met much success among the student population of
Tokyo. In 1905, Hiraiwa suggested that its lack of success, compared
with Ebina Danjō's Hongō Church which attracted large numbers of
Imperial University students, stemmed from an organizational flaw
that put a Canadian missionary in charge of evangelistic work and a
Japanese pastor in charge of the Japanese congregation.[47] True
though this might be, it would seem just as reasonable to suggest that
the Canadian Methodists did not have either a missionary or a
Japanese pastor of the stature or reputation of Ebina Danjō or Uemura
Masahisa to keep a large church filled. The money needed for the
operation of the Central Tabernacle was out of proportion to its
achievement, especially given the successes and needs of smaller
churches of the Canadian Methodist mission.

With the Central Tabernacle falling short of Eby's projections,
Sutherland got his revenge. In 1895, the Mission Board conducted a
special investigation of affairs in Japan, which resulted in Eby's forced
retirement from the mission field after nineteen turbulent years. For
the rest of his long life, Eby worked in pastoral charges in western

Canada, where he could do no harm. The immediate Christianization of Japan would have to wait.

Although Eby was the most dynamic of the Canadian missionaries working during the 1880s, others achieved a good deal with more cautious policies. Eby's dreams were too large for a small mission with a small budget. His excesses led mission authorities to adopt conservative policies. It is possible that, had Eby not been withdrawn from Japan in the mid-1890s, the Canadian Methodist mission might have made a quantum leap in size without great financial support, but it is equally possible that he might have led the mission into more financial quagmires. In one sense, he was cut of the same cloth as George Leslie Mackay and the English Presbyterian Campbell Moody in Taiwan— fiery evangelists, all three. Yet the Taiwanese duo's zeal was tempered by the enervating tropical climate of the island and the steely resistance of the Chinese cultural tradition. Most importantly, they, unlike Eby, were not financially irresponsible. In 1882, a new group of Canadian Methodist missionaries, who proved to be much more financially responsible and more evangelistically committed than the clerics of the Mission Board, began to arrive in Japan. This new group was the Canadian Methodist Woman's Missionary Society, and their chief activity was education.

CHAPTER SIX

Missionary Life in the Japanese Empire

The opportunities for Christianity in the mid-1880s, which Eby sought to exploit through his Self-Support Band and the Central Tabernacle, also saw the missionary movement itself turning from an endeavour dependent upon the efforts of a few pioneers into a large organized movement. From the end of the 1880s onward, the missionary movement developed a distinct missionary lifestyle which remained largely intact until the 1930s. It helped determine the missionary response to the Japanese Empire and maintain the separation of the missionary movement from the indigenous Christian movement.

LIFESTYLE OF THE MISSIONARY

Life in Japan posed distinct cultural and intellectual problems for Canadian missionaries, problems related to their response to an alien culture and also to their relationship to their own Western culture and homeland. Japanese society not only surrounded the missionaries, but also largely isolated them from the regenerating stimulus of their own culture in Canada.

Missionary life reflected these twin tensions. The lifestyle was a natural manifestation of the desire of missionaries to preserve and maintain their own cultural identity. Missionary society was a microcosm of Canadian life transferred overseas, with few concessions to the culture and society which encompassed it. Yet the style of life the missionaries adopted was also their attempt to minimize the difficulties posed by an alien environment. To a great extent, this determined the pattern of missionary contact with the Japanese and their knowledge of Japan. Despite the difficulties a foreign culture and a different language posed, most missionaries found life in Japan relatively agreeable.

Notes for Chapter Six are found on pp. 235-36.

102

Most missionaries shared similar experiences. But major differences in lifestyles did exist between missionaries living in provincial regions and those living in metropolitan areas. The daily environment of provincial and metropolitan missionaries, their friends and acquaintances, their vacations and other aspects of their everyday lives were important influences on the conduct of mission work.

All shared the difficulty of mastering the Japanese language. After the 1870s, though Canadian missionaries spent at least a year in language training, Japanese remained a perpetual problem. C. J. L. Bates, who became president of Kwansei Gakuin in Nishinomiya in 1920, had no more than a limited knowledge of colloquial Japanese. As a young man, when he worked as the evangelistic missionary at the Canadian Methodist Central Tabernacle in Tokyo, he delivered sermons in Japanese, but his inadequate knowledge of the language prevented him from joining in any detailed discussion afterwards.[1] Bates was typical of a large number of missionaries whose linguistic ability was always poor.[2] A minority of missionaries were noted for their knowledge of the Japanese language. Among the pioneers, Davidson McDonald's Japanese was excellent, and among the second generation of Canadian Methodists, H. H. Coates and A. P. McKenzie stand out, as does R. D. M. Shaw who worked for the British Anglicans. Both McKenzie and Shaw were the sons of missionaries and had been brought up in Japan, which obviously contributed greatly to their linguistic success.

An inability to speak Japanese did not necessarily create an insurmountable barrier to effective missionary work, as the early success of the Canadian Methodist pioneer missionaries clearly illustrates. Conversion to Christianity was generally the result, not of a missionary's fluency in Japanese, but rather of his personal contact with the Japanese enquirer. The charisma of the missionary was certainly important. The role of English in the conversion of Japanese enquirers should not be discounted; many Japanese converts were first drawn to missionaries by a desire to learn English. All Japanese Christian workers and priests had some knowledge of English. The letters of Hiraiwa to the Canadian Methodist authorities in Toronto show an excellent grasp of the language. With a limited knowledge of Japanese, most missionaries had to rely very heavily on their Japanese assistants. Because of this communication barrier, the Japanese pastor or catechist acted as a religious comprador between the missionary and the potential convert.

A similar situation existed in Korea and Taiwan and, indeed, in African and Indian mission fields. In Japan, however, the linguistic problem was far greater. Missionaries in British colonies in Africa and India benefited from the fact that English was the language of the colonial power. The language problem in Korea and Taiwan was compounded with the beginning of Japanese colonialism; at least some missionaries had to master not only the local language but also Japanese. In the two Japanese colonies, Canadian missionaries had to propagate a very simple Christian message because of the lower literacy level of their potential converts. In Japan, missionaries were attempting to spread Protestantism in a society with very high literacy levels. Simplistic explanations would not suffice.

As late as 1939, when the British Embassy made a survey of male British subjects in Japan and Taiwan who might be linguistically competent to act as interpreters in Japanese (there were remarkably few), the idea of using Canadian female missionaries was raised.[3] By and large, female missionaries were more proficient in spoken Japanese than their male counterparts, perhaps because single female missionaries had more contact with the Japanese people than their married male colleagues.

Because of language difficulties, only a minority of missionaries engaged in direct evangelistic work. These difficulties did not put great limitations on those missionaries who worked as school teachers, administrators, or even priests in charge of parishes, provided they were well served by Japanese assistants. The Japanese assistants performed the vital tasks of translating sermons and, if necessary, acted as interpreters. They also bore most of the burden of parish visiting. It was one of the main tasks of missionaries to organize and stimulate their assistants to become active evangelists. In a sense, a missionary acted as a team leader and was only as good as the members of his team.

A missionary's knowledge of both the Japanese language and the Japanese people was also in part conditioned by the way he lived. Almost without exception, Canadian missionaries retained their Western lifestyle. In the 1870s, despite the fact that they were teaching in Japanese schools, Cochran and McDonald both lived in Western-style accommodation. In the mid-1870s, George Meacham in Numazu had no choice but to live in a Buddhist temple, but he had his piano and Western furniture. In Hamheung in northern Korea, missionary housing was built in the Korean style, but the interior furnishings were Western. Yet both in Korea and in Japan, missionaries usually built Western-style buildings. W. H. H. Norman described the house of his father, Dan Norman, a Canadian Methodist missionary in Nagano from the turn of the century, as "the embodiment of his mother's protest against the dark huddled Japanese houses of Tokyo."[4] The house Dan Norman designed for his wife and his family in Nagano was a two-storey frame structure similar to those built in many Ontario cities.

The life of the Norman family in Nagano provides a well-documented example of missionary life in provincial Japan in the early twentieth century. Their lifestyle was Western, even to the details of their daily diet. Although it was difficult to obtain Western food locally, items could be easily ordered from Curnow's or Lane and Crawford's in Yokohama or Tokyo.[5] Mrs. Norman liked Magic Baking Powder, a brand unobtainable in Japan, which she ordered directly from Gillett's in Toronto.[6] Vegetables could be grown in the mission compound (thus their purity was guaranteed). Dan Norman is credited with introducing into Nagano Prefecture both apples (for which it is now famous) and white walnuts. As a farmer's son, he knew how to grow things, and as a father with a young family, he wanted good and familiar food. Most Canadian missionaries ate Western food. Though they were not averse to an occasional Japanese meal, it was a rarity.

Malcolm Fenwick introduced new crops to Korea. In 1891, he was the first missionary to settle in Wonsan. He possessed a mission compound with a large garden in which he grew his prize fruit and vegetables. In 1897, his pumpkins, corn, wheat, millet, and oats were greatly admired by his Korean neighbours. That year it was reported that his pumpkins were as large as wash-tubs and that his celery measured twenty-six inches high and seven inches in diameter.[7] In 1901, Fenwick reported an exceptionally fine fruit season in Wonsan: "there is no other place in the East where the apple imported from Europe or America will thrive and not gradually lose its flavor. Wonsan apples grown from American trees are fully equal to those in America."[8] Wonsan apples were selling at very high prices in Vladivostock, and it was predicted that "Korea might become the orchard of the Far East."[9] Fenwick might not have had formal theological training, but he knew how to grow apples, plums, gooseberries, currants, and grapes. The introduction of Western fruits and vegetables and agricultural improvements underlines the fact that the missionary impact on society was much broader than simply the propagation of the Christian message.

Isolation was another problem that confronted Canadian missionaries in provincial centres. In Nagano, the Canadian community after 1902 consisted of the Norman family, two single Canadian Methodist WMS (Women's Missionary Society) missionaries, and the Canadian Anglican Waller family. Once a month, the Canadians met in one of their residences for an English service, followed by tea and cakes.

Missionary children were less affected by a sense of isolation. The Normans had three children, Grace, Howard, and Herbert; the sons were both born after the family moved to Nagano. While they were young children, the two Norman boys played every Saturday with the young Waller children, Wilfred and Gordon,[10] but during the week, they had Japanese playmates. Their Japanese was learned from the maids at home and from their Japanese friends. The Norman children were also free to wander through the town, except during cherry-blossom season when many drunken people roamed about the city.[11] There was virtually no danger from motor vehicles; the first car in Nagano was the Model-T Ford owned by their father, who received it in 1917 as a present from Canadian Methodist supporters at home.

The freedom of the Norman children to play with Japanese friends and to wander about the Japanese city was far different from the experiences of Canadian children living in large centres with a European community. R. C. Armstrong, who taught at the Kwansei Gakuin in the early 1920s, did not allow his young son to have Japanese friends. Many missionaries, including Armstrong, believed that a Western boy or girl might pick up unspecified "bad habits" from Japanese youngsters.[12]

Missionaries did not usually send their children to Japanese schools. Fear of acquiring bad habits aside, this was simply because missionary parents felt that their children would eventually have to make their living at home and thus should be educated there. The Canadian Methodist mission was particularly conscious of the problem of educating missionary children. In 1912, it founded the Canadian (Methodist) Academy in Kobe to provide a Canadian education for the children of its missionaries. This meant that there was no longer a need to send children to Canada until they were ready to enter university.

Despite this general pattern, some missionaries preferred not to send their children to Kobe. P. S. C. Powles, a Canadian Anglican missionary who began work in 1916 in Takata in Niigata Prefecture, decided to have his children educated at home by his wife who had been a school teacher. The Powles children did not attend an organized school, except when the family was on furlough, until they entered university.[13] The Norman children in Nagano were educated at home by their mother, also a school teacher. Later they became boarders at the Canadian Academy in Kobe and matriculated from there into Victoria College, University of Toronto.

Unlike provincial missionaries, missionaries in metropolitan areas were never isolated from Western society. Indeed, they were very much a part of it. Life for missionaries in metropolitan areas was as much within the Western community as it was among the Japanese. George Cochran, for instance, was very much involved with the Western community in Japan through his work with the Evangelical Alliance and as a member of the committee in charge of translating the Old Testament into Japanese. Cochran's colleague, George Meacham, took charge of the Western congregation at the Yokohama Union Church in the 1880s and became an honorary missionary (because he received no stipend from the Canadian authorities). Likewise, Davidson McDonald became an honorary missionary (no stipend as well) when he returned to Japan in 1881, and he made his living as a medical doctor in the Western community in the capital. He had a large practice and also served as a doctor to the British Legation. In Tokyo, McDonald was an active Mason, and when he died in 1904, it was obviously a surprise to some Westerners to learn that he was a missionary as well as a doctor. On the other hand, the Canadian Methodists and the Japan Methodist Church saw him, by the 1890s, strictly as the senior Canadian missionary in Japan and one who controlled mission affairs with an iron hand.

McDonald maintained a link with the British Legation in Tokyo, but how much contact Canadian missionaries had with the British Minister in Japan varied. Sir Harry Parkes (the British Minister from 1868 to 1883) partially influenced the decision of Cochran and McDonald to try to find work outside the confines of the treaty port concessions in the early 1870s. As one of the Western doctors who served the Legation, McDonald had Hugh Fraser (the British Minister from 1889 to 1894) as a patient. In *A Diplomatist's Wife in Japan*, Mary Fraser noted that "many of the Japanese trained nurses have come under the influence of Canadian Methodist missionaries,"[14] another indication of the range of McDonald's activities outside his immediate Christian work.

One of the most traumatic incidents in the history of the Canadian Methodist mission in Japan was the murder in 1890 of T. A. Large, a Canadian missionary teacher at the Tōyō Eiwa Gakkō, the Canadian Methodist mission school for boys founded in Tokyo in 1884. This incident did not escape Mrs. Fraser: "I do not think I was ever more sorry for anybody in my life than for a poor Canadian lady whose husband was murdered in a most horrible way a little while ago."[15] Mrs. Fraser regarded Mrs. Large as one of her friends,[16] which means that Mrs. Large mingled with the highest society in Japan, an especially useful relationship when the Canadian Methodist wished to attract the daughters of leading Japanese figures to their girls' school.

There were other connections between the Canadian missionaries and the British. A. C. Shaw served as chaplain to the British Legation until his death in 1902. During the 1870s, Shaw used diplomatic privilege of this position to enable him to live outside the treaty concessions in Tokyo. Although some British Ministers, like Sir Claude Macdonald, had little to do with Canadian missionaries, usually because they were not ardent churchgoers, others, like Sir Charles Eliot, the British Ambassador during the early 1920s, proved to be open to missionaries. Arthur Hyde Lay, the long-time Consul-General in Seoul, was one of the British consular figures who had a direct connection with Canada; his wife was a relative of Canadian Prime Minister William Lyon Mackenzie King. Whether Lay or his wife were particularly friendly to Canadian missionaries is not known, not is it known whether their ideas about the Japanese had any influence on the opinions of Mackenzie King.

What is clear, however, is that Canadian missionaries were on very good terms with the Canadian Legation in Tokyo after it was established in 1929.[17] As graduates of the University of Toronto, Canadian missionaries had the same alma mater as many of the rising generation of Canadian diplomats. It is not surprising, therefore, that Canadian foreign policy in the postwar era had traces of missionary zeal. Victoria College produced not only D. R. McKenzie, Dan Norman, R. C. Armstrong and other missionaries, but also Lester Pearson, Herbert Norman, Arthur Menzies, and many of the leading figures in the Department of External Affairs during the 1940s and 1950s.

Like most Canadians, the missionaries in Japan spent their holidays in the country and at least part of the hottest summer months in mountain resorts. These summer holidays served the important role of bringing metropolitan and provincial missionaries into social contract. Summer resorts in Japan were a Canadian missionary creation and became a permanent feature of Japanese social life. The first resort, Karuizawa, was discovered and popularized by A. C. Shaw in the late nineteenth century.[18] Its great attraction was a cool highland climate, and for leisure there was tennis, picnicking in the woods, walking, and hill climbing. Missionaries not only from Japan but also from Taiwan and mainland China came to Karuizawa during the summer. By the end of the nineteenth century, this resort in Nagano Prefecture was linked by rail to Tokyo and thus became relatively easy to reach. Karuizawa remained a largely Western resort until the end of the First World War.[19] Later it became popular among the Japanese upper class.

Lake Nojiri, another resort in Nagano Prefecture, was first popularized by Dan Norman of the Canadian Methodist mission.[20] Its climate was hot during the summer, but the lake was ideal for boating and swimming. It could be reached only by road, and throughout this period it remained an exclusively Western resort. Much of the land bordering the lake was owned by an association of missionary shareholders. Although the founder of the resort, Dan Norman, disapproved, the association had a strict policy of not leasing cottages to Japanese.

During the hot months of summer, much Christian work came to a standstill while Western missionaries were on vacation. Christian work in the cities continued, but it was carried on by Japanese clergy and workers. No Protestant missionary was killed in the great Kantō earthquake, which struck Tokyo and Yokohama in the summer of 1923, because the majority of missionaries and their families were on holiday in Karuizawa.

Karuizawa and Lake Nojiri were not the only resorts frequented by missionaries, although they were the most popular. Kamakura, which was close to Tokyo and Yokohama, was convenient for weekend holidays. Atami, the famous hot-springs resort, had Western-style hotels and served as another popular place for missionaries wanting to escape for a few days.

In Korea, Canadian missionaries summered at Wonsan Beach, where there were cottages in a cool pine forest, a sandy beach, and the sea. It was reputed that the natural scenery and climate of Wonsan could not be equalled by any other port in Korea. Beyond the beach were winding valleys formed by low mountain spurs and miles of trails where equestrians, hikers, and bicyclists could enjoy a constant succession of ocean, mountain, and valley scenery.[21]

A summer holiday at Wonsan Beach or Karuizawa sometimes had a serious side. For many missionaries, especially those who lived in the remote areas of Japan, a holiday in Karuizawa was the only time in the year when they met missionaries from their own and other missions. Karuizawa was a frequent venue for annual mission conferences. Because it was not popular among Japanese until after the Great War, it also allowed missionaries to escape for a few weeks from the strains of regular social contact with Japanese.

The summer holiday and activities like mountain and hill climbing, hiking, tennis, and swimming has had a profound influence on Japanese life. Indeed, it is in helping to introduce these leisure pursuits to Japan that Canadian missionaries possibly made some of their most lasting contributions to improving and changing the Japanese way of life. Resorts like Karuizawa and Lake Nojiri and the walnuts and apples planted by Dan Norman represent facets of the Canadian missionary impact on Japan that are as important in their lasting influence upon the broad society as the congregations, schools, and social work that Canadian missionaries established. They represent a side of the missionary that said that life is also for enjoyment and fun, which is by no means a bad contribution to the well-being of Japanese society.

The summer resorts were possible only because missionaries could afford the luxury of extended holidays. Teaching gave most missionaries a long enough vacation to escape to the mountains; as well, they could afford to maintain a standard of living well beyond that of the ordinary Japanese or Korean. Davidson McDonald, when he resided in Shizuoka during the 1870s, had a standard of living equivalent to that of a vice-governor of a province. When he travelled, he usually had two runners in front of his *jinriksha*, a sign of a man of wealth.[22] In itself, the difference in standard of living created a gulf between missionary and ordinary Japanese, including the poorly paid Japanese pastor.

In general, missionaries lived in a solidly middle-class fashion, which included employing servants in house and garden. There was nothing untoward about that situation. In Korea and Taiwan, servants were necessary in order to prevent the theft of belongings, and the mission compound often included very extensive vegetable gardens to ensure that the food on the missionary's table was pure. The spaciousness of the mission compound not only separated the missionary household from the close and perhaps unhealthy confines of the Korean town surrounding the compound wall, but also allowed the missionary land on which to build the ubiquitous tennis court for recreation. In other words, for reasons of health missionaries in Korea and Taiwan had a rather sumptuous lifestyle by Canadian standards. But not every missionary family, especially in Japan, lived in a large compound replete with tennis court. They simply lived well.

Compared to Western businessmen and teachers in government schools in Japan, Canadian missionaries tended to be badly paid. In 1919, D. R. McKenzie, then the senior Canadian Methodist missionary in Japan, complained to Toronto that his salary was only $1,700 per annum, while William Gauntlett (who had come out to Japan in 1888 as a member of the Self-Support Band but had remained as a lay teacher) was receiving in a government school $2,400 a year, with a house supplied and the freedom to supplement his salary. It galled McKenzie that it had taken him seventeen years to pay off a debt of $1,200 to Victoria College for his university education, while Gauntlett, who had no university education, received higher pay.[23] In reality, salaries either for missionaries or for government teachers had not changed greatly from the 1870s.[24] The sharp inflation of the post-First World War period led Canadian Methodist missionaries to ask for a large increase in salary. In July 1920, new pay scales were introduced, and missionaries in Japan received considerably higher wages than Canadian Methodist missionaries working in West China, but not the desired parity with YMCA missionaries working in Japan.[25] While Canadian Methodist missionaries fared relatively badly in comparison with other Westerners in Japan, there is no question that the vast majority of Canadian missionary families were able to maintain a standard of living much higher than their colleagues at home who served as missionaries in western Canada or were ministers of churches in rural Ontario or Nova Scotia.

Although the nature of missionary life in Japan created a gulf between the missionaries and Japanese, it is doubtful whether missionaries would have been any more successful if they had adopted Japanese dress, customs, and standards of living. The Western lifestyle of the missionaries was in itself attractive to many Japanese, particularly the family relationships. In maintaining their own way of life, missionaries undoubtedly adopted the wisest course.

INTELLECTUAL PURSUITS

Intellectual pursuits provided some missionaries with another escape from the pressures of life in the Japanese Empire. Metropolitan missionaries showed greater interest in things intellectual than their provincial colleagues. Despite this, a perceptive missionary observer, Herbert Kelly, a British Anglican who came out to Japan in 1913, criticized the Western community, and by inference the missionary movement, for intellectual poverty. He complained that the Western community was very small, that everybody in it knew each other, and that all their ideas were American, which he considered "very intellectually conventional."[26] Kelly's view of the foreign community was undoubtedly exaggerated, for he was by nature very critical of everybody except himself. Yet it is true that Canadian missionaries in Korea and Taiwan showed a far greater intellectual interest in the culture of those countries than their contemporaries did in Japan.

A fair number of missionaries were members of the Asiatic Society of Japan, an English-language learned society founded in 1872. George Cochran was an officer; Caroline MacDonald, an independent missionary associated with the YWCA during the 1910s, was the first female councillor.[27] The meetings of the Asiatic Society were useful, not only for learning more about the history and culture of Japan, but also for socializing with other Westerners, especially diplomats. A fair number of Canadian missionaries belonged to the Society but few delivered papers; presumably, its social side was the main attraction. It was different in Korea where James Scarth Gale, who served with the American Presbyterian Mission North in Seoul, was one of the founders of the Royal Asiatic Society, Korea Branch, in 1900 and its first corresponding secretary. Gale published in the transactions of the Society papers on a wide range of subjects relating to Korean culture.

The interest of missionaries in the culture of their mission field appears most clearly in their important writings on various aspects of the development of Japan or Korea. It was natural for missionaries to take an interest in Japan's traditional religions. Although the pioneer Canadian Methodist missionaries, who viewed Roman Catholicism in their own country with great bitterness, could be expected to regard Japanese traditional religions with open hostility, the emerging humanitarian concern of their work brought with it a more tolerant attitude toward Buddhism and Shintō. This change was also partially a reflection of growing missionary knowledge of Japanese traditional religions. This new tolerance also revealed the growing influence of liberal theology upon non-Conformist missionaries. While British Anglicans were among the first to study Japanese Buddhism seriously, the change in both the underlying concern of missionary work and the attitude to indigenous faiths were most marked in Canadian Methodists.

Among Canadian Methodist missionaries interested in Buddhism were H. H. Coates and R. C. Armstrong. Armstrong's concern with Buddhism stemmed from being challenged by Japanese scholars to show where Christianity surpassed what the Japanese already possessed in their religions and cultural heritage.[28] H. H. Coates coauthored a life of Honen (1133-1212), the founder of the Pure Land School of Buddhism.[29] R. C. Armstrong, who received his doctorate from the University of Toronto in 1914, was concerned at first with Japanese Confucian studies. This led him to write a life of Ninomiya Sontoku (1787-1866), a peasant sage who stress the efficacy of agrarian life and was a symbol of diligence.[30] Later Armstrong moved to writing general surveys of Japanese Buddhism.[31] Whereas Coates' biography of Honen was a worthwhile contribution to knowledge, Armstrong's works on Buddhism lacked this originality. The Anglican R. D. M. Shaw, the son of A. C. Shaw, was a well-known scholar of Zen Buddhism and translated a number of works into English.[32] Egerton Ryerson was an Anglican from Canada whose interest in *netsuke* led him to publish a study which remains the standard English introduction to that subject.[33] In 1921, when Japanese Buddhism was in vogue (during Sir Charles Eliot's British ambassadorship), Samuel Heaslett, the British Anglican Bishop of South Tokyo, made the acerbic remark, perhaps directed against R. D. M. Shaw, that "if a missionary did not have a gospel to preach, he filled his time by studying Buddhism."[34]

In Korea, James Scarth Gale went far beyond the study of Buddhism. In the introduction to Gale's translation of *The Cloud Dream of the Nine*, published in 1922, Elspeth Keith Robertson Scott, a well-known authority on East Asian culture, described Gale as "the foremost literary interpreter to the West of the Korean mind."[35] In acquiring this mantle, Gale received considerable help; as Robertson Scott noted "the chief native helper of this quiet-eyed missionary in the work of translation has been with him for thirty years."[36] It is partially this help from Koreans that made Gale's magnum opus, the scholarly *History of the Korean People* (1924-1927), such a worthy book.[37] Gale was also a prolific contributor to the *Korean Repository* (1892-1898) and to other magazines. Together with his friend Bishop Mark Napier Trollope of the English Church Mission, whose linguistic gifts and knowledge of Korean culture equalled his, Gale must be regarded as one of the finest Western scholars of Korea. The sheer range of his inquisitiveness into Korean culture (if not also the sheer depth of his understanding) places him in a different class than his Canadian missionary counterparts in Japan, such as Armstrong and Coates, whose interests were largely restricted to Confucianism and Buddhism.

Yet Gale's scholarly interests were only one facet of his literary endeavours. He was the compiler of a Korean-English dictionary which went through a number of editions.[38] In 1895, he translated John Bunyan's *Pilgrim's Progress*, the first Korean translation of this Christian work.[39] He was an active member of the Board of Translators for both the New and Old Testaments (published in 1900 and 1911, respectively).[40] He was also very much involved with and for a time president of the Korean branch of the Christian Literature Society. In Japan, George Cochran served on the Board of Translators for the Japanese-language Old Testament, but he was a member because of his knowledge of the Bible, not because he was a translator. Although articles by Canadian missionaries in Japan appeared in the vernacular press (for example, the essays by Cochran and Eby published in translation in the influential Christian magazine *Rikugō Zasshi*),[41] no first-generation Canadian missionary in Japan could equal Gale's ability and output as a translator.

As there were fewer Westerners in Korea than in Japan, it might be said that Gale had a more open field for research into Korean culture than his counterparts in Japan. Certainly, few books on Japanese intellectual subjects were written by Canadian missionaries after 1905 because there already existed considerable Western literature on many aspects of Japanese society.

After the Russo-Japanese War, the missionary who wished to study Japan no longer had to rely solely on Japanese sources of information. Even in remote areas in Japan, Canadian missionaries could subscribe to one of the English newspapers. During the early twentieth century, the most important of these were the *Japan Times*, which was published in Tokyo and generally reflected the Japanese government's viewpoint; the *Japan Advertiser*, which was also published in Tokyo and reflected the views of its editor Robert Young; and the *Japan Chronicle*, which was published in Kobe and edited by A. Morgan Young. It is difficult to assess the influence of English-language newspapers on missionary opinion. There is no sign of missionary criticism of the editorial position of any of these three journals.

Christian publications also provided some information on secular events. The monthly *Japan Evangelist*, the annual *Japan Mission Year-book* (1903-1910), and annual *Christian Movement in Japan, Formosa and Korea* (1911-1932) normally had some editorial comment on recent events in Japan. As very few missionaries could read Japanese, these English-language newspapers and magazines always played a crucial role in informing missionaries about events in Japan.

It was perhaps more difficult for missionaries to keep fully informed about what was happening in Canada and the West. Furloughs came infrequently. Newspapers and magazines from Canada were out of

date by the time they reached Japan. In Tokyo, the diplomatic community and the Japan correspondents of newspapers, like the London
Times, could help to keep Western residents in touch with what was
happening at home. For those who lived in the provinces, touring
Westerners supplied a link to the world beyond Japan. Westerners
coming to Japan, even those without church connections, looked to
missionaries, especially those in the more remote cities, to provide
advice, information, and often hospitality. G. C. Allen, who later
became an influential British academic specialist on Japanese econom-
ics, described an unnamed Canadian missionary with whom he stayed
when he first arrived in Nagoya in the fall of 1922 to teach in the
Higher Commerical School there:

> A Canadian missionary sufficiently overcame his prejudice against
> Englishmen to invite me to stay with him until I had found perma-
> nent quarters. As he had a long experience of Japan, he taught me
> a good deal about the problems of living in that country, even
> though some of his opinions of Japanese ways naturally reflected
> the bias of his calling. He spent a great deal of effort in raising
> money for his philanthropic ventures. He could never understand
> why anyone with money to spare should spend it in buying a scroll
> painting or what he called an "old bowl" when it might have gone to
> the provision of quarters for the YMCA.[42]

Certainly not all missionaries were interested in Japanese arts and
crafts. The response of many missionaries to Japan obviously did
reflect the bias of their calling, which can be interpreted as narrow-
minded. Despite this, the Canadian did go out of his way to help even
an Englishman. In 1922, there were some fifty Westerners living in
Nagoya: American and Canadian missionaries and teachers, a few
British engineers, even fewer Germans, and a White-Russian family.
Although diverse, it was apparently quite a close-knit society. Allen
noted: "the Americans and Canadians, especially the American Consul
and his wife, were generous in their hospitality. There was a tennis
club. We met for excursions to the seashore, to the nearby mountains
and to beauty spots in the countryside. From time to time *sukiyaki*
parties in Japanese restaurants were arranged."[43] For newcomers, like
Allen, the Western group performed the important function of introducing them to things Japanese. Once they had found their feet in
Japanese society, Allen and other young men under short-term contracts could find other and more stimulating social and cultural
activities with their Japanese friends. To long-term Canadian missionary residents, the Western community provided their main social out-
let.

The lifestyle of missionaries isolated them from the Japanese society.
Missionaries purposely stood aloof in their private lives from the

Japanese; their friends and acquaintances were other missionaries or members of the Western community. They sought to preserve and to maintain their cultural identity in the face of the alien culture that surrounded them. The example of the missionaries of the China Inland Mission in the late nineteenth century, who strove to identify themselves with the Chinese to the extent of adopting their dress, offers a different pattern of missionary lifestyle. Although some missionaries in Korea at the turn of the century were pictured in Korean dress, this approach was never adopted by missionaries in Japan. Canadian missionaries were normally long-term residents and their lifestyle attempted to minimize the pressures of a foreign environment. Nevertheless, outside their Christian work, missionaries were able to exert a considerable long-term influence on the social and leisure activities of millions of Japanese.

CHAPTER SEVEN

Missionaries and Education

While Charles Eby devoted his enormous energy during the 1880s and 1890s to direct evangelism, other Canadian Methodists began to concentrate their attention on the development of mission schools. Education quickly emerged as the major endeavour of the generation of student missionary volunteers. By offering general education with a Western-studies emphasis in the Christian atmosphere of the mission school compound, missionaries hoped to convert the young.

In starting schools which went beyond simply providing theological training for candidates for the clergy, the missions were confronted with the problem of balancing the Christian purpose behind the foundation of their schools with the need to satisfy the demand for high-quality secular education. This balancing act was difficult in Japan, and later in colonial Korea, for mission schools faced very severe competition for students from both private and government schools. Moreover, they were faced with having to abide by stringent government regulations concerning the quality of education if they wished to receive government recognition of their educational program (which was essential if their graduates were to find employment or to go on to further education).

For the missionary, teaching in a mission school provided a stable working environment. Further, it allowed the missionary the opportunity to provide jobs for deserving Japanese or Korean Christians as fellow teachers and administrators. In that sense, mission schools (while part of the missionary movement) helped to sustain indigenous Christian leadership by providing some of them with a possible channel of employment and, importantly, status within the Christian community.

The demand for education in the 1880s offered very considerable prospects of success for the missionary movement. This was especially true in female education.

Notes for Chapter Seven are found on pp. 237-39.

116

SCHOOLS FOR GIRLS

Female education was clearly seen to be one of the major areas in which women missionaries could play a valuable role, particularly because most had teaching diplomas from Canada. According to the Canadian Methodist Woman's Missionary Society (WMS-CM):

> very little can be done in the way of Christian work in this land or any other apart from schools, and it is advised that such be opened as soon as possible, employing native Christian teachers, under the supervision of lady missionaries, who shall visit the home of the children and thereby secure regular attendance, and at the same time gain influence over the parents, winning them to church services.[1]

During the Meiji period, Japanese authorities did much less for female education than for male education. Traditionally, education for Japanese girls was intended to prepare them to fill their subordinate position in life with grace and ease.[2] While the Educational Code of 1872 made elementary education compulsory for both girls and boys, at no time during the Meiji period did females attend elementary schools in the same proportions as males. In the 1870s, the Meiji government did establish certain schools for the education of young women. In 1872, for instance, the Tokyo Jo Gakkō was founded for the education of the daughters of *daimyō* and government officials. Its Western staff was provided, as in the case of a similar school established in Kyoto, by the wives or relations of Western employees of the government or missionaries. Since many of these women teachers were sincere Christians, these first government schools were not without Christian influence. In 1872, the first Japanese women were sent abroad to study. Among the first five was Tsuda Ume, the daughter of the prominent Methodist Episcopalian convert Tsuda Sen. Tsuda Ume later became a leading Christian educator and the founder of Tsuda Juku Daigaku, one of the premier women's colleges in Japan. Unfortunately, the policy of sending females abroad for education was not sustained by the Meiji government after this first trial in 1872. The priorities of the government lay elsewhere. Further, it was unwilling to provide sufficient educational facilities for females in Japan.

The Tokyo Normal School for Girls, founded by Nakamura Keiū in 1875, was an important pioneering effort. Nakamura felt that "the rearing of men and women should be equal, there should not be two different kinds of education. If all human beings want to maintain the highest level of perfection it would be well that men and women receive the same rearing. By doing this, they will progress together. Pure-hearted women must go hand-in-hand with virtuous men."[3] This was a denunciation of the widely held Confucian view of the subordinate position of women, as enunciated by seventeenth-century philosopher Kaibara Ekken in his *Onna Daigaku*. Unlike the case in male education, private individuals and private institutions played a crucial role in providing educational opportunities for girls.

Of private groups involved in female education, the missionary movement was among the most energetic in establishing Western-style educational facilities for girls. By the 1880s, every major centre had a female mission school. But there was still a great demand for more schools, to which the Canadians responded. In 1884, both a girls' school and a boys' school were established in Azabu, Tokyo. Martha Cartmell was the first principal of the girls' school, assisted by Eliza Spencer (later Mrs. T. A. Large) and Susie and Maud Cochran, the daughters of George Cochran, who was the principal of the boys' school.

From the start, the Tōyō Eiwa Jo Gakkō (referred to in English during the late nineteenth century as the Anglo-Japanese or Anglo-Oriental Ladies School) was a resounding success. It opened just as the mid-1880s vogue for things Western, typified by the newly opened *Rokumeikan* in Hibiya with its Western-style receptions and entertainments for government dignitaries, took hold.[4] The Japanese government wanted to impress the Western powers that Japan was receptive to Western influences, hoping that the Unequal Treaties would be revised. The Tōyō Eiwa Jo Gakkō was ready to teach Japanese girls all the Western graces. In its first year, it was reported that "families of wealth and position have sought entrance for their daughters, and have shown their appreciation by repeated and exceedingly kind acts of hospitality to our representatives the teachers."[5] Among the first students were daughters of Iwakura, Itō, Saigō and Date, extremely important political figures.[6] Many of these first girls later married influential men. Vice-Admiral Nire Kagenori's daughter Haruko married Saito Makoto, later Governor-General of Chōsen and Prime Minister of Japan.[7] The daughter of Ushiba Takuzō married into the Arashi family and lived most of her life in the United States. Her granddaughter married American historian and Ambassador to Japan, E. O. Reischauer.[8] It was a school that appealed to the wealthy and upper classes; the social background of the girls at the Tōyō Eiwa Jo Gakkō was much higher than that at its male counterpart. As one of the Japanese teachers points out in 1886:

> though there are eight hundred boys' and girls' schools in Tokio, there is not one school which gives good education of good Japanese, Chinese, English, together except Normal and Empress' school . . . those who wish to receive a good education in Japanese, Chinese, English, fancy works, etiquette, piano etc., must come to our school.[9]

The Tōyō Eiwa Jo Gakkō was able to compete with the very best girls' schools in Tokyo. There were other mission schools where girls could be sent if their parents wanted them to learn English and Western manners, but they provided financial support for many of their students,[10] which did not appeal to wealthy parents. At this stage, the perceptive WMS-CM did not provide bursaries, and so the rich came. The Canadian women missionaries were almost without exception canny; the decision not to offer bursaries allowed them to remain financially solvent.

This did not prevent some girls from Christian families coming to the school. Among them was Takashima Taneko whose Christian father was a merchant in Maebashi in Gumma Prefecture. A year after she graduated from the Tōyō Eiwa Jo Gakkō in 1892, Taneko married Yamaji Aizan.[11] In later life, she was actively involved in women's issues and journalism. A contemporary of Yamaji Taneko was Nomura Michiko who was later very active in the YWCA.[12] In later life, the Christian girls tended to be actively involved in both Christian and women's movements.

Although some parents did not like sending their sons to mission schools because they were Christian, this was not a major consideration when it came to their daughters. Family reputation, which might be ruined if a son became a Christian, was not at stake if a daughter converted. Further, as there was little opportunity for girls to acquire higher education beyond that offered at the mission school, there was not the practical concern about the educational or employment future for a female graduate of a mission school, but it was a prime consideration for males. What Miss Cartmell, her fellow missionary teachers, and the Japanese and Chinese instructors could provide was thorough instruction in the classroom and coaching in Western manners and etiquette inside and outside of class.

The Tōyō Eiwa Jo Gakkō catered to both boarders and day girls. Rigid discipline was maintained. About life at the school during the 1910s, one graduate wrote:

> in those days the school preferred the pupils to live in the dormitory and the smallest ones—a few of them even 6 or 7 years old—were taken to church every Sunday (after Sunday school) to sit through the regular service for adults, and if any of them were bold enough to whisper a word or two to the little friend sitting next and if caught by Miss Blackmore, the child would be ordered, after church, to "stay in bed" without the noon meal. Or, if any of us had forgotten to take in our laundry Saturday evening and it happened to rain Sunday morning, we had to leave it on the lines, as any work—even taking in the laundry was not fit for the Sabbath.[13]

Another graduate of the same period, whose father was in the diplomatic corps, wrote:

> When I was nine, my father put me into the dormitory of the Tōyō Eiwa school where my two elder sisters were already in. There, I was taught for the first time about God and Jesus Christ the Saviour. From morn till night we were in a religious atmosphere, with services twice a day. The principal Miss Blackmore seemed very strict and I was very much afraid of her. Almost everybody felt the same. When we had done something wrong against the rules we were severely punished. For instance, there was a rule "do not run in the corridors," and if anyone ran, she had to repeat writing the rule one hundred times on a sheet of paper and hand to the Office-room. On Sunday mornings we all had to attend the Church service and listen to the sermon. While I was in the primary class, I couldn't understand at all, but gradually I began to realize them.[14]

Discipline was strict, but at least the Minister to Sweden could be content in the fact that his daughters at school in Japan were safe. The discipline was no different from that of contemporary girls' boarding schools in Canada, since the majority of missionary teachers had been trained as teachers in Canada and had merely exchanged the drudgery of working in small rural schools at home for a much more stimulating teaching position in Japan.

As missionaries in Japan, the women of the WMS-CM could develop as independent individuals, as liberated women free from the social constrictions of home, with its pressures to marry. To the very young, the missionary teachers might appear forbidding. But the missionary teachers offered their students many different club activities and invitations to their summer cottages during the holidays,[15] thus not only exhibiting a genuine warmth but also inspiring a tremendous feeling of loyalty toward them and toward the school. A teacher's example did show Japanese girls, perhaps not much to the liking of their parents, that women could lead fulfilling lives as single individuals and that teaching was a worthwhile and pleasant vocation. In that sense, the presence of women missionaries was important because of the alternative that it revealed to Japanese women.

The Tōyō Eiwa grew apace. In 1889, it was proudly reported that

> the Anglo-Oriental Ladies School in Azabu has been in successful operation since the year 1884. Sixteen students have completed the Japanese Course of Study. The average attendance during the past year was about 225. Of these 100 were Christians and are divided into five classes which meet regularly in the school. Besides these there are always a number of enquirers who are seeking the truth. The Sunday School and morning service have an average attendance of over 200. Attendance at these is compulsory. All

expenses of this school except those of the foreign ladies are met by the students' fees etc.[16]

The WMS-CM was hard-pressed during these years to build new facilities at the school to keep pace with the demand for places. Although many of the students would later give up Christianity, the school was an obvious success from an evangelistic standpoint. The more so because it was financially self-supporting, which says much for the business sense of the women missionaries.

During the 1890s, the number of pupils dipped as low as eighty-four. This was rightly recognized at the time not to be the result of a loss of interest in girls' education, or less demand for English, or related to the anti-Western feeling in Japan, but simply the result of the fact that government retrenchment had led to lower salaries for bureaucrats who no longer could afford so much for the education of their daughters.[17] It was not until the turn of the century that attendance reached more than 100 again. Subsequently, the school grew as a composite institution, offering education from kindergarten to high school, with a senior department for the training of teachers. By 1927, the total number of students in all departments was 522.[18] The creation of the Tokyo Woman's Christian College in 1918 by several Protestant denominations, including the Canadian Methodist WMS, helped satisfy the need for higher education for Christian women. The establishment of this interdenominational women's college postponed the need for the Canadians to provide some formal course of general education beyond the high school level. Furthermore, the Canadian Methodists alone very probably could not have afforded the expense of creating their own junior college.

The success of the Tōyō Eiwa Jo Gakkō in Tokyo led to the opening of two other schools in the late 1880s, both located outside the capital. They were adopting an independent policy from the Mission Board, which concentrated its educational efforts solely in Tokyo. The Governor of Shizuoka Prefecture, Sekiguchi Ryūkichi, whose daughter was attending the Tōyō Eiwa Jo Gakkō in Tokyo in order to learn English, and Hiraiwa Yoshiyasu were the prime movers in asking the WMS-CM to establish a school in Shizuoka.[19] In 1887, the WMS-CM was in a position to take up this opportunity. The annual report of the WMS noted, "during the year an offer made in Toronto of a thousand dollars, for the special purpose of opening a school in some other city in Japan. Shizuoka was recommended, a building free of rent, and contributions insuring the Society against loss for two years offered."[20] Miss M. J. Cunningham of Halifax, Nova Scotia, was sent out to teach in the new school, which opened in the fall of 1887 with twenty-three students. In 1888, Miss Kate Morgan was sent out to help Miss Cunningham. In 1889, the school was expanded, with a new building capable of housing as many as fifty boarders and a similar number of day girls, but only twenty-four of the school's seventy-four students were boarders in that year.[21]

Just as Tōyō Eiwa in Tokyo suffered a loss of students at the beginning of the 1890s as a result of government salary cut-backs, so too in 1890 the Shizuoka Eiwa Jo Gakkō's enrollment slipped to twenty-three.[22] In 1890, the Canadian Methodist WMS took over full responsibility for the school because Japanese backers could no longer continue their full financial support. The school was never destined to be as large as its Tokyo counterpart; the number of students for its first thirty years of operation annually averaged about sixty. It was only in the 1920s that enrollment was consistently more than 100. In 1931, the students numbered 135.[23] The low numbers of students meant that the school required a subsidy from the Canadian Methodist WMS in order to cover its running costs. Quite simply, there were not enough rich people in Shizuoka to support the school. Further, there was not the demand for English-language training for girls in the prefecture that there was in Tokyo. The school was, however, still very much a part of the Canadian Methodist commitment to Shizuoka and important to the life of the Christian community. It was, as well, important to the educational life of the city and prefecture because it offered an alternative in female education.

In 1889, a third girls' school was established in Kofu in Yamanashi Prefecture. Like the Shizuoka Eiwa Jo Gakkō, the Yamanashi Eiwa Jo Gakkō was founded following a request from local Christians.[24] It was, as in Shizuoka, a manifestation of the continued Canadian Methodist commitment to their Christian work in that prefecture. Miss Agnes Wintemute (later Mrs. H. H. Coates), who had come out to Japan in 1886 to reinforce the women missionaries in Tokyo, was sent to open the school in Kofu. In 1889, she reported:

> during the winter, enquiries were made as to the best means of sending a lady out there, and the result was that a number of the prominent men of the province of which Kofu is the chief city, formed themselves into a committee of founders, and sent to our council a proposed basis upon which they would be glad to cooperate with our society in establishing and carrying on a Girls' school there. This proposal was taken as a providential opening for us, and after careful consideration, was accepted.[25]

As in Shizuoka, the Japanese provided and furnished the building. The WMS-CM was in charge of the business management of the school and responsible for paying any deficit in the operating costs. The school started with only nine pupils, but the number increased. In 1891, there were thirty-one students, of whom twenty-eight were boarders and nineteen were Christian. In that year, Agnes Wintemute wrote:

Kofu is one of the few places that seems not to have been affected by the general reaction against woman's education. Indeed, we are thankful to be able to report the past year's work as most encouraging in every respect, the school having grown not only in numbers but in the confidence and favor of the people.[26]

Kofu was more isolated from the influences of the capital than Shizuoka, thus it took longer for trends in Tokyo to take effect in Yamanashi Prefecture. At the same time, there was less migration from Yamanashi Prefecture to Tokyo, thus there was a broader commitment to the maintenance of institutions within the prefecture. By the second half of the 1890s, the school had clearly begun to grow. By 1900, it had 105 students and over the next thirty years the average enrollment was more than 150. In 1931, there were 176 students.[27] Consistently, the Yamanashi Eiwa was slightly larger than its Shizuoka counterpart but understandably smaller than the Tōyō Eiwa.

One reason for the relative success of these schools was the fact that government regulation of women's education was not as strict as it was for male education. Girls' schools were unaffected by the Education Department's Instruction of 1899, which prohibited religious instruction in class time at male schools. Perhaps this reflects Meiji attitudes toward women; while many Japanese disapproved of religious instruction for males, they were not concerned about females. This was to some extent surprising, because the type of education in girls' schools was very different from the traditional education of females. Christian education prepared women for an active role in life. This might, and indeed did, cause certain difficulties in adjusting to society at large for some girls once they had graduated.

The three Canadian Methodist schools came to offer education from kindergarten to high school level. Their curriculum was similar to government or other state-recognized schools. Their special strength was the English-language training given by WMS-CM missionaries. The schools offered more hours of English tuition and morals classes than did government girls' high schools.[28] The syllabus of the morals classes extended from the Imperial Rescript on Education to Bible study. It was the latter that received particular stress from the Canadian Methodist missionaries. The emphasis of the Canadian schools on English and morals classes strongly reflected their Western missionary and Christian connections.

The cost of maintaining the three Eiwa schools decreased in real terms as the period progressed.[29] The reduction was achieved, however, by increasing student numbers, which in turn often led to overcrowding. As the numbers of students and receipts from tuition fees rose, the cost of operation of the school for the WMS-CM correspondingly fell.[30] The need to balance the books by increasing student numbers led to a negative difference between the Canadian schools and their government counterparts. In comparison to government schools, not only were the Canadian Methodist institutions over-crowded, but their buildings were often of inferior quality.

Despite this, all the Canadian schools expanded. In 1907, the Yamanashi Eiwa built a new school building in Kofu, which was partially paid for through the sale of the property belonging to the original school site.[31] In 1922, Miss Isabella Blackmore, the principal of the Tōyō Eiwa in Tokyo, noted that the school had an enrollment of 425. In addition, its two kindergartens were over-flowing, and the school was so over-crowded that 200 applicants had been turned away.[32] This vividly illustrates the popularity of the Tokyo school and the substantial demand for missionary education for girls.

The WMS-CM did benefit from maintaining the three schools, since some of their graduates later worked for the mission. In 1922, Isabella Blackmore commented that twenty graduates of the Tōyō Eiwa were working for the WMS-CM mission, either as teachers or in other departments.[33] The kindergartens which the schools provided also had kindergarten-training classes attached to them. In Tokyo, the WMS-CM also supported an orphanage, which accommodated twenty orphans in 1922. This also proved to be a recruiting ground for Japanese workers for the WMS-CM.

In 1922, Miss S. R. Courtice, the principal of the Shizuoka Eiwa, noted with satisfaction that a large percentage of her graduates were eager for more advanced education at the Tokyo Woman's Christian College, the Canadian Methodist Bible School, or its kindergarten-training department. Other graduates had become assistant teachers at the school and also helped in Sunday school work.[34] The WMS-CM missionaries were eager to have their young graduates continue their education at a more advanced level. They also hoped that the Christian graduates of the three schools could do "a great deal as torch bearers for Christianity in non-Christian areas."[35]

Canadian women missionaries helped create a new and independent class of Japanese women who were relatively well educated and interested in pursuing their own careers, usually as teachers. As Loretta L. Shaw, a Canadian Anglican missionary, argued, Japanese women owed "a great debt of gratitude to the missionary societies" for their educational endeavours.[36] In criticizing government schools, Miss Shaw pointed out in the early 1920s:

> Men were, as a matter of course, put in charge of the high schools for girls. Under the influence of the old ideals of the inferiority and subjection of women, they arranged the curriculum on the assumption that girls have not the same mental capacity, power of development, or incentive to study as boys. This unfair idea of

lower standards for girls still pervades the whole system of education in Japan, and is unwise and unmoral.[37]

Although the Tokyo Woman's Christian College, which in 1918 had Nitobe Inazō as its first president, was one example of males retaining prominent positions even in Christian schools, by and large mission schools were run by women. It remains true, however, that the Japanese women's movement gained much of its support from the graduates of Christian schools.[38] Indeed, part of the significance of Christian education for girls was this close relation with the women's movement within the non-Christian society.

Mission schools offered educational opportunities for women who otherwise might not have been able to continue their studies beyond the compulsory level. Government higher schools catered to the educational elite, but those girls who were unable to enter these institutions found an alternative in mission schools. In many cases, like that of the Shizuoka Eiwa, the mission school was the first high school for girls in a particular prefecture. Often the students came from relatively poor backgrounds, and mission school education enhanced the prospect of girls who had to earn their own living after graduation. Mission schools played an important basic function, simply by increasing the number of women who were educated above elementary level. Without this education, the normal fate of women was to exist in a subordinate and dependent position in a male-dominated society. Secondary education gave women a greater degree of independence and unmarried missionary teachers were significant in showing that single women could lead satisfying lives. Although Canadian missionaries considered their mission schools a success as an evangelistic agency, their most important significance may well have been in their contribution to the gradual emancipation of Japanese women.

SCHOOLS FOR BOYS

While the WMS-CM effort in education was marked by growth and sustained success, the Canadian Methodist educational endeavour for boys was, in the long term, much less clear cut. The authorities considered male education much more important, thus the government was prepared to pass regulations concerning the curriculum of private schools, which did much to undercut the primary attraction for missionaries of mission schools, that is, as an evangelistic agency. Unlike their counterparts for girls, whose serious competition came from relatively few government schools, male institutions had to face an impressively broad range of both state and private schools. Lacking the finances of the government to provide excellent facilities, by and large mission schools came to be second-class institutions which attracted second-class students. This was not the case, however, when the Canadian Methodists began their male educational work.

The desire to establish a boys' school stemmed from the unsatisfactory experience of the missionaries working under the control of Japanese employers. In 1884, a site was chosen in Azabu, Tokyo, and land was bought in the name of the Tōyō Eiwa Gakkō Kaisha, of which Asagawa Hiromi was president and Kobayashi Mitsuyasu was secretary. Because foreigners could not own land outside the treaty concessions, the Canadians had to form a Japanese company, legally controlled by their pastors, in order to obtain property. Although the Canadians never had any problems in using such an expedient, some missions had difficulties with their Japanese trustees, as illustrated by the case of the American Board Mission and the Dōshisha school in Kyoto in the mid-1890s.[39]

There was a problem getting government permission to open a Christian school. There was apparently a feeling in government circles that Christianity was to be equated with Republicanism and that the school would cause great trouble, which was all part of the anti-Western mood of the early 1880s. For a time, it was feared that governmental permission to open the Tōyō Eiwa Gakkō would be withheld.[40] As this mood dissipated, permission was granted to open the school in early 1884.

In the summer of 1884, buildings for a boys' preparatory school and the theological institute were erected on the Azabu site. George Cochran returned to Japan from Canada to become the principal of the Tōyō Eiwa Gakkō and teach in the theological department. Robert Whittington, the first of a long line of missionaries whose positions were solely pedagogical, came out to take charge of the lay academic department. The school began operation on December 1, 1884, with eighteen students.[41] The theological department would always remain small, with only six or seven students at the best of times. In the pro-Western atmosphere of the second half of the 1880s, the lay academic department was hugely successful in attracting students. In 1885, the number of academic pupils had risen in the course of a year to 150, of whom eight were boarders. This resulted in an almost continuous expansion of school buildings, which carried on as the school mushroomed in the 1880s.

In 1885, T. A. Large was sent out from Canada to teach mathematics in the expanded school. John Saunby, one of the Self-Support Band, taught there in 1886 before going to teach in a government school in Kofu. Saunby wrote of the school in the late 1880s:

> [its] phenomenal success continued until the Academy became the largest mission school of its day in the capital. It was noted for the

high standard of its Western education made available to the
students who thronged its classrooms. Nor was evangelism allowed
to remain in the background; daily worship, Bible instruction and
Sabbath services were so blessed of God that in one year, 1887, no
less than forty of the students confessed Christ and received baptism.[42]

The Tōyō Eiwa Gakkō was popular because it gave a thorough
education in both Japanese and English.

The aim of the academic department was stated in 1889: "imparting
a thorough training in Japanese and English languages and literatures
and in science and mathematics. It extends over a period of seven
years—three years of Preparatory and four of Collegiate. Candidates
for admission are expected to be graduates of the Elementary
Schools."[43] In its combination of Japanese and English studies, which it
could offer because of its Japanese and Canadian staff, the Tōyō Eiwa
Gakkō was providing a type of education that could not be found in the
majority of government schools. This appealed to those students who
hoped to gain admission to Tokyo Imperial University or institutions
of higher learning overseas.

The teaching staff was an impressive one. Among the early Japanese
teachers was Henry Satoh who had worked with Meacham in Numazu
and now joined him at the Tokyo school. Yamaji Aizan (Yakichi), who
had been converted by Hiraiwa, came from Shizuoka to be both a
student and a teacher at the school.[44] Yamaji's connection with the
Canadian mission is important, for he went on to become one of the
leading Japanese intellectuals of the late Meiji period. Although missionaries found him a difficult person with whom to deal,[45] Yamaji was
a member of the second generation of the Shizuoka Band, and, during
the 1880s and 1890s, he was very close to the Canadian Methodist
mission. At this stage, the Canadian Methodists could draw on a well of
active and competent young men from among their converts to teach at
their new school in Tokyo. And they did.

The initial success of the Tōyō Eiwa Gakkō in the 1880s came to an
end with the economic depression and resurgence of nationalistic and
anti-Western feeling in the early 1890s. It was reported in 1891 that
attendance at the school was particularly bad because of crop failures
the year before and "the false notion of the national attachment or
Kokusui Hōzon Shugi which exerted a powerful influence over the
middle class people and which proved to be a strong barrier against the
introduction of anything that is foreign has reached its climax this year.
All Christian schools especially in Tokyo have suffered from this influence."[46] There was a strong reaction against the indiscriminate borrowing from the West which had characterized the late 1880s. Yet the new
anti-Western feeling was not the only reason for the decline. In 1890,

the promulgation of the Imperial Rescript on Education worked against the influence of Western educational institutions. The Rescript placed morals at the centre of the educational curriculum and particularly stressed *sonnō aikoku* ("reverence for the Emperor and Patriotism"). While the Rescript only affected government schools, the lack of open emphasis upon reverence to the Emperor in mission schools was regarded by some as unpatriotic. Other changes in the Japanese educational system meant that private schools had to be certified in order for their graduates to enter higher government schools. In the early 1890s, the Tōyō Eiwa Gakkō did not have government certification for its curriculum, with the result that its graduates were barred from going to government schools.

This situation changed in 1895 when the government granted the Tōyō Eiwa Gakkō a middle-school status, which allowed its graduates to continue their education at higher government schools. In the same year, Ebara Soroku was made president of the school. To put Ebara in charge of the school was a master stroke, for not only was he a member of the new Diet, which gave him some political influence, but he was also known as a pioneer of Western-style education. His reputation was one of the reasons why a renewed interest in the school developed. Coupled with this was a changed attitude toward the West, brought about by Japan's success in the Sino-Japanese War of 1894 which led to renewed hopes for treaty revision. After 1895, the number of students at the Tōyō Eiwa Gakkō increased very rapidly, and by 1899 there were some 580 students in the academic department.[47]

That was to be the last year of the school's operation as purely a mission school. In 1899, the Mombushō (the Education Ministry) issued an instruction prohibiting religious teaching in any school that had the right to grant government diplomas. The missionary community reacted with dismay. In August 1899, at a meeting in Tokyo of representatives of all Protestant missions engaged in educational work, important points were made, which would have a profound impact on the future of male mission schools. Missionaries felt that it was contrary to the spirit of the constitution to restrict, in a practical sense, the liberty of parents in their decisions about the education of their children. Further, while not objecting to the government's right to pass regulations on religious education in public schools supported by public funds, missionaries argued that putting the same restrictions upon private schools supported by private funds was a grave injustice. The missionary community believed that it would be disloyal to the Christian supporters at home who provided money for the mission schools if missions abided by government regulation and continued to support schools where religious teaching was banned.[48] The missionary movement's response to the new Educational Instruction was either to close their schools or not to seek government recognition of their status. This meant that mission education led to a dead end for the few Japanese students that might come. The Canadian Methodists decided to cut their formal connection with the Tōyō Eiwa Gakkō.

There were certainly hard feelings. E. Crummy, who had served as its headmaster between 1891 and 1897, believed that "the policy of the school was changed too often ... so that with each change we drew further away from what society wanted."[49] It still remains doubtful, however, whether any change made in the Tōyō Eiwa Gakkō would have allowed the Canadian Methodist mission to retain control of the school in the face of the determination of the Mombushō to bring about change in mission schools. Yet in many ways the Canadians came up with a very satisfactory solution under the circumstances. A new school company was formed under Ebara Soroku, and the buildings were taken over at no cost by what was now the Azabu Middle School.[50] The Canadian Methodists still continued to provide teaching support and to evangelize the students outside the classroom, but they were no longer financially committed to the school, now completely under the control of Ebara and the Japanese trustees. The Azabu Middle School continued to flourish. It was no longer a Canadian Methodist institution, but Christian influence remained strong and the missionary presence very close because the missionaries were firmly in control of the Tōyō Eiwa Jo Gakkō next door.

Though the Educational Instruction of 1899 resulted in very considerable missionary protest, the decision about what to do had been taken quickly, and missions had adapted to the new circumstances. The instruction had come swiftly on the heels of the signing of the treaty revision with Great Britain in 1898. In a real sense, it can be seen as an attempt by the Japanese to gain greater control over their internal affairs to offset the changes that would result from the new equal relationship with Britain and the other Great Powers. With the treaty revision, extraterritoriality had disappeared, and Westerners had gained the right to reside in any part of Japan without special permission. The Instruction was the way of protecting Japanese values against undue dislocation as a result of the new opportunities that Westerners had acquired by the final dissolution of the treaty port system. It was an assertion of the greater freedom of action that the Japanese government had achieved. Now the government did not have to look over its shoulder for fear that internal legislation might have an adverse effect on hopes for treaty revision, since treaty revision and diplomatic equality with the West had been fully accomplished.

THE KWANSEI GAKUIN

Having divested themselves of the Azabu Middle School, the Canadian Methodists were loath for some years to engage in educational work. In 1907, however, with the formation of the Japan Methodist Church, the opportunity for co-operation in educational work with the other two Methodist missions reappeared. In 1909, the Methodist Episcopal South mission invited the Canadian Methodists to join them in the educational project they had begun in Nishinomiya, near Kobe.[51] By 1910, this school, the Kwansei Gakuin, consisted of a middle school and a theological seminary, with a total of more than 400 students.

The aim of the proposed united educational endeavour was to build a college of higher learning. The Canadian Methodists agreed to co-operate in this venture, and a college department which gave courses in literature and commercial science was added to the existing middle school. It was a departure for the Canadian Methodists to participate in this educational endeavour, for it was outside their established Tokyo, Shizuoka, and Kofu triangle. Although the Canadian Methodists did help the Methodist Episcopal North mission in Tokyo with the development of Aoyama Gakuin, the opportunity for extensive educational co-operation did not exist there. It was the Methodist Episcopal South mission in Kobe that needed financial help from the Canadians. The Kwansei Gakuin was another departure for the Canadian Methodists; this was the first time they embarked on a major endeavour which was not completely under their control.

The Kwansei Gakuin was jointly managed by the Canadian Methodists and the Methodist Episcopal South mission. Until 1920, J. C. C. Newton of Methodist Episcopal South mission was the president of the college. He was replaced in 1920 by Canadian Methodist C. J. L. Bates, who remained president until 1940. The Canadians had to wait their turn, but once in power it was only political pressure from the government which made them give it up.

The Kwansei Gakuin was very costly to develop. As early as 1913, James Endicott, the Canadian Methodist Foreign Missions Secretary, admitted that the increases in all maintenance charges abroad were so great that they absorbed the entire annual income of the Missionary Society.[52] No money remained for acquiring new property or constructing buildings. Under normal circumstances, funds for new property and buildings would have come from a separate plant and extension fund. But in 1913, a recession in Canada made fund-raising extremely difficult.

In January 1916, D. R. McKenzie informed Toronto of the need for an extension to the college building of the Kwansei Gakuin, and he suggested using money that had originally been allocated for the building of a gymnasium and for college equipment. The need for an extension resulted from a rapid growth in student numbers.[53] McKenzie believed that without an extension some new students would have to be turned away. Echoing a very common missionary plea, he felt that this would be a "fatal mistake."[54]

In response to McKenzie, in February 1916, Endicott pointed out that the prospects were very bleak for funds to buy property or construct buildings in Japan.[55] In 1910, a mission plant fund had been launched specifically to finance the maintenance and expansion of mission property, but this had proved a failure. By 1915, only a little more than half of its $1,500,000 target for the first five years of its operation had been raised, and of this only about a sixth had been received in actual payments (the rest were pledges).[56] This poor performance made Endicott think that other means should be used in the future to raise money for plant development.[57] He did not indicate what those other means might be.

In February 1919, the Japanese government introduced new regulations that intensified the restrictions on religious education in government-recognized schools. Five months later, the Canadian Methodist Japan Mission Council suggested that the Kwansei Gakuin be raised to the status of a university. Because the new regulations would impinge on the middle school section of the Kwansei Gakuin, it was felt that the best way to maintain the institution was to transform it into a university.[58] The Japanese government had indicated that it was going to liberalize its regulations concerning university status to allow a few leading private schools and government colleges outside of Tokyo and Kyoto to become universities. It was not an impossible dream, therefore, that the Kwansei Gakuin might be recognized as a university. For the Canadians, the central objective in their plan was the defence of the school's Christian character, which the Mission Council suggested that its constitution should guarantee. This provision would stipulate that all members of its legal managing and owning body should be Christians.[59]

There were, however, several problems that prevented the Kwansei Gakuin from attaining university status. For some time, it had been hoped that the Protestant missions in Japan would join together to establish a union Christian university. This idea had been aired decades before by Eby, and in 1919 the Canadian Methodist Japan Mission Council still looked forward to such a creation. A union Christian college had always been envisaged as a liberal arts institution. Thus, the Canadian Methodists did not want the Kwansei Gakuin to duplicate the facilities they hoped would be offered in the future by such a university. As a result, the university-level section of the Kwansei Gakuin was projected as a department of commercial studies. It was thought that a literature department should only be started if the plans for the union Christian college did not become a reality.[60] As a union Christian college failed to materialize, a literature department was soon added to the commercial department.

When the future of the Kwansei Gakuin was under discussion in 1919, the Canadian Methodist Japan Mission Council realized that a large endowment would be necessary to sustain their college when it attained university status. It was estimated that an endowment of 5,000,000 yen (approximately $500,000) was needed, with the Canadian Methodists and the Methodist Episcopalians South each providing half the capital sum. This would be needed to supplement the 70,000 yen which each mission was already paying annually to maintain the Kwansei Gakuin. It was thought that the endowment would provide an annual income of 100,000 yen, which would mean that the annual sum needed for the new university from outside funding would be 240,000 yen.[61] If the university departments of literature and commerce were to be established, 1,500,000 yen in gold would have to be placed with the Japanese government. This was the immediate first hurdle.

Although the Methodist Episcopal South mission made rapid progress in raising its share of the endowment, the Canadians were much less successful. In October 1920, James Endicott stated that the Japan Mission could expect to receive only $200,000 from funds raised in a special nation-wide campaign for missions.[62] Thus, there was little hope that the Canadian Methodists would be able to raise sufficient funds for the endowment in the near future. In fact, the Canadians were unable to raise their share of the endowment until 1932, when the Kwansei Gakuin finally attained university status.

During the 1920s, the Kwansei Gakuin was a fairly large institution. In 1922, it had 1,600 students with 850 in the middle school, 750 in the college department, and 30 in the theological seminary.[63] Denominational Christian colleges such as the Kwansei Gakuin clearly satisfied a definite need for post-secondary male education. The Canadian Methodists were fully aware of one major difficulty—maintaining the Christian atmosphere of the college while at the same time responding to the substantial demand for education. Indeed, the Canadians feared that the Kwansei Gakuin might become a completely secular college. Another problem was determining a special role for a Christian college like the Kwansei Gakuin within the framework of Japanese higher education.

According to H. F. Woodsworth, a Canadian Methodist lay missionary who was the dean of the College of Literature, during the 1920s, the special role of the Kwansei Gakuin was to influence central Japan to think along the lines of Christian idealism and to lead its graduates "to give expression to that idealism in Christian service."[64] Yet he also recognized that the Japanese put a great emphasis on education and that parents would often live in poverty in order to send their children to expensive schools. Woodsworth wrote: "Success in school brings gratification throughout the length and breadth of a boy's far-flung family system. Failure is a disgrace that makes life itself almost intolerable."[65] It is probable that Woodsworth felt that the Kwansei Gakuin in the 1920s could provide both a Christian educational alternative and increased educational opportunity for Japanese who might not necessarily want the Christian element.

It is obvious, nevertheless, that the Canadian Methodists were intent on improving the Kwansei Gakuin, for they were firmly committed to raising it to university status. It is also clear that there was a good deal of wishful thinking in this, given the limited resources of the missionary society. Grandiose schemes for the Kwansei Gakuin, which disregarded the limited funds available, can perhaps be taken as a reflection of the frontier spirit which was an important element of Canadian national character. Moreover, the Canadian emphasis on education was an expression of a humanitarian concern, which saw mission work not merely in terms of Christian conversion but also in terms of improving the society in which the missionaries worked. For the Canadians, education was seen as the means by which every class of society could improve itself. They were not interested in providing education solely for the elite.

The Kwansei Gakuin was a denominational college. Among Christian colleges in the Kwansei region, it was second in importance to Dōshisha College in Kyoto, which attained university status in 1920. The Kwansei Gakuin was too small and too underfunded to rival the Imperial universities or the great secular private colleges, such as Keiō or Waseda in Tokyo, which attained university status in the 1920s. Canadian Methodist missionary work in Japan did not receive the large bequests from wealthy Canadian families that might have allowed it to build a well-endowed university. When it came to supporting missions, the Eaton and Massey families, two of the richest Methodist families, contributed to work in China rather than in Japan.

SPECIAL SCHOOLS

While Canadian Methodists largely concentrated on education for the Japanese, one of the most successful of all Canadian missionary educational endeavours was the Canadian Methodist Academy. It opened its doors in Kobe in 1913 to educate the children of Canadian missionaries. The lack of educational facilities for Western children had hampered the Canadian mission in stationing missionaries with large families in rural areas, for they "naturally gravitated" toward the Western communities where facilities for their children were available.[66] Since the Canadian Methodist mission preferred posting married male missionaries, and some missionaries preferred keeping their children with them during the crucial years of adolescence,[67] the creation of the Canadian Academy allowed them to have their children educated in Japan, rather than in Canada, up to university age.

In 1913, the Canadian Academy opened with sixteen pupils. The next year the number had grown to twenty-nine with nine children from the Canadian Methodist mission, ten from other missions, and a further ten from the Kobe business community. The Academy, which had been intended for the Canadian Methodist mission, almost immediately found itself serving a much wider community.[68] It always remained, however, the preserve of Western children.

The school followed the course prescribed by the Education Department of Ontario for ungraded public schools, and in addition gave extra classes in Latin, German, Japanese, manual training, piano, and vocal music.[69] In the second year of its operation, the twenty-nine pupils were spread across six Ontario school grades. In 1915, D. R. McKenzie noted that, if the school did not expand, it would disappoint missionaries who hoped to keep their children in Japan until university age.[70] The Missionary Society in Canada acted promptly and decided that it would enlarge the Academy to embrace high school work.

Because many of the missionary children did not come from the Kobe area, dormitory facilities were needed. In the school's first year, there were six to eight boarders. As the school expanded, the difficulty of accommodating boarders became more acute. In 1920, Senator Lorne Webster of Montreal, who was visiting Japan to attend the World's Sunday School Convention, gave a large donation for a new dormitory building.[71] In the light of the problem of raising money for the Kansei Gakuin endowment, it is somewhat ironic that money was so quickly forthcoming for a Western school.

The first principal of the Canadian Academy was Ethel Misener, the widow of a professor at Victoria College, University of Toronto. Lucy Norman, sister of Dan Norman, the Canadian Methodist missionary in Nagano, was the first matron. Initially, the staff of the school was drawn mainly from the wives of the Canadian Methodist missionaries attached to the Kwansei Gakuin. As well, the Canadian Methodist teachers at the college itself gave occasional help at the school.[72]

In 1920, Reverend G. R. Tench was appointed by the Mission Board in Toronto to teach at the Canadian Academy. By 1922, it was providing a twelve-year course following the Ontario public and high school curriculum, which enabled students to enter the University of Toronto. The Canadian Academy's dormitory facilities provided accommodation for staff and forty-five students. By 1922, the Canadian Academy was educating children not only from its own mission, but also from nineteen other missionary bodies.[73]

By that time, the Academy was also receiving support from other missions. The Methodist Episcopal South, the American Board (Congregationalist), the United Lutheran Church of the U.S.A., and the Presbyterian Church North and South missions all contributed a total annual grant of 6,300 yen. The Canadian Methodist mission itself was providing an annual grant of only 4,000 yen, but since 1913, the Canadian Methodists had invested approximately 150,000 yen in the Academy's buildings and facilities. Thus, while the Canadian Academy had become a union school, it would retain very strong links with the Canadian Methodist mission for many years to come.

The Canadian Academy answered an acute need for educational facilities for the children of Western missionaries in central and southern Japan. Although there were other Western schools in Tokyo, the Academy appealed to Canadian missionaries; it was not unusual for Canadian missionaries in Korea and China to send their children to the school in Kobe. A. R. Menzies, later a distinguished diplomat, was sent to the Academy by his father, a Canadian Presbyterian missionary in China. Among the early students of the Academy was E. Herbert Norman, who became as well a distinguished diplomat in later life and a historian of Japan.[74] Many other graduates went on to successful careers in university teaching, the diplomatic service, and the church. The Canadian Academy and the talented Canadian Methodist women teachers who made up most of its staff gave their students a secondary education as good as that of the very best schools in Canada.

A very different, but equally specialized, school was the Canadian Anglican Blind School (the Kunmoin), located in Gifu. This had its beginnings, following the great Mino-Hide earthquake in 1891, as a blind men's club. At the time, there was only one other school for the blind in Japan. The Kunmoin was an example of Christian work in an important and neglected field, which pointed the way for further Japanese government effort in a necessary field of social work. In the late 1920s, the Kunmoin passed from Canadian Anglican hands into the control of the Japanese government. Until that time, the Canadian Anglican missionaries provided an extremely valuable service to the community. It has to be stressed that one of the major contributions the missionary movement made to Japan was providing a beginning in such areas as a school for the blind. They were a pioneering force in social work that had an impact far greater than the small scale of their institutions might indicate.

MISSION SCHOOLS IN KOREA

Like their colleagues in Japan, Canadian Presbyterians in Korea saw mission schools as an important evangelistic tool. After the annexation of Korea by Japan in 1910, missionaries in Korea faced many of the same problems their counterparts in Japan had dealt with a generation earlier. Education was seen by the Japanese Government-General of Chōsen as being highly important, for through it Japanese values could be disseminated into Korean society. Further, as in Japan, education was perceived as a necessary requirement for the creation of a modern society. After 1910, the Government-General attempted to ensure its control over education by introducing into the peninsula many of the educational reforms that already had been adopted in Japan.

Given the ease with which the various Missionary Societies adjusted to the new circumstances in education in Japan after 1899, the virulent reaction of missionaries in Korea to similar legislation in 1915 is surprising. Control of private education was especially important in Korea because, as Terauchi Masatake, the first Governor-General of Chōsen, reportedly said, "private education in Korea nurtured a national consciousness, which encouraged Koreans to strive for independence from Japan."[75] Yet as far as mission schools were concerned, A. E. Armstrong, the Assistant Foreign Missions Secretary of the Canadian Presbyterian Missionary Society pointed out in 1916 that "it now transpires, or is believed, that the Japanese Government is more concerned about the attitudes of missionaries in Korea towards the Japanese Government than with regard to the teaching of religion or the Bible in the schools."[76] The sensitivity of the Japanese authorities to missionary protest was directly related to Japanese perceptions of the missionaries' ability to influence Western public opinion against Japan. Whether they liked it or not, Japanese governmental reaction to missionaries and their schools was intimately bound to politics. It was not surprising that, following the March 1, 1919, demonstrations, the Government-General introduced educational reforms that allowed missionaries to teach religion once again in their schools. It was good politics to do so.

Yet there is another side to the educational regulations which the Japanese Ministry of Education brought into being in the 1890s and the Government-General of Chōsen brought in twenty years later. This was a matter of educational standards. Educational standards were high in Japan, and in order to attract students, the Canadian Methodists and other Missionary Societies were forced to strive for high standards in their schools from the start. Missionary educational effort was thus concentrated in a relatively small number of schools.

To establish a school in Japan was a serious undertaking. This was not the case in Korea prior to annexation, for in the absence of a national government-sponsored educational system and with no competition from Western-style private schools, church and school were virtually inseparable. Almost every church in the peninsula had its school, often of the most rudimentary type. In 1910, there were some 746 schools run by missionaries in Korea. In 1915, the Canadian Presbyterians maintained some forty-one day schools with 193 high school students and 1,081 primary school students.[77] Theological students, of whom the Canadian Presbyterians had fifteen in 1915, were sent to the united Presbyterian theological seminary in P'yongyang. On the surface, the Canadian Presbyterian effort appears to be far more impressive than the Canadian Methodist endeavour in Japan, as the latter could only afford to maintain a paltry three girls' schools and a half share in a college. The difference, however, was quality.

In all their mission centres, the Canadian Presbyterians tried to maintain schools of a "higher level" for boys and girls to provide an apex to a local church system of Christian primary schools. Most of the latter were most primitive. After annexing Korea in 1910, the new Government-General actively began to develop a governmental educational system and to regulate standards in private schools. Mission schools in Korea had to meet Japanese standards, which demanded teachers who had passed Japanese teacher-training courses and a Japanese curriculum.[78] Mission schools were confronted with very considerable pressure from the Government-General to raise their academic standards. By rigorously applying private-school regulations, the Japanese authorities were able to reduce the number of mission schools by the end of 1914 to 473, almost 300 less than in 1910.[79] As D. A. MacDonald, a Canadian Presbyterian missionary stationed at Hoiryung, wrote in 1914, "the school supported by the local church is so poor that I am expecting it to be closed by the Japanese and our boys sent to the Government school, which is strongly anti-Christian."[80] After 1910, the Canadian Presbyterians and the other missions in Korea were caught by the pressure of modernization, which came in the form of Japanese rule with all its regulations. It was no longer possible, as their Canadian Methodist colleagues in Japan had long known, to maintain schools on a shoestring. This was something that the Korea missionaries should have realized from the experiences of their fellow Canadian Presbyterians in Taiwan, who from the early 1900s had been forced to abide by Japanese colonial educational standards.

There were differences between Korea and Japan; only one was the ability of Korean missionaries to protest more successfully than their counterparts in Japan. Even more important was the continuing vital position that mission schools played in the education of Koreans. Whereas in Japan mission schools were part of a vast competitive network of private schools, in Korea the majority of private schools offering Western-style education remained missionary ones. Further, while a government-recognized diploma was important for higher education, such opportunities existed for only a small minority of Koreans. The bureaucracy of the Government-General was predominantly Japanese; Koreans had little opportunity of holding any but the most minor posts. The educational system the Government-General introduced after 1910 was two-tiered: one tier, an educational system for the Japanese residents, and the other, a system for the Koreans. The apex of the Japanese residents' system was Keijō Imperial University in Seoul, which was open to Japanese from the metropolitan islands as well as those from Korea. The system for Koreans was broad at the elementary level but very narrow at the higher school level. The lack of opportunities for Koreans to go beyond elementary school was deliberate; it was only for the rich who could afford to send their children to Japan that the possibility of higher education existed. What the Japanese wanted in Korea was to inculcate Japanese values and to spread the use of Japanese language, the language of law and government, through elementary school education. As far as possible, the Government-General wished to prevent Koreans from acquiring higher education, for this might lead them to a desire for independence. The underlying theme of Japanese colonialism was assimilation through education, but the ultimate aim was to make Koreans second-class citizens, without the full rights of the Japanese. Despite the attempt to assimilate Koreans, the Japanese were never sure enough of their policies to allow Koreans equal rights, especially when it came to government and the bureaucracy.

The Government-General's educational policies were directed at replacing Korean with Japanese cultural values. The Christian movement in Korea, which by 1910 had reached every corner of the peninsula, found itself as one of the mainstays for the continued existence of Korean culture, and, as such, operated contrary to Japanese policy. Admittedly, the culture was perverted somewhat by putting an emphasis on Christianity. Church services were conducted in Korean. The mission schools, unlike government schools, emphasized the Korean language rather than Japanese. This policy of maintaining Korean culture may have been somewhat contradictory to the central goal of missionaries (which was spreading the gospel), for without a doubt the missionaries irritated the Japanese. It would have been more logical for missionaries to have acted as agents of Japanese cultural imperialism by helping to foster the Japanese language. This would have gained official support from the Japanese, which in turn could have been used to get official support for teaching Christianity in Japanese. However, because there was little opportunity for Koreans or Taiwanese in the

Imperial bureaucracy, certain professions—such as medicine, engineering, and, in Korea, the ministry—became favoured occupations for young men. These occupations, with the exception of medicine which was strictly regulated, allowed their practitioners a degree of personal freedom in their work. In that sense, mission schools were educating Koreans whose ambitions did not lie in pursuing a career in the colonial bureaucracy.

Government regulations over secondary education brought about a similar response from missionaries in both Japan and Korea. They saw higher education as a way of putting their educational activity outside the rigid constrictions of government regulation. In Japan, the Canadian Methodists developed the Kwansei Gakuin as a denominational college. In Korea, the missionary movement was able to create a union college of higher learning. In a sense, the missionary movement in Korea was able to do what Eby had advocated for the missionary movement in Japan in the early 1880s: that is, combine missionary resources to create a major educational institution. While the women's missionary movement in Japan was prepared to join together, as seen by the creation of the Tokyo Woman's Christian College, the male missionaries were not. In Korea, however, a Christian college of higher education was set up following discussions in 1916 by the interdenominational Joint Committee of Christian Education. R. P. MacKay was the Canadian Presbyterian representative during these discussions.[81] In planning for this college, the missionary representatives, like their confreres in the Japan field, were in part hoping to avoid confrontation with government authorities. In 1917, Chōsen Christian College (now Yonsei University) was founded in Seoul.

As a union college, Chōsen Christian College had advantages over the denominational colleges in Japan. Not the least of these was its association with the Underwood family, one of the most famous Korea missionary families (its American branch had established the typewriter company). Not only did successive generations of Underwoods teach at Chōsen Christian College, but their American cousins could be relied upon to give generously for buildings. Private benefactors, as well as the combined income of the missions in the union, were important in making Chōsen Christian College a major force in Korean private education.

The Canadian Presbyterians in Korea were engaged in two other important union educational efforts. The most famous was the Severance Union Medical College in Seoul,[82] which was established as early as 1900 to train Korean Christian doctors and nurses. Like the Chōsen Christian College, the medical school owed much to the generosity of an American philanthropist, the eponymous Louis H. Severance. O. R. Avison, one of the first four unofficial Canadian missionaries to come out to Korea, was the guiding personality behind the medical college and its hospital. Although a Canadian, Avison was supported by the American Presbyterian Mission North. The more purely Canadian Presbyterian commitment to the medical college came from Dr. Frank Schofield, an Englishman who had previously been on the faculty at the Ontario Agricultural College in Guelph and who came out to Korea in 1916 as a Canadian Presbyterian missionary and took up the position of professor of bacteriology. Dr. Schofield and his wife were the only Canadian Presbyterian missionaries living in Seoul. It was not as a bacteriologist, as later events showed, that Schofield would emerge as one of the very few Westerners who have become national heroes in Korea.

The second major union educational endeavour of the Canadian Presbyterians was the Union Christian College (now Soonjun University) in P'yongyang where the Canadians sent candidates for the ministry from their mission field in northern Korea. Like Severance Union Medical College, the P'yongyang school had its roots in pre-Annexation days; a college department was established in 1906. Less nationally prominent than the Chōsen Christian College in Seoul, the P'yongyang Union Christian College was the pinnacle of higher education in northern Korea.

In all these higher educational undertakings, the Canadian Presbyterians played only a minor role as one of the supporting missions. Yet their participation reveals a different approach than Canadian Methodists took in Japan, whose proclivities showed a marked preference for solely Canadian institutions and union work along denominational rather than interdenominational lines. At the expense of exclusive control, joining in union higher educational endeavour allowed the Canadian Presbyterians to participate in institutions that eventually became the leading private colleges in Korea. These Christian colleges, however, did not face the severe competition that confronted the denominational colleges in Japan. For the majority of Koreans who wished Western-style higher education, the Christian institutions were not an alternative or a second or third best to the Imperial universities or elite private universities. The Christian union colleges were the only opportunity.

THE TAIWAN SHOESTRING

In 1895, fifteen years before Korea was annexed, Taiwan became a Japanese colony following the Treaty of Shimonoseki. It was under Japanese rule that the weaknesses and limitations of the missionary endeavour in Taiwan were fully revealed. The missionary effort in education was hindered by the modernization effort of the Japanese

Government-General. Yet even without the Japanese, the educational work of both the English and the Canadian Presbyterian missions in Taiwan had intrinsic flaws which might have yielded problems.

The failure to meet these challenges in education and medical work cannot be blamed on the missionaries themselves or on a deliberately anti-Christian policy of the colonial authorities. Rather, it stemmed from the legacy of the past. Almost singlehandedly, George Leslie Mackay had created in the late nineteenth century a mission in north Taiwan. In the scope of its activities, this mission was as broad as the much larger Canadian Methodist mission in Japan. Mackay had proved that a composite mission, involved in educational, medical, and evangelistic work, could be run on a shoestring budget by one Western missionary. This was not possible under Japanese rule. As in Japan, in Taiwan the Japanese demanded that certain standards be met.

Mackay began educational work in north Taiwan with the creation of Oxford College in Tamsui. In 1900, Oxford College had thirty-seven male students and thirty-four students attending the girls' school. The colonial officials left the educational work of both the Canadian and the English Presbyterians virtually undisturbed, even though they came under private-school regulations. Japanese language was made mandatory in the curriculum, but religious instruction was still allowed.[83] The number of pupils was so small that the Government-General could afford to ignore them, especially when that strategy would help engender the goodwill of the missionaries.[84] While Oxford College was left alone, some of the smaller schools attached to individual congregations were disbanded and their pupils given the opportunity to attend government elementary schools. Apparently, this did not overly disturb the missionaries, for they were pleased at "seeing modern Western-style Japanese education advance at the expense of the 'pagan' Chinese schooling which most of them abhorred."[85] This statement should be taken with a grain of salt, for missionaries did not like to see Christian work closed.

The attempt by the Japanese to engender goodwill among missionaries can be seen in their attitude toward the opening of the middle school in Tamsui. In 1914, the Canadian Presbyterian mission was given permission by the Government-General to open a middle school in Oxford College with G. W. Mackay, the only son of the pioneer missionary, as its principal. At the opening ceremony in April 1914, senior officials of the Government-General were present "purposely to show that the colonial Government-General was pleased to recognize the Christian Middle School."[86] According to Mackay, the new school was at that time the "only high school of any standing" for the three million Chinese on the island.[87] There was, however, some difficulty in maintaining government recognition for the middle school. With the

integration edict of 1922, which aimed at virtually complete Japaniza-
tion of the educational system, it was not until 1938 that the two
Canadian Presbyterian mission schools in Tamsui received official
recognition from the colonial government.[88]

Japanese-language training was a necessity; Taiwanese parents
wanted their children educated in Japanese. In 1915, Milton Jack, a
Canadian Presbyterian missionary in Taipeh, noted:

> for the foreign missionary to have absolutely no knowledge of
> Japanese and thus be unable to advise them [students] in the choice
> of literature, is to be placed at a great disadvantage. Again the
> terminology among the younger generation is fast changing and
> becoming more Japanese in substance, though the Chinese form
> may be retained. It is therefore imperative, in teaching any abstract
> subject to a group of Formosan students who have been trained in
> Japanese elementary and secondary schools, that one should have
> a knowledge of Japanese in addition to Chinese, in order to teach
> with clearness and effectiveness.[89]

Taiwan differed from Korea in that there was a much greater desire
among young Taiwanese to learn Japanese.

A major problem for the Canadian Presbyterians was G. W. Mackay's inability to speak Japanese. Missionary ignorance of Japanese was
seen by the colonial authority as a symbol of pro-Chinese sentiment.
Certainly, Mackay did not get on well with the colonial educational
officials. In 1922, he wrote to R. P. MacKay, the Foreign Missions
Secretary in Toronto: "it is not necessary for me to say much why some
of the Japanese officials dislike and suspect me. Any one who is
friendly to the Chinese is looked upon with disfavour."[90] He maintained that, during his nine years as principal of the Tamsui school, he
had had a "stormy time" with the Japanese, but that he still retained
"the full confidence and respect of all the Chinese in Taiwan of all
classes both Christian and non-Christian."[91] Mackay's suspicions of the
Japanese were perhaps unfounded. Because he was half-Chinese, born
and brought up in Taiwan might explain in part why the Japanese were
suspicious of him and why he was well regarded by the Chinese.
Mackay was a defender of Chinese rights and took pride in seeing one
of the educational changes he had long advocated—the acceptance of
Taiwanese boys into government middle schools—implemented by
the Government-General in 1922.[92] But Mackay's case reveals that, if a
missionary openly sympathized with the Taiwanese in a sensitive area
for the colonial administration, he was courting trouble, all the more so
because the Japanese believed that missionaries and their schools had
actively helped foment anti-Japanese feeling in Korea, which had come
to the fore in the March 1, 1919, movement. Some Canadian missionaries believed that as long as Mackay remained principal of the Tamsui

school it would never be recognized as a middle school by the authorities. But Mackay remained in charge of the school until 1940 and was able to maintain the school's population at around eighty students.

The Canadian Presbyterians also maintained a girls' school, founded as well by George Leslie Mackay in 1883. In 1913, new school buildings were erected which could accommodate upwards of fifty boarders. At the same time, a high school department, in which most of the instruction was carried on in Japanese, was added.[93]

Because the mission schools did not have official recognition, their graduates were prevented from taking examinations for entrance into higher institutions. For the wealthier graduates, this disadvantage was somewhat offset by the opportunities to study in the Christian colleges in Japan. In the interwar years, one missionary estimated that, of the graduates of the Canadian Presbyterian mission schools and their two English Presbyterian sister schools in Tainan, some 200 pupils later studied theology in Taiwan, 300 graduates went on to study medicine either in Taipeh or Japan and practised in Taiwan, a further 100 students went on to become dentists, and a similar number became pharmacists.[94]

As well as its educational work in Taiwan, the Canadian Presbyterian mission also undertook medical work which included training medical assistants and nurses. Medical work begin by George Leslie Mackay in Tamsui was transferred in 1912 to Taipeh, where a new hospital building had been built. The Mackay Memorial Hospital faced very severe problems. It was difficult for the Canadian Presbyterians to attract graduates with government-certified qualifications to work in the hospital because private practice was more lucrative. As Duncan MacLeod, a senior Canadian Presbyterian missionary, pointed out in 1923, "in no department has Formosa made more progress under Japanese rule than in that of medicine."[95] By 1919, the teaching of medical students or assistants, which had been undertaken by missionaries before the First World War, was prohibited because surgical assistants now had to be trained at the Government-General's Medical School in Taipeh.

The Canadian Presbyterian mission also had great difficulty keeping the hospital open because of the lack of missionary doctors. From 1917 until 1924, the hospital was closed; not only were there no doctors, but there were no funds available from the Mission Board in Toronto. The Mackay Memorial Hospital reopened in 1924 with the arrival of Dr. G. Gushue-Taylor, a Newfoundlander who had previously worked for the English Presbyterian mission in south Taiwan. He and his wife, a trained nurse, remained until 1940.

The individual doctor might well have been a skilled surgeon and physician, but the Mackay Memorial Hospital was primitively equipped. As early as 1914, Dr. J. L. Maxwell, who was in charge of the English Presbyterian hospital in Tainan, wrote:

> the doctor is often stationed alone as of old, single handed to run a hospital on modern lines, his own limitations alike of time, ability and knowledge being entirely neglected. In other words we have fallen from the high promise of past days. We are not giving the best to the service of Christ, and we should be laughed out of court anywhere but in a heathen land, where something very far from the best is still infinitely better than the natives possess. But is this a right standard? Is this second-rate (to put it mildly) a proper offering to Christ, a proper presentation of His message.[96]

Though they "should be laughed out of court anywhere but in a heathen land," the English and the Canadian Presbyterians continued with their hospitals. During the late nineteenth century, missionary medical work was conducted by enthusiastic doctors working with primitive equipment. By the early twentieth century, this was no longer possible in the Japanese Empire. In colonial Taiwan, government hospitals and dispensaries were far superior to the Mackay Memorial Hospital or the hospitals of the English Presbyterians in south Taiwan. With funds coming from voluntary contributions in Canada, the Canadian Presbyterians could not compete with the Japanese, who could draw on the resources of a public exchequer. The Missionary Societies themselves were perhaps not prepared to admit that they had "fallen from the high promise of past days." But it was obvious that the old attitude that "something very far from the best is still infinitely better than the natives possess" was no longer valid by the 1920s, even in the remote mission field of Taiwan.

THE CANADIAN CONTRIBUTION

Medical work in Taiwan suffered from underfunding, as did educational work in the Japanese Empire. From the 1880s, educational work developed into the major activity of the Canadian missionary movement. In those educational areas where mission schools faced the least competition from government or private, Western-style schools, Canadian-sponsored schools fared well. Thus, it was in women's education that Canadians made their most significant contribution to education in Japan; before their efforts, Western-style female education had been largely neglected. Mission schools for girls focussed attention on the need for and value of Western-style education, and the example of their unmarried missionary teachers showed Japanese women that they could lead independent, active, and fulfilling lives. The Canadian missionary teachers and the three girls' schools they founded significantly contributed to the broad impact that mission schools had on female education in Japan. In Shizuoka and Kofu, the Canadian schools were the first of their kind in those prefectures, and they were able to sustain a considerable regional importance over the years. In Tokyo, when it was first founded, the Tōyō Eiwa Jo Gakkō was a leading girls' school in the capital and remained a well-known school. Partly because educational opportunities for males were greater than for females, the contribution of Canadian Methodists to male education was less significant than it was for female. The trump card that the Tōyō Eiwa Gakkō, their middle school for boys, possessed was the quality of its English-language training, yet this identification with Western studies made its student enrollment partly dependent upon an open attitude toward the West. More important, however, was that graduates were able to continue their education at a higher level. Few students would come to the school unless its diploma was recognized by the government. The price of this recognition was a prohibition against teaching Christianity as part of the regular curriculum of the school. It was a price which the Canadian Methodists refused to pay, and they closed the Tōyō Eiwa Gakkō.

The involvement of the Canadian Methodists in the Kwansei Gakuin indicated that they still saw evangelistic possibilities in male education. The creation of a college of higher learning was also an attempt to avoid strict government regulation of curriculum. In the 1920s, under new legislation, the Kwansei Gakuin could have achieved university status, but its failure to do so until 1932 underlined the financial weakness of the Canadian Methodist mission. Because of its lack of funds, the Kwansei Gakuin could not compete with the best private colleges, let alone the Imperial universities in Japan. The Canadian Methodists, in supporting the Kwansei Gakuin, were maintaining a college that could only be second-rate in the competitive educational world of Japan. Was this simply a case of missionary aspirations for the institution going beyond the limits of financial resources? There is an element of this in the issue of the Kwansei Gakuin. A major legacy of the late nineteenth century, however, was the belief that mission work in the early twentieth century could still be successfully undertaken on a shoestring. Clearly, as the case of the Kwansei Gakuin revealed, major educational institutions could not be maintained in the Japanese Empire in the 1920s without considerable expense. Yet institutions like the Kwansei Gakuin or the Tamsui Middle School or the schools that Canadian Presbyterians helped maintain in north-eastern Korea should not be seen strictly in terms of educational excellence. They provided, to a greater or lesser extent, a Christian alternative to secular education. Likewise, they increased educational opportunities. In Korea, mission schools, much to the chagrin of the Government-General, obviously inculcated in their students a desire for independence. Nonetheless, the most important contribution of Canadian mission schools lay in helping to change stereotyped Japanese, Korean, or Taiwanese perceptions of Westerners. Few graduates of Canadian mission schools came away without learning to be more understanding and tolerant of sympathetic Westerners. This is not to say that they had a clear idea of what Canadians were or how they differed from Britishers or Americans; however, they knew that Canadians cared enough to establish the school that they attended.

At the same time as educational institutions were being developed, direct evangelism and social work still remained highly important in the Canadian missionary endeavour.

CHAPTER EIGHT

Evangelism and Social Work

The years after Eby's withdrawal from Japan in the mid-1890s saw enormous changes take place in Japanese society, but Canadian missionaries were slow to adapt their evangelistic work to the changing circumstances. This was partly a result of a sense of security in their own position; Canadian missionaries in Japan rarely felt the need to justify their presence. Although some missionaries in Japan speculated on the methods and philosophy of missionary work, there was little systematic discussion of these topics in the missionary community. Missionaries were generally concerned more with pointing out the difficulties confronting Christianity in Japan than with the problem of what they should do to overcome them, perhaps because of the simple but constant need to give their home constituency a reason why they were unable to convert more people.

After the turn of the century, however, Canadian missionaries and especially women missionaries became increasingly involved in social work among the less fortunate in society. The growing concern with social work had as one of its sources of inspiration the theology of the Social Gospel, which was becoming a powerful influence within the church in Canada. Conveniently, social work also provided the missionary in Japan with a new role, for the missionary was being supplanted by Japanese pastors in parish work.

Few missionaries had the oratorical skills in Japanese to be able to rival a well-known Japanese evangelist preacher in open public meetings. Direct evangelistic work sometimes involved preaching every night to non-Christians in open gospel halls in large cities, or three or four nights of consecutive preaching at an individual church, or even tent and street preaching. In order to attract crowds, there was a demand for famous speakers to perform at evangelistic meetings. The great evangelists of Japan, such as Paul Kanamori (Kanamori

Notes for Chapter Eight are found on pp. 239-42.

147

Michitomo) or Uemura Masahisa, never lacked an audience, but very few missionaries could attract large Japanese audiences. It is not surprising that few missionaries displayed much enthusiasm for this very public sort of work; after all, they had to maintain their appearance as respectable members of the community. As was so often the case, it tended to be the women missionaries (less concerned with maintaining appearances) who were the most evangelistic, though there were some able male evangelistic missionaries among the Canadians in Japan. But evangelistic missionaries were a minority group.

Unlike in Japan, where the setting was primarily urban, in Korea Canadian Presbyterian work was largely rural. Until the 1930s, the evangelistic missionary in Korea retained a strong affinity (albeit under the guise of scientific approach to evangelism known as the Nevius Method[1]) with the old circuit rider of early nineteenth-century Ontario. It might be claimed that this evangelistic method was successful, for in the first decade of the twentieth century in Korea a great many converts were made. There was a tremendous optimism among missionaries about the future of Christianity in Korea, an optimism that extended beyond 1910.

In contrast, evangelistic work in Taiwan was more limited than it might have been because the colonial authorities prevented the missionaries from working among the aboriginal tribes who might have been easier to convert than the Chinese. Both in Taiwan and in Korea, in their evangelistic work missionaries had to contend with the fact of Japanese colonialism.

In the early 1900s, Canadian missionaries began paying more attention to the main obstacles confronting the propagation of Christianity. The problems posed by traditional religions and Japanese nationalism were among the most frequent subjects of missionary comment.

PROBLEMS AND OPPORTUNITIES

Many missionaries considered Buddhism as a potential threat to Christian advance. In the 1870s, McDonald had complained about Buddhism in biting terms.[2] In 1905, Arthur Lea, the Canadian Anglican missionary in Gifu (later the Bishop of the diocese of Kyūshū), saw Buddhism in a more reasoned light. In an article dealing with the difficulties of the Japanese accepting Christianity, he noted that the success of Buddhism in Japan was the result of its ability to co-exist with Shintō.[3] He believed that Buddhism would ally itself with Christianity if the latter had an attitude of compromise rather than one of conquest. However, Lea was too orthodox an Anglican to agree to compromise.

C. P. Holmes, a Canadian Methodist missionary, looked for the emergence of a more tolerant attitude toward Buddhism among Christians. In a short, undated article, "The Message for Japan Today" (possibly written in the 1910s), Holmes suggested that the Christian attitude toward Buddhism should be sympathetic without appearing to condone compromise.[4] He thought that the doctrines of Christianity were all present in Buddhist theology. Even though Buddhism used a different word for God, Holmes felt that "Buddhism had everything that Christianity had including incarnation and a trinity except atonement."[5] He thought, however, that atonement was not needed and stressed that no offence should be given in presenting Christianity as a "superior or a more excellent way" than Buddhism.[6] Moreover, Holmes argued that the "superiority of Christianity could not be shown along racial lines" and warned missionaries who attempted this style of argument that they would be confronted with difficult questions from the enquirer.[7] To Holmes, it was "through the humanism of Jesus that the superman was reached and that the credal, the ecclesiastical and the liturgical were valuable so far as they revealed the human."[8] In his view, Christianity was no better than Buddhism, but Jesus was better than Buddha.

Despite the existence of this more tolerant attitude, some missionaries continued to hold a hostile view of Buddhism. This was especially true in rural areas and provincial cities, where traditional values remained strong and Buddhism always appeared as a particularly strong barrier to Christian work. In December 1913, H. E. Walker, the Canadian Methodist missionary in Hamamatsu, believed that Buddhism was especially strong in his district: "while it was said that people in Japan had no religion, they were ardent Buddhists at heart."[9] As late as 1924, F. Ainsworth, the Canadian Methodist missionary in Toyama, noted that a considerable number of people still clung to Buddhist practices even though Buddhism was losing popularity.[10] In the same year, Audrey M. Henty, a British Anglican missionary who was closely associated with the Canadian Anglican mission in central Japan, noted that, despite the material progress of Japan, there was a "dead hand of fear which gripped the Buddhist and ancestor worshipper" and that real progress for Christianity was impossible under these conditions.[11] Although these observers certainly exaggerated Buddhism's role in the life of the Japanese, their misapprehension continued until the end of the period.

Missionaries also saw nationalistic barriers as important obstacles to the acceptance of Christianity in Japan. In 1905, Arthur Lea considered the spirit of Japanese nationalism as the greatest obstacle to the Japanese acceptance of Christianity. He felt that Christianity could not amalgamate with the spirit of Japanese nationalism because Christianity was "unsuited to the history, principles and ideas of which the Japanese nation is the embodiment."[12] Christianity relegated to mythology the story of the divine origin of Japan and the Imperial line, and Lea thought that it would eventually subvert the type of loyalty that was being inculcated through "Imperial myths" by the state educational system. As a result of this, he felt that many Japanese feared Christianity.[13]

Other Canadian Anglicans were conscious of the danger to Christianity posed by nationalism and especially the Emperor cult. In November 1918, J. Cooper Robinson, the veteran Canadian Anglican missionary stationed at Nagoya, considered "Mikadoism" a very serious threat to Christianity. To Robinson, "Mikadoism" was the most prominent aspect of Shintō, which also had two other facets—nature worship and ancestor worship.[14] He thought that the authorities used "Mikadoism" to restrain the Japanese, "who were by nature a rough and ready people with no respect for persons and a fondness of extremities."[15]

In the years immediately following the Russo-Japanese War, the problem of confronting Japanese nationalism and religion was most clearly expressed in the protracted controversy concerning Bushido—the Way of the Warrior. This controversy, which was stimulated by the publication of the 1905 edition of Nitobe Inazō's *Bushido: The Soul of Japan*, centred on the British Anglican diocese of South Tokyo. While the debate did not involve Canadian missionaries directly, it is important in showing a basic Anglican attitude toward Japan which Canadians shared.

In his book, Nitobe attributed Japan's triumph in the Russo-Japanese War to the spirit of the samurai, which he believed to be the most important element in the Japanese cultural heritage. This analysis was romantic, quaint, and unhistorical, but it reflected a growing self-confidence among the Japanese. In response to enquiries about Bushido from Anglicans in Britain, who viewed the concept in surprisingly favourable terms, John Imai, the leading Japanese clergyman in the diocese of South Tokyo, set out to explain the motif of Bushido and to correct the important misconception that it constituted the "soul of Japan."[16] In his article, "Bushido," Imai wrote that the spirit of Japan (or *yamatō damashii*) was a unique Japanese trait, which was a gift to the Japanese race handed down from the remote past and nourished and strengthened under a form of Bushido in the Japanese feudal period.[17] To Imai, Bushido summed up the ethical precepts observed by the Japanese samurai or bushi.[18] He felt that the spirit of the samurai was his sword, and that, except for the army officer corps who were the modern heirs of Bushido, this tradition was of little value to modern Japan. Imai believed that Bushido was a "disembodied spirit," which ran counter to the commercial, legal, and social progress as well as the prevailing utilitarianism of Japan at peace. Moreover, he attacked the harsh precepts of Bushido relating to women and the superior attitude of samurai toward other classes.

Imai stated that Western Christians should not lose interest in Japan through any mistaken idea that Japan under Bushido was better ignored.[19] He firmly believed that "Yamatō damashii—the spirit of Japan—cannot suffice but must be purified, renewed and perfected in its union with Christ."[20] This was an important statement, for it revealed a crucial Anglican attitude toward Japanese culture. For Anglicans, including Canadian ones, Christianity's role was to purify, renew, and perfect what was already in existence in Japan. They believed that there was much that was good in Japanese culture, but that it needed Christianity to perfect it.

The fact that it was a Japanese Anglican rather than a missionary who wrote about Bushido suggests that missionary understanding of its concepts was perhaps incomplete. It is of some interest that Nitobe Inazō, who started the controversy by publishing his book on Bushido, should be criticized by Anglicans. Nitobe was a Quaker and very highly regarded by the missionary movement in Japan, but that did not mean to Anglicans that his views on Bushido were necessarily correct. Indeed, a modern historian of Japan would certainly support the contention that the samurai should not be viewed with uncritical admiration.[21]

Besides traditional religions and aspects of Japanese nationalism, a few missionaries saw that modernization also posed some difficulties for Christianity, difficulties perceived in terms of morality. For instance, H. H. Coates, the Canadian Methodist missionary in Hamamatsu, was disturbed by the corruption in Japanese politics and business life. In 1919, he wrote that this damaging trend had "no panacea but in the Christian Gospel" and that "Japan was doomed nationally and internationally as well as individually without the Saviour."[22] Loretta L. Shaw, a Canadian Anglican missionary writing in 1922, was much less critical than Coates about the Japanese business leadership: "Consciously or unconsciously the Japanese are looking to Christian ideas to guide them in these difficult days of transition. None are more clearly aware of the necessity for new ideals and a new moral sanction for the rising generation of Japan than the keen leaders of finance."[23] There was a tendency among missionaries to assume that Japan would come to realize that it was doomed without Christianity. This meant, of course, that the final victory for Christianity would come about because of this spontaneous realization by Japan, rather than through the individual efforts of evangelistic missionaries.

While business immorality and political corruption might be seen to pose problems for the advance of Christianity, some missionaries realized that many Japanese had difficulty understanding basic Christian concepts. In 1905, Arthur Lea observed that one reason was the character of Japanese education, which he believed was based on a system that was "rigid in the extreme and scientific in the narrowest sense of the word."[24] As a result, many Japanese were strongly prejudiced against Christianity and had particular difficulty accepting its supernatural aspects. He thought that the Japanese people possessed an intensely religious nature,[25] but that their understanding of religion was very different from that of Westerners. In particular, he thought that the Japanese viewed religion as an "instrument or scheme" by which people were influenced to do what was right. For them, it was not necessary for religion to have its foundation in truth.[26]

Lea believed that Christian missions, and even beliefs themselves, also prevented Japanese from accepting Christianity. According to him, some Japanese had difficulty understanding the very purpose of Christian missions, and some even felt that Westerners had a sinister motive in opening and maintaining expensive missions in Japan. Lea thought it was extremely difficult to explain the spiritual aims of Christian missions to a people who supported religion mainly for material benefits.

According to Lea, there were also further difficulties in conveying even the most fundamental ideas, such as the Christian concept of God, to the Japanese people. The Japanese word for God, *kami*, was understood to mean the spirit of an Imperial ancestor or military hero; thus many Japanese did not care to listen to Christian preaching because they thought that it eulogized foreign heroes at the expense of their own.[27] Lea had investigated how the idea of one Christian God had come to Japanese Christians and had found that, without exception, the concept had been new when Japanese Christians had first encountered it in Christian meetings or literature.[28] Educated Japanese also had difficulty understanding the Christian doctrines of the Trinity, the Incarnation, and Atonement.[29] The problem of transferring Christian concepts into Japanese had been faced during the translation of the Bible in the late nineteenth century.[30]

Canadian Methodist missionaries were also conscious of the difficulties of interpreting Christian concepts to the Japanese. At the Japan Mission's WMS-CM annual meeting in July 1914, Miss M. E. Veazey stressed the importance of placing before the Japanese the idea of the Unseen God, impressing this truth upon them, and later bringing them to a knowledge of Christ the Saviour.[31] At the same annual meeting, Miss F. Bird noted that Bishop Hiraiwa Yoshiyasu of the Japan Methodist Church had suggested that, in speaking about Christianity to the Japanese, the WMS-CM missionaries should use Japanese proverbs wherever possible to foster an understanding of the word "sinner" and its significance.[32]

C. P. Holmes would have agreed with much of Miss Veazey's approach. He believed that the Christian message should begin with God, and not with Jesus Christ, because the Japanese mind had no point of contact with the Saviour.[33] He thought that God should be represented as "a person, thinking, willing, planning and working."[34] According to Holmes, one of the problems that prevented the intellectual classes from being attracted to Christianity was the conflict between scientific thought and Christianity. Holmes noted, however (and in doing so revealed his own ignorance of philosophy), that in the West the conflict among science, philosophy, and religion had ended and that now these three disciplines were "profoundly united as to the person of God."[35] To Holmes, therefore, no barrier to Christianity emanated from science. He urged that, in approaching the intellectual classes, missionaries should make more use of experimental psychology in their presentation of God.

Finally, Holmes thought that the importance of Jesus Christ should be stressed only after an initial period in which God had been the central point of missionary presentation. Holmes saw one danger arising in Japan: Christianity might become a movement of Christian work, with its main emphasis on social service.[36] His views were an expression of liberal theological thinking, corresponding with theological trends within the United States, where Protestant theologians had been concerned for some years with developing a form of Christianity that was exportable to the mission field.[37] There is reason to believe that his views were shared by other Canadian Methodist missionaries, as well as by many American Protestants.[38]

Certainly, many problems confronted the Canadian missionary movement. Bishop H. J. Hamilton, of the Canadian Anglican diocese of Mid-Japan, provided an acute analysis of the impediments to the Christianization of Japan. In summarizing the situation, he mentioned:

> insufficiency of workers native and foreign. Pride of intellect, refuse to believe in supernatural. Honest doubt, religious faculty almost dead. Unwillingness to live-up to high standard of Christian morality. Unwillingness to break with environment. Fear of persecution from family, neighbours, employers, Nationalist movement. No one higher than emperor.[39]

Faced with these intricate and complex challenges, it is not surprising that some missionaries were baffled and depressed. In December 1918, Bishop H. H. Montgomery, Secretary of the SPG, wrote to Bishop Mark Napier Trollope of Korea that the Christian movement in Japan was in a "very parlous state. Indeed I hesitate to say much about the Japanese Christian, for I do not know what to make of him. It is the only part of the world in the Far East which I do not want to revisit."[40] Six years later, Montgomery admitted that there was no part of the very broad SPG mission field that was so perplexing as Japan.[41] While these were the reflections of a British Anglican, Montgomery was a very experienced and capable Missions Secretary who supervised missions throughout the world. Of all these, it is significant that Japan was the most perplexing.

Despite this feeling of apprehension and disappointment, James Endicott, the Canadian Methodist Foreign Missions Secretary, remained optimistic. When he visited Japan in 1918 (the same year as Montgomery), he came away much heartened by the prospects of the Christian movement.[42] On this visit, he had interviewed Ōkuma Shigenobu, a former Prime Minister, who had assured him that the future of Christianity in Japan was bright "because of its hold upon the most intelligent people in the country."[43] Such a view from a leading politician, particularly a non-Christian one, undoubtedly gave Endicott hope for the future.

In general, Endicott's optimism was shared by many Canadian Methodist missionaries. In 1919, H. H. Coates believed that "if the eleven Apostles could have turned the Jewish and Roman world upside down within a generation," then his little band of Christian workers could do the same in Hamamatsu and the outlying provinces.[44] Likewise, Dan Norman in Nagano was not discouraged by the fact that the number of local Christians was small; he always remained hopeful for the future.[45]

Hopefulness was characteristic of Canadian missionaries, and set them apart from British Anglican missionaries who, if they did not share the perplexity of Bishop Montgomery, were less optimistic about Christian possibilities in Japan. The generation of student volunteers was aware that their work faced many barriers and few opportunities. In viewing Buddhism or the more vague "Mikadoism" as a barrier, there was a tendency to regard these creeds as being similar to Western religion. D. C. Holtom's pioneer work on national Shintō, *The National Faith of Japan*, was yet to be published.[46] Thus, missionaries had little to guide them about the true nature of "Mikadoism." Arthur Lea was one of the few missionaries who was able to see that Buddhism and Shintō were only part of a greater cultural tradition that opposed Christianity. If Christianity had been willing to compromise, it might have been accepted by this eclectic cultural tradition. Missionary writing often lacked Lea's broad perspective on the difficulties facing Christianity.

The lack of reference to new religions and socialism in missionary correspondence from the turn of the century onward is especially interesting, for the emergence of new religions and the development of socialism were both very important features in the social history of

Japan. Socialism and the new religions had a marked influence on many Japanese people whom Christians might have regarded as potential converts. The omission of any analysis of the threat posed by these new ideas reveals the remoteness of missionaries from the social realities of Japan. It might be conjectured that missionaries preferred to view the barriers to Christianity in the context of familiar concepts and thus were loath to accept the validity of less familiar ideas. As new religions were a relatively new social phenomenon, their importance was discounted. Canadian missionaries were supporters of change in Japan in both social and political matters, but that change was important only because it drew Japan closer to acquiring values that missionaries held dear. Certainly, in their approach to Japanese culture and society, the student volunteers held different views from the jacks-of-all-trades who has preceded them. Among Canadian Methodists, the emphasis was not on the "humanism of Jesus." Yet, for all that, the majority still viewed the barriers to Christianity in a narrow and almost traditional way.

INTERDENOMINATIONAL EVANGELISM

From the earliest days of Protestant missionary activity in Japan, Canadian missions had engaged in interdenominational projects. George Cochran's involvement with the Evangelical Alliance in the 1870s was an early example of this. The Methodist union in 1907, which saw the Canadian Methodist mission join with the two American Methodist Episcopal missions to form the national Japan Methodist Church, was a sign of a Canadian desire for increased co-operation with other missions. Interdenominational co-operation took on much greater impetus after the World Missionary Conference in Edinburgh in 1910. The new atmosphere was reflected in the growing interdenominational activities of the Canadian Methodist missionaries in Japan.

In 1913, this new tendency began with the visit of Tokyo of John R. Mott, one of the chief organizers of the Edinburgh Conference. As a result of his influence, the Japan Continuation Committee was formed, with the goal of realizing the hope of the Edinburgh Conference that its meeting would inaugurate a major evangelistic campaign throughout all the world's mission fields. The Japan Continuation Committee soon proposed a three-year, co-operative campaign to co-ordinate evangelism in Japan, Korea, Taiwan, and China.

In January 1914, D. R. McKenzie wrote to James Endicott in Toronto that the whole of the Protestant missionary body would co-operate in the new campaign, with "the exception of the High Church Anglicans and some American Episcopalians."[47] McKenzie was enthusiastic about the new program and hoped that all of Japan's 800

churches could be covered in the three years of the campaign.[48] The
cost of the campaign was estimated at 50,000 yen ($25,000), approxi-
mately half the normal annual budget of the Canadian Methodist
mission. Half of this amount was provided by John R. Mott, who had
received large donations from individuals and church sources in North
America to support evangelical campaigns.

The evangelical campaign was to embrace a definite and distinct
program of winning converts and was to go well beyond the spreading
of generalized Christian propaganda. McKenzie's optimism continued
well after this ambitious co-operative effort had begun in mid-1914. By
the following year, the campaign was progressing satisfactorily in various parts of Japan and had developed a considerable momentum.[49]

As part of this campaign, ten days of evangelistic meetings were held
in the Canadian Methodists' Central Tabernacle in Tokyo. On the last
two nights, Kimura, a Japanese evangelist who had worked with Billy
Sunday in the United States, led the meeting.[50] On the final night of
this series, fifty people indicated a serious interest in Christianity. Some
days later, about forty people attended a special meeting to welcome
enquirers and candidates.[51] By Japanese standards, these were considerable numbers, and the series of evangelistic meetings appeared to be
a success.

In July 1916, the minutes of the annual meeting of the Canadian
Methodist Japan Mission WMS Council reported that all the WMS-CM
mission stations were "anxiously waiting" for the campaign to help
them extend their work in fields that were already "lying open" for
Christian work.[52] The women missionaries believed the the opportunities for the extension of Christian work had been "greatly widened by
the evangelical campaign."[53]

When the three-year evangelical campaign ended in 1917, it was
clear that it had not been an unqualified success. Although over the
three years some 777,119 people had attended 5,000 meetings, only
27,350 made decisions for Christianity (the precise figures illustrate
the thoroughness of the campaign's organization).[54] Because church
membership grew very little during the course of the campaign, the
movement had failed in its aim of making large-scale conversions.
Information about Christianity had been spread widely throughout
the country, but this was the limit of its achievement. More positively,
the interdenominational nature of the evangelical campaign had
stimulated a new sense of unity and confidence among Japanese Christians.

In these years, the Canadian Methodist mission participated in yet
another interdenominational endeavour, the Federation of Christian
Missions. This organization had a Japanese counterpart, the Japan
Federation of Christian Churches, which was formed in 1911 (that
there were separate organizations for missionaries and Japanese illus-

trates their distinctness). The two federations met annually, and in special committee meetings, to discuss matters of mutal concern. Both organizations maintained a close liaison in planning the best locations for missionaries to ensure the most effective occupation of Japan by Christian forces (again the ultimate decision of where missionaries were sent lay with the individual missionary societies).[55]

Interdenominational activity was also going on in North America. The Missionary Society of the Methodist Church of Canada co-operated with American Missionary Societies supporting missions in Japan. In 1911, this new mood was illustrated by the Committee of Reference and Counsel of the Foreign Mission Board Conference (in North America), which appointed a subcommittee to consider "the advisability of holding a special Japan Missions Conference with the aim of considering from the point of view of the Missions Boards concerned in that field, the present situation there and the question of a uniform missionary policy for the future."[56] In fact, this conference did not take place because the Methodist Episcopal South and other churches were unwilling to work with churches outside their denomination.[57] Nevertheless, the idea of an interdenominational meeting indicated the close contacts which existed among several Missionary Societies in North America.

One important, concrete result of this wider co-operation was the foundation in 1918 of the Tokyo Woman's Christian College. The Canadian Methodists co-operated with the Presbyterian Church of the United States, the American Baptist Church, and the Reformed Church in America in creating a capital fund for the college. The WMS-CM took on three of the sixteen $5,000 shares.[58]

In addition to co-operating with other denominations, Canadian Methodist missionaries and their Japanese Methodist colleagues also joined in discussions with leaders of other religions. In 1912, they attended the Three Religions Conference sponsored by the Home Ministry; the conference's aim was to raise the standard of public morals. That Christians were willing to participate in a conference with Buddhists and Shintōists marked a significant shift from the mutual hostility which had characterized previous relations. Notably, however, when the Anglican Church in Japan was invited to send representatives to the conference, it selected a Japanese member of the American Church mission, for British and Canadian Anglicans disapproved of this meeting.

The Canadian Methodists were in full sympathy with the conference because it provided recognition that religion could indeed play a significant role in the shaping of Japan's moral climate. The Japanese government added prestige to the meeting by organizing a conference dinner, which was attended by Cabinet ministers. Despite the inconclusive discussions of the conference, the support the Japanese Cabinet gave to its meetings left the impression that Christian was no longer seen as inimical to the Japanese state.[59]

The Japanese establishment also showed its recognition of Christianity by providing funds for the convening of the World Sunday School Convention held in Tokyo in 1920. Contributors to the funds included the ubiquitous Ōkuma Shigenobu, the former Prime Minister, and Shibusawa Eiichi, a multimillionaire entrepreneur and banker.[60] Although Ōkuma and Shibusawa were not Christians, they had helped finance the Japanese Christian missionary movement in Korea. The Imperial Household also contributed 50,000 yen ($25,000) to the convention, which cost in total 340,000 yen ($170,000). Clearly, the World Sunday School Convention was seen as an opportunity to project a favourable image of Japan in the West. In the light of the vitriolic criticism of Japanese actions in Korea in 1919 by Western missionaries, it was politically important for the Japanese government to show North American Christians that they considered Christianity to be valuable.

This conference provided many delegates with their first opportunity to visit Japan, and they were suitably impressed. Frank Langdon, a Canadian Methodist representative, even noted that many Westerners who attended were surprised that there was much to be admired in the life and conduct of those Japanese who had not had "the advantage of the teaching of Christianity."[61] Though Langdon was disappointed to hear that Japanese Christians made up less than one half of one per cent of the population,[62] he was deeply impressed by his encounter with the Canadian Methodist missionaries he met at the conference.

The World Sunday School Convention was one of the first major international conferences held in Japan. It was a sign that Christian organizers in the West recognized that the Japanese Christian movement had come of age. It was also an excellent public relations exercise for Japan. The Japanese government was able to project a positive image of the country to most of its Western delegates. The international links which the Japanese Christian movement was able to establish with world Christian organizations (thus becoming the prime source of information about Japan for these international groups) were important to the image of Japan abroad.

While much emphasis was placed on national evangelistic drives and international conferences, evangelistic work also took place at the local level.

LOCAL-LEVEL EVANGELISM

One of the aims of the evangelistic missionary working in an established centre was to create a "revival" when the public mood appeared encouraging with evangelistic meetings and, to a lesser extent, street

preaching. In 1920, A. T. Wilkinson, the Canadian Methodist missionary in Shizuoka, noted that over the past year there had been a desire
among the Shizuoka Church membership for a revival. The Christian
workers had prayed for a revival and he himself had "a longing in his
heart for a revival."[63]

The signs that a revival was about to begin in 1920 were the large
number of Bible teachers who had attended a meeting at Jujieda and
"an air of expectancy which pervaded" Wilkinson's Bible classes.[64]
Although thoughts of revivals provided welcome relief from the
humdrum life of a provincial missionary, none took place in Shizuoka
in 1920. By this time, it had become apparent that the spontaneous
advance of Christianity at the local level had lost its momentum, and
that such advances as there were in Shizuoka could be achieved only by
hard work on the part of the missionary and his Japanese helpers. The
same was true in the other Canadian Methodist mission stations. Many
Japanese Christians hoped for a national revival similar to the one that
had occurred in Korea in the 1920s. It never happened in Japan.

Christian growth at the local level usually came slowly, as a result of
hard but often satisfying work. A. T. Wilkinson in Shizuoka, for
instance, found the Bible classes he gave on three evenings every week
and on Saturday afternoons to be the most personally satisfying part of
his work.[65] In the 1920s, Wilkinson was able to teach the Bible to
teachers and students in the middle school at Kawasaki and to middle
school and commercial school teachers in Shizuoka. During the day, he
taught English at the middle school in Shizuoka, and this gave him an
opportunity for his extracurricular Bible classes. The evangelistic missionary always sought opportunities to speak to groups of people about
Christianity. Dan Norman, the Canadian Methodist missionary in
Nagano since the early 1900s, held meetings for postmen and rail-
waymen. There were no written guidelines about how an evangelistic
missionary should expand his work, which left the missionary bearing
much of the burden for expansion. In 1922, Loretta L. Shaw, a Canadian Anglican, wrote:

> There has been a tendency to think that the mission was responsi-
> ble for all direct aggressive evangelistic effort, and up to the pre-
> sent few of the Churches have started new preaching-places on
> their own initiative and funds, or engaged workers for unopened
> districts. Most Churches, have, of course, either occasional nights
> of special preachings for non-Christians or street preaching, but
> they are content if only a few members are added to the Church
> each year.[66]

This was rather unfair to Japanese Christians. During the late
nineteenth century, many of the first Japanese Christians thought that
Christian belief and preaching the gospel were synonymous. In the

twentieth century, Protestant churches still retained some of this enthusiasm among their members, which was understandable because the aim of these churches was always clearly evangelistic. It has to be remembered, however, that the Japanese cleric at the parish level lacked a long tradition of Japanese Christian ministry. There were only two models for the Japanese pastor to emulate: the first one provided by the Western missionary, and the other, by the Buddhist priest. The impact of the latter model was for the pastor to view his job as teaching a select group of disciples about Christianity. The Japanese pastor was often content, therefore, to have only a small congregation of knowledgeable disciples, for this was in keeping with the traditional Buddhist perception of a priest's function. This clearly hampered expansion and placed the burden for it on the missionary.

A real problem was the shortage of evangelistic missionaries. In 1913, Deaconess A. L. Archer, a Canadian Anglican missionary working in Takata in Niigata Prefecture, noted that she was the only single woman missionary working in an area with a population of two million people. She also complained that, during the previous three years, she had been entirely among Japanese except for the summer vacations.[67] J. G. Waller, one of the pioneer Canadian Anglican missionaries, wrote about three Canadian Anglican single women missionaries who had come out to Japan before the turn of the century:

> It is probable many Canadian women would contemplate almost with a shudder the conditions in which each of these three women lived. Each was alone; in the midst of Asiatic faces, in a house without doors, windows or chimneys, and where all conveniences, sanitary included, were primitive. No basement or furnace in any dwelling even in the largest city. Where a room is heated at all, it is by an improvised stove, the pipe of which carries the smoke off through a hole in the wall. No side-walks in the narrow crowded streets, no street cars. One of them was the only white person in her city. Not another women in that city spoke English, looked as she did, ate the same kind of food, or slept in a bed, sat on chairs or wore the same kind of clothes that white women are accustomed to.[68]

Compared with men engaged in evangelistic activity, women often had to work in conditions of greater isolation from European contact and had to live in less physically comfortable accommodation. Although some lived in a very modest way by choice, it is clear that they were expected to tolerate working and living conditions that would have been unacceptable to the married male missionary. Women missionaries were often more numerous and were usually members of their own women's society, but the male missionary was always regarded as the more important figure.

After the First World War, many missionaries saw new methods of evangelism as more important than old hopes of a revival. Newspaper evangelism was seen as an important new vehicle for reaching a wider audience. The first exponent of newspaper evangelism was American missionary Albertius Pieters. He was followed in 1919 by British Anglican W. H. Murray Walton. During the 1920s, Canadian Methodist Dan Norman effectively used newspaper evangelism as an aid to his work in Nagano Prefecture.[69] The problem with newspaper evangelism was the expense of buying space in secular newspapers. Because of this cost, the Canadian Methodists continued to rely heavily on more traditional methods.

One obvious area for evangelistic activity, which lent itself to traditional methods, was rural work. In 1925, Dan Norman complained that the Japan Methodist Church had failed to realize the importance of rural work, such as he undertook around Nagano. He disapproved of the current view that Christian work should be started by the Japan Methodist Church in Mukden, Sakhalin, and "other far-off places," because work in those places would quickly become self-supporting.[70] He regarded this as an unwholesome policy, since rural work in Japan would suffer as a result. Norman's interest in rural work had its parallel in the Anglican Church. In 1925, the special report on the Anglican Church in Japan, written by Bishop Knight of London, also emphasized the need for more devotion to rural work.[71] This could only encourage Canadian Anglicans whose diocese of Mid-Japan was one with a large rural population. Yet the Anglicans lacked missionaries, and no amount of encouragement was likely to change that.

The stress on self-supporting churches, which Norman mentioned in connection with Japanese missionary work in Manchuria and other places, tended to concentrate work in large cities where self-support was most easily achieved. At the Jerusalem World Missionary Conference of 1928, it was pointed out that the urgency of attaining independence and self-support had partly obscured the paramount duty of the Japanese Christian movement to evangelize.[72] The development of rural work was to be one of the greatest challenges to the Christian movement in Japan after 1931.

For the Canadian Methodists, the main evangelistic centre was the Central Tabernacle in Tokyo. It was close to Tokyo Imperial University, and its work was directed toward Tokyo's student population. The Canadian Methodists realized that graduates of Tokyo Imperial University were Japan's future elite and devoted a good deal of energy to their conversion.[73] Besides its specialized role in evangelism, the Central Tabernacle was somewhat unusual because it was used by two different church organizations. In addition to its place in the Canadian Methodist mission, the Tabernacle also served the Japan Methodist

Church. This dual function caused frequent friction. In 1912, Bishop Hiraiwa of the Japan Methodist Church called for a more aggressive policy of evangelism. He had the temerity to suggest that, if Canadian Methodists were not prepared to adopt more aggressive methods, he would find other Christians to replace them.[74] In 1913, the Canadian Methodist Mission Council responded to Hiraiwa's criticisms and suggested that improvements could be made to the Central Tabernacle. The major suggestion was that the Japanese congregation should be moved to a new church so that the Tabernacle could be used solely for evangelistic purposes.[75] It also proposed that the building should be extended to include sitting-rooms and a library. In spite of these well-considered proposals from Tokyo, the missionary authorities in Toronto were not prepared to vote money to implement these suggestions. The Central Tabernacle would remain a white elephant.

In 1917, C. J. L. Bates, who had been in charge of the evangelistic work at the Tabernacle since 1913, requested two more Canadian missionaries, more Japanese staff, and a regular budget of 6,000 yen to sustain increased evangelistic work. Bates hoped that a special Central Tabernacle lectureship could be instituted to invite eminent British or Canadian Christians to give a series of lectures at the Tabernacle and the Kwansei Gakuin. He wanted sufficient funds to hold these lectures biennially at the two institutions.[76] This smacked of Ebyism. The Missionary Society in Toronto was unprepared to finance such expensive new projects.

Throughout this period, the Central Tabernacle failed to convert many of the elite students of Tokyo Imperial University. Even if Bates' expansionist plans had been implemented, it was doubtful whether the Tabernacle would have been any more successful, for it had to compete with other Christian churches for the attention of Tokyo Imperial University students. The most important of these churches was Ebina Danjō's Hongō Church, which was as close to the university campus as the Tabernacle. With Ebina's reputation as one of the most intellectually distinguished Japanese Christians and the activities of such distinguished church members as Yoshino Sakuzō and Suzuki Bunji, the Hongō Church was better able to attract large numbers of university students than was the Central Tabernacle.

As direct evangelistic work was proving difficult, the Canadian missionaries began to turn their attention to social work.

SOCIAL WORK

Canadian missionaries never engaged in social work on a large scale; what they did undertake was usually nothing more than an expression of an individual's personal social concern and interest. But the significance of their endeavours lay in their pioneering work in areas in which Japanese authorities had taken little interest. In beginning social work in new areas, Canadians and other missionaries undoubtedly spurred Japanese authorities to develop their own programs.

While social work was an evangelistic tool, it was also an expression of a genuine desire to improve the welfare and well-being of the Japanese people. All missionaries in Japan wanted to improve the lot of the ordinary Japanese, but not all denominations saw social work as a necessary part of their missionary work. Canadian Anglicans (especially High Anglicans) did not pursue social work as a conscious policy; much of their activity stemmed primarily from individual initiative which the Anglican missions might eventually support. In contrast, the Canadian Methodist mission developed its social work as a conscious policy; their work stemmed more from a corporate decision than from an individual initiative.

As in direct evangelistic work, women missionaries played a crucial role in social work, which was to some extent an outcome of their working among the ordinary people. Although much of the social work undertaken by Canadian missionaries was directly toward helping female factory workers, it is apparent that women missionaries were more prepared (even expected) to take the initiative in undertaking social work than were their male colleagues. For instance, women missionaries, like British Anglicans Hannah Riddell and Nellie Cornwall Legh, pioneered work among lepers in Japan.[77] The most famous of all missionaries in Japan during the 1920s was the "White Angel of Tokyo," Caroline Macdonald, a Canadian who worked for the YWCA and whose name is associated with the rehabilitation of prisoners.[78] Although the ubiquitous Arthur Lea had pioneered penal rehabilitation in Gifu in the 1890s,[79] it was the activities of women missionaries that tended to attract more publicity.

Health care was a common area of social work for missionaries in Japan. The British Anglicans established leprosaria, for example, and the Canadian Anglicans maintained a sanatorium for people suffering from tuberculosis. Another area in which missionaries shared an interest was kindergartens. The Canadian Anglicans maintained a kindergarten training school at Nagoya which attempted to give its young female students, who were all graduates of a girls' high school, a well-rounded education in which the Bible was emphasized.[80] The Canadian Methodists also trained kindergarten teachers at their three Eiwa schools.

By the First World War, social work in the slums of the larger cities had attracted the attention of many missionaries. The Canadian Methodists were especially active in social work in the slums of East Tokyo, created by the large-scale migration of young people from

rural areas to work in new developing industry.[81] Canadian Methodists
began their work in the slums of East Tokyo by opening a preaching
place in Kameidō ward and by developing a hostel for factory women,
founded by Annie Allen of the WMS-CM in the 1910s.[82] In 1920, the
WMS-CM replaced this hostel with a larger one that included accommodation for twenty girls and a residence for male workers. These welfare
activities led to a limited number of conversions.

In 1920, a grant of $10,000 enabled the Canadian Methodist male
missionaries to acquire land in Ukeji ward, reasonably close to the
WMS-CM hostel in Kameidō. The Tokyo prefectural government was
willing to co-operate with the missionaries; it had opened its own
"model slum settlement" in the Nippori district. In order to reinforce
its own work and increase the number of social workers in Nippori, the
prefectural government helped the Canadian Methodists obtain two
houses in the ward which could be used as a preaching place, a clinic,
and a home for a district nurse, mid-wife, and two Bible women
(female evangelists).[83]

As slum work expanded in 1920, the Mission Council proposed that
a missionary residence should be acquired in the slum quarter, a
suggestion that posed serious difficulties because the slums were considered to be too unhealthy for Westerners. A house was eventually
found in Negishi ward, which bordered on Nippori. It belonged to
Kobayashi Yashichi, a wealthy sugar dealer who had become a Christian while studying the sugar industry in the southern United States. A
member of the Central Tabernacle and a generous man,[84] Kobayashi
donated his house and another property close by (jointly valued at
100,000 yen or $40,000) to the Canadian Methodist mission, on the
condition that his gift would be used for social and religious purposes
for all time.[85] This gift prompted the Mission Board in Toronto to
grant 20,000 yen for remodelling the main Japanese house into a
residence for a Western missionary and for building a kindergarten.

In 1921, the kindergarten was opened and soon had 100 pupils. A
night school was also established and was attended by sixty people. By
the end of May 1921, twenty adults and children had been converted to
Christianity.[86] In the same year, another kindergarten was started on
the Nippori site. Because space was limited at Nippori, Kobayashi
decided to buy extra land and erect a new kindergarten building. He
also guaranteed to finance the Nippori school for five years. At the
time of the great Kantō earthquake in 1923, the new kindergarten had
been almost completely constructed. It was destroyed in the disaster,
and because of his own financial difficulties, Kobayashi was unable to
refinance the project.[87]

Without Kobayashi's generosity, the Canadian Methodists could
not have been as active as they were in the East Tokyo slums. Similarly,

although the Tokyo prefectural government was itself involved in trying to help slum dwellers, its resources were limited. It was not surprising, therefore, that the Tokyo authorities welcomed missionary help. But for both the Japanese authorities and the Canadian Methodists, the great Kantō earthquake was a major setback to their work in Tokyo. Damage to property belonging to the Canadian Methodist mission amounted to $100,000. The Central Tabernacle was destroyed, as was the missionary residence in the East Tokyo slums. The mission escaped with relatively light damage, but the Japan Methodist Church suffered $400,000 damage. Ten Methodist churches and their parsonages were destroyed and five more churches were badly damaged.[88]

The Canadian Methodist mission felt a responsibility to repair its own damaged property and to aid the Japan Methodist Church in any possible way. A special reconstruction fund was opened in Toronto; it was closed in September 1924, a year after the disaster, after raising $125,027.[89] The reconstruction fund covered all losses sustained by the Canadian Methodist mission and allowed for the reconstruction of the Central Tabernacle and other mission buildings. Though the Canadian Methodists were able to make a rapid recovery from the earthquake, the reconstruction fund did not in any significant way contribute to making up the losses of the Japan Methodist Church. Even in a time of disaster, the principle of Canadian funds for Canadian purposes still prevailed in missionary thinking.

Despite this, the Japan Methodist Church grew more rapidly than any other Christian body between 1918 and 1928.[90] While the direct evangelistic and social work endeavours of the Canadian Methodist missionaries might appear paltry in comparison to their more expensive and impressive educational work, their efforts did contribute to the growth of the Japan Methodist Church. The Japan Methodist Church grew partly because of their enthusiasm for interdenominational campaigns to bring new converts into the church. Their Canadian Anglican colleagues were much more ambivalent about such activity. A British Anglican bishop observed about the English Church Mission in Korea: it was " 'the wee modest violet' among Missions. It has a sweet perfume, but the traveller has to hunt for it in order to find it."[91] The same observation could also have been made about the Canadian Church Mission in Japan. Although there were two streams within the Canadian Anglican missionary movement, Anglicans stressed quality before quantity. Numbers of converts were not as important to them as they were to the more uniformly evangelistic Canadian Methodists, who saw quantity as a sign of spiritual strength. In that sense, the Anglicans had more in common with the Buddhists, who believed that a priest's role was to minister to an elite.

During this period, both the Anglicans and the Methodists were confronted by a Japanese society that was rapidly changing. The missionaries' knowledge of the barriers to a successful propagation of Christianity was far from complete; thus they were unable to exploit the changes in Japanese society in their evangelistic work. Furthermore, the conservatism of missionary societies stifled innovation, and shortages of personnel and revenue often prevented the inauguration of new projects. The Canadian Methodist work in the slums of East Tokyo was one new area of evangelistic work that was a clear response to the changing conditions in Japanese society. Because of the sizable gifts from Kobayashi, this did not lead to the transfer of resources from traditional evangelism. But such large bequests were rare. Normally, as old established areas of work were rarely closed down, new projects were merely added to existing work. As a result, a good deal of missionary effort was expended in specialized work; in the long run, this diverted effort from the expansion of orthodox evangelism.

The efficacy of orthodox evangelism was vividly illustrated in Korea.

THE KOREAN CONTRAST

One of the major reasons for the success of orthodox evangelism in Korea was simply that by September 1898, when the first three Canadian Presbyterians arrived in Korea, the missionary movement had already acquired very considerable experience in evangelistic work among East Asians. The evangelistic blueprint which the Canadian Presbyterians applied to Korea was the systematic and scientific Nevius Method, which emphasized individual faith, self-support of congregations, systematic Bible study, and strict discipline. The missionary's role was to ensure the discipline and spirit of the various Korean congregations under his charge. From the first, the Canadians co-operated with the American and Australian Presbyterian missions in Korea, recognizing that united effort was necessary to achieve positive results in the mission field.

In many respects, Korea was an easier field than either Taiwan or Japan. One reason was the relative lack of religious opposition. Unlike in Taiwan and Japan where, respectively, Confucianism and Taoism within the Chinese tradition and Shintōism mitigated against the rapid growth of Christianity, religious opposition to Christianity in Korea was not as powerful a deterrent to Christian growth. Although Shamanism, and new religions like Chondokyo, did have an important impact on religious life, Buddhism was not a vital force in Korea. Christianity might be said to have filled a religious vacuum in Korean life left after the long decline of Korean Buddhism during the Yi dynasty.

On their arrival in Korea, the Canadian Presbyterians were asked by the American Presbyterian societies to undertake work in northeastern Korea. Later, their territory would be extended into the adjacent Manchurian borderland and beyond into Siberia. Grierson, Foote, and McRae, the pioneering trio of missionaries, settled in Wonsan to begin language studies. Wonsan was a major missionary centre with four or five American Presbyterian and Methodist missionaries (including James Scarth Gale), which means the Canadians were by no means isolated. Keen to explore and learn about their mission territory, in the summer of 1900 Dr. Grierson and Duncan McRae went north by steamer to Sungjin) to explore their designated territory and distribute tracts.[92] During this trip, Grierson received a telegram stating that the Korean Court had given special orders to all governors and mayors to execute Christians and missionaries. He returned to Wonsan at once, cycling 240 miles in two days, only to find out that the putative orders to kill Christians and missionaries were forgeries. It was the time of the Boxer Rebellion in China, and Grierson believed that the forged orders were a rare instance of its influence extending to Korea. By 1900, the bicycle had become an important vehicle for the missionary, and under duress, as Grierson's ride illustrated, missionaries could be very energetic pedallers.

In May 1901, Grierson and his wife moved to Sungjin to open a hospital, leaving Foote and McRae in Wonsan. In 1904, the Russo-Japanese War disrupted mission work in the area occupied by the Canadian Presbyterians. A Royal Navy cruiser, HMS *Phoenix*, removed the Griersons and the A. F. Robbs, another Canadian Presbyterian missionary and his family, from Sungjin to the assumed safety of Wonsan.[93] The fact that a British cruiser came to their assistance revealed, not only that the Royal Navy had a long reach, for Sungjin was a remote northern port, but also that concern for the safety of missionaries was at least in part responsible for that long reach.

The Russo-Japanese War also had a profound impact on the future of Christianity in the peninsula. The year before the Russo-Japanese War broke out, a revival began in Wonsan, giving missionaries hope that there would be a very rapid rise in Christian numbers. In 1907, a great revival took place in P'yongyang and spread from there throughout the peninsula. Prior to the great revival, the early converts to Protestantism had largely come from the *yangban*, *hyganban*, and *soja* classes within Korean society, that is, from the educated higher classes. The first Korean Protestants were comparable in societal status to their Japanese counterparts of the late nineteenth century whose social background was largely lower samurai. The great revival in Korea broadened the base of Christianity since most of its new converts were farmers and agricultural workers. Christianity in Japan never achieved such a broad base; it was primarily an urban, white-collar movement. In Korea, converts were drawn from all strata of society, but Christianity's strength lay in the rural north.

The cause of the great revival was political. As J. C. Crane, an American missionary, later admitted:

> in 1907 the prevailing motive, or cause of the movement toward the Church, [aside from the Spirit's direct work] was evidently a hope to find a way out of Japanese sovereignty, to enlist its [Christianity] organization and the prestige and influence of its foreign relations on behalf of national existence [of an independent Korea].[94]

Despite this, the very success of gaining converts on a large scale gave rise to a great spirit of achievement and success among missionaries. In 1908, Horace Underwood, an American Presbyterian missionary, wrote:

> for almost ten years the story of the work in Korea has been entrancing. It has read almost like a fairy tale, and veritably it has seemed like a chapter from the Acts of the Apostles. Steadily and regularly, with an ever-increasing momentum, the work has been growing faster and faster, exceeding the brightest visions of the most optimistic students of missionary work.[95]

Statements like this and the growth in the number of Christians generated a feeling in the West that Korea was one of the most hopeful mission fields in Asia. In 1909, an evangelistic campaign began in Korea to continue the momentum of the great revival. This campaign took as its slogan "A million souls for Christ" and involved the "whole Korean Church with the exercise of personal evangelism." Each Christian was expected to contribute a number of days to evangelistic work and the distribution of Christian literature.[96] Although it failed to reach its objective of a million converts, the campaign did strengthen church life and was beneficial to the general morale of the Christian movement.[97]

Although there were only about 200,000 Christians in Korea in 1910, the Protestant movement was highly organized on a nation-wide scale. Three years earlier, in 1907, the Korean Presbyterian Church, which the Canadian Presbyterians supported, was created and became the largest Protestant denomination in the peninsula. All its officials were Korean, except for its moderator and treasurer. In 1907, its membership included 7 pastors, 53 elders, 989 congregations, 19,000 communicants, and 70,000 believers;[98] and it was aided by 38 Western missionaries. Five years later, the First General Assembly of the Presbyterian Church of Korea held in P'yongyang was attended by 52 pastors, 125 elders, and 44 Western missionaries.[99] In that short time, the

Presbyterian Church made remarkable strides in increasing the numbers of its Korean clergy, important strides because of what the church meant politically in Korea. Apart from the Government-General, the Protestant movement was the largest national organization in Korea. As it was under Korean leadership, the Government-General regarded the Protestant movement as a threat to its colonial control and prestige. The Christian movement in Korea had an important influence on the life of the colony. Indeed, as one Korean scholar has noted, the independence and cultural movements of the 1910s and 1920s would have been impossible without the influence of the many mission schools in Korea.[100]

After the annexation of Korea in 1910, Christian growth proceeded at a much slower pace. Annexation destroyed the belief of many Korean Christians that their faith could help Korea retain its independence. Moreover, although the Japanese Christian movement itself joined in missionary work in Korea with the support of the Government-General, it was obvious that the Government-General was becoming increasingly antagonistic toward the Korean Christian movement as a whole.[101] This is clearly seen in the fact that the majority of defendants in the Conspiracy Trial of 1912 (which resulted from charges of planning the assassination of Governor-General Terauchi Masatake) were Christians. Similarly, large numbers of Korean Christians were imprisoned or harassed in the aftermath of the independence demonstrations of 1919.

It was not obvious to the Canadian Presbyterians that much of their success was linked to the relationship between Christianity and the defence of Korean nationalism and culture. Few Canadian missionaries were given to speculation, for they were primarily men of action and not by nature deep thinkers. In 1909, the great revival in Korea was described at the Canadian Presbyterian General Assembly in joyful tones: "it may be said without exaggeration that at the present moment the eyes of the Christian world are on Korea, and that many of those who are in a position to understand the situation best are looking for Korea's speedy evangelization."[102] In other words, the Canadians were prepared to take the success in Korea at face value. The question of why Korea was proving to be a more fruitful field than Japan or Taiwan did not seem to concern them.

Canadian Presbyterian missionaries were largely concerned with how their mission could take advantage of the great revival. The major difficulty for the Canadians was their own lack of missionaries. In 1909, missionaries from the Western [Ontario] Division of the Presbyterian Church of Canada were sent out, which allowed the church to occupy both eight counties in North Hamkyung province and the districts of Manchuria known as Chientao (Kandō, Kantō) and Hoon-

choon. Before the Western Division missionaries took the field, their
fellow Maritimes Division missionaries had established forty-four rural
churches in the area. By 1913, three mission stations had been established by Western Division missionaries at Kyungsung, Hoiryung, and
Lungchingtsun (Yonjung, Ryūseison) in Manchuria. This expansion of
work across the Tumen River into Manchuria followed the path of
Korean emigration. In 1913, William Rufus Foote, one of the pioneer
Canadian Presbyterian missionaries, noted:

> Kandō [Chientao] was only a name to us three years ago and we
> never considered it an important part of our field. It was a largely
> unoccupied tract of land, capable under cultivation of sustaining a
> large population. After the Japanese rule in Korea became oppres-
> sive many natives moved there until now some estimate the Korean
> population at 500,000.[103]

Prior to this expansion into new territory, missionaries from other
Protestant denominations had questioned whether Canadian Presbyterians had sufficient resources to cope satisfactorily with their existing
field. In 1912, J. M. Scott reported that there was a feeling among some
other missions that, unless a serious movement was undertaken to
improve the work of the Canadian Presbyterian mission in Korea,
some of its territory would have to be transferred to others.[104] Obviously, the Canadian Presbyterians were seen to be the poor sisters of
other missions in Korea, and there was a matter of face involved in
ensuring that the church pulled its weight.

After 1912, the Canadian Presbyterian Church responded quickly to
these criticisms and the pressing needs of the mission in Korea. During
1913 and early 1914, Canadian Presbyterians in Korea were reinforced
by thirteen new missionaries. The authorities in Toronto were fortunate in responding so swiftly to the call for more missionaries; it
would have been extremely difficult for them to send out large numbers of missionaries once the Great War had begun. Significant
increases of money were also given to the mission by the home church
after 1912. In that year, the Western Division estimates were $17,002;
$5,327 for general purposes and $11,675 for building.[105] By 1919, the
estimates had climbed to $61,975 for general purposes and $13,500 for
buildings. In the same year, the WMS-CP spent $13,603 for general
purposes.[106] The consequence of this injection of money and staff into
the mission was apparent in the rapid growth of its Korean congregations.

In the six years from 1909, the Canadian Presbyterian mission had
virtually doubled its size. In 1909, the mission consisted of a missionary
staff of 14, including four wives, serving a total Christian community of
5,594 people.[107] Six years later, there were 24 missionaries, 10 wives,
and five ordained Korean priests now caring for over 10,000 Chris-

tians.[108] Canadian missionaries were resident in five centres—Wonsan (Genzan), Hamheung (Kanko), Sungjin (Seishin), Hoiryung (Kainei), and Lungchingtsun—from which they would constantly visit the outlying Korean churches and Christian groups. Although it was still a small mission, by 1915 it was approximately the same size as the Canadian Methodist Japan Mission.

By the early 1920s, the Canadian Presbyterian mission was again faced with serious financial problems. These were, in part, the result of financial difficulties at home and a general decline in the strength of the home church. In August 1922, the deficit of the various mission-supporting bodies of the home church totalled $350,000.[109] Three years later, a solution to the financial problems of the Canadian Presbyterian Church came with the formation of the United Church of Canada. Yet even then the debts of the Presbyterians, which the new United Church had to absorb, caused financial embarrassment just when it was expected to launch a great missionary campaign among the new immigrants in Western Canada.[110]

This financial situation meant that the Canadian Presbyterian mission could not look forward to any expansion. In 1923, the twenty-fifth anniversary of the Canadian Presbyterian Korea Mission, the total appropriations were $108,789, out of a total budget for all the missionary work of the Canadian Presbyterian Church of $585,000.[111] It was still said, however, that the Canadian mission was one of the worst managed and equipped in the peninsula and that its territory was one of the furthest from complete evangelization.[112]

Nevertheless, Canadian Presbyterian missionaries had much to celebrate in 1923 when they commemorated their first twenty-five years of work. Their mission territory had been organized into three presbyteries, with 24 Korean ministers, 140 elders, and 80 unordained helpers. There were 363 churches with 6,500 communicants and a total church membership of 21,000. In addition, the Canadian Presbyterian mission was involved in union work at the Pyeng Yang Union Theological College, at the Severance Union Medical College, and at Chōsen College in Seoul.[113]

At the time of church union in Canada, the Canadian Presbyterians had the choice of either joining the United Church of Canada or continuing in association with the rump of the Canadian Presbyterian Church. The Presbyterian missionaries in Korea chose to join the United Church, and the new mission in Korea was henceforth called the Korean Mission of the United Church of Canada. Its relation with the other evangelical missions in Korea remained unchanged. The new United Church mission continued its membership in the General Assembly of the Korean Presbyterian Church.

The Canadian Presbyterians were working in a remote rural area of Korea. As the last major Western Presbyterian church to enter mission work in the peninsula, perhaps they received the least desirable of regions to evangelize. It was among the rural people of northern Korean, however, that the major Christian advances were made during the great revival. The Canadian-served territory was potentially an area where considerable Christian growth could take place, which might well have given strength to the recurring complaint that the Canadian Presbyterian mission was understaffed and badly equipped. The Canadian Presbyterian Church made a significant effort to provide funds and indeed personnel for its Korean mission. Approximately one-fifth of the church's funds for overseas mission work went to support the work in Korea. The problem was not one of the willingness of the home church to provide money for Korea. It was simply that the home church, with missions in Taiwan, China, the West Indies, and the South Seas, was over-committed and thus could not provide adequately for any of its missions. This was especially so by the 1920s, when the home support for the church itself, let alone for its overseas missions, was declining.

The degree to which the Canadian Presbyterian missionaries succeeded in bringing Koreans to Christianity was not simply a function of lack of funds and personnel. What is very clear in the Korean case is that the political situation in the peninsula had a direct impact on the attractiveness of Christianity to the Koreans. During the five years immediately after the Russo-Japanese War, Koreans looked to Christian missions to help restore their nationhood and protect them from the Japanese. Once annexation had taken place, Christian growth in Korea slowed, because of the Korean realization that Christianity had not preserved their country's independence. The death knell to the identification between Christianity and Korean aspirations for political freedom was the failure of the March 1, 1919, movement to achieve Korean independence. Passive resistance was seen to be ineffective in bringing about the end of Japanese rule, but the Korean Christian movement could not condone violence. There is a link between the decline of the church and the rise of the Communist movement. By the end of the 1920s, the Communist movement, because it would support armed struggle, had supplanted the Christian movement as the leading Korean force opposed to Japanese colonialism. As this change took place, the rate of growth of the Christian movement slowed.

The pattern of growth of the Canadian Presbyterian missions follows this broad outline with some slight variations. The Canadian Presbyterian mission, reinforced with new missionaries after 1909, did in fact grow significantly in the years immediately after annexation. This growth in the number of converts also coincided with the expansion of the Canadian mission into the Chientao district of Manchuria. It is apparent that the Koreans in Manchuria continued to view the missionaries and the Christian church as an important protective bulwark against the Japanese, from whom they were endeavouring to escape by migrating across the Tumen River. In looking to Canadian missionaries to protect them, the Koreans in Manchuria found extremely tenacious defenders. But the Canadian Presbyterian mission was not isolated from the influences which were infiltrating the nationalist movement in Korea and drawing the young away from Christianity.

While the evangelistic work in Korea differed very dramatically from that in Japan, the case of Taiwan differs from both.

EVANGELISM IN TAIWAN

Just as in rural Korea, the Canadian Presbyterians in Taiwan propagated the gospel in the most simple terms. The majority of Taiwanese Christians came from the lowest social classes, and Christians were regarded as outcasts by the rest of the Chinese population. At times of xenophobic tension, as during the French blockade of the island in 1884-1885 or during the Black Flag fighting against the Japanese in 1894-1895, Christians were killed by hostile crowds. The Taiwanese Christians were considered to be traitors during these emergencies and were regarded as lackeys of the foreigners.[114] This attitude reflected the mainland Chinese view of Christians, and it differed from the Japanese and Korean view, which did not openly criticize Christians in those terms. Christians in Taiwan were generally scapegoats, and their position in Taiwanese society was generally very low.

The aborigines were a constant source of interest for the missionaries. George Leslie Mackay noted: "the Chinese in Formosa have great contempt for the aborigines, and treat them very much as the Americans have treated the Indian tribes, bartering with them, cheating them and crowding them back into their mountain strongholds."[115] Plain curiosity and an unquenchable scientific interest drove Mackay and other missionaries to undertake perilous expeditions into areas frequented by headhunters, often accompanied by an adventurous British naval officer or consular official. But little evangelistic work was possible among the headhunting aborigines. Though reasonable success was achieved by Mackay among the Sinicized aborigines living on farms on the Kaptsulan plain in north Taiwan, this was an exception to the general rule. By 1888, Mackay had established 16 chapels and had over 500 converts among the Sinicized aborigines.[116] The Sinicized aborigines in north Taiwan are an example of an oppressed group who saw protection coming from the missionary presence. Yet it was the Chinese in Taiwan, rather than the aborigines, whom the missionaries wanted most to convert.

Early Presbyterian missionaries in Taiwan viewed the religious life of the Chinese in Taiwan as idolatrous and heathen. In 1907, Campbell N. Moody, an English Presbyterian missionary, noted:

> [the Taiwanese] bow down before Buddhist and Taoist idols indiscriminately, while they recite the teachings of Confucius, who scarcely taught of any divinity but God and Heaven, and did not worship idols at all. They worship obscure local deities, or make pilgrimages to distant shrines, paying attention to any and all who seem to promise effectual aid, and transferring their allegiance to the end in view, as we go to different shops for different goods, or according to the rise and fall of the idol's celebrity, just as we forsake one shop for another which offers better value.[117]

Moody's views were common to both English and Canadian Presbyterian missionaries at the time. Missionaries recognized the importance of ancestral tablets to the Chinese, and in Taiwan they allowed Christian enquirers to retain them. Nevertheless, possession of the tablets became a measure of the strength of an enquirer's Christian conviction; if the man became a firm believer in Christianity, then he would naturally discard his ancestral tablets.

As in Japan, Christians in Taiwan almost automatically became outcasts from their families. In view of the difficulties missionaries faced in trying to convert the Chinese to Christianity when the island was under Manchu administration, it is understandable that both the English and Canadian missionaries welcomed the Japanese occupation. They felt that Japanese rule must be superior to Chinese administration (in their view any other government would be better than the Chinese). Most missionaries would have agreed with the view of Thomas Barclay, the senior English Presbyterian missionary, that the destruction of Chinese administration and the discrediting of Confucianism would assist the propagation of Christianity.[118] The change-over to Japanese rule did bring about a rapid growth in numbers of converts. During the decade between 1895 and 1905, the Christian movement in the island "witnessed remarkable advance which was indicated by the doubling of the Church membership from 8,000 to 16,000."[119] The Japanese officials did show more sympathy toward Christianity than their Manchu predecessors had. Indeed, one English missionary noted that "not a few [Taiwanese] entered the Church because it was safer to be known as a Christian."[120]

Various parallels can be drawn between Taiwan in these years and Korea after 1905. In both colonies, the Christian movement represented an organization that was outside Japanese control. It is of some interest that 1905, the year which marked the end of rapid Christian growth in Taiwan, was also the year when effective control was achieved by the Japanese authorities. In Korea, 1910 saw the end of hope for the maintenance of Korean independence.

With the assumption of government by the Japanese, the Presbyterians in Taiwan took on the role of protectors of the Chinese. The Canadian and English missions served the Chinese, and their hospitals and educational institutions were also directed toward them. The Chinese language was the medium of communication and instruction. The Presbyterian missions, therefore, offered an alternative to similar institutions administered by the colonial power, institutions in which opportunities for Taiwanese were often limited. In this sense, they played a role which resembled that of the missionary movement in Korea.

It would be a mistake, however, to claim too much for the missionary movement in Taiwan. The Presbyterian missions in Taiwan, unlike those in Korea, were never closely identified with Chinese nationalism. Prior to Japanese rule, the attitude of the Chinese administration to the Presbyterian missions had been largely antagonistic. In fact, the relationship of the Presbyterian missions and their Chinese converts to the Japanese Government-General in Taiwan after 1895 was always cordial and friendly. Unlike in Korea, in Taiwan the Presbyterian Church never acted as an informal opposition to the Government-General.

The Canadian Presbyterians in Taiwan carried out their Christian work in political and cultural circumstances that were largely unfavourable to Christian growth. Although the missionaries were enthusiastic workers and often evangelists of the highest order, they were able to attract only the very poor and members of the lowest social classes. Like their colleagues on the Chinese mainland, they essentially failed to penetrate the barriers posed by the Chinese Confucian tradition. In the years after 1905, the missionaries in Taiwan were faced with new and different problems stemming from the rapid modernization of the island by the Japanese.

From an organizational standpoint, the most important event in Taiwan after 1905 was the formation of the Presbyterian Synod of Formosa in 1912, which determined the general policy of the Presbyterian Church. Despite the union, both the English and the Canadian Presbyterian missions remained responsible to their respective Foreign Missions Committees in London and Toronto and retained their own Mission Councils to formulate policy and to guide development.

In 1925, the rump of the Presbyterian Church in Canada, which did not join the United Church of Canada, continued to operate the Canadian Presbyterian mission in Taiwan. Certain Canadian Presbyterian missionaries, including Duncan MacLeod, felt that their loyalty lay with the new United Church of Canada. They continued to work in Taiwan, but under the auspices of the English Presbyterian mission and as members of the United Church of Canada.

The two major centres of Canadian work in north Taiwan were Tamsui and Taipeh. From these centres, missionaries took itinerant tours to the outlying Christian groups and churches. The Canadian Presbyterian mission had always been understaffed. In June 1914, R. P. MacKay, the Canadian Presbyterian Foreign Missions Secretary in Toronto, noted that, although the Canadian Presbyterians were eager to join their English colleagues in attempting to work among Sinicized Ami tribe aborigines on the east coast of Taiwan, the Canadians were having difficulty finding men for their established work, let alone for new work.[121] The First World War further curtailed such evangelistic work as the Canadian Presbyterians had been able to undertake prior to 1914 because some missionaries volunteered for war service.

One of the consequences of the First World War was inflation, which affected missionaries in Taiwan as much as those in Japan. In October 1919, G. W. Mackay complained to Toronto that he was being paid the same salary that his father had received when he had been "a boy and things cheap."[122] Mackay wanted an increase of forty per cent to offset recent price increases. Furthermore, he pointed out that certain Taiwanese ministers' families had nothing to eat except soft-boiled rice and salt, even though some ministers had received salary increases of up to a hundred per cent over the five years since 1914.[123] In Taiwan, the Canadian Presbyterians made the same mistake as their Anglican and Methodist counterparts in Japan, which was failing to make adequate provisions for an acceptable stipend for the Japanese or Taiwanese clergy. The result was the greatest difficulty in attracting men into the ministry. Missionaries held to the belief that the church abroad should become self-supporting as soon as possible. Being self-supporting was a laudable aim for any mission church, but over-emphasizing that goal could seriously undermind an embryonic church. This was particularly the case when such a policy obstructed the payment of adequate salaries for clergy and lay helpers.

One man had been responsible for establishing and maintaining Canadian Presbyterian mission work in north Taiwan during much of the late nineteenth century. During the first three decades of the twentieth century, although new Canadian missionaries were sent to Taiwan, the mission was unable to become more than just a small mission in a colonial backwater. In a sense, because George Leslie Mackay had singlehandedly achieved so much, the Canadian Presbyterian Church perhaps felt that there was little need to allocate more personnel or funds to Taiwan. In the early twentieth century in Taiwan, such an attitude had the gravest consequences for the well-being of the mission. As far as their evangelistic work was concerned, the Canadian missionaries in Taiwan could do little more than maintain the size of the Christian community served by their mission. However, the cultural tradition of the Chinese, the educational and colonial policies of the Japanese, and the lack of nationalistic feeling meant that, even if the mission in Taiwan had obtained the same number of missionaries as there were in Japan, it is unlikely whether the number of Taiwanese Christians would have been significantly higher.

Japan, Korea, and Taiwan offer examples of evangelistic work undertaken under different circumstances. Korea alone represented a mission field where favourable conditions existed for rapid Christian growth, at least during the first decade of the twentieth century. The urban, industrial setting of missionary work in Japan allowed missionaries to adopt some forms of evangelistic work, such as the interdenominational evangelistic rallies featuring famous Christian figures, which were common in North America at the time. In their development of social work, Canadians in a sense were transferring to a Japanese setting the types of projects Christians were fostering among the underprivileged in the slums of larger North American cities. In undertaking this social work, missionaries often provided valuable service to the Japanese by supplementing over-taxed government resources or, more importantly, by bringing attention to the need for social work in particular areas. In Korea and Taiwan, specialized social work, such as the Canadian Methodists undertook in the East Tokyo slums, simply was not necessary. In both colonies, evangelistic work mainly consisted of itinerant tours along rural circuits. In all three areas, it is clear that all the Canadian missions were understaffed and lacked the resources to do little more than gradually increase the size of the Christian constituency they served in the mission field.

CHAPTER NINE

Democracy and Imperialism

The educational and evangelistic work of Canadian missionaries was affected by political and social changes taking place in the Japanese Empire. This is clearly seen in the regulations concerning schools in the Japanese Empire and also in the impact of the Japanese political influence on Christianity in Korea. While the attitudes of missionaries toward political and social affairs in the Japanese Empire were closely interlinked with their aspirations for Christianity, this was not the only factor that determined their judgements. In their analysis of secular changes, missionaries also brought to bear the values and prejudices of their particular social backgrounds in Canada. Indeed, the fact that they were Canadian, rather than the fact that they were missionaries, was often the chief force that determined their attitudes toward events.

As observers of political and social affairs, missionaries had some advantages over other Westerners. They were normally long-term residents. Their day-to-day work, as well as their contact with Japanese or Korean Christian workers, gave them access to a broader spectrum of people than usually encountered by diplomats or merchants. Missionaries were regarded as experts on Japan, Korea, and Taiwan by their constituents at home. Their opinions were likely to be respected and trusted, even by Westerners who had no ties with the church, because they were clergymen. In remote areas, missionaries were often the only resident Westerners and so were sometimes the only source of information about incidents in those particular locales. Likewise, the peripatetic cavalcade of tourists, journalists, and naval officers who took advantage of a missionary's presence in a town would undoubtedly cross-examine him about the "current situation" as well as accept his hospitality. Except in the very large centres, like Tokyo, Osaka, Kobe, and Yokohama, where there was a developed Western community of which the missionary group was only a small part, the mission-

Notes for Chapter Nine are found on pp. 242-47.

ary acted as the key conduit through which a Western visitor or new arrival learned about Japan or Korea. Their influence went far beyond what was published.

Missionary views on political events in the Japanese Empire became increasingly pronounced in the years after the Russo-Japanese War. Prior to 1905 missionaries had been more or less content with Japan's political direction. Modernization of the country was seen to be breaking down the traditional barriers to Christianity. Although Canadian missionaries might not always agree with Japanese Government policies on all issues, prior to 1905 missionaries were in the main supportive of government polities. Added to their appreciation of modernization was the simple fact that missionaries genuinely admired some of the Meiji political leadership, most particularly, and rather surprisingly in view of his private life, Itō Hirobumi. The feelings of friendship were capped in 1902 by the promulgation of the Anglo-Japanese Alliance and further cemented by the universal support that missionaries gave to Japan in its struggle with Russia two years later.

Attitudes started to change after 1905, and especially after the annexation of Korea in 1910. One major reason for this change was Japanese cultural imperialism in Korea. Not surprisingly, Japanese colonial actions in Taiwan were thought to have less consequence, for the occupation of Taiwan in 1895 had not brought about missionary protest. The Taiwan missionaries had been simply glad to see the end of Manchu rule on the island. Indeed, the initial reaction of Canadian missionaries in Korea was to welcome Japanese colonial rule because it would accelerate the modernization of the peninsula. The missionaries' pro-Japanese view, however, quickly changed to an implacable anti-Japanese feeling. One of the most significant reasons for this was the impact of the First World War.

Wilsonianism clearly infected the missionary community with a desire to see the Japanese Empire changed. The political idealism of President Wilson easily meshed with the social idealism which the student volunteers brought to their missionary work. This combined with the Canadian characteristics missionaries had always manifested: support for the colonial underdog and insistence on fair play. Canada, after all, had been a colony in the living memory of some of the missionaries, and Canadians felt an empathy with peoples under colonial rule. The impact of these different influences, however, had profoundly dissimilar results on missionaries in Japan and Korea. The Japan missionaries continued to maintain a pro-Japanese attitude toward the political changes they saw taking place in post-1918 Japan. On the other hand, the missionaries in Korea became virulently critical of the Japanese and their colonial rule. The paradox, of course, was that these two different reactions to the Japanese stemmed from a similar *Weltanschauung*.

Canadian missionaries in Korea were among the most severe critics of the Japanese Government-General in the aftermath of the March 1, 1919, demonstrations. In 1920-1921, Canadian missionaries were involved in a serious confrontation with the Japanese military establishment over atrocities committed by the Japanese during their punitive expedition against Korean residents living in the Chientao region of Manchuria. These two incidents represent the first time that Canadian missionaries had been at the centre of an international protest against a colonial regime.

Although the missionaries in Korea were highly critical of Japanese colonial policies, their colleagues in Japan were desperately trying to combat rising Western anti-Japanese feeling. The two missionary groups were working unwittingly at cross-purposes, for the anti-Japanese sentiments of the one could not help but undermine the positive sentiments projected by the other. The missionaries in Japan saw Japan gradually developing into a modern state with a political system based on parliamentary democracy. They felt that as parliamentary democracy flourished so too would the Christian movement in Japan. They also believed that Canadians could no longer see the Japanese as a "primitive" or "backward" people. Canadian missionaries perceived racism against the Japanese as an obstacle to the development of democracy in Japan and thus to the growth of Christianity. Their crusade against anti-Japanese feeling was tied to their hopes for Christianity and democracy in Japan. However, there was also a broader church-related reason for the missionary advocacy of fair treatment for Japanese. There was a Japanese community in Canada which the Canadian churches wished to Christianize.

MISSIONARIES AND JAPANESE IMMIGRATION TO CANADA

The Canadian Methodists, Anglicans, and Presbyterians all maintained missions in western Canada for the Christianization of Oriental people. The churches' stand on the issue of East Asian immigration to Canada was predicated on a belief that all immigrants should become Christian and be assimilated into Canadian society. A further early concern of the Canadian Methodists was the prohibition of the opium trade, which was allegedly carried on in Canada by Chinese and Japanese immigrants.[1] As a result of these concerns, the Canadian Methodist Church asked the Japan Methodist Church to supply Japanese pastors for the Japanese residents in Vancouver and other western cities.[2] It later became a tradition for Japanese pastors to serve their compatriots who were settled in Canada. As well as the Japanese Church supplying pastors, both the Canadian Anglican and Methodist churches maintained missions working among the Japanese on the west coast. These complex concerns made the Canadian Methodist apprehensive about the Ottawa government taking measures against Japanese immigrants. Such measures might in turn stimulate anti-Canadian feeling in Japan to the detriment of missionary activity.

The issue of racism against the Japanese was taken up in the last year of the First World War by C. J. L. Bates and John Saunby, two of the more thoughtful Canadian Methodist missionaries. In February 1918, Bates saw Japan's future in Asia as extremely bright. He felt that Japan would be the leading power in the Far East for the next twenty-five years and that no decision in the region could be made without taking it into account.[3] Bates also noted that Japan's victories over China in 1894 and Russia in 1905 had revealed to all "coloured peoples" the possibility of throwing off the "overlordship of the white races" and establishing their own national independence. Bates did not see any basis for the idea of the "Yellow Peril," which he believed was a purely German invention.[4] Nor did he believe that the Japanese had ever given official support to any anti-European movements among subject peoples in East Asia. Bates believed that the basic tenet of Japanese foreign policy was to prevent any western power from establishing itself in force on the "Far Eastern coast of Asia." He saw that the Anglo-Japanese Alliance and the Lansing-Ishii agreements both unequivocally affirmed the territorial integrity of China and recognized Japan's special place in East Asia. Likewise, he stressed that it was Japan's determination to prevent the domination of China by any Western power that lay behind Japanese foreign policy, rather than any desire to colonize China. Although Bates admitted that the Twenty-One Demands of 1915 had been "badly worded," he thought that their real intention was the prevention of Western domination of China.[5] Few other people were as lenient as Bates in their attitude toward the Twenty-One Demands, but he wished to remove any apprehension that Japan might become a dangerous threat to the Western powers and China in the postwar world. He also realized that there was concern about Japan in Canada which had to be mollified. It is significant that Bates alluded to the "overlordship of the white races," for this was an element in world politics that received no attention in the contemporary writings of British missionaries. As Canada was not the centre of a multi-racial empire, as a Canadian, Bates could freely write about such a concept.

In April 1918, another Canadian Methodist, John Saunby, highlighted the racial aspect of the relationship between Japan and North America. He noted that people on the west coast would have to prepare themselves for "the mingling of races because the East was becoming a mighty competitor in manufactured goods" and that trade relations were annually becoming more extensive.[6] Saunby argued that Canadians had to be ready for "the coming of the Oriental to our own shores, that we may not imperil all that we hold most dear, and at the same time throw the doors open to such classes as will best respond to Christian influences and take on the best traits of our western civilization."[7] In view of the problems of East Asian immigration, which affected both Canada and the United States, it is not surprising that race relations were always an important element in Canadian Methodist thinking in both Canada and Japan.

In 1922 the Canadian Methodists again turned their attention to the problems of Japanese immigration. In March 1922 A. T. Wilkinson at Shizuoka roundly condemned discriminatory immigration laws.[8] He thought that the Japanese had the ability to become loyal Canadian citizens. He also felt that there was no reason why a Japanese immigrant could not be successfully assimilated into Canadian society. Moreover, Wilkinson believed that the onus of assimilation lay with the Canadians themselves.[9] In making such a suggestion, he introduced an idea that had not previously been considered in other missionary articles on the immigration problem. However, Wilkinson considered the great question in 1922 to be the problem of bringing East and West together. He thought that the emergence of a new national conscience in Japan, India, and China, which demanded self-expression and self-determination, necessitated a rethinking of Western attitudes toward those countries. Wilkinson was perhaps hoping for too much if he thought that Canadians would quickly reconstruct their thinking about the Japanese. Yet, in attempting to predict the future, he envisaged the Pacific becoming "the most important theatre of the world's future civilization"; he also believed that "Vancouver will be a mightier city than Montreal, and the whole of Canada will feel the thrill of a new life, of a nation which will before the close of the century contain probably 100,000,000 people."[10] Though the latter prediction might have been a pipe dream, his vision of the future gave a further impetus to his concern of bringing East and West together.

More concerned with the immediate rather than the future, the foreign missions secretaries of the Canadian Methodist, Anglican, and Presbyterian churches wrote a joint letter in April 1923 to Prime Minister W. L. Mackenzie King, expressing their disapproval of discriminatory laws against Oriental residents. As an example, they cited the Chinese Head Tax which had been abolished earlier in the year. To these Christian leaders, immigration from East Asia was acceptable, provided that it was limited to such numbers as the Canadian church could hope to convert and assimilate.[11] To Canadian churchmen, Christianity was inherent in the notion of Canadian citizenship.

In 1924 the ubiquitous C. J. L. Bates wrote to the Canadian Prime Minister opposing the notion of any new restrictions on Japanese immigration.[12] Bates' letter defended the Japanese against all charges that might be brought against them. He was very concerned that Canada would follow the lead of the United States, which in 1924 had passed discriminatory legislation against Japanese immigration. Although events in the 1930s would sorely test Bates' sympathies for the Japanese, his gesture in defending the Japanese against racism was typical of the sympathetic concern of Canadian missionaries for all Japanese.

Much earlier than most other Canadians, the missionaries in Japan advocated the need for racial tolerance, for they foresaw the "mingling of races" in western Canada. While they had the prescience to foresee a multi-racial Canada, they were advocates neither of unrestricted East Asian immigration nor of a multicultural Canada. Indeed, it was seen as the role of the church in Canada to convert and assimilate these immigrants, and only once that had been achieved would they be worthy of becoming Canadian citizens.

In dismissing the idea of a "Yellow Peril" and supporting fair treatment for Japanese immigrants to Canada, the Japan missionaries were acting in their own self-interest. They wanted to try to ensure that anti-Japanese feeling in Canada would not harm their own missionary work in Japan. The missionaries were also conscious of the resentment among Japanese caused by the passage of the American Immigration Bill in 1924. Five years earlier, Japanese diplomats had failed in their bid to have the question of racial equality discussed at the Versailles Peace Conference. Although their own attitudes toward Koreans and Chinese were often tempered by racism, the Japanese were understandably very sensitive to racial discrimination directed against themselves. The emergence of democratic government was seen by missionaries as helping to change Western attitudes toward Japan. Such a change would result in the West becoming less discriminatory. As they also believed that liberal democracy would benefit the growth of Christianity, Canadian missionaries became increasingly enthusiastic about the political trends within Japan.

THE MOVEMENT TOWARD DEMOCRACY

Canadian Methodist missionaries wanted to see the establishment of parliamentary democracy in Japan. This was made clear in early 1913 by a missionary who wrote under the pen name of "Sayonara." As Japan entered into a new reign following the death of the Meiji Emperor, "Sayonara" wrote about his hopes for the future:

> we are not of those who think that a republican form of government is the best in the world, and certainly not for Japan. It is a blessing for this country just now that there is such a close alliance

with Britain, and it is so immensely popular. May the outcome of it all be that eventually representative government, modelled after that obtaining in the British Empire, shall find an abiding home here in these beautiful Isles of the far Pacific.[13]

In June 1914 another Canadian Methodist, C. P. Holmes, expressed the hope that the development of democracy in Japan would assist the Christian movement. He noted that

> a new democracy of thought is growing up. The man in the street is beginning to think, and we know it takes a thinking man to make a Christian. A year and a half ago Count Ōkuma [then Prime Minister of Japan] said that the present Emperor's reign would be remarkable for one thing and that would be the growth of democracy.[14]

This political development toward democracy was all the more welcome because of serious social problems within Japan. In February 1912 "Sayonara" noted that there was a possibility of serious social disturbances if Japan's industrial problems were not soon resolved. He thought that the exceedingly heavy war tax and war establishment might result in civil disturbances if Japanese workers felt that they were not getting a "square deal."[15] Taxation was very high because of new Imperial and international responsibilities which had emerged after the Russo-Japanese War. Parliamentary democracy would help the ordinary people of Japan get a "square deal."[16] "Sayonara" and his fellow Canadian missionaries were genuinely concerned with the welfare of the ordinary Japanese.

In fearing that social problems might turn into serious political difficulties for the Japanese, Canadian Methodists might have had in mind the High Treason Incident that led to the execution of twelve Japanese socialists in January 1911 for allegedly plotting to assassinate the Meiji Emperor. One of those executed, Oishi Seinosuke, had been a Christian enquirer from Nagano who had been in contact with Daniel Norman. While Norman dissociated himself from this man after the arrest, obviously it was an experience which Canadian Methodists wished to forget.

The First World War was a turning point for Canadians and their hopes for Japan. At the beginning of the war, Canadians in Japan probably agreed with the opinions offered by James Endicott in writing to D. R. McKenzie in August 1914. Endicott expressed the hope that the end of the war might bring a "crystallization of enlightened convictions throughout the world," which in turn would lead to an effort to prevent war. At the same time, Endicott considered that "Britain had done her best" to preserve peace and had entered the war with "a clear conscience and at the call of honour."[17]

Within a few months of Japan's entry into the war, its role had become an important subject of missionary comment. In April 1915 the *Christian Guardian*, the Methodist newspaper published in Toronto, applauded Japan's positive service to Britain "by clearing the Germans out of China."[18] There was some criticism of the Twenty-One Demands, but the newspaper reminded its readers that the Anglo-Japanese Alliance guaranteed the independence and integrity of the Chinese Republic and that Japan in the future would continue to honour the Alliance.

Yet once the Japanese military campaign in China had come to an end, missionaries began to consider the impact of the war on their Christian work. In March 1916, J. G. Waller, the Canadian Anglican missionary in Nagano, thought that, with the destruction of German power in the Pacific in 1914, Japan, although still one of the Allies, had "virtually become a neutral."[19] However, unlike British missionaries who felt betrayed by Japan's lack of support for the Allies after the China campaign and the existence of widespread pro-German feeling, Canadian missionaries considered Japan a loyal ally and remained optimistic about its democratization.

In April 1919 a Canadian Methodist commentator writing under the nom de plume of "Kosai" took the opportunity to criticize Japan in an article about the Paris Peace Conference.[20] Although he favoured the Japanese resolution calling for racial equality to be guaranteed by the Covenant of the League of Nations, he believed that such a resolution could not be accepted until Japan improved its "own moral conditions."[21] Daniel Norman also expressed sympathy for Japanese racial aspirations and felt that it was foolish to show a "spirit of disdain or resentment" while Japan was "in the throes of social and political ferment and evolution."[22]

Despite the social and political ferment, Canadian Methodists regarded political developments in Japan as highly promising. In the same article in which he had questioned the racial equality clause, "Koasi" mentioned the beginning of a new era of growing democracy. He saw the emergence of the Hara Kei Cabinet, based upon the parliamentary majority of a single party, as the beginning of a new era of democratic politics.[23] "Kosai" held that "the word democracy was on every lip."[24]

The positive image of a changing Japan, which Canadian missionaries in Japan wished to project at home, was clearly illustrated in the opinions expressed by Canadian Anglican Loretta L. Shaw in 1922:

> Before the world the transformation is well nigh complete. The Japanese flag is to be seen in almost every harbour; her goods appear in every market; she has gained brilliant victories over every enemy she has yet encountered; her empire has rapidly

expanded; she scrupulously adheres to the present codes of international conduct. In all world problems Japan is a force that must be considered.

Within the nation also great changes have taken place. Japan seldom invents, but she is quick to seize new ideas and to adapt them to her own needs. Western democratic ideals are influencing the national life increasingly. Business is expanding and developing on western lines; education has made great strides; women in the home and in public life are gaining freedom.[25]

Though this was a somewhat idealized view of Japan, it legitimately summed up the feelings of the missionaries in Japan toward the strides the country had made up to 1922, but also throughout the rest of the decade. The Japan which Miss Shaw described was a Japan that was coming close to being the type of modern country that missionaries wanted to create. It was, however, very much a perception of a resident in metropolitan Japan. The attitude of Canadian missionaries living in Korea was dramatically different.

CANADIAN PRESBYTERIANS AND THE BEGINNINGS OF JAPANESE RULE IN KOREA

Before 1905 Canadian Presbyterian missionaries were introduced by other North American missionaries to such Korean Christians as Syngman Rhee and Philip Jaisohn, men who later became leading figures in the American-based Korean independence movement and in the provisional government of Korea, which was established in Shanghai in 1919.[26] Despite this early connection with Korean nationalists, missionaries were still initially sympathetic to the Japanese, although they were disappointed to learn in 1905 of the establishment of the Japanese Residency-General.[27] In terms reminiscent of missionary attitudes toward the Manchu administration in Taiwan, the missionaries in Korea saw the declining Korean bureaucracy as "corrupt, blind and predatory" and the Korean government as possessing little sympathy for the welfare of its people.[28] The Japanese were welcomed as modernizers just as in Taiwan. However, this swiftly changed.

The establishment of the Residency-General in Korea meant that from 1905 onwards a good many Japanese *mauvais sujets* moved into the peninsula. Many were simple carpetbaggers in search of a quick fortune, but others were Japanese settlers attracted to Korea by the simultaneous opening of all unsettled land to Japanese settlement and the formation of the Oriental Development Company to foster Japanese immigration. The influx of Japanese inevitably led to bitter hostility on the part of the Koreans.

Throughout this and subsequent friction, the Canadian Presbyterians were deeply sympathetic to the local population. Robert Grierson, the missionary doctor in Sungjin, compared the feats of the Righteous Armies, who fought a guerrilla war against the Japanese in northern Korea after 1907, to the feats of the ancient Greeks.[29] Since much of this guerrilla war was being fought in the mission territory of the Canadian Presbyterians, the Canadians could not help but hear about it. Of the Japanese military operations against the Righteous Armies on the Manchurian border, Grierson noted that "word had come out that the troops in there were acting badly, treating the people as if they were a defeated enemy, forcibly taking chickens, pigs, vegetables etc., and, worst of all, committing rape on women in the secluded far-away farms."[30] In their quest to destroy the Righteous Armies (they had succeeded by 1912), the Japanese military was prepared to act brutally toward Koreans living in remote areas where atrocities might well pass unnoticed. Even before the annexation of Korea by Japan in 1910, the Canadian Presbyterians had good reason to loathe the Japanese.

The assassination in October 1909 of Itō Hirobumi, the Japanese Resident-General in Korea, came as a great shock to missionaries in Japan. The esteem in which Japan missionaries held Itō was clearly expressed as late as four years after his death. In April 1913 a Canadian Methodist commentator thought that Itō's administration had been more wise, broadminded and sympathetic than any other in East Asia. Further, he believed that Korea's worst enemy was the Korean who had assassinated Itō in Harbin.[31] However, the assassination was one of the reasons why the Japanese decided to annex the peninsula. Indeed, the fact that Itō had been killed by a Christian made the new Japanese colonial overlords suspicious of Christians. This was clearly seen in the so-called Conspiracy Case of late 1911, which followed the arrest of some ninety-eight Korean Christians for allegedly taking part in a plot to assassinate the Governor-General, Terauchi Masatake. Although torture was used to extract confessions,[32] the charges against these Korean Christians were proven to be false. Canadian Methodist opinion, with which in this instance the Canadian Presbyterians would possibly have concurred, was that the Christian church in Korea was somewhat feared by the Japanese Government-General because its Korean leadership might overshadow the Japanese civil authority.[33]

After the Conspiracy Case, the Government-General always continued to be suspicious of Korean Christians. In June 1914, D. A. MacDonald reported that there was a "lack of progress" in the rural districts near Hoiryung because "the people have been rather intimidated by the Japanese gendarmes in the past."[34] William Scott believed that the regulations concerning religious propaganda had led to the constant harassment of Christian workers by local Japanese officials and the intimidation of communities that welcomed Christians.[35] In the case of educational regulations, the Japanese were more concerned with the attitude of missionaries in Korea toward the Japanese government than with the teaching of religion and the Bible in the schools.[36] As Sir Charles Eliot, the British ambassador to Japan, wrote in 1921 about the difficulties between missionaries and the Japanese in Korea, one of the main problems was that the young American and Canadian missionaries brought with them political ideas and sympathies which they passed on to their pupils.[37] As a result of mission school education, a type of Korean intensely distasteful to Japanese officials was being produced. The democratic ideas which American and Canadian missionary teachers were subconsciously passing on to their students ran counter to the aim of the Japanese administration in Korea. Mission schools posed a serious threat to the success of Japanese colonial policy in Korea. Despite the repeated assurances by Western missionaries that they were not anti-Japanese, it was from the graduates of mission schools that many of the leading opponents of the Japanese came, for which missionaries had to take some responsibility. The problems between missionaries and the Japanese Government-General came to a head with the March 1, 1919, movement.

THE MARCH 1, 1919, MOVEMENT

Although some missionaries realized that there were going to be demonstrations for independence in Seoul, and other centres in Korea, at the time of the funeral of Kojong, the former Korean monarch, no missionary had any part in planning the demonstrations. This does not mean, however, that missionaries were not involved in the independence movement or that they remained aloof from the movement's political issues. Although missionaries repeatedly and vigorously denied that they in any way encouraged or aided the Korean demonstrators, they maintained no neutrality where brutality was concerned.[38] In March 1919, A. E. Armstrong, the Assistant Missions Secretary of the Canadian Presbyterian Church, noted that all the Western missionaries in Korea were united in their disapproval of Japanese actions and wished to see justice done.[39] On March 16, 1919, just prior to returning home from an extended tour of East Asia, Armstrong had met in Seoul with some thirty representatives from the various Mission Boards working in Korea. They asked him to publicize the atrocities; it was felt that it was only through publicity that justice could be secured for the Korean people.

As it turned out, Canadian Presbyterians were among the most active critics of the treatment of Koreans by the Japanese in the aftermath of the independence demonstrations. In early April 1919, by then at home in Canada, Armstrong began to tell people about the Japanese reaction to the independence movement. He made his own view clear in a letter to John R. Mott, the famous YMCA leader:

> the cause of the poor defenceless Korean is on my heart and conscience and I would be doing them a very great wrong if I did not do all in my power to help them secure those sweeping reforms which the World will demand as the right of all peoples henceforth. It is no exaggeration whatever to call the present military system in Korea the "GERMAN MACHINE." The American Consul says so, the missionaries declare it to be so and the Japanese whom I met in Tokyo admitted it. We ought to lend every assistance to the democratic movement in Japan which has gained such prestige through the Allied victory for the principles of democracy, righteousness, justice and freedom.[40]

Armstrong and the other Canadian Presbyterians saw themselves as the champions of democracy fighting against the evils of militarism. In a letter of April 9, 1919, to N. W. Rowell, a leading Cabinet minister, R. P. MacKay, the Canadian Presbyterian Missions Secretary, took up the same themes as Armstrong. Japan was a "German Machine" which was repeating the Armenian atrocities by its actions against the Koreans.[41] Rowell had been chairman of the Laymen's Missionary Movement and was an obvious, as well as a well-known, politician to approach. That Mackay involved Rowell was part of the Presbyterians' strategy to bring Japanese actions to the attention of the Canadian and other Western governments. Armstrong himself had suggested to Mott that an approach ought to be made to the British and American governments to intercede and to have the Korean question brought before the Paris Peace Conference.[42]

At the same time, it was clear that Armstrong was not an advocate of Korean independence. In May 1919 he wrote to George Paik, who was later to become a famous Korean Christian but who was then a student in Missouri, that he hoped reforms would be granted in the government of Korea. However, Armstrong insisted that the Koreans would have to show that they could maintain a stable government before expecting to be granted the privilege of governing their own country.[43] In July 1919, in a letter to Takahashi Motoguchi, a Japanese Parliamentarian, Armstrong clearly outlined what he would like to see:

> Japan build up an Empire in the East like the British Empire,— Koreans, and Japanese and Formosans, on an equal footing,— as English Canadians and Australians are, for example. Indeed—I would like to go further and see Japan, Korea, and China working together in the development of the Orient, even as the British and American people are working more and more closely together, and I trust in the interests of world-wide humanity.[44]

In May 1919 Armstrong wrote to William Scott in Lungchingtsun that he had faith in democracy in Japan but that militarism was dying hard. By implication, it is clear that he felt that militarism was the cause of the difficulties in Korea.[45] Armstrong wanted the Government of Japan to announce quickly the adoption of a new liberal policy toward Koreans.[46] This new policy in the peninsula would also help, he felt, the Japanese in China where they were confronted with a boycott of Japanese goods stemming from the May 4, 1919, demonstrations in Peking.

Although Armstrong did not question Japan's right to have Korea as a colony, the publication of Japanese atrocities in Korea obscured this fact and benefited those who were virulently opposed to Japanese rule in the peninsula. Armstrong can be accused, along with the Canadian Presbyterians in Korea, of being naive in assuming that the Japanese would share his belief that the publication of anti-Japanese stories was for Japan's own benefit. Likewise, in viewing the events in Korea as a struggle between democracy and militarism which should be debated in the forum of international public opinion, Armstrong and his missionary colleagues can be accused of wishing to play the part of judge, jury, and executioner. Even though it was only a few months since the end of the First World War, and the disillusionment at the inability of world governments to fulfill the Allies' democratic ideals had not yet set in, neither Armstrong nor other missionary critics attempted to understand the difficulties and point of view of the Government-General in Korea.

In mid-April 1919 the Federal Council of the Churches of Christ's Commission on Relations with the Orient began to meet in New York to discuss the Korean situation. The Japanese Consul-General in New York agreed to raise the issue of Korea with the Japanese government, on the understanding that Armstrong's views on Korea should not be made public until the Japanese government had time to reply to the Commission.[47] It was only in July 1919 that the Japanese government made a reply to the Commission. In this reply, Hara Kei, the Japanese Prime Minister, made it clear that the Japanese government was seriously investigating the charges of abuses committed by its agents in Korea and was endeavouring to formulate a comprehensive plan of reforms in the colonial administration in order to promote the lasting welfare of the Korean people.[48] The Commission could not have hoped for a better response from the Japanese government. Yet before a reply could come from Tokyo, details of Armstrong's views on Korea were somehow made public and published in the New York *Times*.[49] At the same time, different stories about events in Korea also began to appear in North America. Armstrong himself was under very great pressure to publish the increasing number of atrocity stories which were reaching him from Canadian Presbyterian missionaries in Korea.[50]

These stories often portrayed brutality. As Robert Grierson remembered, on the day after the peaceful demonstrations for independence in Sungjin "quite early, a squad of Japanese firemen, armed with fire axes, and police armed with rifles, paraded up from their settlement to the quietly resting Korean villages . . . beating, hacking, shooting. Soon casualties began to come into the hospital, adding to our usual heavy Monday clinic."[51] From this it would appear as if the local Japanese communities were taking matters into their own hands and beating up Koreans indiscriminately. A. H. Barker in Hoiryung reported to R. P. MacKay in late March 1919 that

> many non-Christians & many Christians have been arrested. Tonight 15 or so of our Hoi Ryung Christians are in jail. Some of them are said to have had no part in the waving of flags and in shouting for independence, but were arrested nevertheless. The Japanese authorities say they did have part in it.[52]

As Barker indicated, Christians were being arrested whether or not they were guilty of participating in the independence demonstration. This was certainly confirmed in May 1919 in a letter A. R. Ross, who worked in Sungjin, wrote to W. M. Royds, the acting British Consul in Seoul. Ross reported that Korean Christians in villages in the hinterland had been forced, after beatings by Japanese gendarmes, to sign written statements renouncing their Christianity. Further, a church had been damaged by the Japanese gendarmes.[53] Much more serious were events that had taken place in Lungchingtsun in Manchuria.

A. H. Barker had mentioned to R. P. MacKay in late March that "in Yong Jung [Lungchingtsun] the Chinese troops fired on the crowd and 14 Koreans were killed & 18 seriously wounded."[54] The Canadian Presbyterians found themselves in the middle of what was in fact one of the most famous March demonstrations. Dr. S. H. Martin, who worked in the Canadian Presbyterian hospital in the town, wrote to the British Consul in Mukden about the independence demonstration which had taken place on March 12:

> You will be interested to know that in the demonstration made here by Koreans—about 8,000 in a perfectly harmless manner, with speeches and waving flags—they were fired on by Chinese troops using Mauser rifles. Fourteen were killed outright, mostly shot through the brain, others so badly wounded that they will probably die. Our hospital is full and all the Britishers are doing what they can in the way of Red Cross work. We did six amputations last week and three other operations to save life. Over forty are severely wounded. Of course we are all accused of taking part in this thing; as a matter of fact we did our best to restrain our

> people, and we always aim to keep out of things politically. The
> Chinese were under the control of Japs otherwise the Japs would
> have brought in infantry from across the border.[55]

The fact that the Chinese troops used Mauser rifles clearly fitted the
image of the "German machine." The acting British Consul in Mukden
agreed with Martin that the Chinese troops acted the way that they did
because they were afraid that Japanese troops might have otherwise
come across the border.

William Scott, another of the Canadian Presbyterian missionaries in
Lungchingtsun, wrote to complain that Japanese plainclothes policemen had been trespassing on the mission compound, hoping to arrest
some of the Korean workers in the mission hospital.[56] The issue at stake
here was the fact that Lungchingtsun was in Manchuria and that the
mission compound and all within it were protected by the extraterritoriality which still applied in China. Apparently the Japanese police
believed that an independence newspaper was being printed in the
compound on a mimeograph machine belonging to the missionaries.
Scott also complained about the beatings Japanese police had given the
Koreans they had interrogated. Some unfortunate Koreans, like one of
the teachers at the mission school for girls, had been held in prison for
ten days without being questioned even once. As a result of this sort of
treatment, Scott believed that the Koreans in Lungchingtsun had been
reduced to living in a state of terror. He was not about to let the
Japanese police come into the mission compound, which he considered
to be British territory.[57] Although Scott wrote that the Canadian missionaries in Lungchingtsun tried to keep as free from politics as possible,[58] it is clear that Korean Christians in the town were deeply involved
in the independence movement.

Although the missionaries might not have been aware of the full
details of the involvement, it would be highly surprising if they had no
inkling of Christian activities in support of the independence movement. The Myong Dong (Meitō) Christian school, which was the main
Canadian Presbyterian middle school in Lungchingtsun, was an especially important centre of independence activity where an independence newspaper was published (thus the suspicion of the Japanese
police about the non-existent mission mimeograph). The school's
headmaster, Kim Yaku-jon, who later became influential in the socialist
movement, was closely watched by the Japanese police. He had been a
representative from the Chientao (Kantō) region at the All Russia
Korean Peoples' Congress held in Vladivostock. This meeting discussed sending representatives to France to press the case for Korean
independence at the Paris Peace Conference and also began planning
for independence demonstrations to coincide with the memorial services for ex-King Kojong.[59] The proclamation issued by the All Russia

Korean Peoples' Congress served as the basis for the alliance of Christians, Tendōkyoists, and Confucianists for independence. Among the leading female organizers who had delivered one of the four speeches to the crowd at Lungchingtsun on March 12 was the teacher whom Scott reported as being held by the Japanese. The Japanese were certainly correct in assuming that the Korean Christians in Lungchingtsun were actively involved in the anti-Japanese movement. For the moment, however, it was not the Manchurian border that captured attention, but rather events in the capital.

The most famous of Canadian Presbyterian missionaries involved in the March 1, 1919, movement was Dr. Frank W. Schofield, who was attached to the Severance Union Medical College in Seoul. Schofield was one of the most hostile missionary critics of Japanese rule in Korea. He bombarded the British Foreign Office with reports and pictures of atrocities. Undoubtedly, this erstwhile veterinarian from the Agricultural College at Guelph was a pest to both the Japanese authorities and the British Foreign Office. Unlike Scott, Martin and the others in northern Korea and Manchuria who provided the Foreign Office with information, Schofield did not know when to stop.

A photographer, Schofield took many pictures of the actual demonstration in Seoul on March 1, 1919. Later he photographed Japanese atrocities outside the city. However, he was unable to convince the Japanese authorities in Korea to change their conduct toward Koreans. So he went to Japan, where he interviewed Prime Minister Hara Kei and other influential Japanese, and wrote many articles for Japanese newspapers.[60] He also informed the Foreign Office in London of his actions and provided them with evidence of Japanese atrocities.

Schofield was appalled by the torture used by the Japanese gendarmes against innocent Koreans.[61] Korean figures estimate that some 2,023,098 people took part in independence demonstrations throughout Korea and the Chientao region. Of these, 7,509 were killed, 15,981 wounded and 46,948 imprisoned.[62] In June 1919 General Kojima, Chief of the Gendarmerie in Korea, admitted to Schofield that 20,000 persons had been arrested since the disturbances had begun and that 11,000 had been flogged.[63] What made Schofield so infuriated was the attitude of the Japanese toward such actions.

As he informed Cecil Harmsworth at the Foreign Office in London, the Japanese Prime Minister had excused the atrocities as acts of minor, out-of-control policemen and illiterate soldiers. Schofield believed that this was an utter lie because the atrocities had continued for two months.[64] He gained no satisfaction from Hara Kei, and he fared no better with the highest military officials. They too offered excuses for everything and made no attempt to investigate his charges. About police actions, Schofield wrote: "the police always allowed the coolies with their pick axe handles, the fire men with their hooks and the sportsmen with their shotguns to have a good time shooting and killing the crowds."[65] It is apparent from Grierson's description of the assault of the Japanese firemen on the Korean community in Sungjin that it was open season on Koreans.

It was also open season on Schofield. Admiral Saitō Makoto, who was appointed Governor-General of Chōsen shortly after the March demonstrations, was quoted by the English-language *Japan Advertiser* as saying: "Mr. Schofield is a most dangerous man, assiduously carrying on the independence agitation in Korea, and even among the missionaries there are many who look askance at his vehement methods."[66] Apparently Saitō felt that it was an undeniable fact that Christian missions were behind the disturbances in Korea and that Schofield was one of the most pronounced independence agitators. Eventually, a belated *démenti* did appear saying that the Governor-General had been misunderstood and had never asserted that missionaries had been behind the disturbances.[67] Schofield himself went to see the Governor-General, who denied it all and who was most courteous to him. However, Schofield noted: "I have an idea who were behind things (The Police), they hate me like poison since, because I have recently been exposing their torture stunts. However I prayed & others prayed & the Lord worked things out right. The beggers [*sic*] thought they had me. I pity anyone who gets into the hands of the police here."[68] Schofield's brother, who lived in England, was certainly worried about his sibling's safety in Korea and expressed his concern to the Foreign Office.[69] C. H. Bentinck at the Foreign Office noted on John Schofield's letter that "Dr. Schofield is a very well-known man in Seoul and has supplied us with many reports on Japanese atrocities. Had the Japanese asked to arrest him, I fancy they would have done so long ago, but I gathered that he was wise enough never to go too far."[70] The Japanese authorities did arrest some missionaries for their alleged support of the independence. Those arrested included two female missionaries with the Australian Presbyterian mission in Pusan and one American Presbyterian missionary in P'yongyang, E. M. Mowry, who was sentenced to six months in prison for concealing five Korean students in his home.[71] Schofield undoubtedly was too well known to be touched.

Yet Schofield did have an Achilles heel, and that was his zealousness. His accusations against the Japanese were not simply restricted to the gruesome facts of the atrocities. Prior to the independence rallies, Schofield had been carrying out a determined campaign against the system of licensed prostitution imported from Japan into Korea. In his zeal to get at the Japanese, he issued this accusation: "Japan instead of civilizing the Koreans was 'syphilizing' them."[72] As Beilby Alston at the

British Embassy in Tokyo noted in a letter to Lord Curzon of Keddle-ston, the British Foreign Secretary, "correct though the statements probably are which Dr. Schofield marshals in support of his charge that the conquerors are striving to force prostitution on the conquered, he produces no evidence, statistical or other, in support of his accusation of 'syphilization'."[73] Schofield had overplayed his hand. He even offended the British Foreign Office; he was a dedicated opponent of colonialism generally and criticized British colonial rule.[74] It was perhaps with some relief to both the Japanese and the British Foreign Office that Schofield left Korea for Canada at the end of 1919.

Schofield and the other Canadian Presbyterian missionaries had hoped that the British Foreign Office might make representations to the Japanese government after learning of the atrocities. But the Foreign Office viewed Japan as sovereign in Korea and thus able to act as it pleased, just as Britain could in India or Ireland.[75] Even so, the Foreign Office attempted to placate the missionaries. In Tokyo, Alston drew the attention of the Japanese government to the necessity of reform in Korea. In London, Lord Curzon interviewed the Japanese Ambassador in July 1919.[76] So stormy was the meeting that the Japanese apparently for a time considered withdrawing their ambas-sador from London.[77]

The reasons for this were evident. Curzon had told the Japanese Ambassador:

> I had lying before me pages of evidence describing the most barbarous and revolting atrocities, the publication of which would produce a sensation in the civilized world and would rebound to the discredit of the Japanese Government. To such an extent had matters gone that the missionaries in Korea had seriously consid-ered a suggestion to leave the country en masse, by way of public protest; and it had even been proposed that a boycott of Korea by all foreigners should be arranged in order to make the public sense of the situation. Nor was this a matter that affected the Japanese and the Koreans alone. The persecution of the Koreans had assumed an anti-Christian form, and deeply affected all foreign nations whose subjects were either resident or interested in that country.[78]

Curzon went on to tell the Japanese Ambassador that his government should adopt without delay a more liberal system of government in Korea. It is very clear that Curzon had in front of him Schofield's reports and photographs. It has to be pointed out, however, that Max Muller of the Foreign Office, who wrote a memorandum on Japanese policy in Korea in early July, relied very heavily on the opinions of Bishop Mark Napier Trollope, the British Anglican Bishop of Korea. In sharp contrast to the vehemence of the Canadian Presbyterians,

Trollope was very moderate in his attitude toward the Japanese and constructive in his suggestions about what reasonable forms they might undertake.[79] Because his views demanded no action and agreed with those of the Foreign Office, it is highly probably that Trollope's opinions carried much more weight with Curzon and the Foreign Office officials than did those of Schofield.

The Canadian Presbyterians did make a stand. As a letter of July 10, 1919, from the Korean Mission of the Presbyterian Church in Canada to Field Marshal Hasegawa, then Governor-General of Chōsen, stated, the missionaries believed that atrocities committed by the Japanese should be made known because "we feel that not only do these injustices reflect upon the honour of Japan but upon us who are British subjects in special treaty relationships with Japan."[80] While this was true, as Canadians they were not restrained as were the British (because they were colonial overlords themselves) from criticizing the Japanese. The Canadian Presbyterians were at the very centre of publicizing the atrocities the Japanese had committed against the Koreans. In Frank Schofield, Canada produced a hero in South Korea equal in stature to that Norman Bethune would later acquire in China.

Although Schofield returned to Canada, the March 1 movement was not over for the Canadian Presbyterian mission. In the fall of 1920, the Canadian Presbyterians were once again at loggerheads with the Japanese military over atrocities committed against Koreans during the Chientao Punitive Expedition (Kantō Shuppei).

THE CHIENTAO INTERVENTION

During March 1919, Lungchingtsun and other important towns in North and West Chientao were the sites of important independence demonstrations. William Scott and the other Canadian Presbyterian missionaries had been appalled by the killing of demonstrators in Lungchingtsun by Chinese soldiers and had reacted vigorously to the highhanded actions of the Japanese following the demonstration there. However, the independence movement in Chientao did not end with the suppression of the March demonstrations.

The failure to obtain the swift independence of Korea by peaceful means led some within the independence movement to become increasingly more radical and militant. The change in the nature of the independence movement was exemplified by the power struggle between the two major factions within the Provisional Government of Korea, which was formed in Shanghai in the early summer of 1919. One faction, led by Syngman Rhee and drawing its support largely from the Korean ex-patriates in the United States, advocated the use of diplomatic means to achieve independence by exerting international pressure on Japan. The other faction, led by Yi Tong-hwi and supported by socialists and nationalists in Siberia and Chientao, advocated the intensification of armed struggle. By the end of 1919, Yi's faction was in control of the provisional government in Shanghai. In Chientao province, following the March demonstrations, anti-Japanese peoples' organizations had been formed. One of the most important was the Hunchun (Konshung) branch of the Great Korea Peoples' Congress. This single branch had the support of some 20,000 people in the district surrounding Hunchun and was subordinate to the provisional government.[81] Many Christians supported this branch. By August 1920, the Hunchun branch was providing support for about 450 guerrillas, and about 2,600 partisans were operating in North Chientao.[82]

These developments obviously disturbed the Japanese. Although a few, like Prime Minister Hara, had dismissed the notion that the independence movement was motivated by a desire for self-determination as a baseless rumour,[83] others felt the movement had a deep intellectual foundation.[84] Moreover, it was felt by some that the independence movement in Korea had acted in concert with the movements in Chientao, Vladivostock, and Shanghai.[85] In this triangle outside of Korea, the nationalists in Chientao were seen to be particularly important because of the financial support they gave to the independence movement.[86] In response to the March demonstrations, the Japanese had despatched six battalions and some 450 military police across the border into North Chientao to help subjugate the independence movement.[87] However, Japanese efforts were hampered by the fact that the Chinese authorities were in *de jure* control of this region of Manchuria. Nevertheless, the Japanese were prepared to send large numbers of troops and gendarmes into Chientao if an opportunity arose. They saw that by fully subjugating Chientao they could indirectly deal a severe blow to the independence groups in Siberia and Shanghai. The appropriate opportunity came with the Second Hunchun Incident in October 1920.

Although the anti-Japanese activities of Korean nationalists were of primary importance in precipitating the Chientao intervention, there were others as well. Also important were the deteriorating situation in the Siberian conflict (the Hunchun district was of considerable strategic importance to Japan because of its situation immediately behind Vladivostock) and an element of revenge against Chang Tso-lin, the Manchurian warlord, for upsetting Japanese designs in North China.[88] Japanese annoyance was further heightened by the collapse of the White Russian forces under General D. L. Horvath in October 1920, which allowed the control of the Harbin and the Chinese Eastern Railway to fall into the hands of Chang Tso-lin.[89] It was against this background of serious reverses in Manchuria, North China and Siberia during 1920 that the Japanese government reached its decision to send an expeditionary force into Chientao province.

As early as April 1920, the Japanese residents in Yongjung had petitioned Army Minister Tanaka Giichi to ensure both their personal safety and Japanese commercial interests.[90] In the light of the Nikolaevsk Incident of May 1920, and the inability of the Chinese forces to deal with the anti-Japanese partisans despite Japanese assistance, the Japanese Army was sympathetic. By August 1920 the Japanese military had begun to make preparations for an invasion.[91]

On September 12, 1920, the First Hunchun Incident took place: some 400 to 500 mounted bandits attacked the town but were beaten off by Chinese and Japanese police and soldiers. Across the border in Korea, the 19th Division had been warned to be ready to march to protect the Japanese residents in Hunchun if the Japanese Consul deemed that such action was warranted. On October 2, 1920, in the Second Hunchun Incident, some 300 mounted bandits attacked the town and burned the Japanese Consulate. The Japanese responded quickly by despatching large numbers of troops to Hunchun and commencing a general invasion of Chientao.

The Japanese had decided beforehand to invade Chientao, and the Second Hunchun Incident was a pretext to do so. Indeed, it has been described as a "frame up."[92] At the time, however, it was the Japanese version of what happened that was publicized. On December 20, 1920, the Japanese Consul-General in Ottawa wrote in the Toronto *Globe*:

> on October 2 last a large crowd, consisting of Korean revolters, Chinese bandits and Russian Bolsheviki, suddenly attacked the Japanese Consulate at Hunchun, burned the buildings, set fire on the premises of the "foreign trade quarter" and massacred the inhabitants, including Japanese police officers, men, women and children.[93]

There was evident scepticism about this announcement in London. Miles Lampson, an official in the British Foreign Office, on hearing similar reports, noted that "we know that brigands can be created by Japan when she wishes to."[94] Despite such scepticism, faith in these "brigands" remained strong. As late as February 1921, the British Consul-General in Seoul reported that the *Japan Chronicle*, the most independent-minded and thoughtful of English-language newspapers in Japan, had mentioned that there were 600 freebooters under a Chinese leader (named as Chang Hao Chiang) operating from a base on Mount Potai on the Korean side of the Tumen and raiding villages on the Chinese side of the river.[95]

The presence of "bandits" could justify the continued need for Japanese troops across the Tumen. Student demonstrations in Peking against the Japanese intervention were to be expected;[96] what was unexpected was the foreign press in the Far East giving prominence to the accusations brought by Canadian Presbyterian missionaries against Japanese troops in Chientao.[97]

In a letter published in the Toronto *Globe* on December 23, 1920, William Scott, on furlough from Lungchingtsun, rebutted the earlier statements of the Japanese Consul-General.[98] Scott reported that he had travelled extensively in the spring of 1920 in the area south of the Hunchun district and had seen no signs of "Chinese bandits." Indeed, Scott had seen only two small groups of armed Koreans who were extorting money from Korean farmers for the provisional government in Shanghai. He believed that Chinese military patrols prevented the formation of Korean revolutionary bands. Further, although he had no firsthand evidence about the Hunchun Incidents, Scott had witnessed the burning of a Japanese Consulate elsewhere in Chientao, and this had been perpetrated by disgruntled Korean police attached to the Consulate guard and not by any Korean revolutionaries.[99] Scott flatly contradicted the Japanese claim, which was supported by Korean nationalist groups themselves, that Chientao was seething with armed revolutionaries. Again, while he admitted seeing the two small groups of armed revolutionaries, the fact that they were extorting money from Korean farmers in itself casts some doubt on the popular support for the provisional government found in Chientao province. For their own purposes, both the Japanese and the Korean nationalists might have exaggerated somewhat the numbers of partisans operating in Chientao, but it remains true that considerable numbers were in fact there. Scott must have been either wilfully blind or unusually insensate not to have known what was going on in his mission area.

By the end of October 1920, letters from W. R. Foote, Emma Palethorpe, and S. H. Martin had come to the attention of S. Shimazu, the Japanese Consul-General in Ottawa.[100] These letters attacked the burning of churches and such schools as the Myung Dong Christian school. Further to this, the letters gave details of atrocities and murders committed by the Japanese Army during October 1920. The army could hardly deny burning churches, but the stock answer was that the buildings were used as meeting places by the independence movement. As to the killings, the excuse was always that those killed were independence activists who had offered resistance. Linguistic problems also aided the Japanese; missionaries in their letters referred to incidents that took place in villages with romanized Korean names. The Japanese used Chinese characters. Some incidents, therefore, could be conveniently lost in linguistic confusion.[101] It goes without saying that Japanese records do not substantiate any of the claims of the missionaries about atrocities or murders.[102]

An example of the type of atrocity that the missionaries reported appears in a letter from Dr. S. H. Martin, the young physician at the mission hospital in Lungchingtsun. In his letter, which was published in January 1921 by the Toronto *Globe*, Martin wrote:

> Japan, under the strongest protest from China, has sent over 15,000 troops into this part of China, with the seeming intention of wiping out of existence, if possible, the whole Christian community, especially all young men. Village after village is daily being methodically burned and the young men shot, so that at present we have a ring of villages surrounding this city [Lungchingtsun] that have suffered from fire or wholesale murder, or both.[103]

Martin detailed the atrocities committed by the Japanese troops. He reported that either Koreans had been murdered or houses had been burned by Japanese troops in 32 villages. In one village, as many as 145 inhabitants had been killed. In another, 14 people had been positioned in front of a large grave and then shot, and their corpses burned.[104] There is no Japanese record that 145 people were killed in any one village. Moreover, it is very difficult to substantiate the charge that the Japanese were aiming to wipe out the entire Christian community. What was apparent to the Japanese, however, was that many Korean Christians were deeply involved in the independence movement. This was irrefutable. For their part, the Canadian Presbyterian missionaries were intent on protecting Christians and church property.

In response to the accusations of committing atrocities, the Japanese Army established in November 1920 a military commission under Colonel Mizumachi, who had been military attaché in Washington, to investigate the charges. The protests of the missionaries likely would not have attracted undue Western attention, especially as the findings of the military commission did not substantiate their claims, had it not been for the naiveté of the Japanese Army in its dealings with the Canadians in Lungchingtsun. Undoubtedly, William Foote, who was one of the original three Canadian Presbyterian missionaries and possessed a robust and strong personality, offended the Japanese officers stationed in Lungchingtsun. No diplomat, Foote spoke his mind. The upshot was that the Japanese Army accused the missionaries of fomenting revolution. On December 7, 1920, the London *Times* reported that Major-General Satō of the War Department in Tokyo had stated:

> it is a curious circumstance that most of the insurgents are Christians while the mission schools are their headquarters. It is a matter of regret that some missionaries entertain the mistaken notion that the Japanese Army is persecuting Christians. We may suppose that the insurgents consider it to their own advantage to rely on foreigners in order to further their aims, flocking together under the

shelter of missionaries and assuming the name of Christians with the same design. The missionaries and mission schools have exceeded the bounds of duty. Some directly encouraged the insurgent bands, the schools being training places. The missionaries, while accusing the Japanese troops of inhumanities and taking photographs to substantiate what they say, are themselves the cause of the tragedy that has befallen the insurgents.[105]

Major-General Satō then went on to say that the Japanese might be forced to remove the missionaries: "Japan grants freedom of religious belief, but cannot allow treason that threatens to undermine the foundations of the Empire."[106] There was an element of truth in what Satō said; Korean Christians had been active in the independence movement and the teachers and students in Christian schools had helped in its organization. However, there is absolutely no evidence that the missionaries themselves actively encouraged the independence movement. Further, a Japanese Army officer had no right to threaten to stop the activities of Christian missionaries in a foreign land in which his own army was an unwanted aggressor. These accusations by a senior officer in the Japanese Army created a diplomatic incident, for Chientao was a sovereign part of China.

Satō was not alone in his accusations against the Canadians. In a letter written in November 1920, Colonel Mizumachi, who headed the military commission, also accused the missionaries of encouraging the independence movement. By alluding to the actions of General Dyer at Amritsar, he pointed out that the British record in terms of atrocities was by no means blameless. The Colonel also made it clear that, if missionaries persisted in their accusations against the Japanese Army, the Japanese would have no alternative but to support anti-British movements in British colonies, arguing that Japanese Buddhists could not sit idly by seeing the oppression of their co-religionists.[107]

The Canadian Presbyterians and the British and Canadian governments took the matter of the Mizumachi letter very seriously. As Foote wrote to A. E. Armstrong in March 1921, "we took the ground that Colonel Mizumachi's letter, and the issues raised by the conduct of the Japanese Punitive Expedition were of an inter-national character, and, that we, without instructions from our Consul, should take no action apart from protest, reporting the facts, and helping the destitute."[108] The question of the personal safety of missionaries also worried Armstrong, for it was apparent that Colonel Mizumachi would not give Foote permission to travel in Chientao for fear that the Japanese troops would kill him.[109] This matter was taken up by R. P. MacKay. He wrote to Sir Joseph Pope in the Department of External Affairs in Ottawa in December 1920 asking for the Foreign Office's interpretation of the rights of Canadian missionaries in China.[110]

The Canadian Presbyterian Church considered this matter serious enough to attempt to secure the legal services of N. W. Rowell. A. E. Armstrong felt that the Presbyterian Church needed such a counsel because it was dealing with the Japanese government through the Consul-General in Ottawa and with the British government through the Secretary of State in Ottawa. Rowell declined because his government and the British government faced the possibility of having to take some part in the issue.[111] In itself, Rowell's refusal showed how seriously the Dominion government was taking the matter.

The Canadian Presbyterians in Toronto pressed their case because they felt that Japanese accusations against missionaries had important ramifications for Christian work in Korea. Armstrong wrote to Sidney L. Gulick of the Churches of Christ's Commission on Relations with the Orient that

> many questions are involved which must be settled satisfactorily for the sake of future missionary operations in Korea and among Koreans in China. It is intolerable that a foreign Power has the right to dictate to missionaries in China, when there is a perfectly proper procedure if they have complaints to make, namely through the Consuls under whose jurisdiction the missionaries concerned carried on their work.[112]

As early as December 1920, Armstrong hoped that the Canadian Presbyterians could press the British government into including adequate guarantees of protection for Christians in Korea and Manchuria in any treaty for the renewal of the Anglo-Japanese Alliance. He felt that this was necessary to ensure that Korean Christians were not arbitrarily brutalized by Japanese troops and that the right of missionaries to pursue their Christian work went unhampered.[113] By February 1921, Armstrong was confident that this would be achieved.[114]

Some missionaries were totally opposed to the Anglo-Japanese Alliance and felt that Japan had utilized it only to hide its own aims. In December 1920 Duncan McRae, one of the three original missionaries with Foote and Grierson, wrote to Armstrong that he had "told the Japanese authorities I am ashamed to have my country allied with a nation like Japan, who treat human beings as they treat Koreans." He further added that "through the 'Anglo-Japanese Alliance' Britain has forfeited too much of her good name, and confidence among these people [in East Asia], to satisfy the 'Prussianism' of Japan."[115] McRae believed that the Japanese had purposely engineered the Chientao intervention because they hoped to bring about the destruction of China.

In March 1921 R. W. Foote, on furlough in North America, had a meeting in New York with two Japanese officials, the Japanese Consul-General and Mr. Shirakami, Secretary to Saitō Makoto, the

Governor-General of Chōsen. The Japanese apparently expressed horror at the atrocities Foote described, but doubted "as to whether they were possible, being so contrary to Japanese nature."[116] When questioned by the Japanese, Foote was unable to give them adequate answers about the events that had forced Japan to undertake a punitive expedition into Manchuria. Moreover, Foote admitted that he had not personally seen the shootings and cremations nor the wounded Koreans. For that information, he had relied upon Korean statements as reliable.[117] In simple terms, Foote had come off badly in his interview in New York with the Japanese, and far from believing him, they probably viewed his remarks and attitudes as perniciously anti-Japanese. In their evaluations of what had happened in the Chientao region, the two sides were as far apart as ever.

There was, of course, one party that was prepared to accept the missionary accounts—the Korean patriots and their Western sympathizers. Armstrong's views on the future of Korea were just as unacceptable to them in 1921 as they had been in 1919. Armstrong was not opposed to the actual invasion of Chientao, for he believed that the colonial rulers of Korea had as much right "as Britain would have in defending her government in India by making provision in Persia or Thibet against Russians promoting sedition among Indians."[118] What Armstrong opposed was the brutality of the Japanese and their use of terrorism against the Koreans. In January 1921 he wrote to Philip Jaisohn, a leading figure in the Korean independence movement living in the United States, that he did not think Korea should gain independence in the immediate future. Instead, Armstrong felt that Korea should "attain a similar dominion status to that enjoyed by Canada or Egypt in the British Empire."[119] To Jaisohn, this position was unacceptable because he felt that it was impossible for the Japanese to treat Korea in the way that the British had treated Canada.[120] Writing in July 1921 to H. T. Owens, an American missionary in Seoul, Armstrong noted that, although he had corresponded with Syngman Rhee, who had been President of the provisional government, "as you know, I have little sympathy for the independence movement, just because I question the ability of the Koreans to govern themselves without falling into various factions as India would do if she were given complete self-government."[121] At the same time, he thought that there was a great need for the Conference on Pacific matters, which President Harding was calling for in Washington. He also believed that "undoubtedly Japan needs to adopt a Foreign policy and a colonial policy more in order with International ideas and ideals."[122] Yet, as he told F. A. McKenzie, the Anglo-Canadian journalist and a leading advocate of Korean rights, "the time has come when there must be more than courteous words of protest to the military part in Japan which has been treating the Koreans so atrociously."[123] Armstrong was obviously a moderate in his political views whose humanitarian concern for Koreans had pushed him to adopt a far from moderate position on events in Chientao.

As in 1919 the British government brought the Chientao atrocities to the attention of the Japanese government. Lord Curzon spoke to the Japanese Ambassador in London about the charges against Canadian missionaries.[124] In contrast to 1919, this time the British Foreign Office had to appear to be taking action, for at least some Canadians were not satisfied with the way that the British Consular service treated Canadian missionaries. In December 1920 S. D. Chown, a Canadian Methodist, wrote in the Toronto *Globe* that he had heard many complaints about British consuls from Canadian missionaries in China and felt that "Canadians were not given the consideration due them as a nation within the Empire."[125] Chown also gave Canadian Methodist support to the Presbyterian protest against Japanese inhumanity toward the Koreans. He believed that the methods adopted by the Japanese to oppress the Koreans "far exceed the Anglo-Saxon conception of humanitarian justice, even to a rebellious people."[126] Nor were such remarks confined to non-governmental circles.

The problem of British consular treatment of Canadian missionaries in China was brought up by Loring Christie, technical adviser to Prime Minister Arthur Meighen, in an interview with Miles Lampson at the Foreign Office in July 1921. Lampson wrote of this interview that "there was again the question of the Canadian missionaries in Chientao, that no doubt has made considerable stir in Canada but we had gone into the matter with the greatest care."[127] Christie went away reassured that Canadian missionary interests in China were not being neglected by the British consular service. However, there was a feeling among some Canadians that, if the British Foreign Office did not look after the rights of Canadians properly, then Canada should have its own representatives abroad. This was something that the Foreign Office wished to avoid.

It is clear, though, that the Canadians were well served by the British in the Chientao intervention. Winston Churchill, the Colonial Secretary, and L. S. Amery, his deputy, seemed at pains throughout 1921 to keep the Canadian government informed about this crisis through the Governor-General.[128] It was a major concern of the Foreign Office to ensure that no Canadian property was destroyed. Some churches had been destroyed, but these were found to have belonged, in accordance with the Nevius Method, to Korean Christians rather than to the Canadian Presbyterians.[129] Thus, in fact, mission property had not been damaged. According to the Foreign Office, some 7,000 Japanese troops (not the 15,000 of Martin's letter) had been involved in the

Chientao invasion.[130] By May 1921 all Japanese troops had been withdrawn into Korea, except for a very small number of officers.

In June 1921 the Foreign Office sent W. B. Cunningham to Lungchingtsun to report on conditions in Chientao and to investigate the various charges brought against the Canadian Presbyterians by the Japanese military. One of the points Cunningham made in his report was that the Mizumachi letter and the difficulties between the Japanese military and the Canadian missionaries were

> as much the result of the different personalities and character of the parties concerned as of anything else, as the somewhat rough and ready ways of the Canadian missionaries must be very liable to be misunderstood by Japanese officials with their love of formality of all kinds. At the same time there is little doubt that the military authorities while in the district acted in a most high-handed manner.[131]

Although there were personality clashes between Canadians and Japanese, Cunningham found no evidence to substantiate the charges of Colonel Mizumachi against the Canadian missionaries.

As to the Japanese military attitude toward Korean Christians in the Chientao region, Cunningham concluded that Korean Christians were undoubtedly viewed with suspicion by the Japanese and, in certain instances, they had been deliberately singled out for persecution. However, Cunningham believed that this persecution was not motivated by anti-Christian sentiments, so much as by the conviction that Korean Christians as a body were supporters of the independence movement. He noted that because of the superior education and broader outlook of many Christians, as a rule they manifested a greater interest in politics and were more patriotic than the average Korean, although he qualified this by adding that not many Christians were active partisans in the independence movement.[132]

To Cunningham, it was also clear that the Japanese had invaded the Chientao region with every intention of permanently occupying the area. Yet, as he noted, "after about a fortnight of general burning and destruction the whole thing ceased as suddenly as it had begun, probably because the Japanese found that the news of what they were doing was finding its way to the outside world."[133] It was the international protest that made them withdraw. In this context, Canadian Presbyterians have to be given considerable credit for bringing about the cessation of destruction and saving Chientao for China, albeit only for a few more years. The impression of the Foreign Office was that "if a favourable opportunity again presented itself, Japan would not hesitate to avail herself of it to add both the Chientao and Hunchun districts to her possessions" and that this "would in all probability merely whet the appetite of Japan for further conquests in Manchuria."[134] This, indeed, had been their opinion at the time of the March 1919 demonstrations in Lungchingtsun. Japanese actions in the Chientao region presaged their eventual acquisition of Manchuria.

As far as the Canadian Presbyterians were concerned, Cunningham had been "very favourably impressed with the work which missionaries were doing in Chientao, and especially that of Dr. Martin. Their withdrawal from the district would be a calamity for its Korean inhabitants."[135] Cunningham's superior, F. E. Wilkinson, the British Consul in Mukden, hoped that Cunningham's investigation would help improve relations between the Canadians and the Japanese. He believed that it would at least prevent a recurrence of any unpleasant incidents like the publication of the Mizumachi letter. However, Wilkinson also thought that "owing to the incurably suspicious trend of the Japanese mind, I have no hope that the Japanese themselves will ever be convinced that their charges against the missionaries were unfounded."[136]

The Chientao intervention is an early example of the missionaries' power to influence events in remote areas by publicizing their views in the international press and by pressing the Foreign Office. Without the Canadian missionaries in Lungchingtsun, it is very unlikely that the Japanese explanation of its actions in Chientao would have been questioned. Certainly, the intervention would not have had, as the Under-Secretary of State for External Affairs wrote to Armstrong, the "unfortunate effect which such proceedings are bound to have both in the Mother Country and in the Dominions at a time when that opinion is particularly susceptible of such matters."[137] Following hard on the heels of the atrocities committed by the Japanese in the aftermath of the March 1919 demonstrations, the Chientao crisis occurred at an inopportune time, as the Japanese and the British government were negotiating the renewal of the Anglo-Japanese Alliance. What happened in Chientao could have only contributed to Canadian public antipathy toward the renewal of the Alliance.

Canadian missionaries' attitudes toward both the 1919 demonstrations and the Chientao intervention were simple and straightforward. They wanted to protect innocent Koreans, both Christian and non-Christian, from the brutality of the Japanese military. The missionaries might have been naive in not realizing that their protests had far-reaching political implications. Armstrong might tell Philip Jaisohn that he was not opposed to Japanese colonialism, only to its oppressive methods, and that he was not an advocate of Korean independence, only of Korean greater self-government. It is very clear, however, that both those Koreans who supported the independence movement and the Japanese authorities who opposed them understood the actions of missionaries as support for the independence movement.

There is no doubt that the majority of Canadian Presbyterian missionaries in Korea were virulently anti-Japanese. In terms of the

Chientao intervention, they were certainly prepared to accept the Koreans' stories of atrocities committed by the Japanese. The Canadian Presbyterians were motivated by humanitarian feeling. As S. H. Martin wrote in February 1921, "it's pathetic to meet these poor people wandering over these cold bleak hills and plains persecuted and beaten, wounded and slaughtered like helpless sheep."[138] In this letter, Martin wrote a short poem about the desolation of Chientao; the two concluding lines were "Mankind has a country/Korea the grave."[139] This illustrates the depth of feeling that the suffering of the Koreans at the hands of the Japanese had evoked among Canadian missionaries.

The sense of outrage that this feeling engendered drove the Canadians to publicize what had happened. In his February 1921 letter, Martin told Armstrong: "I have been so busy writing to the P[eking] and Tientsin *Times* and the Kobe *Chronicle* that I didn't get time to write home. At the time of the Jap. expedition here I spent hours every day informing the Papers and British Minister at Peking by letter and telegram."[140] Martin was as zealous as Schofield had been the year before.

There is absolutely no doubt that the 28th Brigade committed atrocities against Koreans in Chientao. Since the days of fighting the Righteous Armies in north Korea before annexation, Canadians knew that the Japanese Army was quite prepared to commit atrocities against Koreans. Terrorism was one tactic the Japanese used against insurgents, and it cannot be condoned. Yet the missionaries must have realized that Korean Christians were very much involved in the independence movement. In their reports about the Chientao intervention, the missionaries revealed to the outside world only that Koreans were being brutalized and killed by the Japanese; there was no attempt to point out that the Japanese did have cause, in the light of the activities of Korean partisans, to take military steps to ensure the security of the border with Manchuria. To say that the Koreans were simply innocent victims, which is how the Canadians portrayed them, is to deny the truth of the armed struggle against the Japanese. Both the Koreans and the Japanese believed that partisan activity in Chientao following the March 1919 demonstrations was important. There was probably less anti-Japanese activity than either the Koreans or the Japanese believed. Nevertheless, the missionaries' view of events in Chientao was highly subjective, and it is legitimate to question the reliability of their reports. In a situation where their converts were being beaten, tortured, and killed by Japanese soldiers, why should missionaries be reliable chroniclers of events? Yet Canadians at home never challenged the veracity of the Presbyterians' one-sided version of the Chientao intervention.

The Chientao region was strategically very important both to Korean partisans and to the Japanese military. It was the fate of the

Canadian Presbyterians to be serving the Korean community in an area that was a battleground until 1945. In 1921 the Japanese were seen as the aggressors, but eleven years later it was different. In December 1932 E. J. O. Fraser wrote to Armstrong:

> there is a lot of disturbance in the country west of Lungchingtsun, and most of the people, Chinese and Korean, have left, and the country is pretty well deserted. Korean communists, desperate Yellows, armed, are doing a lot of slaughter among the Koreans, and in return the Japanese consular police and the soldiers are catching as many of the communists as they can, and putting an end to them.[141]

The Japanese had become the protectors of Koreans against the atrocities committed by partisans.

The antipathy of Canadian Presbyterians in Korea toward Japanese colonialism was not shared by their colleagues in Taiwan. This was the result of differing situations. While the Canadians had only a short experience of working in a Korea that was not under Japanese control, the Presbyterians in Taiwan had had a relatively long exposure to a Taiwan under Manchu rule. As modernizers whose presence would help break down the barriers of the Chinese cultural tradition, the Japanese were welcomed in 1895 when Taiwan became a Japanese colony following the Treaty of Shimonoseki. Most importantly, the Japanese colonial overlords represented law and order. At the simplest level, the missionaries welcomed the Japanese because most believed that any ruler would be better than the Manchus.

THE TAIWANESE CONTRAST

Outwardly at least, cordial and friendly relations on a personal level were maintained between missionaries and the highest officials in the Japanese administration in Taiwan. Three English Presbyterian missionaries working in southern Taiwan were decorated by the Japanese with the Order of the Rising Sun (Fifth Class). Of these, Duncan Ferguson and Thomas Barclay were decorated for their part in helping to arrange the peaceful surrender of Tainan to General Nogi in 1895.[142] The third, William Campbell, was decorated in 1915 for "efforts which have increased the intelligence and loyalty of many people in Formosa, and for some valued literary contributions on subjects relating to the Island."[143] Though these decorations were not high awards, they were an indication of the respect the Government-General accorded these Scotsmen. The esteem in which Campbell was held is clear; the Governor-General travelled to Tainan to bid him farewell when he retired in 1918 after serving 47 years as a missionary in Taiwan.[144] It was good public relations on the part of the Japanese. Canadian Presbyterian missionaries were not awarded decorations, partially because, once George Leslie Mackay had died, the Canadians did not possess missionaries of the longevity of Campbell and Barclay.

Though it is clear that missionaries realized that the Japanese sometimes treated the Taiwanese population harshly, they were often ill-informed about specific atrocities or injustices committed by the colonial authorities. There were frequent localized rebellions against the Japanese in the initial period of colonial rule. However, the Silaian Incident in the summer of 1915, which was suppressed with almost 2,000 casualties, marked the end of serious revolts. The Japanese authorities never hesitated to use the Summary Court Ordinance (*Rinjū Hōin Jorei*) in cases of revolt. This measure enabled the colonial officials to mete out a summary justice, which included the death penalty. By 1915 these methods had effectively stamped out armed resistance. In other words, the colonial authorities could be as harsh as their colleagues in the Government-General of Chōsen. The degree of violence was different, however, in the sense that Taiwan was an island with a small population. Further, the Taiwanese people did not have the strong nationalistic spirit that the Koreans most certainly possessed. This expressed itself after 1915 in the fact that the Taiwanese realized the futility of armed resistance against the Japanese colonial overlords, while the Koreans never gave up the anti-Japanese struggle. While the Canadian Presbyterians in north Korea were situated in an area in which Koreans were constantly fighting the Japanese, it has to be remembered that half of Taiwan was inhabited by aboriginal headhunters and closed to both Taiwanese and Western visitors. Though the Japanese admitted that armed punitive expeditions entered this area, what transpired there could be learned only from Japanese accounts. The absence of criticism of these punitive expeditions against the aborigines was probably due to lack of knowledge. The same must also be true of many Taiwanese rebellions before 1915. It was also rare that missionaries commented on events taking place in other parts of the Japanese Empire.

However, one event in Korea did have repercussions in Taiwan. In 1912 William Gauld in Taipeh made an interesting comment about the impact of the Korean Conspiracy Case on attitudes of young Taiwanese students in Taipeh toward Christianity:

> now more than ever they are somewhat embittered against Christianity because of that trouble in Korea. Not a few are saying that Christianity leads to anarchy; that the Christian Church resents the government by the state, in other words resents too much official oversight or (interference), that it is "a power within a power" etc. etc.[145]

It is difficult to judge what effect this sentiment had on evangelistic work. It does show, however, that some young Taiwanese supported the Japanese argument in the Korean Conspiracy Case. The fact that the case had an impact in Taiwan reveals the connection between colonialism in Taiwan and in Korea. Again, if Taiwanese Christians were known to be involved in revolutionary activity against Japanese rule, there was every reason to believe that the Taiwanese Government-General would have acted harshly against them. What happened in one colony was a warning to the other.

In January 1916 G. W. Mackay reported that a serious uprising, the Silaian Incident, had taken place in the south of the island in the previous year. He wrote: "the genesis of the outbreak of hostilities was caused by the ill treatment of the natives in a village by an over jealous [sic] policeman. The villagers who were ignorant folks could think of nothing else but how to get rid of this objectionable personage and his associates."[146] Mackay went on to describe the rebels' planning, which took place in a Buddhist temple to avoid detection; he added "some Chinese became impatient and attacked the police and the rest of the Japanese in the village killing about forty men and women."[147] Of the consequences to the villagers, he wrote: "at once soldiers were despatched to the scene, villages were burnt and hundreds of people shot. Arrest became wholesale and for months afterwards executions of the plotters were common occurrences. In all about five hundred Chinese were put to death."[148] Apparently, the Government-General's investigation of the uprising had revealed that "the people were ignorant and led to believe in magic and other black arts."[149]

It would apear that Mackay's description of the Silaian Incident was largely correct, except that his statistics on the number of Taiwanese killed was low. According to a modern source, 866 were executed after the uprising was quelled.[150] Yet it is not the killing of Taiwanese that is the main impression produced by Mackay's letter; rather, it is his concern with the quasi-religious aspects of the uprising. His relief that no Christians were involved is very apparent. Despite this, there is no doubt that the uprising had been a very serious affair in which many people were killed.

What is very surprising is the different reaction these killings provoked compared with the reaction following similar events in Korea three and four years later. A cynical view of the different reactions might be that missionaries were not prepared to publicize atrocities because no Christians were involved. Another reason was that the identification of Japanese militarism with the "Prussian machine" had not yet taken place. That the Great Was was a war fought to end militarism was not yet a commonly held notion. The Allies still looked to Japan for aid in their common struggle against Germany. Thus, criticism of Japan's conduct in its colonies was best avoided. Again, because Western attention was concentrated on the war in Europe, it was probable that few would become concerned with atrocities committed in far-off Formosa. Nevertheless, it is clear that missionaries were selective in the atrocities they publicized. Perhaps there was some reason for the Japanese authorities in Korea to be suspicious of missionary motives in March 1919. Such a response was unprecedented in the Japanese Empire, despite the fact that, as the Silaian Incident illustrated, missionaries and Westerners well knew that the Japanese treated uprisings with the sword and summary justice. That there was no protest about the Taiwan uprising and so much about the March 1 movement shows the enormous change in Western thinking that had taken place in three years.

What is also clear about Japanese rule in Taiwan is the material changes that took place. In 1912 G. W. Mackay noted that "Taiwan had all the necessary accessories that went to make up a civilized country," a great transformation from the days of his boyhood in the island.[151] Of course, it was precisely because of this modernization of Taiwan under Japanese rule that the English and Canadian Presbyterians were confronted with one of their most serious challenges.

It is, therefore, not totally surprising that, despite the material advances made under Japanese colonial rule, some missionaries noticed that the "Formosan people still regard themselves with no little sorrow, as a subject race."[152] Even so, Duncan MacLeod wrote optimistically in 1923 about the possibilities of voting rights for the Taiwanese:

> though convinced that under Japanese rule they are much more prosperous, there is still left the painful feeling that they are governed by an alien power. This feeling has been asserting itself in recent years, not through rebellion, but through the expressed hope that the Formosans may be recognized as citizens with complete franchise entitling them to share in the administration of affairs in their own native island. Steps are being taken to meet this general aspiration among the more educated and intelligent. The younger generation, however, is becoming so rapidly Japanese in manners, language and dress, through education and constant association with the Japanese, that one can readily conceive of the final merging of the two races in Formosa. The recent removal of hindrances to intermarriage will accelerate the process of assimilation.[153]

MacLeod was, of course, too optimistic about the Taiwanese receiving the franchise. Yet this optimism was not without some grounds. In 1920 a movement had been founded in Tokyo to advocate the establishment of a Taiwanese legislature which would supervise the budget of the Government-General. Indeed, in 1921, as one of his last political acts, the aged Ebara Soroku, who was a member of the House of Peers in the Imperial Diet, submitted a petition to the House of Peers calling for a Taiwanese legislature.[154] Between 1921 and 1934 the League for the Establishment of a Taiwan Parliament petitioned the Imperial Diet 15 times.[155] To the Japanese colonial administrators, and to the Japanese government, the idea of a Taiwanese Parliament was incompatible with their basic policy: Taiwan's integration with Japan.[156] As Wakatsuki Reijiro, the Japanese Prime Minister, noted in 1926, "Japan, including Formosa, is one country. There cannot be two legislative bodies."[157] It was clear to Duncan MacLeod that the Japanese policy of assimilation was achieving success.

The success of assimilation was a major reason why there was not the Canadian antipathy toward Japanese colonialism in Taiwan that there was in Korea. The Japanese were more successful colonizers in Taiwan than they were in the Korean peninsula, and the Taiwanese were relatively content under Japanese rule. This is not to say that the Japanese in Taiwan were any less brutal in putting down opposition to their rule than they were in Korea. Just as it was a testing ground for colonial policies later applied to Korea, Taiwan acted as a harbinger of the Japanese oppression in Korea after 1910. Yet the violence in Taiwan never reached the level it did in Korea in the wake of the March 1919 demonstrations. The response of Taiwanese to Japanese colonialism was different because the cultural, geographical, and political conditions in the two colonies were different.

Though the situations were different, the reaction of missionaries in the two colonies and in metropolitan Japan to the issues of democracy and imperialism sprang from the same ideological viewpoint. By the end of the Great War, missionaries in all three areas believed in democracy. By democracy they meant parliamentary democracy of the Canadian and British type. While some Canadian missionaries were anti-colonial in principle, among whom should be numbered Frank Schofield, Armstrong and MacKay in Toronto, they did not want to see Korea gain instant independence in 1919. Armstrong clearly wanted Japan to create an empire similar to Britain's with its self-governing dominions. Though his opinion might appear moderate to an extreme in light of the atrocities the Japanese had committed in Korea, there is no doubt that the majority of Canadian missionaries in Korea agreed with him. The successful achievement of democracy in Japan was seen as the means to solve the question of Japanese brutality in Korea. As Canadians, whose country had undergone a colonial experience, they felt a special sympathy for other peoples still under the yoke of colonialism. Further, they were "rough and ready," which meant that they were prepared to speak their minds. Foote and the others in Lungchingtsun were not predisposed to be polite to the Japanese. Regardless of how their actions might be interpreted by the suspicious Japanese, what the missionaries wanted was fair treatment for the Koreans.

Although the missionaries' concern for the social welfare of the people among whom they worked might well lead them to a Christian socialist political stance, their views were, by no stretch of the imagination, either radical or revolutionary. In 1919 and 1920 they were appalled by the brutality of the Japanese; their concern was a humanitarian one. But to the Japanese and the Korean nationalists their motivation was political, not humanitarian; the Canadians were identified as supporters of Korean independence. This is not what they were. What they were, instead, was naive. The danger of their actions being misinterpreted, even to the detriment of their church work, was seemingly not important. What was important was to protest the outrages committed against Koreans, regardless of the consequences to their Christian work. In their zeal to see justice in the court of international public opinion, missionaries were gullible in accepting without question Korean accounts of atrocities. Undoubtedly, whether they denied it or not, the views of the Canadian Presbyterians in Korea were coloured by their anti-Japanese feelings. The same, of course, is equally true of the Canadian Methodists in Japan, whose views of events were strongly influenced by their very positive feelings for the Japanese. And the passage of time also had an effect. In 1919, with the Great War at an end, the time was right for such a protest. While the Japanese authorities might well have been surprised by the vehemence of missionary protest in 1919, with hindsight it should not have been unexpected. Relations between the Government-General and missionaries had not been good from the time of the Conspiracy Case onwards, and the issue of educational reform had done little to bring the two sides together. The 1919 protest was in that sense a culmination of the longstanding missionary grievances against the Japanese.

Canadian Presbyterian missionaries in Korea were among the most outspoken of Western missionaries. In many ways, it was their finest hour. What was important to the future is that in 1919 and 1920, regardless of the consequences, missionaries were prepared to protest vigorously. As individuals, little harm came to them, and their protest was important in bringing about diplomatic pressure on Japan to make reforms in Korea. Nevertheless, it would be wrong to attach too much importance to the influence of this missionary protest on Canadian opposition to the continuation of the Anglo-Japanese Alliance. Still, the Chientao intervention came at a particularly bad time for those British and Japanese who wished to see the Alliance renewed. And, clearly, the Canadian government took seriously the Chientao intervention and the accusations of Colonel Mizumachi against Canadian missionaries. The Foreign Office in London and British diplomats and consuls in the field not only performed well but also served Canadian interests well. They did what they could.

The publicity missionary letters and reports received in the international press was also important in bringing international attention to Korea and the Manchurian borderland. In its turn, international public opinion was undoubtedly important in helping to convince the Japanese of the need for changes in the colonial administration of Korea. Without the presence of Canadian missionaries in Chientao, it is highly unlikely that the actions of the Japanese punitive expedition against Koreans would have attracted much outside attention. Indeed, one of the aspects of the missionary movement was that it brought remote places to the attention of ordinary people in North America. The protest against the Chientao intervention illustrates that the missionary movement could link the world just as closely in the 1920s as modern technology can link it today.

CHAPTER TEN

Toward the Future

The Canadian missionary movement in the Japanese Empire began at a time when many Canadians believed that the onward march of Western civilization made not only the Europeanization of Africa and Asia a possibility but also the Christianization of the entire world an inevitability. As the years passed, the continuation of this link between Canada and Japan took on a momentum of its own, became a captive of its own history. Despite the personal optimism of missionaries that the Christianization of the Japanese would come about in the near future, by 1931 it was apparent that the world would not become Christian.

The missionary movement did not have to justify its existence in terms of success or failure or productivity. It mattered not a whit whether Japan modernized or not as a result of missionary effort. Insofar as changes in society helped the cause of Christianity or bettered the physical, material, and spiritual lot of Japanese, such changes were welcomed. However, missionary work was undertaken as much for the benefit of the Home Church as it was for the Japanese. The history and concerns of the missionary movement in Japan were different from those of the Japanese Christian movement. It was all to the good if missionaries were able to report back to Toronto that their mission work was growing by leaps and bounds. In the final analysis, however, what mattered was the link between the Canadian churches and the expansion of Christianity in the Japanese Empire which the missionary movement provided.

The achievements of the Canadian missionary movement in the Japanese Empire between 1872 and 1931 were considerable, despite its failure to convert many people to Christianity. From small beginnings, the missionary endeavour grew to include hundreds of Canadian workers in Japan, Korea, and Taiwan. Canadian missionaries founded churches, schools, hospitals, and other specialized institutions. And the

Notes for Chapter Ten are found on p. 247.

social work of Canadians drew the attention of the Japanese authorities to hitherto neglected areas. Even in their leisure activities, Canadian missionaries had significant influence on Japanese society; they introduced the idea of the summer cottage to the Japanese and focussed interest in healthy outdoor activities like hiking, mountain-climbing, and tennis. The translation of *Anne of Green Gables* made a story of childhood in Prince Edward Island a favourite for generations of young Japanese girls. Missionaries themselves wrote books, which are still being read, about *netsuke*, Japanese Buddhism, and the history of the Korean people.

The achievements of Canadian missionaries were appreciated by the staff of the Canadian Legation in Tokyo. In a preface to a report on Canadian missionary activities prepared in 1933 for the Tokyo Legation, K. P. Kirkwood noted that the Canadian Minister and his officers realized "the profound influence of Canadian missionary activity in strengthening the international bonds and goodwill between Canada and Japan."[1]

For much of this period, the missionary movement provided the only vehicle for continuous contact between Canada and the peoples of Japan, Korea, and Taiwan. Missionaries exerted influence at an individual and personal level. As a result, their impact was cumulative rather than immediate. They linked ordinary people living in small provincial towns in the interior of Japan or rural communities in northern Korea to the outside world. They were living encyclopedias of things Western and microcosms of Canadian society. Their presence in the Japanese Empire demonstrated that Canadians cared about the welfare of East Asians. By their actions, missionaries showed the common people that they not only were sympathetic to their problems but were also prepared to strive actively to improve their material well-being. For example, they showed Japanese women that they had alternatives other than marriage. Most importantly, they revealed that Westerners shared a common humanity with Japanese.

The vast majority of missionaries came from Scottish or English stock. They were, in a real sense, overseas representatives of the Anglo-Scottish element in Canadian society. They were as Canadian as Sir John A. Macdonald, Sir Andrew MacPhail or Stephen Leacock. They were different from both Britons and Americans but did not deliberately stress their uniqueness. Since Japanese perceptions of foreigners tend to be conditioned by military and industrial power, they had a clear idea of the American and the British cultural identities but no clear concept of a separate and distinct Canadian cultural identity. What is clear is that the problem of national identity did not overly worry missionaries. The Nova Scotian Presbyterian pioneers who went to northern Korea were rugged individualists with a great zest and optimism for life. As Japanese Army officers learned in Lungchingtsun in 1921, Canadian missionaries did not mince words. It is a Canadian characteristic to stand up for the underdog and help the underprivileged. The two most well-known Canadians in postwar Japan were probably E. H. Norman and Norman Bethune, both of whom impressed the Japanese because they championed the weak. But there was certainly a number of other figures of equal stature among missionaries in Japan. As a result of the missionary movement in the Japanese Empire, there is a deep well of individuals and Canadian-founded institutions which have made significant contributions to the improvement of Japanese society.

Despite obvious achievements and failures, the lasting legacy of the Canadian missionary movement between 1872 and 1931 is a controversial one. Within ten years of the Mukden Incident, the missionary movement had voluntarily withdrawn from the Japanese Empire, and the world was on the verge of the Pacific War. In retrospect, the impact of the missionary movement appears, at first glance, to have been remarkably short-lived. And Canadian racial hatred toward the Japanese, which manifested itself in 1942 with the forced movement of Japanese-Canadians from the west coast, casts doubt on the missionaries' ability to impart understanding about and knowledge of Japan to their compatriots.

One way of putting all this in perspective is to look briefly at the Canadian missionary response to both the developing East Asian crisis of the late 1930s and the religious policies of the government. The responses of Canadians to these challenges in the late 1930s also vividly illustrate many of the strengths and weaknesses of the missionary movement prior to 1931. The key to understanding the different missionary responses to the East Asian crisis in the 1930s is the missionaries' strong sense of commitment and identification with their converts, a quality which had existed from the beginning of Canadian missionary work in the Japanese Empire. The dilemma of Japan missionaries over the beginning of the Sino-Japanese War is illustrated in a letter written in December 1937 by H. W. Outerbridge, a Kwansei Gakuin professor, to H. L. Keenleyside. Outerbridge wrote: "it was hard for us to realize this summer on the peaceful shores of Lake Nojiri that the holocaust reported in our daily papers was so closely related to us."[2] Outerbridge, who had devoted 27 years of his life to missionary work in Japan, found it difficult to take the anti-Japanese view of the Marco Polo Bridge incident of July 1937 which marked the beginning of the Sino-Japanese War. While he saw Japan's faults, he also saw its virtues and appreciated its difficulties. Professor Cyril Powles has argued that the problem the missionaries had in distinguishing between their identification with the Japanese people and support of government policies was a significant factor in weakening their "ability to act as ambassadors of the people."[3] Although this assumes that the Japanese people were opposed to their government's policies for China (which is questionable), one of the reasons why Canadians did not heed the missionaries' opinions about the East Asian crisis was their obviously pro-Japanese bias.

Missionaries in Japan were not the only missionaries who identified with their converts. This was one of the strengths of the missionary movement in Korea, and one of the reasons for its success. In late October 1945 from Lungchingtsun, Reverend Chairin Moon wrote to A. E. Armstrong: "the Christians in Kantō and Korea, especially in North Korea are waiting your missionaries because they have some trouble from the R. Movement."[4] Obviously, Moon was confident that the trouble from the Communist movement would disappear once Canadian missionaries returned to Lungchingtsun. He was so confident, in fact, that Canadian missionaries would quickly settle any problem in northern Korea that already "his soul was wandering the streets of Toronto" in anticipation of his return to Emmanuel College. In the past, Rufus Foote, William Scott, and others had always attempted to protect Korean Christians from the Japanese military or Communist partisans. Prior to 1931 missionaries had won the respect of Korean nationalists because the Canadians protested vigorously against the brutal treatment of Korean Christians by the Japanese military. By chance rather than by calculation, the Christian movement was identified with Korean nationalism.

However, it was the immediate protection of Korean Christians that concerned missionaries and not the broader issue of the Korean struggle against Japanese imperialism. This was clearly illustrated by their support of the Japanese military occupation of Chientao province in 1931 because Korean Communist partisans had been killing innocent Korea Christians.[5] This support, a volte-face from their opposition to the Japanese ten years before, ran counter to Korean nationalist feeling. It revealed that missionaries did lose touch with the forces at work in Korean society. As it turned out, the Japanese military was able to bring peace to Chientao province through much of the 1930s. Further, the completion of the Kainei (Hoiryung)-Kirin railway by the Japanese helped create considerable prosperity in this agriculturally rich region. However, once peace had come to northern Korea and Chientao, Canadian missionaries in northern Korea found themselves once again at loggerheads with the Japanese authorities, this time over the religious issue of shrine worship.

Before 1931 Canadians had been exposed to two different opinions about the Japanese. On the one hand, missionaries in Japan had stressed that the Tokyo Government was moving toward parliamen-

tary democracy. On the other, missionaries in Korea had publicized the
atrocities committed by the Japanese Army. After 1937 the missionaries in China (the most numerous of Canadian missionaries) spoke out
against Japanese aggression in China in order to defend their Christian
converts. For many Canadians, Japanese aggression in metropolitan
China was the last straw. Although missionaries in Japan argued for
fair play—they strove to explain the Japanese reasons for the policies
in China—Canadians were tired of being tolerant. In light of this, it is
highly doubtful if missionaries in Japan could have influenced Canadian opinion about the East Asian situation. After the Marco Polo
Bridge Incident, the bulk of missionary writing about the situation in
East Asia was highly critical of Japanese aggression.

In 1937, in a rare action, the Archbishop of Canterbury expressed
Western Anglican dissatisfaction by taking a public stand against
Japanese actions in China. The Japanese government then cast a
suspicious eye on the Anglican Church in Japan. A crisis was averted
only because the Japanese clergy insisted that the Nihon Seikōkai
adopt a stand of enthusiastic support for the government's position on
the China issue. After 1937, in the Nihon Seikōkai there was a very
rapid internal process of dissociation from the Church of England
(with which it had always maintained close links) and of replacing
Western bishops. The Salvation Army also came under great pressure
to sever all connections with England. Outside criticism of Japan's
China policies resulted in governmental pressure on the Japanese
Christian movement to rid itself of Western missionaries. For fear of
bringing further harm to Christian movement in Japan, the missionaries did not protest.

The exigencies of the East Asia situation were most important in
creating the conditions that caused Canadian missionaries to withdraw
from the Japan Empire before the beginning of the Pacific War. However, the 1930s also saw the coming together of various trends both in
the Christian movement and in government policies toward Christianity. Government pressure, in the form of legislation, and the implied
threat of punishment, from the thought-control police, were most
important in the creation of a single Protestant denomination (the
Nihon Kirisutokyōdan) in June 1941. Nevertheless, it is doubtful
whether the Kyōdan could have come into being so swiftly and easily
without the existence of internal opinion within the Japan Christian
movement itself which was moving toward the achievement of a similar
goal. A precondition of the success of the government-forced amalgamation of Protestant denominations was the strong movement for
church union led by the Japanese National Council of Churches. Yet in
the decade that preceded the formation of the Kyōdan, the government had an almost uncanny ability to strike responsive chords within

the Christian movement, of which the internal desire for church union was only one. By its policies, the government freed the church in Japan from real or imaginary vestiges of Western control, and it gave the Nihon Kirisutokyōdan the hope of a vital role in the expansion of Christianity in East Asia. Distaste for any form of foreign control, as well as a desire for a special role in leading the Christian movement in East Asia, had been very powerful forces in the history of the Christian movement.

Since the 1880s the missionary movement had been separated from the Japanese Christian movement. Canadian missionaries had refused to give up their control over money received from Canada. They had retained the principalships and deanships of the schools and colleges Canadians had founded. For over half a century, missionaries had maintained a privileged position free from Japanese control. In the 1930s the missionary movement paid the price for its separation from the Christian movement. Faced with pressure from the government to rid the Christian movement of Western influence, Japanese Christian leaders (who did not have the intense loyalty to individual missionaries that Hiraiwa, Ebara, and Tsuchiya had displayed) were loath to defend the need for a missionary presence in Japan. They believed that the missionary movement was no longer essential to the continuation of the Christian movement. In justifying their withdrawal, missionaries in Japan felt that their continued presence might cause either the gendarmerie to threaten Japanese Christians or the government to proscribe Christianity.

In their concern to protect the Christian movement in Japan by leaving the mission field, missionaries showed that they were prepared to sacrifice the Korean Christian movement. Traditionally, Korean Christians in Chientao and northern Korea looked to Canadian missionaries for protection. Without this protection, the Korean Christian movement was defenceless against persecution by the Japanese. The ingrained Korean hatred of the Japanese meant that the Japanese Christian leaders in charge of the Korean Church would be viewed with the greatest suspicion. Furthermore, given the acquiescence of Japan Christian leaders to the demands of their government at home, it was extremely doubtful that they would have the courage to challenge any government regulations in order to protect Korean Christians. Yet there was little missionary protest.

In the late 1930s the Japanese government's interest in the Christian movement was part of a more general concern with the mobilization of national spirit in response to increasingly critical external situations. Debate about religious change was conducted within the parameters of an entirely new set of conditions. Christian resistance to the religious policies of the government could be interpreted as opposing national solidarity during a time of crisis and foreign threat. During the late 1920s, when the Christian movement had been unified in its opposition to the religious bills of the Wakatsuki and Tanaka Cabinets, the issues had been simply ones of defending religious freedom and opposing government interference in religion. By the late 1930s, in opposing government religious policies a choice had to be made between religious principles and loyalty and patriotism to the nation. The Christian movement followed the path of least resistance. Christian leaders revealed themselves as only too human when they gave in to the pressure of nationalism and patriotism instead of standing fast on Christian principle.

The missionaries in Japan can be criticized for not taking a firmer stand against Japanese government policies on both China and religion. In that respect, they failed to follow in the footsteps of their colleagues in Korea who demonstrated greater courage. However, nothing could have prepared missionaries in the Japanese Empire for the grave challenges of the 1930s. They were the first Canadian casualties in a war the Japanese waged to prevent Western ideas from infiltrating their cultural traditions.

The missionary movement in colonial Korea was not a thing of violence (and as a result failed to retain an important role within the Korean Revolution in which violence was necessary to bring about liberation). That still unfinished revolution led to the destruction of the Korean Christian movement in the northern part of the peninsula. The example of colonial Korea bodes ill for the future of the Christian movements in Africa and Latin America. Be that as it may, the missionary movement was in the past, and should remain in the future, one of persuasion, hard work and revival. The Canadian missionary movement in the Japanese Empire had its finest hours with McDonald in Shizuoka and Cochran in Koishikawa.

Notes

PREFACE

1 Max Warren, *Social History and Christian Mission* (London: SCM Press, 1967), pp. 56, 66ff.

2 See W. P. Livingstone, *Mary Slessor of Calabar* (1915; London: Hodder and Stoughton, 1935).

3 See Stephen Neill, *A History of Christian Missions* (Harmondsworth: Penguin Books, 1971), pp. 333ff. Numerous books have been written on Hudson Taylor; his own autobiography remains a classic missionary account: James Hudson Taylor, *To China . . . with Love* (Minneapolis: Dimension Books, n.d.).

4 The writings of the Bickersteth family on British Anglican work in Japan include: Samuel Bickersteth, *Life and Letters of Edward Bickersteth, Bishop of South Tokyo* (London, 1899); Mrs. Edward Beckersteth, *Japan* (London: Mowbray 1908); May Bickersteth, *Japan as We Saw It* (London: Sampson Low, 1893).

5 George Leslie Mackay, *From Far Formosa: The Island, Its People*, ed. J. A. Macdonald (Chicago: Fleming H. Revell, 1896), p. 6n.

6 Rosalind Goforth, *Goforth of China* (1937; Minneapolis: Dimension Books, n.d.). For Mackay's influence on Goforth's decision to become an overseas missionary, see pp. 28-29.

7 Elizabeth A. McCully, *A Corn of Wheat or the Life of Rev. W. J. McKenzie of Korea*, 2nd ed. (Toronto: Westminster Press, 1904).

8 Rosetta (Sherwood) Hall, ed., *The Life of Rev. William James Hall, M.D., Medical Missionary to the Slums of New York; Pioneer Missionary to Pyong Yang, Korea* (New York: Press of Eaton & Mains, 1897).

9 Nathaniel Burwash, *Reverend Davidson Macdonald D.D.* (Toronto: Women's Missionary Society, 1917). Following Macdonald's death in 1904, the Tokyo-based magazine, *Japan Evangelist*, published a large number of tributes in "Davidson MacDonald M.D.," *Japan Evangelist* 12, no. 3 (1905): 72-80. This says much for Macdonald's standing among missionaries in Japan, for the death of no other missionary had previously attracted such attention in the influential magazine. The independent Canadian missionary, Caroline Macdonald, was the subject of a short pamphlet: John McNab, *The White Angel of Tokyo: Miss Caroline Macdonald* (Toronto: Centenary Committee of the Canadian Churches, n.d.). Malcolm C. Fenwick, who worked as an independent Baptist missionary in Korea, wrote his own autobiography: *The Church of Christ in Corea: A Pioneer Missionary's Own Story* (New York: George H. Doran Company, 1911).

10 For example: William Elliot Griffis, *Honda, the Samurai: A Story of Modern Japan* (Boston: Congregational Sunday School and Publishing Society, 1890); *A Maker of the Orient, Samuel Robline Brown: Pioneer Educator in China, America and Japan* (New York: Revell, 1902); *Verbeck of Japan: A Citizen of No Country* (New York and Chicago: Revell, 1900); *Hepburn of Japan and His Wife and Helpmates* (Philadelphia and New York: Westminster Press, 1913).

11 Munro Scott, *McClure: The China Years* (Markham: Penguin Books, Canada, 1979); Stephen Endicott, *James G. Endicott: Rebel in China* (Toronto: Univ. of Toronto Press, 1980).

12 Richard Rutt, *James Scarth Gale and His History of the Korean People* (Seoul: Royal Asiatic Society, Korea Branch in conjunction with Taewon Publishing Company, 1972).

13 Ushiyama Setsuai. *Kirisutokyō shinkō dendō shi: Wara Chōrō, dendō no kiseki* (Nagano: Ginga Shobō, 1980); W. Howard Norman, *Nagano no Noruman*, trans. H. Hirabayashi (Tokyo: Fukuinkan, 1965).

14 Austin Fulton, *Through Earthquake, Wind and Fire: Church and Mission in Manchuria, 1867-1950* (Edinburgh: The Saint Andrew Press, 1967).

15 See, for example, Iida Hiroshi, *Shizuoka ken eigaku shi* (Tokyo: Kodansha, 1967).

16 *Basis of Union in Japan Agreed Upon by the Joint Commission Representing the Methodist Episcopal Church, the Methodist Episcopal Church, South and the Methodist Church, Canada* (Buffalo, 1906).

17 Nihon seikōkai rekishi hensan iinkai hen, *Nihon Seikōkai hyakunen shi* (Tokyo: Nihon Seikōkai kyōmuin bunshokyoku, 1959).

18 Kuranaga Takashi, *Kanada Mesojisuto Nihon dendō gaishi* (Tokyo: Kanada Gōdō Kyōkai, Senkyōshikai, 1937).

19 See, for instance, the recent history of Japanese Protestantism: Dohi Akio, *Nihon Purotesutanto Kirisutokyōshi* (Tokyo: Shinkyō Shuppansha, 1982).

20 See *Proceedings of the General Conference of Protestant Missionaries in Japan Held in Osaka, Japan, 1883* (Yokohama: Meiklejohn, 1883).

21 See *Proceedings of the General Conference of Protestant Missionaries in Japan, 1900* (Tokyo: Methodist Publishing Co., 1901).

22 Wilburn T. Thomas, *Protestant Beginnings in Japan: The First Three Decades 1859-1889* (Tokyo and Rutland, Vt.: Charles E. Tuttle Company, 1959).

23 Charles W. Iglehart, *A Century of Protestant Christianity in Japan* (Tokyo: Charles E. Tuttle, 1959); Richard H. Drummond, *A History of Christianity in Japan* (Grand Rapids, Mich.: William B. Eerdmans Publishing Company, 1971).

24 K. S. Latourette made the transition from missionary in China to professor at Yale.

25 Max Warren, *The Missionary Movement from Britain in Modern History* (London: SCM Press, 1965); Warren, *Social History and Christian Mission*.

26 Warren, *Social History and Christian Mission*, p. 11.

27 Stephen Neill, *Colonialism and Christian Mission* (London: Lutterworth Press, 1966).

28 George Shepperson and Thomas Price, *Independent African—John Chilembwe and the Origins, Setting and Significance of the Nyasaland Native Rising of 1915* (Edinburgh: Edinburgh Univ. Press, 1958).

29 See Neill, *Colonialism and Christian Mission*.

30 Paul A. Varg, *Missionaries, Chinese and Diplomats: The American Protestant Missionary Movement in China, 1890-1952* (Princeton: Princeton Univ. Press, 1958).

31 John King Fairbank, ed., *The Missionary Enterprise in China and America* (Cambridge, Mass.: Harvard Univ. Press, 1974), p. 19.

32 Paul A. Cohen, *China and Christianity: The Missionary Movement and the Growth of Chinese Antiforeignism, 1860-1870* (Cambridge, Mass.: Harvard Univ. Press, 1963); Ellsworth C. Carlson, *The Foochow Missionaries, 1847-1880* (Cambridge, Mass.: Harvard Univ. Press, 1974); Irwin T. Hyatt, Jr., *Our Ordered Lives Confess: Three Nineteenth Century American Missionaries in East Shantung* (Cambridge, Mass.: Harvard Univ. Press, 1976).

33 James Reed, *The Missionary Mind and American East Asia Policy 1911-1915* (Cambridge, Mass.: Harvard Univ. Press, 1983).

34 Valentin H. Rabe, *The Home Base of American China Missions, 1880-1920* (Cambridge, Mass.: Harvard Univ. Press, 1978).

35 Jesse Gregory Lutz, *China and Christian Colleges, 1850-1950* (Ithaca, N.Y.: Cornell Univ. Press, 1971).

36 Jane Hunter, *Gospel of Gentility: American Women Missionaries in Turn-of-the-Century China* (New Haven and London: Yale Univ. Press, 1984).
37 Robert S. Schwantes, *Japanese and Americans: A Century of Cultural Relations* (1955; Westport, Conn.: Greenwood Press, 1976).
38 F. G. Notehelfer, *American Samurai: Captain L. Janes and Japan* (Princeton: Princeton Univ. Press, 1985); Edward R. Beauchamp, *An American Teacher in Early Meiji Japan* (Honolulu: Univ. Press of Hawaii, 1976).
39 Hazel J. Jones, *Live Machines: Hired Foreigners and Meiji Japan* (Vancouver: Univ. of British Columbia Press, 1980).
40 Ardath W. Burks, *The Modernizers: Overseas Students, Foreign Employees, and Meiji Japan* (Boulder: Westview Press, 1985).
41 Notehelfer, *American Samurai*, p. 5.
42 Irwin Scheiner, *Christian Converts and Social Protest in Meiji Japan* (Berkeley: Univ. of California Press, 1970).
43 See, for example, John F. Howes, "The Non-Church Christian Movement in Japan," *Transactions of the Asiatic Society of Japan* third series, 5 (December 1957): 119-37; John F. Howes, "Japan's Enigma: The Young Uchimura Kanzo" (unpublished Ph.D. thesis, Columbia Univ., 1965).
44 See, for example, Ōta Yuzō, *Uchimura Kanzō—sono sekaishugi to Nihonshugi o megute* (Tokyo: Kenkyūsha Shuppan, 1977); Ōta Yuzō, *Taiheyō no hashi to shite Nitobe Inazō* (Tokyo: Misuzu Shobō, 1986); Carlo Caldarola, *Christianity: The Japanese Way* (Leiden: E. J. Brill, 1979).
45 Fred G. Notehelfer, "Ebina Danjō: A Christian Samurai of the Meiji Period," *Papers on Japan* 2 (August 1963), and *Kōtoku Shūsui: A Portrait of a Japanese Radical* (Cambridge: Cambridge Univ. Press, 1971).
46 Cyril Hamilton Powles, *Victorian Missionaries in Meiji Japan, the Shiba Sect: 1873-1900*, Publication Series vol. 4, no. 1 (Toronto: Univ. of Toronto–York Univ. Joint Centre on Modern East Asian Studies, 1987). See also Cyril Hamilton Powles, "Victorian Missionaries in Meiji, Japan: The Shiba Sect 1873-1900" (Ph.D. thesis, Univ. of British Columbia, 1968).
47 William Scott, *Canadians in Korea: Brief Historical Sketch of Canadian Mission Work in Korea: Part One, To the Time of Church Union* (Toronto: United Church of Canada Board of World Mission, 1970); Gwen R. P. Norman and W. Howard Norman, *One Hundred Years in Japan: A History of the Canadian Methodist and United Church of Canada Missions in Japan, 1873-1973*, 2 vols. (Toronto: United Church of Canada Board of World Missions, 1981).

INTRODUCTION

1 Sir Herbert Marler to Secretary of State for External Affairs, May 22, 1936, RG 25 G1, vol. 1668, file 537, Public Archives of Canada, Ottawa (hereafter cited as PAC).
2 M. S. Gewurtz and P. M. Mitchell, "Canadians and East Asia: The Missionary Experience" (typescript, dated 1981), p. 1.
3 See Matsuzawa Hiroaki, "History and Prospect of Canada-Japan Relations: Through My Personal Experiences," *Hokudai Hōgaku Ronshū* 36 (October 1985): 623-40, 643-44.
4 Cyril H. Powles, "The Development of Japanese-Canadian Relations in the Age of Missionary Activity, 1873-1930," *Kanada Kenkyū Nempō/Annual Review of Canadian Studies* (Tokyo, 1980): 146-65; Matsuzawa, "History and Prospect," pp. 632-33.
5 Scheiner, *Christian Converts*, p. 30.
6 Ibid.
7 Matsuzawa, "History and Prospect," p. 632.
8 Lutz, *China and Christian Colleges*, p. 89.
9 *Fifty-Seventh Annual Report of the Missionary Society of the Methodist Church of Canada* (Toronto: Methodist Church of Canada, 1882), p. xxxi.

10 Powles, "Victorian Missionaries in Meiji Japan," p. 220.

11 Ibid., abstract. For a discussion of the different reactions of Anglicanism compared with other denominations to Japanese culture and society, see Powles, *Victorian Missionaries in Meiji Japan*, pp. 1-18.

12 E. Wood and I. Taylor to G. Cochran, January 3, 1873, HIS G4, folder 190, United Church of Canada Archives, Victoria College, University of Toronto, Toronto (hereafter cited as UCCA).

13 *Uchimura Kanzō eibun shosaku zenshū, The Japan Christian Intelligencer*, vol. 4, with notes and comments by Taijiro Yamamoto and Yoichi Muto (Tokyo: Kyobunkwan, 1972), pp. 25-29.

14 M. S. Murao and W. H. Murray Walton, *Japan and Christ: A Study in Religious Issues* (London: Church Missionary Society, 1928), p. 141.

15 Arthur J. Brown, *The Mastery of the Far East* (New York: Scribner's Sons, 1919), p. 660.

16 John R. Mott, *Addresses and Papers*, vol. 2 (New York, 1941), p. 437.

17 Kozaki Hiromichi, *Reminiscences of Seventy Years: The Autobiography of a Japanese Pastor*, trans. Nariaki Kozaki (Tokyo: Kyobunkwan, 1934), passim, especially pp. 364-74.

18 The attitude of many Japanese toward Japanese Christians in the late nineteenth century might be likened to the attitude of many Canadians to Hare Krishna adherents in the late 1960s.

19 Tsunakawa Banri, *Ebina Danjō, Uemura Masahisa: Nihon no daihyōteki Kirisutosha 2* (Tokyo: Tōkai Daigaku Shuppankai, 1965), p. 178.

20 Dohi Akio, "Christianity and Politics in the Taisho Period of Democracy," *Japanese Religions* 7, no. 3 (July 1972): 42-68, especially 42.

21 Ibid., pp. 52-53. See also Yoshino Sakuzō, "Demokurashi to Kirisutokyō," in Takeda Kyoko, ed., *Gendai Nihon Shisō Taikei*, vol. 6: *Kirisutokyō* (Tokyo: Chikuma Shobō, 1975), pp. 236-41.

22 Dohi, "Christianity and Politics," p. 64.

23 Sumiya Mikio, *Nihon no shakai shisō: kindaika to Kirisutokyō* (Tokyo: Tokyo Daigaku Shuppankai, 1968), p. 16.

24 Kano Masanao, *Nihon no rekishi 27: Taishō Demokurashii* (Tokyo: Shōgakukan, 1976), pp. 329-30.

25 Drummond, *A History of Christianity in Japan*, p. 227.

26 Cyril H. Powles, "Abe Isoo and the Role of Christians in the Founding of the Japanese Socialist Movement, 1895-1905," *Papers on Japan*, vol. 1 (Cambridge, Mass., 1961), pp. 89-109, especially p. 102.

27 Kagawa was the subject of a number of sympathetic hagiographic monographs written by missionaries which established his undoubted high reputation in Europe and North America. One of the most important of these was William Axling, *Kagawa* (London: Student Christian Movement Press, 1932).

28 One of the most influential books in making Caroline Macdonald's name well known in Western Christian circles was Caroline Macdonald, trans., *A Gentleman in Prison: With the Confessions of Tokichi Ishii Written in Tokyo Prison* (London: Student Christian Movement, 1923).

CHAPTER ONE

1 See H. H. Walsh, *The Christian Church in Canada* (Toronto: Ryerson Paperbacks, 1968), p. 214. The overseas mission work of the Presbyterian Church in Canada was still carried on separately by the two divisions of the Presbyterian Church until 1909. The Eastern Division (Maritimes) opened missions in British Guiana in 1885 and in Korea in 1898. The Western Division (Ontario and Quebec) began missions in Indian in 1877, Honan (China) in 1888, and in South China in 1901.

2 In 1891 the Canadian Methodists began their West China mission in Szechuan; it became the largest overseas mission of the Canadian Methodist Church.

3 Walsh, *The Christian Church in Canada*, p. 208. The British Anglican Society for the Propagation of the Gospel in Foreign Parts (SPG) continued to support mission work in Western Canada until the beginning of the Second World War.

4 Ibid., pp. 264-85 passim.

5 Not until the advent of the Laurier Government in 1896, some ten years after the completion of the Canadian Pacific Railway, did the migration of people into the vacant spaces of western Canada become important.

6 Walsh, *The Christian Church in Canada*, p. 8.

7 In the 1890s the Japanese leadership of the Kumiai Church outnumbered the American Congregationalist missionaries in the various committees and assemblies of the Church, with the result that the Japanese could decide how to manage Dōshisha College whose buildings and facilities had been given by American donors for the furtherance of Christian education in Japan (Albert Carman, *Report of the General Superintendant's Official Visit to the Mission in Japan, April to June 1898* [Toronto: Methodist Book and Publishing House, 1898], pp. 14-15). For a Japanese view of the Dōshisha controversy, see Kozaki, *Reminiscences of Seventy Years*, pp. 98-117 passim.

8 Walsh, *The Christian Church in Canada*, pp. 290-91.

9 Information concerning the structure of the Japan Methodist Church comes from *Basis of Union in Japan Agreed Upon by the Joint Commission Representing the Methodist Episcopal Church, the Methodist Episcopal Church, South, and the Methodist Church, Canada* (Buffalo, N.Y., 1906).

10 John G. Waller, *Our Canadian Mission in Japan* (Toronto: Joint Committee on Summer Schools and Institutes of the Church of England in Canada, 1930), p. 18.

11 Stephen Neill, *The Cross over Asia* (London: Canterbury Press, 1968), p. 62.

12 A. Sutherland to Mrs. J. Gooderham, January 17, 1882, H11d-e, United Church of Canada Archives (hereafter cited as UCCA). Two books are useful for the detailed history of the Canadian Methodist WMS: H. E. Platt, *The Story of the Years, 1881-1906* (Toronto: Woman's Missionary Society of the United Church of Canada, 1930), and Mrs. F. C. Stephenson, *One Hundred Years of Canadian Methodist Missions, 1824-1924*, 2 vols. (Toronto: Missionary Society of the Methodist Church, 1925). Both Canadian Methodists and Presbyterians referred to their women's missionary societies as WMS. To avoid confusion, the designations WMS-CM and WMS-CP have been used.

13 Longevity of service of mission secretaries was not unusual. Alexander Sutherland was General Secretary of the Missionary Society of the Methodist Church of Canada between 1878 and 1910. R. P. MacKay was the Foreign Missions Secretary of the Presbyterian Church of Canada between 1892 and 1926.

14 The co-operation between Canadian Presbyterians and American missionary societies in Korea also meant Canadian involvement with the interdenominational Commission on Relations with the Orient of the Federal Council of the Churches of Christ, which played an influential part in expressing the protests of North American churches against Japanese actions in the aftermath of the March 1, 1919, independence demonstrations in Korea.

15 Walsh, *The Christian Church in Canada*, p. 279.

16 Alvyn J. Austin, *Saving China: Canadian Missionaries in the Middle Kingdom 1888-1959* (Toronto: Univ. of Toronto Press, 1986), p. 99.

17 Andrew Thomson, *The Life and Letters of Rev. R. P. MacKay: A Record of Faith, Friendship and Good Cheer* (Toronto: Ryerson Press, 1932). Robert MacKay came from Zorra and as a boy attended the same church and school as the slightly older George Leslie Mackay.

18 For American missionary logistics see Valentin H. Rabe, "Evangelical Logistics: Mission and Support and Resources to 1920," in John King Fairbank, ed., *The Missionary Enterprise in China and America* (Cambridge, Mass.: Harvard Univ. Press, 1974), pp. 56-90.

19 No documentary evidence was found relating to the foundation of any of the missions under discussion in which the matter of the future maintenance cost of the proposed mission after its initial establishment was discussed.

20 The main factor in the acceptance or rejection of prospective candidates for the Japanese Empire was seemingly whether the Missionary Society had the funds to support them. A few missionaries were self-supporting, and this helped to increase numbers. J. McQueen Baldwin, a graduate of Wycliffe College, who served as a Canadian Anglican missionary between 1889 and 1922 was one. There were always more self-supporting women missionaries than male.

21 Yamanashi Eiwa Gakuin shi hensan iinkai, *Yamanashi Eiwa Gakuin hachijū nen shi* (Kofu: Yamanashi Eiwa Gakuin, 1969), p. 29.

22 Alexander Sutherland, *Methodist Church and Missions in Canada and Newfoundland: A Brief Accout of the Methodist Church in Canada, What It Is and What It Has Done* (Toronto: Young People's Forward Movement for Missions, 1906), p. 220.

23 *The Christian Guardian*, October 16, 1872. See also Shizuoka Eiwa Jo Gakuin Hachijūnenshi hensan iinkai, *Shizuoka Eiwa Jo Gakuin hachijūnen shi* (Shizuoka: Shizuoka Eiwa Jo Gakuin, 1971), p. 3.

24 *Wesleyan Missionary Notices* 17 (November 1872): 258.

25 Ibid.

26 For bibliographical details about McDonald see "Davidson Macdonald M.D.," *Japan Evangelist* 22, no. 3 (March 1905): 72-80.

27 Nihon Seikōkai rekishi hensan iinkaihen, *Nihon Seikōkai hyakunen shi*, p. 146.

28 Details of early Canadian Anglican missionaries can be found in Ushiyama, *Kirisutokyō shinkō dendō shi*, pp. 33-39.

29 Tōyō Eiwa Jo Gakuin hyakunen shi hensan jikkō iinkai, *Tōyō Eiwa Jo Gakuin hyakunen shi* (Tokyo: Tōyō Eiwa Jo Gakuin hyakunen shi hensan jikkō iinkai, 1984), p. 13.

30 Constitution of the WMS-CM in *First Annual Report of the Woman's Missionary Society* 1 (1881): 32.

31 A. Sutherland to Mrs. J. Gooderham, January 17, 1882, H11 d7 (UCCA).

32 Tōyō Eiwa Jo Gakuin hyakunen shi, *Tōyō Eiwa Jo Gakuin hyakunen shi*, pp. 48-49.

33 Ibid., pp. 52-53.

34 Ushiyama, *Kirisutokyō shinkō dendō shi*, pp. 35-39.

35 William Scott, *Canadians in Korea*, p. 67.

36 Mackay, *From Far Formosa*, pp. 300-302. See also Austin, *Saving China*, pp. 31-32.

37 Kuranaga Takashi, *Hiraiwa Yoshiyasu den* (Tokyo: Kyobunkwan, 1939), p. 42.

38 Rutt, *James Scarth Gale*, pp. 65-66.

39 L. G. Paik, *A History of Protestant Missions in Korea 1880-1910*, 2nd ed. (Seoul: Yonsei Univ. Press, 1971), p. 190.

40 Fenwick, *The Church of Christ in Corea*.

41 Sherwood Hall, *With Stethoscope in Asia: Korea* (McLean, Va: MCL Associates, 1978), p. 10 passim.

42 Paik, *History of Protestant Missions in Korea*, p. 213.

43 James Scarth Gale, *Korean Sketches* (New York: Fleming H. Revell, 1898), p. 253. The high regard in which other missionaries in Korea held McKenzie can be seen in the obituary by G. H. Jones, "Rev. William J. McKenzie: A Memoir," *Korean Repository* 2 (August 1895): 295-98. In the last months of his life McKenzie wrote one of the few contemporary English-language descriptions of the Tonghak Rebellion: "Seven Months among the Tong Haks," *Korean Repository* 2 (June 1895): 201-208.

44 Paik, *History of Protestant Missions in Korea*, p. 277.

45 Ibid.

46 Ibid., p. 206.

47 See, for instance, Fulton, *Through Earthquake, Wind and Fire*, pp. 27-31.

48 These treaties signed in 1858 and 1860 respectively allowed for missionary residence in the treaty ports in the interior of China.

CHAPTER TWO

1 Inoue Kiyoshi, *Nihon no rekishi 20: Meiji Ishin* (Tokyo: Chuōkoron, 1974), p. 247.

2 See Komura Jutarō, "My Autobiography," handwritten 10-page manuscript dated

1874, Box 17, William Elliot Griffis Special Collection, Rutgers University, New Brunswick, New Jersey, U.S.A. (hereafter cited as WEGC).

3 Matsuzawa Hiroaki, "Japanese Civilization as Viewed by Japanese Intellectuals," 22-page typescript in the possession of the author, p. 2.

4 Ibid., p. 4.

5 Jones, Live Machines, p. 5.

6 Schwantes, Japanese and Americans, pp. 193-94. See also Sugii Mutsurō, "Yokoi Saheida to Yokoi Daihei no Amerika ryūgaku: Oranda Kaiseiha kyōkai senkyōshi Ferubeki no katsudō," Shakai Kagaku, 11 (1970): 1, 110, 84-85.

7 For William Wheeler, see Watanabe Masao, "Wm. Wira: W. S. Kuraku no wakiyaku," in Nihon Kagakushi Kenkyū, no. 109 (1974): 26-31.

8 W. E. Griffis later wrote that nothing was said in his contract about religion (William Elliot Griffis, The Mikado's Empire, 9th ed. [New York: Harper and Brothers, 1899], p. 402). However, it is clear that he never attempted to propagate the Gospel outside the confines of his own house.

9 E. W. Clark to W. E. Griffis, November 27, 1871, AC 2064, WEGC.

10 Takahashi Masao, Nakamura Keiū (Tokyo: Yoshikawa Kobunkan, 1967).

11 Ibid., pp. 60-71.

12 Scheiner, Christian Converts, p. 62. For Nakamura and Confucianism, see Earl H. Kinmonth, "Nakamura Keiu and Samuel Smiles: A Victorian Confucian and a Confucian Victorian," American Historical Review 85, no. 3 (June 1980): 535-56.

13 In 1858 treaties were signed by which the Great Powers established the rights of trade and residence of Westerners at the ports of Hakodate, Kanagawa (for which Yokohama was later substituted), and Nagasaki. In 1868 Osaka and Kobe and in the next year Niigata and Tsukiji (Tokyo) were opened. The rights of freedom of worship for Westerners was stipulated in these treaties and Western clergymen were permitted to reside in the treaty ports. Westerners could obtain permission from the Japanese authorities to go outside the treaty ports for short periods, using the excuse that it was necessary for reasons of health.

14 Ōta Aito and Takaya Michio, Yokohama Bandō hanashi (Tokyo: Tsukiji Shokan, 1981), p. 71.

15 Letter from George Cochran, April 22, 1874, Wesleyan Missionary Notices 24 (August 1874): 377. A. C. Shaw, on the advice of Sir Harry Parkes, the British Minister Plenipotentiary, decided that his Anglican work should be undertaken in Tokyo (Powles, Victorian Missionaries in Meiji Japan, pp. 61-62).

16 As will be seen, the teaching of English was a very important means by which missionaries made converts.

17 For Edward Warren Clark, see A. Hamish Ion, "Edward Warren Clark and Early Meiji Japan: A Case Study of Cultural Contact," Modern Asian Studies 11, no. 4 (1977): 557-72. For a short summary of the development of the Gakumonjo school see Yamamoto Yukinori, "Shizuoka han ōyatoi gaikōkujin kyōshi E. W. Clark: Shizuoka bandō seiritsu no haike," Kirisutokyō Shakai Mondai Kenkyū 29 (March 1981): 114-56, especially 116-20.

18 Ōta, Meiji Kirisutokyō no ryūiki, p. 94. See also Shizuoka Mesojisuto Kyōkai rokujūnen shi hensan iinkai, Shizuoka Mesojisuto Kyōkai rokujūnen shi (Shizuoka: Shizuoka Mesojisuto Kyōkai, 1937), p. 5.

19 Letter from George Cochran, January 21, 1874, Wesleyan Missionary Notices 23 (May 1874): 355.

20 Ōta, Meiji Kirisutokyō no ryūiki, p. 94; Shizuoka Mesojisuto Kyōkai rokujūnen shi hensan iinkai, Shizuoka Mesojisuto Kyōkai rokujūnen shi, p. 4. In declining Cochran suggested that the Shizuoka authorities would receive a favourable response if they offered the teaching post to McDonald.

21 Fiftieth Annual Report of the Missionary Society of the Wesleyan Methodist Church in Canada in Connection with the English Conference, UCCA, p. xxxvi.

22 Ibid.

23 See John F. Howes, "Japanese Christians and American Missionaries," in Marius B.

Jansen, ed., *Changing Japanese Attitudes toward Modernization* (Princeton: Princeton Univ. Press, 1969), pp. 337-68, especially 351.
24 Takahashi, *Nakamura Keiū*, pp. 128-30.
25 Grace Fox, *Britain and Japan, 1858-1883* (Oxford: Clarendon Press, 1969), p. 522. See also Nihon Seikōkai rekishi hensan iinkai, *Nihon Seikōkai hyakunen shi*, pp. 59-60.
26 Burwash, *Reverend Davidson Macdonald, D.D.*, p. 8.
27 Thomas R. H. Havens, *Nishi Amane and Modern Japanese Thought* (Princeton: Princeton Univ. Press, 1970), p. 72.
28 Yamamoto, "Shizuoka han ōyatoi gaikōkujin kyōshi E. W. Clark," pp. 135-36.
29 Iida, *Shizuoka ken eigaku shi*, p. 11.
30 Ōta, *Meiji Kirisutokyō no ryūiki*, p. 12.
31 Yamamoto, "Shizuoka han ōyatoi gaikōkujin kyōshi E. W. Clark," p. 122.
32 Edward Warren Clark, *Life and Adventures in Japan* (New York: American Tract Society, 1878), pp. 41-42.
33 Takahashi, *Nakamura Keiū*, pp. 53-114.
34 Iida, *Shizuoka ken eigaku shi*, p. 28.
35 Shizuoka Mesojisuto Kyōkai rokujūnen shi, *Shizuoka Mesojistuto Kyōkai rokujūnen shi*, p. 5.
36 Ibid., p. 6.
37 Ibid., pp. 6-7; Iida, *Shizuoka ken eigaku shi*, p. 30. The textbooks McDonald used included G. P. Quackenbos' *Natural Philosophy*, Tyler's *Elements of General History*, Gray's *Botany*, and Roscoe's *Chemistry*. For the use of Canadian textbooks for English-language training and science, see Ōta, *Kirisutokyō no ryūiki*, p. 95.
38 Ibid., p. 97.
39 John W. Saunby, *The New Chivalry in Japan: Methodist Golden Jubilee, 1873-1923* (Toronto: The Missionary Society of the Methodist Church, 1923), p. 63; Shizuoka Mesojisuto Kyōkai rokujūnen shi, *Shizuoka Mesojistuto Kyōkai rokujūnen shi*, p. 12.
40 Ōta, *Kirisutokyō no ryūiki*, pp. 68, 67-69.
41 Kuranaga, *Kanada Mesojisuto Nihon dendō gaishi*, pp. 94-95.
42 Matsuzawa Hiroaki, "Kirisutokyō to chishikijin," in Iwanami Kōza, *Nihon Rekishi 16, Kindai 3* (Tokyo: Iwanami Shoten, 1976), passim.
43 Ōta, *Kirisutokyō no ryūiki*, p. 68.
44 Letter from Davidson McDonald, October 1, 1874, *Missionary Notices*, third ser. (January 1875): 7.
45 Henry Satoh, *My Boyhood: A Reminiscence*, 2nd ed. (Tokyo: Japan Times Publishing Co., 1921), p. 79.
46 Ōta, *Kirisutokyō no ryūiki*, pp. 98-99.
47 Fukamachi Masakatsu, *Nihon Kirisutokyōdan Shizuoka Kyōkai hachijūgonen shi* (Shizuoka: Shizuoka Kyōkai, 1959), pp. 3-4.
48 Letter from Davidson McDonald, October 1, 1874, *Missionary Notices*, third ser. (January 1875), p. 8.
49 Letter from Davidson McDonald, *Missionary Notices*, third ser., no. 2 (April 1876): 382-83.
50 Ōta, *Kirisutokyō no ryūiki*, p. 103.
51 Iida, *Shizuoka ken eigaku shi*, p. 53.
52 Letter from Davidson McDonald, April 7, 1876, *Missionary Notices*, third ser., no. 4 (August 1876), p. 150.
53 Yamamoto Yukinori, "Yamaji Aizan to kirisutokyō: Meiji Nijūnendai o chushin to shite," *Kirisutokyō Shakai Mondai Kenkyū* 26 (December 1977): 102-62, especially 109.
54 Ibid., p. 109.
55 Letter from Davidson McDonald, March 1875, *Missionary Notices*, third ser., no. 3 (June 1875): 46.
56 *Fifty-Fourth Annual Report of the Missionary Society of the Methodist Church of Canada*, p. xxxi.
57 Letter from Davidson McDonald, November 22, 1875, *Missionary Notices*, third ser. (March 1876): 91.

58 Ibid.
59 Amenomori (Matsubara) Nobushige to W. E. Griffis, July 23, 1876, WEGC.
60 Ibid.
61 *Fifty-Second Annual Report of the Missionary Society of the Methodist Church of Canada,*
    p. xxxvi.
62 Matsuzawa, "Kirisutokyō to chishikijn," p. 291.
63 Letter from Davidson McDonald, November 22, 1875, *Missionary Notices,* third ser.
    (March 1876): 91.
64 Shizuoka Mesojisuto Kyōkai rokujūnen shi, *Shizuoka Mesojistuto Kyōkai rokujūnen shi,*
    pp. 7-8.
65 Letter from Davidson McDonald, March 1875, *Missionary Notices,* third ser., no. 3
    (June 1875): 46.
66 Ibid.
67 Shizuoka Mesojisuto Kyōkai rokujūnen shi, *Shizuoka Mesojistuto Kyōkai rokujūnen shi,*
    p. 8; Iida, *Shizuoka ken eigaku shi,* p. 31.
68 Burwash, *Reverend Davidson Macdonald D.D.,* p. 12.
69 Beauchamp, *An American Teacher in Early Meiji Japan,* pp. 53-54.
70 *Fifty-Second Annual Report of the Missionary Society of the Methodist Church of Canada,*
    p. xxxviii.
71 A. Sutherland to G. Cochran, April 18, 1976, Sutherland Letter Book H11 d, UCCA.
72 Saunby, *The New Chivalry in Japan,* pp. 70-73.
73 A. Sutherland to G. Cochran, February 8, 1878, Sutherland Letter Book H11 d3,
    UCCA.
74 Hiraiwa Yoshiyasu, "The Relation of Rev. George C. Cochran D.D. to the Ushigome
    Church," typescript, H13 F4, UCCA.
75 Shizuoka Mesojisuto Kyōkai rokujūnen shi, *Shizuoka Mesojistuto Kyōkai rokujūnen shi,*
    p. 20.
76 Fukamachi, *Nihon Kirisutokyōdan Shizuoka Kyōkai hachijūgonen shi,* p. 6.
77 Iida, *Shizuoka ken eigaku shi,* p. 48.
78 Shizuoka Mesojisuto Kyōkai rokujūnen shi, *Shizuoka Mesojistuto Kyōkai rokujūnen shi,*
    p. 45.

CHAPTER THREE

---

1 Kuranaga, *Hiraiwa Yoshiyasu den,* pp. 21-23.
2 Takahashi, *Nakamura Keiū,* p. 128. For the founding of the Evangelical Alliance in
   Japan, see S. R. Brown to J. M. Ferris, December 5, 1878, Box 747.4N, in Archives of
   the Japan Mission of the Reformed Church of America, Gardiner Sage Library, New
   Brunswick Theological Seminary, New Brunswick, New Jersey, U.S.A. (hereafter
   cited as AJMRCA).
3 Letter from G. Cochran, April 22, 1874, *Wesleyan Missionary Notices* 24 (August 1874):
   377.
4 Ibid.
5 Scheiner, *Christian Converts,* p. 62. In 1875 Nakamura annotated the Chinese text of
   Martin's book for Japanese readers (Takahashi, *Nakamura Keiū,* pp. 136-37).
6 Ogihara Takahashi, *Nakamura Keiū to Meiji keimō shisō* (Tokyo: Waseda Daigaku
   Shuppanbu, 1984), p. 214.
7 Kuranaga, *Hiraiwa Yoshiyasu den,* p. 260.
8 Ogihara, *Nakamura Keiū to Meiji keimō shisō,* p. 215.
9 See Ion, "Edward Warren Clark," pp. 557-72, 564-65.
10 Otis Cary, *A History of Christianity in Japan,* vol. 2 (New York: Fleming H. Revell,
    1909), p. 25.
11 Ogihara, *Nakamura Keiū to Meiji keimō shisō,* p. 149.
12 Takahashi, *Nakamura Keiū,* p. 94.
13 Griffis, *The Mikado's Empire,* p. 548.
14 Takahashi, *Nakamura Keiū,* pp. 129-30.
15 Letter from G. Cochran, April 22, 1874, *Wesleyan Missionary Notices* 24 (August 1874):
    377.

16 Ibid., p. 378.
17 S. R. Brown to J. M. Ferris, February 19, 1874, Box 747.4N, AJMRCA.
18 Ibid.; for S. R. Brown and the Yokohama Band, see Ōta and Takaya, *Yokohama Bandō hanashi*, especially pp. 69-82.
19 Edward Warren Clark, *Katz Awa, Bismarck of Japan*, p. 77.
20 Letter from G. Cochran, April 22, 1874, *Wesleyan Missionary Notices* 24 (August 1874): 379.
21 Ibid.
22 As the Governor of Tokyo, Ōkubo had the legal right to persecute Japanese Christians but never did.
23 Letter from G. Cochran, April 22, 1874, *Wesleyan Missionary Notices* 24 (August 1874): 380.
24 Nihon Seikōkai rekishi hensan iinkai, *Nihon Seikōkai hyakunen shi*, p. 59.
25 Wade Crawford Barclay, *Widening Horizons 1845-95*, vol. 3 of *The Methodist Episcopal Church 1845-1939* (New York: The Board of Foreign Missions of the Methodist Church, 1957), p. 673.
26 Letter from G. Cochran, October 5, 1874, *Missionary Notices*, third ser., no. 3 (January 1875): 6.
27 *Fifty-First Annual Report of the Missionary Society of the Methodist Church of Canada*, p. xxxii.
28 Ibid.
29 Letter from G. Cochran, March 31, 1875, *Missionary Notices*, third ser., no. 3 (June 1875): 42; Kuranaga, *Hiraiwa Yoshiyasu den*, p. 20.
30 Ibid., p. 43.
31 Masaaki Kosaka, comp. and ed., *Japanese Thought in the Meiji Era*, trans. and adapted by David Abosch (Tokyo: Pan Pacific Press, 1958), pp. 64-65.
32 Minutes of the Committee of Consultation and Finance, April 1874-April 1890, H11 c10, UCCA.
33 Nihon Mesojisuto Shitaya Kyōkai rokujūnen shi hensan iinkai shusai, *Nihon Mesojisuto Shitaya Kyōkai rokujūnen shi* (Tokyo: Rekishi hensan iinkai, 1939), p. 51.
34 Ebara Sensei denki hensan iinkai hen, *Ebara Soroku Sensei den* (Tokyo: Ebara Sensei denki hensan iin kai, 1924), p. 161.
35 Letter from G. Cochran, March 22, 1876, *Missionary Notices*, third ser., no. 4 (June 1876): 125. For a description of Kawamura Isami see Edward Warren Clark, *Life and Adventures in Japan*, p. 209.
36 Kawamura Isami's mother became a leading supporter of the Canadian Methodist Mission's girls' school, the Tōyō Eiwa Jo Gakkō, which was founded in 1884. See *The Missionary Outlook* 4 (May 1886): 75. It is apparent that Kawamura's father was of very high social rank.
37 Kuranaga, *Hiraiwa Yoshiyasu den*, passim.
38 The author is grateful to Professor Jerry K. Fisher of Macalester College for this information.
39 Kuranaga, *Hiraiwa Yoshiyasu den*, p. 5.
40 Ibid., p. 23.
41 Hiraiwa, "The Relation of Rev. George Cochran D.D. to the Ushigome Church."
42 Ibid.
43 Kuranaga, *Hiraiwa Yoshiyasu den*, p. 34.
44 The author is grateful to the Rev. Iwai Hiraku of the Japanese United Church, Montreal, for providing this quotation.
45 Letter from G. Cochran, March 22, 1876, *Missionary Notices*, third ser., no. 4 (June 1876): 125.
46 *Canadian Methodist Magazine and Review* (July 1901): 91.
47 Letter from G. Cochran, March 22, 1876, *Missionary Notices*, third ser., no. 4 (June 1876):
48 Ibid., pp. 126-27.
49 Nihon Mesojisuto Shitaya Kyōkai rokujūnen shi, *Nihon Mesojisuto Shitaya Kyōkai rokujūnen shi*, p. 24.

50 Hiraiwa, "The Relation of Rev. George Cochran D.D. to the Ushigome Church."
51 Letter from Charles S. Eby, October 24, 1876, *Missionary Notices*, third ser., no. 4 (January 1877): 175.
52 Ibid.
53 Letter from G. Cochran, May 1877, *Missionary Notices*, third ser., no. 4 (September 1877): 239.
54 A. Sutherland to G. Cochran, September 8, 1877, H11 d3, UCCA.
55 A. Sutherland to G. Cochran, October 2, 1878, H11 d3, UCCA.
56 Letter from Charles S. Eby, October 24, 1876, *Missionary Notices*, third ser., no. 4 (January 1877): 175.
57 A. Sutherland to G. Cochran, October 2, 1878, H11 d3, UCCA.
58 Ibid.
59 Hiraiwa, "The Relation of Rev. George Cochran D.D. to the Ushigome Church." See also Kuranaga, *Hiraiwa Yoshiyasu den*, p. 26. In 1876 Akai Yu, a student at the Kaisei Gakkō, wrote to Margaret Griffis that "with one of my schoolmates, a pupil of Captain Janes in the Kumamoto Ei-Go-Gakkō, I go to the Christian Society, which is held every Wednesday afternoon" (Akai Yu to M. C. Griffis, December 10, 1876, AC. 2083, WEGC).
60 Letter from G. Cochran, March 22, 1876, *Missionary Notices*, third ser., no. 4 (June 1876): 127.
61 George B. Sansom, *The Western World and Japan: A Study in the Interaction of European and Asiatic Cultures* (New York: Vintage Books, 1973),. p. 472.
62 Letter from G. Cochran, May 1877, *Missionary Notices*, third ser., no. 4 (September 1877): 240.
63 Letter from G. Cochran, August 8, 1977, *Missionary Notices*, third ser., no. 4 (February 1878): 240.
64 A. Sutherland to G. Cochran, February 8, 1878, H11 d3, UCCA.
65 *Journal of Proceedings, General Conference of the Methodist Church Canada, 1874 and 1878*, p. 104.
66 Nihon Mesojisuto Shitaya Kyōkai rokujūnen shi, *Nihon Mesojisuto Shitaya Kyōkai rokujūnen shi*, p. 26.
67 Nihon Seikōkai rekishi hensan iinkai, *Nihon Seikōkai hyakunen shi*, p. 60.
68 J. S. Motoda, *Nippon Seikōkai Shi* (Tokyo: Fukosha, 1910), p. 30.
69 Unpublished letter to Secretary of the Society for the Propagation of the Gospel in Foreign Parts, December 27, 1875, quoted in Carmen Blacker, *The Japanese Enlightenment: A Study of the Writings of Fukuzawa Yukichi* (Cambridge: Cambridge Univ. Press, 1969), p. 150.
70 MSS.SPG (D.41 Asia, 1875), Shaw to SPG, Yedo, May 17 and August 30, 1875, *Mission Field* (December 1875): 357, footnoted in Fox, *Britain and Japan*, p. 522.
71 *Mission Field* (June 1877): 422, footnoted in Fox, *Britain and Japan*, p. 31.
72 Motoda, *Nippon Seikōkai Shi*, p. 31.

CHAPTER FOUR

1 Kuranaga, *Kanada Mesojisuto Nihon dendō gaishi*, p. 108.
2 Ebara sensei den hensan, *Ebara Soroku sensei den*, p. 203.
3 Iida, *Shizuoka ken eigaku shi*, p. 117.
4 Ibid., p. 118. For a short mid-career biographical sketch of Ebara Soroku by a Canadian Methodist missionary, see John Scott, "Hon. Soroku Ebara M.P.," *Japan Evangelist* 9, no. 2 (1902): 42-46.
5 The author is grateful to the Rev. Iwai Hiraku, late of the Japanese United Church, Montreal, for this information.
6 Ebara Sensei denki hensan, *Ebara Soroku Sensei den*, p. 161. Yūki Reiichirō, *Kyūbaku shinsensō no Yūki Muhimitsu* (Tokyo: Chūbunko, 1976), p. 88.
7 Scott, "Hon. Soroku Ebara M.P.," p. 42.

8 Life Sketches of Missionaries in Japan: Sketch of George Meacham, Box 4, Folder 52, H13 F, UCCA.

9 Letter from G. Meacham, October 19, 1876, *Missionary Notices*, third ser., no. 4 (January 1877): 171.

10 Ibid., p. 172.

11 Letter from G. Meacham, January 20, 1877, *Missionary Notices*, third ser., no. 4 (April 1877): 195.

12 Scott, "Hon. Soroku Ebara M.P.," p. 45.

13 Ebara sensei den hensan, *Ebara Soroku sensei den*, p. 205.

14 Ibid.

15 Kuranaga, *Kanada Mesojisuto Nihon dendō gaishi*, p. 108.

16 Nihon Mesojisuto Shitaya Kyōkai rokujūnen shi, *Nihon Mesojisuto Shitaya Kyōkai rokujūnen shi*. p. 35.

17 Kuranaga, *Kanada Mesojisuto Nihon dendō gaishi*, p. 82.

18 See A. Sutherland to G. Cochran, July 10, 1878, H11 d3, UCCA. Eby was almost perpetually in debt; two years after his arrival in Japan he was still paying off his Canadian debts. Unfortunately, Eby had the same attitude toward Mission funds as he had to his own. Eventually in 1895 Sutherland and McDonald saw to it that Eby was withdrawn from the Japan field.

19 "Interesting Journal of a Missionary Tour in Japan 1877," *Missionary Notices*, third ser., no. 3 (1877): 258.

20 Kuranaga, *Kanada Mesojisuto Nihon dendō gaishi*, p. 147.

21 Kuranaga, *Hiraiwa Yoshiyasu den*, p. 26.

22 "Interesting Journal of a Missionary Tour in Japan," p. 262.

23 Ibid., p. 263.

24 Ibid., p. 262.

25 Letter from C. S. Eby, March 7, 1878, *Missionary Notices*, third ser., no. 3 (1878): 305. 305.

26 *Minutes of the Japan Conference of the Methodist Church of Canada, 1899*, p. 16.

27 C. S. Eby to A. Carman, August 31, 1898, H13 F1, Folder 3, UCCA.

28 Ibid.

29 A. Sutherland to D. McDonald, March 10, 1880, H11 d4, UCCA.

30 *The Missionary Outlook* 1 (1880): 47.

31 *Fifty-Seventh Annual Report of the Missionary Society of the Methodist Church of Canada*, p. xi.

32 *Minutes of the Japan Conference of the Methodist Church of Canada, 1899*, p. 16.

33 The author is grateful to Dr. William J. Richardson for this information.

34 Mackay, *From Far Formosa*, p. 316.

35 Hollington K. Tong, *Christianity in Taiwan: A History* (Taipeh: China Post, 1972), p. 46.

36 Austin, *Saving China*, pp. 33-34.

37 Ibid., p. 32.

38 Duncan MacLeod, *The Island Beautiful: The Story of Fifty Years in North Formosa* (Toronto: Board of Foreign Missions of the Presbyterian Church in Canada, 1923), p. 75.

39 Yamaji Aizan, *Gendai Nippon Kyōkai shiron*, reprinted in Gendai Nihon Bungaku taike, no. 6, *Kitamura Tokoku Yamaji Aizan Shū* (Tokyo: Chikuma Shobō, 1972), pp. 223-71.

40 Ibid., p. 230.

41 Ibid., p. 231.

42 Scheiner, *Christian Converts*, p. 25.

43 Sugii Mutsurō, *Tokutomi Sohō no kenkyū* (Tokyo: Hosei Daigaku Shuppankyōku, 1977), p. 47.

44 Sumiya, *Nihon no shakai shisō*, pp. 19-20.

45 Ibid., pp. 5-9.

46 Scheiner, *Christian Converts*, pp. 41-44, especially 43.

47 Dohi, *Nihon Purotesutanto Kirisutokyōshi.*

48 There were some other Christian Bands formed in the 1870s in such places as Hirosaki, Niigata, and Tokyo, not to mention Shizuoka and Yamanashi Prefectures. It is not simply a matter of lack of records that more attention has not been paid to the other groups. It is more often a matter of denomination involved and nationality of missionary worker.

49 Ōhama Tetsuya, *Meiji Kirisutokyō kaishi no kenkyū* (Tokyo: Yoshikawa Kōbunkan, 1979).

CHAPTER FIVE

1 Kuranaga, *Hiraiwa Yoshiyasu den*, pp. 35-37.

2 Ibid., p. 5.

3 Edward S. Morse, *Japan Day by Day 1877, 1878-79, 1882-83*, vol. 1 (Boston: Houghton Mifflin, 1917), pp. 39-40.

4 Robert S. Schwantes, "Christianity versus Science: A Conflict of Ideas in Meiji Japan," *Far Eastern Quarterly* 12 (1952-53): 123-32, especially 124-25.

5 Ibid., p. 126. See also Morse, *Japan Day by Day*, vol. 2, pp. 428-29.

6 *Fifty-Seventh Annual Report of the Missionary Society of the Methodist Church of Canada*, p. xxxi. See also Schwantes, "Christianity versus Science," p. 126.

7 Letter from Y. Hiraiwa to G. Cochran, June 2, 1882, *The Missionary Outlook* 2 (September 1882).

8 Nara Shoitsuro, *Nihon YMCAshi* (Tokyo: Nihon YMCA Domei, 1968), p. 4.

9 Ibid., p. 4.

10 G. F. Verbeck, "Review of the Rikugo Zasshi," *Chrysanthemum* 1 (April 1881): 150-53. See also Sugii Mutsurō, "Kozaki Hiromichi no Tokyo dendō to Rikugo Zasshi no hakken," in Dōshisha Daigaku Jibun Kagaku Kenkyujo/Kirisutokyō Shakai Mondai Kenkyūkai hen, *Nihon no Kindaika to Kirisutokyō* (Tokyo: Shinkyō Shuppansha, 1973), pp. 131-66, especially 147.

11 "Japanese Lectures: Fukuzawa's Lecture on Religion (Delivered at Mita, Tokyo, Last Summer: Christianity a National Injury (Delivered Recently in Kioto)," trans. and condensed by Merriman C. Harris, *Chrysanthemum* 1 (1881): 392-96, especially 394.

12 Ibid., p. 394.

13 Letter from Y. Hiraiwa to G. Cochran, June 2, 1882, *The Missionary Outlook* 2 (September 1882).

14 *Fifty-Seventh Annual Report of the Missionary Society of the Methodist Church of Canada*, p. xxxi.

15 Kuranaga, *Hiraiwa Yoshiyasu den*, p. 39.

16 Ebisawa Arimichi and Ōuchi Saburō, *Nihon Kirisutokyō shi* (Tokyo: Nihon Kirisutokyōdan Shuppan Kyōku, 1970), p. 315

17 Fox, *Britain and Japan*, p. 516.

18 Kozaki, *Reminiscences of Seventy Years*, p. 373.

19 Charles S. Eby, *Christianity and Humanity: A Course of Lectures Delivered in Meiji Kuaido, Tokio, Japan, Including One Lecture Each by J. A. Ewing and J. A. Dixon* (Yokohama: Meiklejohn, 1883), p. 33.

20 Ibid., pp. ii-iii.

21 Reported in *The Missionary Outlook* 3 (July 1883): 99.

22 Charles S. Eby, *The Eastern Pioneer of Western Civilization and the Recognition Her Efforts Receive* (Yokohama, 1884).

23 Cary, *A History of Christianity*, vol. 1, p. 176. See also letter from Y. Hiraiwa to G. Meacham, August 13, 1884, *The Missionary Outlook* 4 (October 1884): 158.

24 Matsuzawa, "Japanese Civilization as Viewed by Japanese Intellectuals."

25 John D. Pierson, *Tokutomi Sohō 1863-1957: A Journalist for Modern Japan* (Princeton: Princeton Univ. Press, 1980), pp. 123-24.

26 Kozaki, *Reminiscences of Seventy Years*, p. 73.

27 Letter from Y. Hiraiwa to Mrs. G. Cochran, *The Missionary Outlook* 4 (June 1884): 96.
28 Charles S. Eby, *The Immediate Christianization of Japan: Prospects, Plans, Results* (Tokio: Japan Mail, 1884). See also Cary, *A History of Christianity*, p. 176.
29 C. S. Eby to A. Carman, August 31, 1898, H13 F1, Box 3, UCCA.
30 Ibid.
31 A. Sutherland to C. S. Eby, May 30, 1887, H11 e4, UCCA.
32 Ibid.
33 Stenographic Report of Proceedings re Japan Affairs at the Annual Meeting of the General Board of Missions of the Methodist Church, held in Montreal, October 3-11, 1895, p. 23, H13 F1, Box 2, Folder 27, UCCA.
34 Clifton J. Phillips, "The Student Volunteer Movement and Its Role in China Missions, 1886-1920," in John King Fairbank, ed., *The Missionary Enterprise in China and America* (Cambridge, Mass.: Harvard Univ. Press, 1974), pp. 91-109, especially p. 92. See also Rutt, *James Scarth Gale*, p. 10.
35 D. R. McKenzie, "Off to Japan," 8-page typescript in the possession of Miss Constance Chappell.
36 C. S. Eby to A. Carman, August 31, 1898, H13 F1, Box 3, UCCA.
37 *Sixty-Sixth Annual Report of the Missionary Society of the Methodist Church of Canada*, 1890, p. xv.
38 Dr. and Mrs W. H. H. Norman, "Japan Mission of the Methodist Church of Canada," 103-page typescript in the possession of Mrs. G. R. P. Norman, p. 88.
39 Ibid.
40 *The Missionary Outlook* 9 (November 1889): 162-63.
41 *Sixty-Sixth Annual Report of the Missionary Society of the Methodist Church of Canada*, p. xv.
42 *Minutes of the Japan Mission Conference of the Methodist Church of Canada, 1889*, p. 6, H13 g3, UCCA.
43 *The Missionary Outlook* 9 (November 1889): 162-63.
44 C. S. Eby to A. Carman, August 31, 1898, H13 F1, Box 3, UCCA.
45 A. Sutherland to G. Cochran, January 4, 1888, H22 e5, UCCA.
46 *Sixty-Fifth Annual Report of the Missionary Society of the Methodist Church of Canada, 1889*, p. xxiii.
47 Y. Hiraiwa to A. Sutherland, March 22, 1905, H11 i2, Box 3, Folder 61, UCCA.

CHAPTER SIX

1 Interview with Mrs. de Metral, C. J. L. Bates's daughter, December 1971.
2 Both Professor Cyril H. Powles and Dr. W. H. H. Norman concurred with this view in interviews.
3 British Foreign Office, FO 371/23571 1939, Public Record Office, Kew, England (hereafter cited as PRO).
4 Norman, *Nagano no Noruman*, p. 21.
5 Ibid., p. 22.
6 D. Norman to G. S. Patterson, T. E. Egerton Shore Papers, Japan Mission, Box 9, 1907-1912, H13 C1, File 170, UCCA.
7 *The Korean Repository* 5 (February 1898): 77.
8 *The Korean Review* 1, no. 11 (November 1901): 512.
9 Ibid., p. 17.
10 Norman, *Nagano no Noruman*, p. 34.
11 Ibid., p. 37.
12 Interview with the Rev. Egerton Armstrong of Montreal concerning his boyhood in Japan, October 1971.
13 The author is grateful to Professor Cyril H. Powles for this information.
14 Mrs. Hugh (Mary) Fraser, *A Diplomatist's Wife in Japan: Letters from Home to Home* (London: Hutchinson, 1899), p. 389.
15 Ibid., p. 189.
16 Ibid., p. 409.

17 Hugh L. Keenleyside, *Tokyo no sora ni Kanada no hata o: Memoirs of Hugh L. Keenleyside: Hammer the Golden Day*, trans. Iwasaki Tsutomu (Tokyo: Seimuru Shuppankai, 1984), pp. 145-58.
18 There is a monument to A. C. Shaw in Karuizawa.
19 Interview with Miss Constance Chappell, October 1971.
20 Interview with W. H. H. Norman, May 1974. There is a monument to A. P. McKenzie at Lake Nojiri.
21 *The Korean Review* 1, no. 2 (February 1901): 60.
22 Interview with Miss Constance Chappell, October 1971.
23 D. R. McKenzie to J. Endicott, September 1, 1919, H13 F1, Box 1, File 15, UCCA.
24 In 1919 the salary of YMCA workers with five to ten years' experience was $2,250, while Canadian Methodist missionaries received only $1,500 (Japan Mission, Minutes of Council Meetings, October 3-4, 1919, H13 F3, Box 3, File 43, UCCA). Under the new scales introduced in July 1920, married men with eight to fifteen years' experience received $1,900. Those in the West China Mission had to do with $1,500 (J. Endicott to D. R. McKenzie, October 13, 1920, Japan Mission, General Correspondence, 1920-1925, H13 F2, Box 2, File 16, UCCA).
25 Ibid.
26 Alan William Jones, "Herbert Hamilton Kelly S.S.M. 1860-1950: A Study in Failure (A Contribution to the Search for a Credible Catholicism)" (unpublished Ph.D. thesis, Nottingham Univ., 1971), pp. 212-13.
27 The author wishes to thank D. M. Kendrick for this information.
28 Robert Cornell Armstrong, *An Introduction to Japanese Buddhist Sects* (Toronto: Oxford Univ. Press, 1950; privately printed), p. ix.
29 Harper H. Coates with Ryugaku Ishizuka, *Honen, the Buddhist Saint: His Life and Teachings*, trans, with an historical introduction and explanatory and critical notes, 2nd ed. (Kyoto, 1925).
30 Robert Cornell Armstrong, *Just Before the Dawn: The Life and Work of Ninomiya Sontoku* (New York: Macmillan, 1912), and *Light from the East: Studies in Japanese Confucianism* (Toronto: Univ. of Toronto Press, 1914).
31 Armstrong, *An Introduction to Japanese Buddhist Sects*.
32 R. D. M. Shaw, *Enlightenment and Salvation* (London, 1930); R. D. Shaw, ed. and trans., *The Blue Cliff Record, the Hekigan Roku* (London: Michael Joseph, 1961); and R. D. M. Shaw, trans., *Hakuin Zenji, the Embossed Tea Kettle* (London: Michael Joseph, 1963).
33 Egerton Ryerson, *The Netsuke of Japan* (London: G. Bell, 1958).
34 Quoted in A. C. Hutchinson, "Autobiography of A. C. Hutchinson," typescript in the possession of Canon A. C. Hutchinson, Bristol, England.
35 Kim Man-chong, *The Cloud Dream of the Nine: A Korean Novel: A Story of the Times of the Tangs of China about 840 A.D.*, trans. James Scarth Gale with an introduction by Elspeth Keith Robertson Scott (London: Daniel O'Connor, 1922), p. x.
36 Ibid., p. xi.
37 James Scarth Gale's *The History of the Korean People* (Seoul: Christian Literature Society, 1927) first appeared in serial form in the *Korean Mission Field*, a monthly magazine published in Seoul between July 1924 and September 1927.
38 James Scarth Gale, comp., *A Korean-English Dictionary* (Yokohama: Kelly and Walsh, 1897).
39 Rutt, *James Scarth Gale*, p. 27.
40 Ibid., pp. 379-83; Harry A. Rhodes, ed., *The History of the Korean Presbyterian Church U.S.A. 1884-1934* (Seoul: Chōsen Mission Presbyterian Church U.S.A., 1935), pp. 411-13.
41 Yamamoto Yukinori, "Rikugō Zasshi to Hiraiwa Yoshiyasu," in Dōshisha Daigaku Jibun Kagaku Kenkyūjo hen, *Rikugō Zasshi no kenkyū*, vol. 1 (Tokyo: Kyobunkan, 1984), pp. 233-75, especially p. 252.
42 George C. Allen, *Appointment in Japan: Memories of Sixty Years* (London: Athlone Press, 1983), p. 10.
43 Ibid., p. 133.

CHAPTER SEVEN

1 *Second Annual Report of the Woman's Missionary Society* [WMS-CM] 1882, Eg. F5, UCCA.
2 Robert S. Schwantes, "American Influence in the Education of Meiji Japan" (unpublished Ph.D. dissertation, Harvard Univ., 1950), pp. 185-86.
3 Quoted in Kosaka, comp. and ed., *Japanese Thought in the Meiji Era*, p. 120.
4 Tōyō Eiwa Jo Gakuin hyakunen, *Tōyō Eiwa Jo Gakuin hyakunen shi*, pp. 33-35.
5 *Fourth Annual Report of the Woman's Missionary Society* [WMS-CM] 1884, Eg F5, UCCA.
6 Tōyō Eiwa Jo Gakuin hyakunen, *Tōyō Eiwa Jo Gakuin hyakunen shi*, p. 36; Tōyō Eiwa Jo Gakuin nanajūnen shi henshū iinkai, *Tōyō Eiwa Jo Gakuin nanajūnen shi* (Tokyo: Tōyō Eiwa Jo Gakuin, 1955), p. 9.
7 Tōyō Eiwa Jo Gakuin hyakunen, *Tōyō Eiwa Jo Gakuin hyakunen shi*, pp. 134-35.
8 Ibid., p. 135. See also Haru Matsukata Reischauer, *Samurai and Silk: A Japanese and American Heritage* (Cambridge, Mass.: Belknap Press of Harvard Univ. Press, 1986), p. 231.
9 *The Missionary Outlook* 6 (June-July 1886): 101.
10 Ibid., p. 101.
11 Tōyō Eiwa Jo Gakuin hyakunen, *Tōyō Eiwa Jo Gakuin hyakunen shi*, pp. 151-52.
12 Ibid., p. 156.
13 Reminiscences of Mrs. Yoshiko Matsuo, in the possession of Miss Constance Chappell.
14 Reminiscences of sister of Takagi Katsuo (née Uchida), in the possession of Miss Constance Chapell.
15 The author is grateful to Miss Constance Chappell for this information.
16 *Minutes of the Japan Conference of the Methodist Church of Canada, 1889*, p. 40.
17 *Minutes of the Japan Conference, 1891*, p. 45.
18 Tōyō Eiwa Jo Gakuin hyakunen, *Tōyō Eiwa Jo Gakuin hyakunen shi*, p. 27.
19 Shizuoka Eiwa Jo Gakuin hachijūnen shi hensan iinkai, *Shizuoka Eiwa Jo Gakuin hachijūnen shi*, pp. 22-24.
20 *Sixth Annual Report of the Woman's Missionary Society* [WMS-CM] 1886, Eg F5, UCCA.
21 Shizuoka Eiwa Jo Gakuin hachijūnen shi hensan iinkai, *Shizuoka Eiwa Jo Gakuin hachijūnen shi*, p. 44.
22 Ibid., p. 70.
23 Ibid., p. 201.
24 *Minutes of the Japan Conference, 1889*, p. 40.
25 Ibid.
26 *Minutes of the Japan Conference, 1891*, p. 44.
27 Yamanashi Eiwa Gakuin shi hensan iinkai, *Yamanashi Eiwa Gakuin hachijūnen shi*, p. 516.
28 Shizuoka Eiwa Jo Gakuin hachijūnen shi hensan iinkai, *Shizuoka Eiwa Jo Gakuin hachijūnen shi*, p. 189.
29 Ibid., p. 192.
30 Ibid., pp. 204, 206.
31 Yamanashi Eiwa Gakuin shi hensan iinkai, *Yamanashi Eiwa Gakuin hachijūnen shi*, pp. 183-84.
32 Saunby, *The New Chivalry in Japan*, p. 159.
33 Ibid.
34 Ibid., p. 179.
35 Ibid.
36 Loretta L. Shaw, *Japan in Transition* (London: Church Missionary Society, 1922), p. 52.
37 Ibid., p. 52.
38 Kano, *Nihon no rekishi 27*, pp. 43-44.
39 Carman, *Report of the General Superintendant's Official Visit*, p. 23.
40 *The Missionary Outlook* 7 (1888): 45.
41 *The Missionary Outlook* 5 (1893): 12.

42 Saunby, *The New Chivalry in Japan*, pp. 99-100.
43 *Minutes of the Japan Conference of the Methodist Church of Canada, 1889*, p. 40.
44 Ōta, *Meiji Kirisutokyō no ryūiki*, p. 132.
45 An example of this was a disturbing incident in 1901 when Yamaji was responsible for charging a young married missionary in Nagano with having sexual relations with his Japanese maid. Although the Canadian was cleared of these charges, he did not return to Japan after his first furlough. Yamaji's motives for bringing forward this serious accusation were apparently related to his underlying desire for Japanese independence from the Canadian Church.
46 *Minutes of the Japan Conference, 1891*, p. 30.
47 *Minutes of the Japan Conference, 1899*, p. 63.
48 Benjamin Chappell to the Rev. Dr. Smith, August 19, 1899, copy contained in the Journal of Benjamin Chappell, 1898-99, in the possession of Miss Constance Chappell. Benjamin Chappell was a Canadian serving with the Methodist Episcopal Church, North mission in Tokyo. He was present at the meeting of missionaries held in Tokyo on August 16, 1899 to discuss the issue of the missionary response to the Instruction.
49 Ebara Sensei denki hensan, *Ebara Soroku Sensei den*, p. 292.
50 *Minutes of the Japan Conference, 1900*, p. 46. For the Azabu Middle School see also Kirisutokyō Gakkō Kyōiku Domei Hen, *Kirisutokyō Kyōikushi* (Tokyo: Sobunsha, 1977), p. 123.
51 Saunby, *The New Chivalry in Japan*, p. 301.
52 J. Endicott to D. R. McKenzie, September 19, 1913, H13 F1, Box 1, File 13, UCCA.
53 D. R. McKenzie to J. Endicott, January 5, 1916, H13 F1, Box 1, File 13, UCCA.
54 Ibid.
55 J. Endicott to D. R. McKenzie, February 8, 1916, H13 F1, Box 1, File 13, UCCA.
56 Ibid.
57 Ibid.
58 Japan Mission Council, Minutes of Meeting, Tokyo, July 1-3, 1919, H13 F3, Box 3, File 43, UCCA.
59 Ibid.
60 Ibid.
61 Ibid.
62 J. Endicott to D. R. McKenzie, October 28, 1920, H13 f2, Box 2, File 16, UCCA.
63 Saunby, *The New Chivalry in Japan*, p. 302.
64 Ibid., p. 308.
65 Ibid., p. 305.
66 Ibid., p. 312.
67 D. Norman to G. S. Patterson, May 30, 1912, T. E. Egerton Shore Papers, Japan Mission Box 9, UCCA.
68 Saunby, *The New Chivalry in Japan*, p. 313.
69 D. R. McKenzie to J. Endicott, September 1, 1915, enclosure Report of the Canadian Methodist Academy, H13 F1, Box 1, File 1, UCCA.
70 Ibid.
71 Saunby, *The New Chivalry in Japan*, p. 314.
72 Ibid., pp. 312-13.
73 Ibid., p. 316.
74 See Roger W. Bowen, ed., *E. H. Norman: His Life and Scholarship* (Toronto: Univ. of Toronto Press, 1984).
75 E. Patricia Tsurumi, *Japanese Colonial Education in Taiwan, 1895-1945* (Cambridge, Mass.: Harvard Univ. Press, 1977), p. 164.
76 A. E. Armstrong to T. E. Mansfield, May 5, 1916, PCC GA41 B6K, Box 3, File May 1916, UCCA.
77 *Acts and Proceedings of the General Assembly of the Presbyterian Church in Canada, 1915*, p. 100.
78 Tsurumi, *Japanese Colonial Education in Taiwan*, p. 165.

79 Ibid.
80 D. A. MacDonald to A. E. Armstrong, June 1914, PCC GA41 B6K, Box 2, File June 1914, UCCA.
81 A. E. Armstrong to T. G. Mansfield, May 5, 1916, PCC GA41 B6K, Box 2, File May 1916, UCCA.
82 H. B. Gordon, the Toronto architect who had been the convener of the Harkness Committee which had initially supported Robert Harkness in Korea, designed the first building for the Severance Hospital.
83 Tsurumi, *Japanese Colonial Education in Taiwan*, p. 35.
84 Ibid.
85 Ibid., p. 36.
86 G. W. Mackay to A. E. Armstrong, May 20, 1914, PCC GA41 B6K, Box 4, File April-June 1914, UCCA.
87 Ibid.
88 Tsurumi, *Japanese Colonial Education in Taiwan*, p. 125.
89 M. Jack to R. P. MacKay, August 17, 1915, PCC GA41 B6K, Box 4, File July-September 1915, UCCA.
90 G. W. Mackay to R. P. MacKay, March 14, 1922, PCC GA41 B6F, Box 6, File January-March 1922, UCCA.
91 Ibid.
92 Ibid.
93 MacLeod, *The Island Beautiful*, pp. 191-92.
94 Tong, *Christianity in Taiwan*, p. 160.
95 MacLeod, *The Island Beautiful*, p. 39.
96 J. L. Maxwell, "The Mission Hospital of the Future," dated February 1914, Tainan, PCE Box 98, File 5, in United Reformed Church Archives, Tavistock Place, London, England.

CHAPTER EIGHT

1 The Nevius Method was named after its originator, John Nevius of Cheefoo. The Method stressed personal evangelism and wide itineration by missionaries. It also emphasized self-propagation, self-government, self-support among Christians. It put great emphasis on Bible study and strict discipline enforced by Bible penalties (Spencer J. Palmer, *Korea and Christianity: The Problem of Identification with Tradition* [Seoul: Hollym Corporation, 1967], pp. 27-28).
2 *Fifty-Second Annual Report of the Missionary Society of the Methodist Church of Canada*, 1876, p. xxxvi.
3 Arthur Lea, "Some Difficulties of the Japanese in Accepting Christianity," *South Tokyo Diocesan Magazine* 9, no. 28 (December 1905): 84-88.
4 C. P. Holmes, "The Message for Japan To-Day," H13 G4 F1, Box 7, File 112 Literature, UCCA.
5 Ibid.
6 Ibid.
7 Ibid.
8 Ibid.
9 H. E. Walker to F. C. Stephenson, December 11, 1913, H13 F1, Box 1, UCCA.
10 F. Ainsworth, Individual Annual Reports 1923-24, H13 F4, Box 4, File 60, UCCA.
11 A. M. Henty, Church Missionary Society [CMS], *Japan Quarterly* (June 1924): 1.
12 Lea, "Some Difficulties of the Japanese in Accepting Christianity," p. 86.
13 Ibid., p. 87.
14 J. Cooper Robinson, in *Mission World* 16, no. 11 (November 1918): 421.
15 Ibid., p. 422.
16 John Imai, "Bushido," *South Tokyo Diocesan Magazine* 9, no. 28 (December 1905): 78-84. See also John Imai, *Bushido in the Past and in the Present* (Tokyo: Kanazashi, 1906).

17 Imai, "Bushido," p. 79.
18 Ibid.
19 John Imai, quoted in P. Y. Saeki, "The Sources of Bushido," *South Tokyo Diocesan Magazine* 12, no. 35 (March 1908): 5-12, especially 6.
20 Imai, "Bushido," p. 83.
21 See for instance Egerton Herbert Norman, *Japan's Emergence as a Modern State: Political and Economic Problems of the Meiji Period* (New York: Institute of Pacific Relations, 1940), pp. 16-18.
22 H. H. Coates, Individual Annual Reports 1919-20, H13 F4, Box 4, File 57, UCCA.
23 Shaw, *Japan in Transition*, p. 30.
24 Lea, "Some Difficulties of the Japanese in Accepting Christianity," p. 87.
25 Ibid., p. 88.
26 Ibid.
27 Ibid., p. 86.
28 Ibid.
29 Ibid., p. 88.
30 Fujiwara Fujio, *Seisho no wayaku to buntairon* (Tokyo: Kirisuto Shinbunsha, 1974), passim.
31 Japan Mission WMS Council Minutes 1914-21, Annual Meeting 1914, July 14, 1914, MC GC1 W8, UCCA.
32 Ibid.
33 Holmes, "The Message for Japan To-Day."
34 Ibid.
35 Ibid.
36 Ibid.
37 William R. Hutchinson, "Modernism and Missions: The Liberal Search for an Exportable Christianity, 1875-1935," in John King Fairbank, ed., *The Missionary Enterprise in China and America* (Cambridge, Mass.: Harvard Univ. Press, 1974), pp. 110-31, passim.
38 Holmes, "The Message for Japan To-Day."
39 Undated jotting in Bishop H. J. Hamilton's Notebook in Anglican Church of Canada Archives, Church House, 600 Jarvis Street, Toronto, Ontario.
40 H. H. Montgomery to M. N. Trollope, October 22, 1918, SPG Series F in United Society for the Propagation of the Gospel in Foreign Parts Archives, Tufton Street, Westminster, England (hereafter cited as USPGA).
41 H. H. Montgomery Papers, Memorandum of Bishop Montgomery on mission and politics in Japan, China, Africa, and Singapore after an interview with J. H. Oldham, H.9, USPGA.
42 J. Endicott, "Can Christianity Make Good in Japan?," *Christian Guardian*, June 5, 1918.
43 Ibid.
44 H. H. Coates, Individual Annual Reports 1919-20, H13 F4, Box 4, File 57, UCCA.
45 D. Norman, Individual Annual Reports 1924-25, H13 F4, Box 4, File 61, UCCA.
46 D. C. Holtom, *Shintō: The National Faith of Japan* (London: Kegan Paul, 1938).
47 D. R. McKenzie to J. Endicott, January 9, 1914, H13 F1, Box 1, File 10, UCCA.
48 Ibid.
49 D. R. McKenzie to J. Endicott, June 10, 1915, H13 F1, Box 1, File 10, UCCA.
50 D. R. McKenzie to J. Endicott, June 3, 1915, H13 F1, Box 1, File 12, UCCA.
51 Ibid.
52 Japan Mission WMS Council Minutes 1914-21, Annual Council Meeting 1916, July 22, 1916, MC GC1 W8, UCCA.
53 Ibid.
54 Drummond, *A History of Christianity in Japan*, p. 245.
55 D. R. McKenzie to T. E. Egerton Shore, July 12, 1912, H13 F1, Box 1, File 8, UCCA.
56 T. E. Egerton Shore to A. J. Brown, February 23, 1911, T. E. Egerton Shore Papers, Japan Mission, 1907-12, H13 C2, Box 10, File 190, UCCA.

57 A. B. Leonard to T. E. Egerton Shore, May 29, 1911, T. E. Egerton Shore Papers, Japan Mission, 1907-12, H13 C2, Box 10, File 190, UCCA.

58 WMS, Methodist Church of Canada, Overseas Missions, Japan, Secretary-Treasurer, 1909-25, File Japan 1914-21, Women's Christian Union College of Japan, UCCA.

59 The Three Religions Conference was attended by representatives from 52 Buddhist sects, 13 Shintō sects, and 7 representatives from the various Protestant denominations and the Roman Catholic Church.

60 Kozaki, *Reminiscences of Seventy Years*, p. 276.

61 Frank Langdon, "Impressions from the World's Sunday School Convention and the Far East," *Christian Guardian*, December 22, 1920.

62 Ibid.

63 A. T. Wilkinson, Individual Annual Reports 1919-20, H13 F4, File 57, UCCA.

64 Ibid.

65 Ibid.

66 Shaw, *Japan in Transition*, p. 95.

67 Deaconess A. L. Archer, in *Mission World* (1918).

68 J. G. Waller, "Our Canadian Mission in Japan," 27-page pamphlet issued by the Joint Committee on Summer Schools and Institutes of the Church of England in Canada, 1930, p. 14.

69 Norman, *Nagano no Noruman*, pp. 128-29.

70 D. Norman, Individual Annual Reports 1924-25.

71 Murao and Walton, *Japan and Christ*, pp. 121-22.

72 Ibid., p. 114.

73 C. J. L. Bates, "A Challenge from Japan," *Christian Guardian*, November 21, 1917.

74 Japan Mission, Notes on Council Minutes 1913, Minutes of Meeting, H13 F3, Box 3, File 36, UCCA.

75 Ibid.

76 Bates, "A Challenge from Japan."

77 Nihon Seikōkai rekishi hensan iinkaihen, *Nihon Seikōkai hyakunen shi*, pp. 301, 302-303.

78 Murao and Walton, *Japan and Christ*, p. 57.

79 The author wishes to thank Professor Cyril H. Powles for this information.

80 Waller, "Our Canadian Mission in Japan," p. 20.

81 The number of factory operatives increased from 165,000 males and 257,000 females in 1900 to 855,000 males and 970,000 females in 1929 (George C. Allen, *A Short Economic History of Modern Japan 1867-1937: With a Supplementary Chapter on Economic Recovery and Expansion 1945-1960* [London: George Allen & Unwin, 1966], p. 197).

82 Keenleyside, *Tokyo no sora ni Kanada no hata o*, p. 150; Saunby, *The New Chivalry in Japan*, p. 142.

83 J. W. Saunby to J. Endicott, March 20, 1920, H13 F2, Box 2, File 16, UCCA.

84 Saunby, *The New Chivalry in Japan*, p. 149.

85 J. W. Saunby to J. Endicott, March 20, 1920, H13 F2, Box 2, File 16, UCCA.

86 Saunby, *The New Chivalry in Japan*, p. 151.

87 D. R. McKenzie to J. Endicott, September 21, 1923, H13 F2, Box 2, File 23, UCCA.

88 Ibid.

89 WMS Methodist Church of Canada, Overseas Mission Japan, Japan Emergency 1924, Secretary-Treasurer 1920-25, File Joint Committee re Japan Emergency 1924, UCCA.

90 Murao and Walton, *Japan and Christ*, p. 103.

91 "Journal of Tour of the Far East 1911," p. 107, Bishop H. H. Montgomery Papers, H9, USPGA.

92 Robert Grierson, "Episodes on a Long, Long Trail," 92-page typescript in the possession of Dr. Horace Underwood, Seoul, Korea.

93 Ibid., pp. 20

94 FO 371/6698 (Political Far Eastern Japan 1921), F2325/1641/23, PRO; Grierson, "Episodes on a Long, Long Trail," pp. 38-40ff.

95 Palmer, *Korea and Christianity*, p. vii.
96 Eui Whan Kim, "The Korean Church Under Japanese Occupation with Special Reference to the Resistance Movement within Presbyterianism" (unpublished Ph.D. dissertation, Temple Univ., 1966), p. 86.
97 Ibid., p. 87.
98 Ibid., pp. 59-60.
99 Ibid., p. 62.
100 The author wishes to thank Professor Chi Mekan for this information.
101 Matsuo Takayoshi, "Nihon Kumiai Kirisutokyōkai no Chōsen dendō," *Shisō* (July 1968): 949-65, passim.
102 Quoted in Scott, *Canadians in Korea*, p. 63.
103 Ibid., p. 74.
104 J. M. Scott to R. P. MacKay, November 12, 1912, FMC Western Section, Korean Mission, Correspondence 1895-1912, PCC GA41 86K, Box 1, UCCA.
105 *Acts and Proceedings of the General Assembly of the Presbyterian Church in Canada*, vol. 24.
106 *Acts and Proceedings of the General Assembly of the Presbyterian Church in Canada, 1918-1919*, p. 43.
107 Scott, *Canadians in Korea*, p. 62.
108 *Acts and Proceedings of the General Assembly of the Presbyterian Church in Canada, 1915*, p. 100.
109 R. P. MacKay to W. Scott, August 17, 1922, PCC GA41, Box 7, File August 1922, UCCA.
110 Walsh, *The Christian Church in Canada*, p. 304.
111 *Acts and Proceedings of the General Assembly of the Presbyterian Church in Canada, 1922-1923*, vol. 35, p. 41.
112 *Acts and Proceedings of the General Assembly of the Presbyterian Church in Canada, 1923*, p. 137.
113 Ibid.
114 Edward Band, *Barclay of Formosa* (Tokyo: Christian Literature Society, 1936), pp. 87-97, passim.
115 Mackay, *From Far Formosa*, p. 103.
116 Ibid., pp. 215-25, passim.
117 Campbell N. Moody, *The Heathen Heart: An Account of the Reception of the Gospel among the Chinese of Formosa*, pp. 99-100.
118 Band, *Barclay of Formosa*, p. 109.
119 Edward Band, *Working Out His Purpose: The History of the English Presbyterian Mission 1847-1947* (Taipeh: Ch'eng Wen Publishing Company, 1972), p. 127.
120 Ibid., p. 128.
121 R. P. MacKay to W. Dale, June 30, 1914, PCC GA41 B6F, Box 4, File April-June 1914, UCCA. William Dale was the Foreign Missions Secretary of the Missionary Society of the Presbyterian Church of England.
122 G. W. Mackay to R. P. MacKay, October 19, 1919, PCC GA41 B6F, Box 6, File October-December 1919, UCCA.
123 Ibid.

CHAPTER NINE

1 W. L. Mackenzie King to S. D. Chown, November 1, 1908, Samuel Dwight Chown Papers, Box 10, Manuscripts, Correspondence, General Material, H8 12, File 212, UCCA. Japanese immigration to Canada was limited by the Gentlemen's Agreement negotiated by the Canadian Minister of Labour, R. Lemieux, in 1908.
2 J. Endicott to D. R. McKenzie, August 11, 1914, H13 F1, Box 1, UCCA.
3 C. J. L. Bates, "Japan's Place in the Orient," 11-page typescript, dated February 1918, H13 G4, Box 7, File 112, UCCA.
4 Ibid.

5 Ibid.
6 J. W. Saunby, "The Question of Japanese Immigration," *The Christian Guardian*, April 24, 1918.
7 Ibid.
8 A. T. Wilkinson, "What Do the Japanese Want?," *The Christian Guardian*, March 29, 1922.
9 Ibid.
10 Ibid.
11 Mission Secretaries to W. L. Mackenzie King, April 3, 1923, H13 F2, Box 2, File 23, UCCA.
12 C. J. L. Bates to W. L. Mackenzie King, June 12, 1924, MT. 382.345, Taishō 13 (1924), vol. 2 in Gaimushō Gaikō Kan, Tokyo, Japan.
13 "Sayonara," *The Christian Guardian*, April 9, 1913.
14 C. P. Holmes, "Address to the Hamilton Conference, June 9, 1914," H13 F1, Box 1, UCCA.
15 "Sayonara," *The Christian Guardian*, March 6, 1912.
16 Ibid.
17 J. Endicott to D. R. McKenzie, August 11, 1914, H13 F1, Box 1, UCCA.
18 *The Christian Guardian*, April 28, 1915.
19 J. G. Waller, March 1916, Canadian Anglican Missionary Society Report, 1916.
20 "Kosai" and "Far Eastern Table-Talk: Japan and the Peace Conference," *The Christian Guardian*, April 16, 1919.
21 Ibid.
22 D. Norman, "Political Change in Japan Influenced by Christian Teaching," *The Missionary Bulletin* 15, no. 4 (October-December 1919): 577-83, especially 579.
23 "Kosai" and "Far Eastern Table-Talk: Japan and the Peace Conference."
24 Ibid.
25 Shaw, *Japan in Transition*, pp. 8-9.
26 See O. R. Avison, "Autobiography," 2-volume typescript in the possession of Dr. Samuel H. Moffett, Seoul, Korea, vol. 2, pp. 259-79.
27 Scott, *Canadians in Korea*, p. 57.
28 Ibid.
29 Grierson, "Episodes on a Long, Long Trail," p. 45.
30 Ibid.
31 "Sayonara," *The Christian Guardian*, April 16, 1913.
32 Allen D. Clark, *A History of the Church in Korea* (Seoul: The Christian Literature Society of Korea, 1971), p. 188.
33 Ibid., p. 189.
34 "Sayonara," *The Christian Guardian*, April 16, 1913.
35 D. A. MacDonald to A. E. Armstrong, June 1914, PCC GA41 B6K, Box 2, UCCA.
36 A. E. Armstrong to T. D. Mansfield, May 5, 1916, PCC GA41 B6K, Box 3, File May 1916, UCCA.
37 Sir C. Eliot to Lord Curzon, July 2, 1921, FO 371/6586, China 1921, PRO.
38 Frank Baldwin, "Missionaries and the March First Movement: Can Moral Man be Neutral?," in Andrew C. Nahm, ed., *Korea under Japanese Colonial Rule: Studies of the Policy and Techniques of Japanese Colonialism* (Kalamazoo: Center for Korean Studies, Western Michigan Univ., 1973), pp. 193-219, especially p. 200.
39 A. E. Armstrong to J. R. Mott, April 9, 1919, PCC GA41 B6K, Box 4, File April 1919, UCCA.
40 Ibid.
41 R. P. MacKay to N. W. Rowell, April 9, 1919, PCC GA41 B6K, Box 4, File April 1919, UCCA.
42 A. E. Armstrong to J. R. Mott, April 9, 1919, PCC GA41 B6K, Box 4, File April 1919, UCCA.
43 A. E. Armstrong to G. Paik, May 12, 1919, PCC GA41 B6K, Box 4, File May 1919, UCCA.

44 A. E. Armstrong to Takahashi Motoguchi, July 9, 1919, PCC GA41 B6K, Box 4, File July 1919, UCCA.
45 Ibid.
46 Ibid.
47 Baldwin, "Missionaries and the March First Movement," p. 204.
48 Japanese Ministry of Foreign Affairs, 1868-1945, Micro. 11, MT 1.5.3.14 270; Reply to Commission on Relations with the Orient, n.d.
49 New York Times, April 23, 1919.
50 A. E. Armstrong to W. Scott, May 16, 1919, PCC GA41 B6K, Box 4, File May 1919, UCCA.
51 Grierson, "Episodes on a Long, Long Trail," pp. 64-65.
52 A. H. Barker to R. P. MacKay, March 27, 1919, PCC GA41 B6K, Box 4, File March 1919, UCCA.
53 A. R. Ross to W. Massey Royds, May 27, 1919, FO 371/3818/766, PRO.
54 A. H. Barker to R. P. MacKay, March 27, 1919, PCC GA41 B6K, Box 4, File March 1919, UCCA.
55 Quoted in P. E. O'Brien-Butler to Sir J. N. Jordan, April 11, 1919, FO 371/3818/766/90971, PRO.
56 W. Scott to P. E. O'Brien-Butler, April 14, 1919, FO 371/3818/766, PRO.
57 Ibid.
58 Ibid. Dr. Paul Hobom Shin has noted that the leaders of the Chientao wing of the March First 1919 independence movement drafted their version of Korea's independence declaration in the basement of the Canadian Mission Hospital. See Paul Hobom Shin, "The Korean Colony in Chientao: A Study of Japanese Imperialism and Militant Korean Nationalism, 1905-1932" (unpublished Ph.D. dissertation, Univ. of Washington, 1980), p. 278.
59 Hara Kishi, "Kyokutō Roshia ni okeru Chōsen dokuritsu undō to Nihon," San Sen Ri 17 (Tokushū San Ichi Undō Rokujū Shunen) (1979): 47-53, especially 50.
60 F. W. Schofield to C. Harmsworth, May 20, 1920, FO 371/6352/766, PRO.
61 Ibid.
62 Paku Wuon Shiku, Tōyō bunko 216: Chōsen dokuritsu undō no ketsu shi, trans. Kan Doku Sen, vol. 1 (Tokyo: Heibonsha, 1978), p. 183.
63 Quoted in W. M. Royds to B. Alston, June 11, 1919, FO 371/3818/766, PRO.
64 F. W. Schofield to C. Harmsworth, May 20, 1920, FO 371/6352/766, PRO.
65 Ibid.
66 B. Alston to Earl Curzon of Kedleston, December 9, 1919, enclosure no. 2, Japan Advertiser, December 17, 1919, FO 371/3818/766/177945, PRO.
67 Ibid.
68 F. W. Schofield to Bob (R. P. MacKay?), December 16, 1919, PCC GA41 B6K, Box 4, File December 1919, UCCA.
69 S. J. Schofield to Secretary, Foreign Office, October 11, 1919, FO 371/3818/766/140262, PRO.
70 C. H. Bentinck minute, October 13, 1919, FO 371/3818/766/140262, PRO.
71 Baldwin, "Missionaries and the March First Movement," p. 200.
72 B. Alston to Earl Curzon of Keddleston, December 19, 1919, enclosure no. 2, Japan Advertiser, December 17, 1919.
73 Ibid.
74 C. H. Bentinck minute, June 14, 1920, FO 371/5352, PRO.
75 Lord Curzon to B. Alston, July 22, 1919, FO 371/3818/109885, PRO.
76 Memorandum by Mr. Max Muller on Japanese Policy in Korea, July 5, 1919, FO 371/3818/766, PRO.
77 The author wishes to thank Professor Ian H. Nish for this information.
78 Lord Curzon to B. Alston, July 22, 1919, FO 371/3818/109885, PRO.
79 Memorandum by Mr. Max Muller on Japanese Policy in Korea, July 5, 1919. See also M. Muller to M. N. Trollope, May 10, 1919, Bishop Mark Napier Trollope

Papers, USPGA. Trollope jotted a number of ideas in the margin of Muller's letter which later appear in Muller's Memorandum.

80 Scott, *Canadians in Korea*, pp. 87-88.

81 Paku Kyon Shiku, *Heibonsha senshō 49: Chōsen san ichi dokuritsu undō* (Tokyo: Heibonsha, 1976), p. 211.

82 Ibid., p. 212.

83 Taiheyō Sensō Ge'in Chōsabu, Nihon Kokusai Seiji Gakkai, *Taiheyō sensō e no michi—kaisen gaikōkshi*, vol. 1 (Tokyo: Asahi Shimbunsha, 1963), p. 178.

84 Ibid.

85 Ibid.

86 Ibid.

87 Ibid.

88 E. Edmund Clubb, *Twentieth Century China* (London and New York: Columbia Univ. Pres, 1964), p. 102.

89 Ibid., pp. 93-94.

90 *Gendai shi shiryō*, vol. 26 (Tokyo: Misuzu Shobō, 1963), pp. 61-64, especially p. 62.

91 Ibid., pp. 116-22.

92 Ibid., p. xi.

93 *Toronto Globe*, December 8, 1920.

94 M. W. Lampson Memorandum for V. Wellesley, October 1920, FO 371/6585/F1640/3/10, PRO.

95 Consul-General Lay to Sir Charles Eliot, February 25, 1921, FO 371/6585/F1640/3/10, PRO.

96 *Times* (London), November 20, 1920.

97 Ibid., December 15, 1920.

98 *Toronto Globe*, December 23, 1920.

99 Ibid.

100 *Gendai shi shiryō*, vol. 26, pp. 670-78.

101 Ibid., pp. 678-81.

102 Ibid.

103 *Toronto Globe*, January 20, 1921.

104 Ibid.

105 *Times* (London), December 7, 1920.

106 Ibid.

107 *Gendai shi shiryō*, vol. 26, pp. 692-93, 691-94.

108 W. R. Foote to A. E. Armstrong, March 21, 1921, PCC GA41 B6K, Box 6, File March 1921, UCCA.

109 A. E. Armstrong to Sir Charles Eliot, December 15, 1920, PCC GA41 B6K, Box 5, File December 1920, UCCA.

110 R. P. MacKay to Sir J. Pope, December 21, 1920, PCC GA41 B6K, Box 5, File December 1920, UCCA.

111 N. W. Rowell to A. E. Armstrong, January 1920, PCC GA41 B6K, Box 6, File January 1921, UCCA.

112 A. E. Armstrong to Sidney L. Gulick, January 14, 1921, PCC GA41 B6K, Box 6, File January 1921, UCCA.

113 A. E. Armstrong to W. Scott, December 27, 1920, PCC GA41 B6K, Box 5, File December 1920, UCCA.

114 A. E. Armstrong to S. H. Martin, February 2, 1921, PCC GA41 B6K, Box 6, File February 1921, UCCA.

115 D. M. McRae to A. E. Armstrong, December 24, 1920, PCC GA41 B6K, Box 5, File December 1920, UCCA.

116 S. L. Gulick to A. E. Armstrong, March 22, 1921, PCC GA41 B6K, Box 6, File March 1921, UCCA.

117 Ibid.

118 A. E. Armstrong to E. McLellan, December 14, 1920, PCC GA41 B6K, Box 5, File December 1920, UCCA.

119 A. E. Armstrong to P. Jaisohn, January 31, 1921, PCC GA41 B6K, Box 6, File January 1921, UCCA.

120 Ibid.

121 A. E. Armstrong to H. T. Owens, July 15, 1921, PCC GA41 B6K, Box 6, File July 1921, UCCA.

122 Ibid.

123 A. E. Armstrong to F. A. McKenzie, February 18, 1921, PCC GA41 B6K, Box 6, File January 1921, UCCA.

124 Ibid.

125 *Toronto Globe*, December 16, 1920.

126 Ibid.

127 M. W. Lampson interview with L. Christie, July 14, 1921, FO 371/6586/F2576/3/10, PRO.

128 See RG 7 G21 volume 393, RG 25 G 1 volume 1279, File 1491, PAC. These volumes contain copies of some of the most important correspondence between the British diplomatic and consular officers in Japan and China and the Foreign Office in London concerning the Chientao Crisis.

129 M. W. Lampson minute, December 22, 1920,

130 C. Harmsworth to Sir R. Newman, December 21, 1920, FO 371/5346/F3336/2358/10, PRO.

131 Sir B. Alston to Lord Curzon, June 17, 1921, enclosure no. 2, W. B. Cunningham to F. E. Wilkinson, June 7, 1921, FO 371/6586/230, PRO.

132 Ibid.

133 Ibid.

134 Ibid.

135 Ibid.

136 Ibid., enclosure no. 1, F. E. Wilkinon to Sir B. Alston, June 1921.

137 Under-Secretary of State for External Affairs to A. E. Armstrong, April 1921, RG 25 G1 volume 1279, File 1491, PAC.

138 S. H. Martin to A. E. Armstrong, February 4, 1921, PCC GA41 B6K, Box 6, File February 1921, UCCA.

139 Ibid.

140 Ibid.

141 E. J. O. Fraser to A. E. Armstrong, December 6, 1932, United Church of Canada, Korea Mission, Box 2, File 54, December 1932, UCCA.

142 Band, *Barclay of Formosa*, p. 102.

143 Band, *Working Out His Purpose*, p. 155.

144 Ibid., pp. 155-56.

145 W. Gauld to R. P. MacKay, December 3, 1912, PCC GA41 B6F, File October-December 1912, UCCA.

146 G. W. Mackay to A. E. Armstrong, January 30, 1916, PCC GA41 B6F, Box 5, File January-March 1916, UCCA.

147 Ibid.

148 Ibid.

149 Ibid.

150 Edward I-te Chen, "Japan: Oppressor or Modernizer? A Comparison of the Effects of Colonial Control in Korea and Formosa," in Andrew C. Nahm, ed., *Korea under Japanese Colonial Rule: Studies of the Policy and Techniques of Japanese Colonialism* (Kalamazoo: Center for Korean Studies, Western Michigan Univ., 1973), pp. 251-60, especially p. 254.

151 G. W. Mackay to A. E. Armstrong, PCC GA41 B6F, File April-June 1912, UCCA.

152 MacLeod, *The Island Beautiful*, p. 41.

153 Ibid., pp. 41-42.

154 Tsurumi, *Japanese Colonial Education in Taiwan*, p. 187.

155 Edward I-te Chen, "Formosan Political Movements under Japanese Colonial Rule, 1914-1937," *Journal of Asian Studies* 21, no. 3 (May 1972): 477-98, especially 485.

156 Edward I-te Chen, "Japanese Colonialism in Korea and Formosa: A Comparison of its Effects upon the Development of Nationalism" (unpublished Ph.D. dissertation, Univ. of Pennsylvania, 1968), p. 306.
157 Chen, "Formosan Political Movements," p. 489.

CHAPTER TEN

1 Report on Canadian Missionary Activities in the Japanese Empire, 1933, Prepared by Kenneth P. Kirkwood for the Tokyo Legation, RG 25 G1 volume 1668, File 547-33, PAC.
2 H. W. Outerbridge to H. L. Keenleyside, December 9, 1937, United Church of Canada, Board of Foreign Missions, Japan Mission, Box 4 (microfilm).
3 Powles, "Development of Japanese-Canadian Relations, p. 158.
4 C. R. Moon to A. E. Armstrong, October 26, 1945, United Church of Canada, Board of Foreign Missions, Korea Mission, Box 6 (microfilm).
5 D. A. Macdonald to A. E. Armstrong, January 13, 1932, United Church of Canada, Board of Foreign Missions, Korea Mission, Box 2, File 50 (microfilm).

Select Bibliography

PRIVATE PAPERS
---

1. *In the Possession of Miss Constance Chappell, Toronto*

Journal of Benjamin Chappell (1898-1900). Benjamin Chappell was a Canadian attached to the Methodist Episcopal (North) mission in Japan. He was dean of the Anglo-Japanese College, Aoyama, Tokyo, 1898-1907.
Letters concerning the early days of the Tōyō Eiwa Jo Gakkō.
D. R. McKenzie, "Off to Japan," 8-page typescript, 1934.

2. *In the Possession of Canon A. C. Hutchinson*

"Autobiography of A. C. Hutchinson." This describes Hutchinson's life as a CMS missionary in Japan, 1909-1940.

3. *In the Possession of Mrs. G. R. P. Norman, Toronto*

"Japan Mission of the Methodist Church of Canada," 103-page typescript covering the period from 1873 to 1900.

4. *In the Possession of Dr. Samuel H. Moffett, Seoul, Korea*

"Autobiography of O. R. Avison," 2-volume typescript. This contains much interesting material about Avison's life in Korea (1892-1941).

5. *In the Possession of Dr. Horace Underwood, Seoul, Korea*

"Episodes on a Long, Long Trail," 92-page typescript. A colourful autobiography of Dr. Robert Grierson's life in Korea, originally intended as a memoir for his family.

ARCHIVES
---

1. *General Synod Archives, The Anglican Church of Canada, Church House, 600 Jarvis Street, Toronto, Ontario*

Annual Reports of the Missionary Society of the Church of England in Canada.
Official Minutes of the Missionary Society of the Church of England in Canada.
Mission World (monthly magazine).
Bishop H. J. Hamilton Notebook.

2. *Gaimushō Gaikō Shiryō Kan, Tokyo, Japan*

MT.382.345. Taishō 13 (1924). Volume 2 contains C. J. L. Bates to W. L. Mackenzie King, June 12, 1924.

3. *William Elliot Griffis Special Collection, Rutgers University, New Brunswick, New Jersey, U.S.A.*

Correspondence and Manuscripts: Boxes 8-18
   AC. 2064. Family Correspondence.
   AC. 2065. M. C. Griffis Journal (1871-1873).
   AC. 2083. Correspondence from Japanese to W. E. and M. C. Griffis (1874-1905).

4. *Korean Research Center, Seoul, Korea*

Japanese Ministry of Foreign Affairs, 1868-1945, Micro. 11, MT1.5.3. 14 270.

5. *Public Archives of Canada, Ottawa*

RG 7 G21. Governor-General's Office.
RG 25 G1. External Affairs Central Registry Files.

6. *Public Record Office, Kew, England*

FO 371. General Correspondence: Political.

7. *The Reformed Church of America Archives, Gardiner Sage Library, New Brunswick Theological Seminary, New Brunswick, New Jersey, U.S.A.*

Records and Letters of G. F. Verbeck (1860-1880). Box 747.3N.
Letters of Samuel R. Brown (1859-1880). Box 747.4N.

8. *United Church of Canada Archives, Victoria College, University of Toronto, Toronto, Ontario*

a. Printed Materials

Acts and Proceedings of the General Assembly of the Presbyterian Church in Canada (1873-1925).
Proceedings of the General Conferences of the Methodist Church of Canada (1876-1914).
Minutes of the Foreign Mission Committee (Western Division) of the Presbyterian Church in Canada (1888-1925).
Annual Reports of the Missionary Society of the Wesleyan Methodist Church of Canada (1870-1874).
Annual Reports of the Missionary Society of the Methodist Church of Canada (1874-1925).
Annual Reports of the Woman's Missionary Society of the Methodist Church of Canada (1881-1925).
Annual Reports of the Woman's Missionary Society of the Presbyterian Church in Canada.
Minutes of the Toronto Annual Conference of the Methodist Church of Canada (1873-1889).
Minutes of the Japan Conference of the Methodist Church of Canada (1889-1906).
Minutes of Conferences of the United Church of Canada (1926-1931).

b. Periodicals

Wesleyan Missionary Notices (1870-1874).
Missionary Notices (1875-1878).
Canadian Methodist Magazine (1875-1906).
The Missionary Outlook (1881-1914).
The Missionary Bulletin (1903-1925).
The Christian Guardian (1844-1925).
The New Outlook (1925-1939).
The Presbyterian Record.

c. Manuscript Materials

i. *Canadian Methodist*

Samuel Dwight Chown Papers. H8 12.
Davidson MacDonald (McDonald) Letter Books. 1895-1901.
J. Endicott and J. Arnup Papers. 1910-1925.
F. C. Stephenson Papers. 1894-1940.
T. E. Egerton Shore Papers. 1906-1913. H13 C2.
Alexander Sutherland. Letter Books. 1875-1910. H11 d2-H12 c3.
————. Papers. 1904-1910.
Japan Mission. General Correspondence. 1894-1925. H13 F1-F2.
————. Minutes of Council Meetings. H13 F3.
————. Individual Annual Reports. H13 F4.
wms Methodist Church of Canada. Overseas Missions, Japan. Secretary-
    Treasurer. 1909-1925.
wms Council Minutes. 1914-1921. MCGCLW8.

ii. *Canadian Presbyterian*

Presbyterian Church in Canada. Board of Foreign Missions. Formosa.
    1868-1923. PCC GA41 B6F.
8888 . Foreign Mission Committee. Korea. 1895-1925. PCC GA41 B6K.

iii. *United Church of Canada*

Board of Foreign Missions. Japan. 1931-1948. Boxes 4-7.
————. Korea. 1931-1950. Boxes 2-5.

9. *United Reformed Church Archives, Tavistock Place, London, England*

Presbyterian Church of England. Formosa Mission. Correspondence.

10. *United Society for the Propagation of the Gospel in Foreign Parts Archives, 15 Tufton Street, Westminster, England*

Bishop H. H. Montgomery Papers.
Bishop M. N. Trollope Papers.
Letters from SPG to field, SPG Series F, 1874-1928.

BOOKS

Addison, A. P. *The Heart of Japan.* Toronto: Young People's Forward Move-
    ment for Missions, 1905.
Allen, George C. *A Short Economic History of Modern Japan 1867-1937: With a
    Supplementary Chapter on Economic Recovery and Expansion 1945-1960.*
    London: George Allen & Unwin, 1966.

_____ . *Appointment in Japan: Memories of Sixty Years*. London: Athlone Press, 1983.

Armstrong, Robert Cornell. *Just Before the Dawn: The Life and Work of Ninomiya Sontoku*. New York: Macmillan, 1912.

_____ . *Light from the East: Studies in Japanese Confucianism*. Toronto: Univ. of Toronto Press, 1914.

_____ . *Progress in the Mikado's Empire*. Toronto: The Missionary Society of the Methodist Church, 1920.

_____ . *An Introduction to Japanese Buddhist Sects*. Toronto: Oxford Univ. Press, 1950. Privately printed.

Austin, Alvyn J. *Saving China: Canadian Missionaries in the Middle Kingdom 1888-1959*. Toronto: Univ. of Toronto Press, 1986.

Axling, William. *Kagawa*. London: Student Christian Movement Press, 1932.

Band, Edward. *Barclay of Formosa*. Tokyo: Christian Literature Society, 1936.

_____ . *Working Out His Purpose: The History of the English Presbyterian Mission 1847-1947*. Taipeh: Ch'eng Wen Publishing Company, 1972.

Barclay, Wade Crawford. *The Methodist Episcopal Church 1845-1939*. Vol. 3, *Widening Horizons 1845-95*. New York: The Board of Foreign Missions of the Methodist Church, 1957.

Barratt, Glyn. *Russian Shadows on the British Northwest Coast of North America*. Vancouver: Univ. of British Columbia Press, 1983.

Basis of Union in Japan Agreed Upon by the Joint Commission Representing the Methodist Episcopal Church, the Methodist Episcopal Church, South, and the Methodist Church, Canada. Buffalo, N.Y., 1906.

Beauchamp, Edward R. *An American Teacher in Early Meiji Japan*. Honolulu: Univ. Press of Hawaii, 1976.

Berger, Carl. *The Sense of Power: Studies in the Ideas of Canadian Imperialism 1867-1914*. Toronto: Univ. of Toronto Press, 1976.

Bickersteth, Mrs. Edward. *Japan*. London: Mowbray, 1908.

Bickersteth, May. *Japan as We Saw It*. London: Sampson Low, 1893.

Bickersteth, Samuel. *Life and Letters of Edward Bickersteth, Bishop of South Tokyo*. London, 1899.

Blacker, Carmen. *The Japanese Enlightenment: A Study of the Writings of Fukuzawa Yukichi*. Cambridge: Cambridge Univ. Press, 1969.

Bowen, Roger W., ed. *E. H. Norman: His Life and Scholarship*. Toronto: Univ. of Toronto Press, 1984.

Brown, Arthur J. *The Mastery of the Far East*. New York: Scribner's Sons, 1919.

Burks, Ardath W. *The Modernizers: Overseas Students, Foreign Employees, and Meiji Japan*. Boulder: Westview Press, 1985.

Burwash, Nathaniel. *Reverend Davidson Macdonald D. D.* Toronto: Woman's Missionary Society, 1917.

Caldarola, Carlo. *Christianity: The Japanese Way*. Leiden: E. J. Brill, 1979.

Carlson, Ellsworth C. *The Foochow Missionaries, 1847-1880*. Cambridge, Mass.: Harvard Univ. Press, 1974.

Carman, Albert. *Report of the General Superintendant's Official Visit to the Mission in Japan, April to June 1898*. Toronto: Methodist Book and Publishing House, 1898.

Cary, Otis. *A History of Christianity in Japan*. 2 vols. New York: Fleming H. Revell, 1909.

Chi, Mekan. *Kankoku gendai shi to kyōkai shi*. Tokyo: Shinkyō Shuppansha, 1975.

Clark, Allen D. *A History of the Church in Korea*. Seoul: The Christian Literature Society of Korea, 1971.

Clark, Edward Warren. *Life and Adventures in Japan*. New York: American Tract Society, 1878.

————. *Katz Awa, Bismarck of Japan, A Story of a Noble Life*. New York: B. F. Buck, 1905.

Clubb, E. Edmund. *Twentieth Century China*. London and New York: Columbia Univ. Press, 1964.

Coates, Harker H., with Ryugaku Ishizuka. *Honen, the Buddhist Saint: His Life and Teachings*. Trans. with an historical introduction and explanatory and critical notes. 2nd ed. Kyoto, 1925.

Cohen, Paul A. *China and Christianity: The Missionary Movement and the Growth of Chinese Antiforeignism, 1860-1870*. Cambridge, Mass.: Harvard Univ. Press, 1963.

Dohi, Akio. *Nihon Purotesutanto Kyōkai no seiritsu to tenkai*. Tokyo: Nihon Kirisutokyōdan Shuppan Kyōku, 1975.

————. *Nihon Purotesutanto Kirisutokyōshi*. Tōkyō: Shinkyo Shuppansha, 1982.

Dōshisha Daigaku Jimbun Kagaku Kenkyūjo/Kirisutokyō Shakai Mondai Kenkyūkai hen. *Nihon no Kindaika to Kirisutokyō*. Tokyo: Shinkyō Shuppansha, 1973.

Drummond, Richard H. *A History of Christianity in Japan*. Grand Rapids, Mich.: William B. Eerdmans Publishing Company, 1971.

Duus, Peter. *The Rise of Modern Japan*. Boston: Houghton Mifflin Company, 1976.

Ebara Sensei denki hensan iinkai. *Ebara Soroku Sensei den*. Tokyo: Ebara Sensei denki hensan iinkai, 1924.

Ebisawa, Arimichi, and Ōuchi Saburō. *Nihon Kirisutokyō shi*. Tokyo: Nihon Kirisutokyodan Shuppankyoku, 1970.

Eby, Charles S. *Christianity and Humanity: A Course of Lectures Delivered in Meiji Kuaido, Tokio, Japan, Including One Lecture Each by J. A. Ewing and J. A. Dixon*. Yokohama: Meiklejohn, 1883.

————. *The Eastern Pioneer of Western Civilization and the Recognition Her Efforts Receive*. Yokohama, 1884.

————. *The Immediate Christianization of Japan: Prospects, Plans, Results*. Tokio: Japan Mail, 1884.

————. *Methodism and the Missionary Problem: A Lecture Delivered Before the Theological Union of Victoria University, May 10th, 1886*. Toronto: Wm. Briggs, 1888.

————. *The Forward Movement in Japan: An Address to the Methodist Church*. Toronto: Christian Guardian, 1889.

Endicott, Stephen. *James G. Endicott: Rebel in China*. Toronto: Univ. of Toronto Press, 1980.

Fairbank, John King, ed. *The Missionary Enterprise in China and America*. Cambridge, Mass.: Harvard Univ. Press, 1974.

Fenwick, Malcolm C. *The Church of Christ in Corea: A Pioneer Missionary's Own Story*. New York: George H. Doran Company, 1911.

Fox, Grace. *Britain and Japan, 1858-1883*. Oxford: Clarendon Press, 1969.

Fraser, Mrs. Hugh (Mary). *A Diplomatist's Wife in Japan: Letters from Home to Home*. London: Hutchinson, 1899.

Fujita, S. *Ishin no seishin*. Tokyo: Misuzu Shobō, 1974.

Fujiwara, Fujiro. *Seisho no wayaku to buntairon*. Tokyo: Kirisuto Shinbunsha, 1974.

Fukamachi, Masakatsu. *Nihon Kirisutokyōdan Shizuoka Kyōkai hachijūgonen shi*. Shizuoka: Shizuoka Kyōkai, 1959.

Fulton, Austin. *Through Earthquake, Wind and Fire: Church and Mission in Manchuria, 1867-1950*. Edinburgh: The Saint Andrew Press, 1967.

Galbraith, John Kenneth. *A Life in Our Times: Memoirs*. Boston: Houghton Mifflin Company, 1981.

Gale, James Scarth. *Korean Sketches*. New York: Fleming H. Revell, 1898.

————. *The Vanguard*. New York: Fleming H. Revell, 1904.

————. *The History of the Korean People*. Seoul: Christian Literature Society, 1927.

————, comp. *A Korean-English Dictionary*. Yokohama: Kelly and Walsh, 1897.

Gendai Nihon Bungaku taike 6, Kitamura Tokoku Yamaji Aizan Shū. Tokyo: Chikuma Shōbō, 1972.

Gendai shi shiryō. Vols. 25-26. Tokyo: Misuzu Shobō, 1963.

Goforth, Rosalind. *Goforth of China*. Minneapolis: Dimension Books, n.d.

Griffis, William Elliot. *Honda, the Samurai: A Story of Modern Japan*. Boston: Congregational Sunday School and Publishing Society, 1890.

————. *The Mikado's Empire*. 9th ed. New York: Harper and Brothers, 1899.

————. *Verbeck of Japan: A Citizen of No Country*. New York and Chicago: Revell, 1900.

————. *A Maker of the Orient, Samuel Robline Brown: Pioneer Educator in China, America and Japan*. New York: Revell, 1902.

————. *Hepburn of Japan and His Wife and Helpmates*. Philadelphia and New York: Westminster Press, 1913.

Hall, Rosetta (Sherwood), ed. *The Life of Rev. William James Hall, M.D., Medical Missionary to the Slums of New York; Pioneer Missionary to Pyong Yang, Korea*. New York: Press of Eaton & Mains, 1897.

Hall, Sherwood. *With Stethoscope in Asia: Korea*. McLean, Va.: MCL Associates, 1978.

Havens, Thomas R. H. *Nishi Amane and Modern Japanese Thought*. Princeton: Princeton Univ. Press, 1970.

Hewitt, Gordon. *The Problems of Success: A History of the Church Missionary Society 1910-1942*. Vol. 2, *Asia: Overseas Partners*. London: SCM Press, 1977.

Holtom, D. C. *Shintō: The National Faith of Japan*. London: Kegan Paul, 1938.

Hunter, Jane. *Gospel of Gentility: American Women Missionaries in Turn-of-the-Century China*. New Haven and London: Yale Univ. Press, 1984.

Hyatt, Irwin T., Jr. *Our Ordered Lives Confess: Three Nineteenth Century American Missionaries in East Shantung*. Cambridge, Mass.: Harvard Univ. Press, 1976.

Iglehart, Charles W. *A Century of Protestant Christianity in Japan*. Tokyo: Charles E. Tuttle, 1959.

Iida, Hiroshi. *Shizuoka ken eigaku shi*. Tokyo: Kodansha, 1967.

Imai, John. *Bushido in the Past and in the Present*. Tokyo: Kanazashi, 1906.

Inoue, Kiyoshi. *Nihon no rekishi 20: Meiji Ishin*. Tokyo: Chuōkoron, 1974.

Iwanami Kōza. *Nihon Rekishi 16 Kindai 3*. Tokyo: Iwanami Shoten, 1976.

Jansen, M., ed. *Changing Japanese Attitudes toward Modernization*. Princeton: Princeton Univ. Press, 1969.

Jones, Hazel J. *Live Machines: Hired Foreigners and Meiji Japan*. Vancouver: Univ. of British Columbia Press, 1980.

Kan, Juon. *Heibonsha senshō 90: Chōsen kindai shi*. tokyo: Heibonsha, 1986.

Kan, Ujō. *Nihon toji shita Chōsen no shukyō to seiji*. Tokyo: Seibunsha, 1976.

Kano, Masanao. *Nihon no rekishi 27: Taishō Demokurashii*. Tokyo: Shogakukan, 1976.

Keenleyside, Hugh L. *Tokyo no sora ni Kanada no hata o: Memoirs of Hugh L. Keenleyside: Hammer the Golden Day*. Trans. Iwasaki Tsutomu. Tokyo: Seimuru Shuppankai, 1984.

Kim, Man-chong. *The Cloud Dream of the Nine: A Korean Novel: A Story of the Times of the Tangs of China about 840 A.D.* Trans. James Scarth Gale with an introduction by Elspeth K. Robertson Scott. London: Daniel O'Connor, 1922.

Kirisutokyō Gakkō Kyoiku Domei Hen. *Kirisutokyō Kyōikushi*. Tokyo: Sobunsha, 1977.

Kosaka, Masaaki, comp. and ed. *Japanese Thought in the Meiji Era*. Trans. and adapted by David Abosch. Tokyo: Pan Pacific Press, 1958.

Kozaki, Hiromichi. *Reminiscences of Seventy Years: The Autobiography of a Japanese Pastor*. Trans. Nariaki Kozaki. Tokyo: Kyobunkwan, 1934.

Kuranaga, Takashi. *Kanada Mesojisuto Nihon dendō gaishi*. Tokyo: Kanada Gōdō Kyōkai, Senkyōshikai, 1937.

_____. *Hiraiwa Yoshiyasu den*. Tokyo: Kyobunkwan, 1938.

Kuyama, Y., ed. *Kindai Nihon to Kirisutokyō: Taishō, Showa hen*. Tokyo: Kirisutokyō Gakuto Kyōdai dan, 1970.

Langdon, Frank. *The Politics of Canadian-Japanese Economic Relations 1952-1982*. Vancouver: Univ. of British Columbia Press, 1984.

Livingstone, W. P. *Mary Slessor of Calabar*. 1915. London: Hodder and Stoughton, 1935.

Lutz, Jesse Gregory. *China and Christian Colleges, 1850-1950*. Ithaca, N.Y.: Cornell Univ. Press, 1971.

Macdonald, Caroline, trans. *A Gentleman in Prison: With the Confessions of Tokichi Ishii Written in Tokyo Prison*. London: Student Christian Movement, 1923.

Mackay, George Leslie. *From Far Formosa: The Island, Its People*. Ed. J. A. Macdonald. Chicago: Fleming H. Revell, 1896.

McCully, Elizabeth A. *A Corn of Wheat or the Life of Rev. W. J. McKenzie of Korea*. 2nd ed. Toronto: Westminster Press, 1904.

McKenzie, F. A. *Korea's Fight for Freedom*. London: Simpkin, Marshall and Co., 1920.

Maclay, A. C. *A Budget of Letters from Japan: Reminiscences of Work and Travel in Japan*. New York: A. C. Armstrong, 1885.

MacLeod, Duncan. *The Island Beautiful: The Story of Fifty Years in North Formosa*. Toronto: Board of Foreign Missions of the Presbyterian Church in Canada, 1923.

McNab, John. *The White Angel of Tokyo: Miss Caroline Macdonald*. Toronto: Centenary Committee of the Canadian Churches, n.d.

Maruyama, Masao. *Nihon no shisō*. Tokyo: Iwanami Shoten, 1973.

Mathews, Basil. *John R. Mott: World Citizen*. London: Student Christian Movement, 1934.

Matsuo, Takayoshi. *Taishō Demokurashii*. Tokyo: Iwanami Shoten, 1974.

May, Earnest R., and J. C. Thomson, Jr. *American-East Asian Relations: A Survey*. Cambridge, Mass.: Harvard Univ. Press, 1972.

Moody, Campbell N. *The Heathen Heart: An Account of the Reception of the Gospel among the Chinese of Formosa*. Edinburgh and London: Oliphant, Anderson & Ferrier, 1907.

Morse, Edward S. *Japan Day by Day 1877, 1878-79, 1882-83*. 2 vols. Boston: Houghton Mifflin, 1917.

Motoda, J. S. *Nippon Seikōkai Shi*. Tokyo: Fukosha, 1910.

Mott, John R. *Addresses and Papers*. 2 vols. New York, 1941.

Murao, M. S., and W. H. Murray Walton. *Japan and Christ: A Study in Religious Issues*. London: Church Missionary Society, 1928.

Nahm, Andrew C., ed. *Korea under Japanese Colonial Rule: Studies of the Policy and Techniques of Japanese Colonialism*. Kalamazoo: Center for Korean Studies, Western Michigan Univ., 1973.

Nara, Shoitsuro. *Nihon YMCA shi*. Tokyo: Nihon YMCA Domei, 1968.

Neill, Stephen. *Colonialism and Christian Mission*. London: Lutterworth Press, 1966.

——. *The Cross over Asia*. London: Canterbury Press, 1968.

——. *A History of Christian Missions*. Harmondsworth: Penguin Books, 1971.

Nihon Kirisutokyōdan shi hensan iinkai hen. *Nihon Kirisutokyōdan shi*. Tokyo: Nihon Kirisutokyōdan Shuppan Kyōku, 1967.

Nihon Mesojisuto Shitaya Kyōkai rokujūnen shi hensan iinkai shusai. *Nihon Mesojisuto Shitaya Kyōkai rokujūnen shi*. Tokyo: Rekishi hensan iinkai, 1939.

Nihon seikōkai rekishi hensan iinkai hen. *Nihon Seikōkai hyakunen shi*. Tokyo: Nihon Seikōkai kyōmuin bunshokyoku, 1959.

Nish, Ian H. *The Anglo-Japanese Alliance: The Diplomacy of Two Island Empires*. London: Athlone Press, 1966.

——. *Alliance in Decline: Anglo-Japanese Relations, 1908-1923*. London: Athlone Press, 1972.

Norman, Egerton Herbert. *Japan's Emergence as a Modern State: Political and Economic Problems of the Meiji Period*. 2 vols. New York: Institute of Pacific Relations, 1940.

Norman, Gwen R. P., and W. Howard Norman. *One Hundred Years in Japan: A History of the Canadian Methodist and United Church of Canada Missions in Japan, 1873-1973*. 2 vols. Toronto: United Church of Canada Board of World Missions, 1980.

Norman, W. Howard. *Nagano no Noruman*. Trans. H. Hirabayashi. Tokyo: Fukuinkan, 1965.

Notehelfer, F. G. *Kōtoku Shūsui: A Portrait of a Japanese Radical*. Cambridge: Cambridge Univ. Press, 1971.

——. *American Samurai: Captain L. Janes and Japan*. Princeton: Princeton Univ. Press, 1985.

Ogihara, Takahashi. *Nakamura Keiu to Meiji keimō shisō*. Tokyo: Waseda Daigaku Shuppanbu, 1984.

Ōhama, Tetsuya. *Meiji Kirisutokyō kaishi no kenkyū*. Tokyo: Yoshikawa Kōbunkan, 1979.

Ōta, Aito. *Meiji Kirisutokyō no ryūiki: Shizuoka Bandō to bakushintachi*. Tokyo: Tsukiji Shokan, 1979.

——, and Takaya Michio. *Yokohama Bandō hanashi*. Tokyo: Tsukiji Shokan, 1981.

Ōta, Yuzō. *Uchimura Kanzō—sono sekaishugi to Nihonshugi o megute.* Tokyo: Kenkyūsha Shuppan, 1977.

————. *Taiheyō no hashi to shite no Nitobe Inazō.* Tokyo: Misuzu Shobō, 1986.

Paik, L. G. *A History of Protestant Missions in Korea 1880-1910.* 2nd ed. Seoul: Yonsei Univ. Press, 1971.

Paku, Kyon Shiku. *Heibonsha senshō 49: Chōsen san ichi dokuritsu undō.* Tokyo: Heibonsha, 1976.

Paku, Wuon Shiku. *Tōyō bunko 216: Chōsen dokuritsu undō no ketsu shi.* Trans. Kan Dokusen. 2 vols. Tokyo: Heibonsha, 1978.

Palmer, Spencer J. *Korea and Christianity: The Problem of Identification with Tradition.* Seoul: Hollym Corporation, 1967.

Pierson, John D. *Tokutomi Sohō 1863-1957: A Journalist for Modern Japan.* Princeton: Princeton Univ. Press, 1980.

Platt, H. E. *The Story of the Years, 1881-1906.* Toronto: Women's Missionary Society of the United Church of Canada, 1930.

Powles, Cyril Hamilton. *Victorian Missionaries in Meiji Japan, the Shiba Sect: 1873-1900.* Publication Series vol. 4, no. 1. Toronto: Univ. of Toronto– York Univ. Joint Centre on Modern East Asian Studies, 1987.

Pringsheim, Klaus H. *Neighbours across the Pacific: The Development of Economic and Political Relations between Canada and Japan.* Westport, Conn.: Greenwood Press, 1983.

Proceedings of the General Conference of Protestant Missionaries in Japan Held in Osaka, Japan, 1883. Yokohama: Meiklejohn, 1883.

Proceedings of the General Conference of Protestant Missionaries in Japan, 1900. Tokyo: Methodist Publishing Co., 1901.

Rabe, Valentin H. *The Home Base of American China Missions, 1880-1920.* Cambridge, Mass.: Harvard Univ. Press, 1978.

Reed, James. *The Missionary Mind and American East Asia Policy 1911-1915.* Cambridge, Mass.: Harvard Univ. Press, 1983.

Reischauer, Haru Matsukata. *Samurai and Silk: A Japanese and American Heritage.* Cambridge, Mass.: Belknap Press of Harvard Univ. Press, 1986.

Rhodes, Harry A., ed. *The History of the Korean Presbyterian Church U.S.A. 1884-1934.* Seoul: Chōsen Mission Presbyterian Church U.S.A., 1935.

Robinson, J. Cooper. *The Island Empire of the East: Being a Short History of Japan and Missionary Work therein with Special Reference to the Mission of the M.S.C.C.* Toronto: Prayer and Study Union of the Church of England in Canada, 1912.

Rutt, Richard. *James Scarth Gale and His History of the Korean People.* Seoul: Royal Asiatic Society, Korea Branch in conjunction with Taewon Publishing Company, 1972.

Ryerson, Egerton. *The Netsuke of Japan.* London: G. Bell, 1958.

Sansom, George B. *The Western World and Japan: A Study in the Interaction of European and Asiatic Cultures.* New York: Vintage Books, 1973.

Satoh, Henry. *My Boyhood: A Reminiscence.* 2nd ed. Tokyo: Japan Times Publishing Co., 1921.

Saunby, John W. *The New Chivalry in Japan: Methodist Golden Jubilee, 1873-1923.* Toronto: The Missionary Society of the Methodist Church, 1923.

Scheiner, Irwin. *Christian Converts and Social Protest in Meiji Japan.* Berkeley: Univ. of California Press, 1970.

Schwantes, Robert S. *Japanese and Americans: A Century of Cultural Relations.* 1955. Westport, Conn.: Greenwood Press, 1976.

Scott, Munro. *McClure: The China Years*. Markham: Penguin Books, Canada, 1979.

Scott, William. *Canadians in Korea: Brief Historical Sketch of Canadian Mission Work in Korea: Part One to the Time of Church Union*. Toronto: United Church of Canada Board of World Mission, 1970.

Shaw, Loretta L. *Japan in Transition*. London: Church Missionary Society, 1922.

Shaw, R. D. M. *Enlightenment and Salvation*. London, 1930.

—————, ed. and trans. *The Blue Cliff Record, the Hekigan Roku*. London: Michael Joseph, 1961.

—————, trans. *Hakuin Zenji, the Embossed Tea Kettle*. London: Michael Joseph, 1963.

Shepperson, George, and Thomas Price. *Independent African—John Chilembwe and the Origins, Setting and Significance of the Nyasaland Native Rising of 1915*. Edinburgh: Edinburgh Univ. Press, 1958.

Shizuoka Eiwa Jo Gakuin hachijūnen shi hensan iinkai. *Shizuoka Eiwa Jo Gakuin hachijūnen shi*. Shizuoka: Shizuoka Eiwa Jo Gakuin, 1971.

Shizuoka Mesojisuto Kyōkai rokujūnen shi hensan iinkai. *Shizuoka Mesojisuto Kyōkai rokujūnen shi*. Shizuoka: Shizuoka Mesojisuto Kyōkai, 1937.

Stephenson, F. C. (Mrs.). *One Hundred Years of Canadian Methodist Missions, 1824-1924*. 2 vols. Toronto: Missionary Society of the Methodist Church, 1925.

Sugii, Mutsurō. *Tokutomi Sohō no kenkyū*. Tokyo: Hosei Daigaku Shuppan-kyōku, 1977.

Sumiya, Mikio. *Nihon shakai to Kirisutokyō*. Tokyo: Tokyo Daigaku Shuppankai, 1956.

—————. *Nihon no shakai shisō: kindaika to Kirisutokyō*. Tokyo: Tokyo Daigaku Shuppankai, 1968.

—————. *Nihon Purotesutanto shiron*. Tokyo: Shinkyō Shuppansha, 1983.

Sutherland, Alexander. *Methodist Church and Missions in Canada and Newfoundland: A Brief Account of the Methodist Church in Canada, What It Is and What It Has Done*. Toronto: Young People's Forward Movement for Missions, 1906.

Taiheyō Sensō Ge'in Chōsabu, Nihon Kokusai Seiji Gakkai. *Taiheyō sensō e no michi—kaisen gaikōkshi*. 7 vols. Tokyo: Asahi Shimbunsha, 1963.

Takahashi, Masao. *Nakamura Keiu*. Tokyo: Yoshikawa Kobunkan, 1967.

Takeda, Kyoko, ed. *Gendai Nihon Shisō Taikei*, vol. 6: *Kirisutokyō*. Tokyo: Chikuma Shobō, 1975.

Taylor, J. Hudson. *To China ... with Love*. Minneapolis: Dimension Books, n.d.

Thomas, Wilburn T. *Protestant Beginnings in Japan: The First Three Decades 1859-1889*. Tokyo and Rutland, Vt.: Charles E. Tuttle Company, 1959.

Thomson, Andrew. *The Life and Letters of Rev. R. P. MacKay: A Record of Faith, Friendship and Good Cheer*. Toronto: Ryerson Press, 1932.

Tong, Hollington K. *Christianity in Taiwan: A History*. Taipeh: China Post, 1972.

Tōyō Eiwa Jo Gakuin nanajūnen shi henshū iinkai. *Tōyō Eiwa Jo Gakuin nanajūnen shi*. Tokyo: Tōyō Eiwa Jo Gakuin, 1955.

Tōyō Eiwa Jo Gakuin hyakunen shi hensan jikkō iinkai. *Tōyō Eiwa Jo Gakuin hyakunen shi*. Tokyo: Tōyō Eiwa Jo Gakuin hyakunen shi hensan jikkō iinkai, 1984.

Tsunakawa, Banri. *Ebina Danjō, Uemura Masahisa: Nihon no daihyōteki Kirisutosha 2*. Tokyo: Tōkai Daigaku Shuppankai, 1965.

Tsurumi, E. Patricia. *Japanese Colonial Education in Taiwan, 1895-1945.* Cambridge, Mass.: Harvard Univ. Press, 1977.

Ushiyama, Setsuai. *Kirisutokyō shinkō dendō shi: Wara Chōrō, dendō no kiseki.* Nagano: Ginga Shobō, 1980.

Varg, Paul A. *Missionaries, Chinese and Diplomats: The American Protestant Missionary Movement in China, 1890-1952.* Princeton: Princeton Univ. Press, 1958.

Waller, John G. *Our Canadian Mission in Japan.* Toronto: Joint Committee on Summer Schools and Institutes of the Church of England in Canada, 1930.

Walmsley, Lewis C. *Bishop in Honan: Mission and Museum in the Life of William C. White.* Toronto: Univ. of Toronto Press, 1974.

Walsh, H. H. *The Christian Church in Canada.* Toronto: Ryerson Paperbacks, 1968.

Warren, Max. *The Missionary Movement from Britain in Modern History.* London: SCM Press, 1965.

————. *Social History and Christian Mission.* London: SCM Press, 1967.

Yamaji, Aizan. *Gendai Nippon Kyōkai shiron.* Reprinted in Gendai Nihon Bunyaku taike, no. 6, *Kitamura Tokoku Yamaji Aizan Shū.* Tokyo: Chikuma Shobō, 1972.

Yamamoto, Taijirō, and Yoichi Muto, comps. *Uchimura Kanzō eibun shosaku zenshū.* 7 vols. Tokyo: Kyobunkwan, 1971-72.

Yamanashi Eiwa Gakuin shi hensan iinkai. *Yamanashi Eiwa Gakuin hachijūnen shi.* Kofu: Yamanashi Eiwa Gakuin, 1969.

Yūki, Reiichirō. *Kyūbaku shinsensō no Yūki Muhimitsu.* Tokyo: Chūbunko, 1976.

ARTICLES AND DISSERTATIONS

Armstrong, Robert C. "The Effect of the Earthquake on Christian Work." *Japan Evangelist* 30 (November-December 1923): 127-33.

Bamba, Nobuya. "Nikka bunka koshōshi josetsu: Kanada Mesojisuto Mishyon to Meiji no shisōkatachi." *Kokusai Kankei Gaku Kenkyū* 3 (1977).

————. "Nippon Kanada kankei no tenkai: sono kaiko to tenbō." *Kokusai Mondai* (February 1977).

Baldwin, Frank. "Missionaries and the March First Movement: Can Moral Man be Neutral?" In Andrew C. Nahm, ed., *Korea under Japanese Colonial Rule: Studies of the Policy and Techniques of Japanese Colonialism*, 185-219. Kalamazoo: Center for Korean Studies, Western Michigan Univ., 1973.

Bates, C. J. L. "A Challenge from Japan." *Christian Guardian*, November 21, 1917.

Chen, Edward I-te. "Formosan Political Movements under Japanese Colonial Rule, 1914-1937." *Journal of Asian Studies* 21, no. 3 (May 1972): 477-98.

————. "Japan: Oppressor or Modernizer? A Comparison of the Effects of Colonial Control in Korea and Formosa." In Andrew C. Nahm, ed., *Korea under Japanese Colonial Rule: Studies of the Policy and Techniques of Japanese Colonialism*, 251-60. Kalamazoo: Center for Korean Studies, Western Michigan Univ., 1973.

————. "Japanese Colonialism in Korea and Formosa: A Comparison of its Effects upon the Development of Nationalism." Unpublished Ph.D. dissertation, Univ. of Pennsylvania, 1968.

Cholmondeley, Lionel B. "A Review of Japan's Attitude Towards Christianity." *The Contemporary Review* 105 (January-June 1914): 220-26.

Coates, Harper H. "The Second Japanese Bishop." *Japan Evangelist* 29, no. 5 (1911): 217-20.

"Davidson Macdonald M.D." *Japan Evangelist* 12, no. 3 (1905): 72-80.

Dohi, Akio. "Christianity and Politics in the Taisho Period of Democracy." *Japanese Religions* 7, no. 3 (July 1972): 42-68.

Endicott, J. "Can Christianity Make Good in Japan?" *Christian Guardian*, June 5, 1918.

Fisher, Galen. "Recent Labor Movements in Japan." *Christian Movement in Japan, Korea and Formosa* (1919): 198-210.

―――. "The Missionary Significance of the Last Ten Years." *International Review of Missions* 11 (April 1922): 193-211.

Grajdanzev, A. "Formosa (Taiwan) under Japanese Rule." *Pacific Affairs* 15, no. 3 (September 1941): 311-24.

Heaslett, Samuel. "The Present Spiritual Conflict." *Christian Movement in Japan, Korea and Formosa* (1923): 59-70.

Hamilton, Heber J. "The Diocese of Mid-Japan." *Mission World* 15 (November 1917).

Hara, Kishi. "Kyokutō Roshia ni okeru Chōsen dokuritsu undō to Nihon." *San Sen Ri* 17 (Tokushū San Ichi Undō rokujū shunen) (1979): 47-53.

Harris, Merriman C., trans. and condenser. "Japanese Lectures: Fukuzawa's Lecture on Religion (Delivered at Mita, Tokyo, Last Summer); Christianity a National Injury (Delivered Recently in Kioto)," *Chrysanthemum* 1 (1881): 392-96.

Howes, John F. "The Non-Church Christian Movement in Japan." *Transactions of the Asiatic Society of Japan* third series, 5 (December 1957): 119-37.

―――. "Japan's Enigma: The Young Uchimura Kanzo." Unpublished Ph.D. thesis, Columbia Univ., 1965.

―――. "Japanese Protestant Stereotypes and the Role of the Missionary." *Japan Christian Quarterly* 33, no. 3 (1967): 151-61.

―――. "Japanese Christians and American Missionaries." In Marius B. Jansen, ed., *Changing Japanese Attitudes toward Modernization*, 337-68. Princeton: Princeton Univ. Press, 1969.

Hutchinson, Archibald C. "The Present Conditions." CMS *Japan Quarterly* 10, no. 6 (April 1920): 199-202.

Hutchinson, William R. "Modernism and Missions: The Liberal Search for an Exportable Christianity, 1875-1935." In John King Fairbank, ed., *The Missionary Enterprise in China and America*, 110-31. Cambridge, Mass.: Harvard Univ. Press, 1974.

Imai, John. "Bushido." *South Tokyo Diocesan Magazine* 9, no. 28 (December 1905): 78-84.

Ion, A. Hamish. "Edward Warren Clark and Early Meiji Japan: A Case Study of Cultural Contact." *Modern Asian Studies* 11, no. 4 (1977): 557-72.

Jones, Alan William. "Herbert Hamilton Kelly S.S.M. 1860-1950: A Study in Failure (A Contribution to the Search for a Credible Catholicism)." Unpublished Ph.D. thesis, Nottingham Univ., 1971.

Jones, G. H. "Rev. William J. McKenzie: A Memoir." *Korean Repository* 2 (August 1895): 295-98.

Kagawa, Toyōhiko. "The Cooperative Movement in Japan." *Japan Christian Quarterly* 5 (July 1930): 240-48.

260 THE CROSS AND THE RISING SUN

Kan, Juon. "1919 nen no San Ichi Chōsen Dokuritsu Undō." *San Sen Ri* 17 (Tokushu San Ichi Undō rokujū shunen) (1979): 26-38.

Kim, Eui Whan. "The Korean Church under Japanese Occupation with Special Reference to the Resistance Movement within Presbyterianism." Unpublished Ph.D. dissertation, Temple Univ., 1966.

Kinmonth, Earl H. "Nakamura Keiu and Samuel Smiles: A Victorian Confucian and a Confucian Victorian." *American Historical Review* 85, no. 3 (June 1980): 535-56.

Langdon, Frank. "Impressions from the World's Sunday School Convention and the Far East." *Christian Guardian*, December 22, 1920.

Lea, Arthur. "Some Difficulties of the Japanese in Accepting Christianity." *South Tokyo Diocesan Magazine* 9, no. 28 (December 1905): 84-88.

———. "Church Membership." *Japan Christian Quarterly* 5 (January 1930): 17-23.

Matsuo, Takayoshi. "Nihon Kumiai Kirisutokyōkai no Chōsen dendō." *Shisō* (July 1968): 949-65.

Matsuzawa, Hiroaki. "Japanese Civilization as Viewed by Japanese Intellectuals." 22-page typescript in the possession of the author.

———. "Kirisutokyō to chishikijin." In Iwanami Kōza, *Nihon Rekishi 16, Kindai 3*, 282-320. Tokyo: Iwanami Shoten, 1976.

———. "History and Prospect of Canada-Japan Relations: Through my Personal Experiences." *Hokudai Hōgaku Ronshū* 36 (October 1985): 644-723.

McDonald, G. "George Leslie MacKay: Missionary Success in Nineteenth-Century Taiwan." *Papers on China* 21 (Cambridge, Mass.).

McKenzie, William J. "Seven Months among the Tong Haks." *Korean Repository* 2 (June 1895): 201-208.

Nitobe, Inazō. "The Penetration of Japanese Life and Thought by Christianity." *Japan Christian Quarterly* 4 (October 1929): 299-306.

Norman, Dan. "Political Change in Japan Influenced by Christian Teaching." *Missionary Bulletin* 15, no. 4 (October-December 1919): 577-83.

Norman, Gwen R. P. "Evangelism in Yamanashiken, 1877-1881." *Alaska and Japan: Perspectives of Past and Present* (1972): 136-49.

Norman, W. Howard H. "They Went Before... Daniel Riel McKenzie (1861-1935)." *Japan Christian Quarterly* (1955): 74-76.

Notehelfer, Fred G. "Ebina Danjō: A Christian Samurai of the Meiji Period." *Papers on Japan* 2 (Cambridge, Mass.) (August 1963): 1-56.

———. "Leroy Lansing Janes and the American Board." In Dōshisha Daigaku Jimbun Kagaku Kenkyūjo/Kirisutokyō Shakai Mondai Kenkyūkai hen. *Nihon no Kindaika to Kirisutokyō*, 3-51. Tokyo: Shinkyō Shuppansha, 1973.

Phillips, Clifton J. "The Student Volunteer Movement and Its Role in China Missions, 1886-1920." In John King Fairbank, ed., *The Missionary Enterprise in China and America*, 91-109. Cambridge, Mass.: Harvard Univ. Press, 1974.

Powles, Cyril Hamilton. "Nihon seikōkai no keisei ki ni okeru: Kanada seikōkai no koken 1873-1900." *Shingaku No Koe* 7 (1964): 1-8.

———. "Victorian Missionaries in Meiji, Japan: The Shiba Sect 1873-1900." Ph.D. thesis, Univ. of British Columbia, 1968.

———. "Foreign Missionaries and Japanese Culture in the Late Nineteenth

Century: Four Patterns of Approach." *North East Asia Journal of Theology* (1969): 14-28.

————. "Trinity's First Man to Japan." *Trinity* 9, no. 2 (1971): 6-7.

————. "The Development of Japanese-Canadian Relations in the Age of Missionary Activity, 1873-1930." *Kanada Kenkyū Nempō/Annual Review of Canadian Studies* (Tokyo, 1980): 146-65.

————. "Abe Isoo and the Role of Christians in the Founding of the Japanese Socialist Movement, 1895-1905." *Papers on Japan*, vol. 1 (Cambridge, Mass., 1961), pp. 89-109.

Rabe, Valentin H. "Evangelical Logistics: Mission Support and Resources to 1920." In John King Fairbank, ed., *The Missionary Enterprise in China and America*, 56-90. Cambridge, Mass.: Harvard Univ. Press, 1974.

Saeki, P. Y. "The Sources of Bushido." *South Tokyo Diocesan Magazine* 12, no. 35 (March 1908): 5-12.

Saunby, J. W. "The Question of Japanese Immigration." *The Christian Guardian*, April 24, 1918.

Schwantes, Robert S. "American Influence in the Education of Meiji Japan." Unpublished Ph.D. dissertation, Harvard Univ., 1950.

————. "Christianity versus Science: A Conflict of Ideas in Meiji Japan." *Far Eastern Quarterly* 12 (1952-53): 123-32.

Scott, John. "Hon. Soroku Ebara M.P." *Japan Evangelist* 9, no. 2 (1902): 42-46.

Shin, Paul Hobom. "The Korean Colony in Chientao: A Study of Japanese Imperialism and Militant Korean Nationalism, 1905-1932." Unpublished Ph.D. dissertation, Univ. of Washington, 1980.

Sugii, Mutsurō. "Yokoi Saheida to Yokoi Daihei no Amerika ryūgaku: Oranda Kaiseiha Kyōkai senkyōshi Furubeki no katsudo." *Shakai Kagaku* 11 (1970): 1-110.

————. "Kozaki Hiromichi no Tokyo dendō to Rikugo Zasshi no hakken." In Dōshisha Daigaku Jibun Kagaku Kenkyūjo/Kirisutokyō Shakai Mondai Kenkyūkai hen. *Nihon no Kindaika to Kirisutokyō*, 131-66. Tokyo: Shinkyō Shuppansha, 1973.

————. "Kumamoto Bandō. Doshisha to bungaku: Doshisha bungaku no taidō." *Bungaku* 47, no. 4 (1979): 167-86.

Trollope, M. N. "The Japanese Treatment of Corea." *The East and the West* 12 (1923): 57-63.

Verbeck, G. F. "Review of the Rikugo Zasshi." *Chrysanthemum* 1 (April 1881): 150-53.

Watanabe, Marao. "Wm. Wira: W. S. Kuraku no wakiyaku." *Nihon Kagakushi Kenkyū* 2, 13, 109 (1974): 26-31.

Wilkinson, A. T. "What Do the Japanese Want?," *The Christian Guardian*, March 29, 1922.

Yamamoto, Yukinori. "Yamaji Aizan to kirisutokyō: Meiji Niju nendai o chushin to shite." *Kirisutokyō Shakai Mondai Kenkyū* 26 (December 1977): 102-62.

————. "Shizuoka han ōyatoi gaikokujin kyōshi E. W. Clark: Shizuoka bandō seiritsu no haike." *Kirisutokyō Shakai Mondai Kenkyū* 29 (March 1981): 114-56.

————. "Rikugō Zasshi to Hiraiwa Yoshiyasu." In Dōshisha Daigaku Jibun Kagaku Kenkyūjo hen, *Rikugō Zasshi no kenkyū*. 2 vols. Tokyo: Kyobunkan, 1984.

Index

Abe, Isoo, 11

Africa, British missionary movement in, xvii; Calabar mission in, xiv; Christian movements in, 221

Ainsworth, F., 149

Allen, G. C., 114

Allen, Annie, 164

Alston, Beilby, 194-95

Amenomori, Nobushige, 46

American Baptists, 39, 157

American Board Mission, xvi-xvii, xix, 21, 65, 126, 135

American Church Mission (Protestant Episcopalian), xv, 39, 68, 155

American Dutch Reformed Church Mission, xvi, 39, 55

American East Asia Policy, xvii

American Immigration Bill (1924), 183

American Missionary Societies, 157

American Presbyterian Mission (North) in Korea, xvi, 13, 32, 39, 111, 135, 140, 157, 166, 167

American Presbyterian Mission (South) in Korea, 13, 135, 167

Amery, L. S., 204

Ami Tribe, Taiwan, 176

Ancestor worship, 149-50

Amritsar, 201

Anglican Church of Canada, see also Canadian Anglican, xx, 2, 19; and Japanese immigrants in Canada, 180-81

Anglo-American world and East Asia, 2

Anglo-Japanese Allliance, 179, 181, 202, 206, 213

Anglo-Oriental Ladies School, see Tōyō Eiwa Jo Gakkō

Anne of Green Gables, 216

Aoyama Gakuin, 130

Archbishop of Canterbury, public stand against Japanese actions in China (1937), 219

Archer, Deaconess A. L., 31; picture, xxv

Arminians, xvi

Armstrong, A. E., 26, 106, 112, 136, 188-90, 201-203, 206-208, 212, 218

Arnup, Jesse, 26

Arthur, William, 74

Asagawa, Hiromi, 48-49, 59-60, 62-63, 69, 73-74, 76, 126; picture, xxi

Asiatic Society of Japan, 111

Atami, 109

Austin, Alvyn, 81

Australian Presbyterian Mission in Korea, 166

Avison, Dr. Oliver R., 32, 137, 140; and Korean independence movement, 32; and Severance Hospital, 32

Azabu (Tokyo), 30, 126; Azabu Middle School, 43, 129-30

Barclay, Thomas, 82, 208-209

Barker, A. H., 191

Bates, Charles J. L., xxv, 103, 130, 162, 181-83

Beauchamp, Edward, xix

Bethune, Norman, 217

Bickersteth, Bishop Edward, xiv

Bird, Miss F., 152

262

Blackmore, Isabella, 119-20, 124

Boxer Rebellion, 167

Brinkley, Frank, 91-92

British Anglican Missions in Japan, xiv-xv, xx, 7, 9, 29, 687, 111, 149, 151, 155, 157, 161, 163, 181, 183; diocese of Kyūshū, 148; diocese of South Tokyo, 29, 223

British Anglican Missions in Canada, 19

British Consul in Mukden, 191-92; in Seoul, 191

British Foreign Office, 193-96, 198, 201, 204-206, 214; Legation in Japan, 39, 104, 107

British Wesleyan Methodist Church, 63

Brown, S. R., 61; description of Bible Class at Dōjinsha, 55

Buddhism, 46-47, 74, 111-12, 148-49, 154, 157, 160, 165, 201; antipathy toward Christianity, 9; Canadian missionaries' interest in, 112; in Korea, 112, 166; potential threat to Christian advance, 148

Bunyan, John, 112; Pilgrim's Progress, 113

Burks, Ardath W., xix

Burns, William Chalmers, 33

Bushido, 150-51

Caldarola, Carlo, xix

Calvinism, xvi

Campbell, William, 82, 208-209

Canada, 130, 144; and Japanese immigration problem, 182-83; empathy with people under colonial rule, 179; government of, 201; forced movement of Japanese Canadians in, 217; Protestant churches in, 18; racial hatred toward Japanese in, 217; role of Church to convert and assimilate East Asian immigrants, 183

Canadian Academy, 106, 133-35

Canadian Anglicans in Japan, xv-xvi, 13, 19, 22-24, 28-31, 106, 135, 148-51, 157-58, 160-61, 163, 165-66, 176, 185, 219; diocese of Mid-Japan, 19, 22, 153; kindergarten training school (Nagoya), 163; sanatorium for tuberculosis sufferers, 163; Women's Auxiliary of the Church of England in Canada (WA), 29-31

Canadian Church Missionary Society (CCMS), 29

Canadian Embassy in Tokyo, establishment, 1, 108, 216

Canadian-Japanese relations, xiii, 102

Canadian Methodist Church, 27, 38, 59, 67, 83, 93, 99; and prohibition of opium trade in Canada, 180; formation, 19; General Conference (1878), 67; Missionary Conference within, 97

Canadian Methodists in China, 26, 110

Canadian Methodist Mission in Japan, xiv-xvi, 2, 4, 6-7, 12, 15, 20-25, 30-36, 38-40, 68, 76, 77, 84, 96, 100-101, 107-108, 110-11, 123, 127, 129-30, 133, 136-37, 140-41, 147, 149, 154-55, 182-85, 187, 204, 213; advocate need for racial tolerance, 183; contribution to male education, 145; damage to property in Kantō Earthquake, 165; formation, 20, 28-29; Japan Conference, 98-99, 157; Japan District, 49, 63; Japanese language abilities of missionaries, 103; missionary concern for the welfare of the Japanese people, 70; optimism about Christianization of Japan, 12; proposed union with Methodist Episcopal (North) mission (1878), 67; union with Methodist Episcopal missions, 21, 155; slum work in Tokyo, 12, 163-64, 166, 177

Canadian Methodist Mission Board, 48, 59, 64-65, 67, 95, 97, 99, 100-101, 121, 134, 164

Canadian Methodist Mission Council, 131-32, 162, 164

Canadian Methodist Missionary Society (CMMS), 25, 95, 134, 157; Committee of Finance and Consultation, 66; reduced expenditures, 48

Canadian Methodist Toronto Conference, 49, 67

Canadian Methodist Young People's Forward Movement, 26-27

Canadian Methodist Woman's Missionary Society (WMS), 29-30, 101, 117, 119-23, 125, 135, 152, 157; contribution to female education in Japan, 117, 144-45; Japan Mission WMS Council, 156; slum work in Tokyo, 164

Canadian missionaries, and introduction of Western fruits, grains and vegetables in Japan and Korea, 105; background of, 2-3, 5; criticism of Japanese colonial rule in Korea, 14-15; in China, 1

Canadian Presbyterian Church, 2, 175; General Assembly and Great Revival in Korea, 169; Maritimes Division and mission in Korea, 19, 22-23; unwilling to finance Avison, Gale, Harkness, and Hardie, 32; Western Division of, 169-70

Canadian Presbyterian Missionary Society, and educational crisis in Korea in 1916, 136; Maritimes Division of, 33

Canadian Presbyterian Mission Board, 143

Canadian Presbyterian Mission in Chientao, 206

Canadian Presbyterian Mission in Korea, 13, 22, 24, 31, 136-37, 139, 140, 144, 148, 166-68, 173, 190-91, 196, 200-201, 205-206, 211, 213; and union of higher educational endeavours, 140; champions of democracy against militarism, 189; protest against Japanese atrocities, 196, 213

Canadian Presbyterian Mission in Taiwan, xiv-xv, 15, 22, 24, 31, 33, 34, 173-76, 208-209; and girls' school, 141, 143; medical work, 143

Carlson, Ellsworth, xviii

Carman, Albert, and Alexander Sutherland, 25; opposition to union of Canadian Methodist mission with Methodist Episcopal missions, 20-21

Cartmell, Martha J., 30, 118-19; picture, xxiii

Cary, Otis, xvi

Cassidy, F. A., 49, 95

Central Tabernacle, 100, 103, 156, 161-62

Chang Hao Chiang, 198

Chang Tso-Lin, 197

Chientao (Kantō) Province, 13, 169, 180, 192, 197-99, 201, 218; Intervention, 202-207, 214; Punitive Expedition in, 14, 196, 201

Chilembwe, John, xvii

China, 33-34, 167, 182, 190, 205; academic interest in American China missions, xvii-xix; barrier to Christianity, 208; cultural tradition, 166; issue, 218; Japanese foreign policy and, 181; missions in, 33-34; Revolution (1911), xvii; Western domination of, 181

China Inland Mission, xiv, 94, 114

Chinese Eastern Railway, 197

Chinese head tax, 182

Chondōkyo, 166

Chōsen, Government-General of, 14, 169, 190, 209, 213; and assimilation through education, 138; and missionaries, 14

Chōsen Christian College, 139-40

Chōshū, 73

Chown, S., 95, 204

Christian Guardian, 96, 185

Christian Movement in Japan, Formosa and Korea, 113

Christian movement in Korea, 169
Christianity, and nationalism, 84; and Shakai Minshutō, 11; and socialism, 10-11; and Westernization, 84; English language and propagation of, 49; in Japan and Korea compared, 167-68; prohibition in Japan, 37
Christie, Loring, 204
Churchill, Winston, 204
Church Missionary Society (CMS), xvii
Church of England in Canada, *see* Anglican Church of Canada, Canadian Anglican
Clark, Edward Warren, 38-39, 42-44, 49-54, 56, 58, 60-61, 70, 88; and Cochran, 39, 52, 55; and Hiraiwa, 60-61; and Gakumonjo, 42, 51-52; and Kaisei Gakkō, 60, 61; and Nakamura, 42-43, 51-56
Clark, W. S., 37-38
Coates, Harper H., 95, 103, 112, 151, 154
Cochran, George, xv, 3-4, 28, 34-36, 38-39, 40, 48, 50, 53, 60, 62, 71, 83, 85, 87, 118, 126, 155, 221; and E. W. Clark, 39, 52, 55; and Hiraiwa, 60-61; and Kaisei Gakkō, 55, 58, 60; and Nakamura Keiū, 40, 48, 50-59, 66; and Old Testament translation committee, 113; and Self-Support Band, 96-99, 104, 106-107, 111, 113; and Tōyō Eiwa Gakkō, 68; at Dōjinsha, 52, 54, 55-57; background, 2, 29; complains about lack of Canadian support for Japan mission, 62, 63; elected chairman of Japan District, 63; experience at Dōjinsha compared with Shaw's at Keiō Gijuku, 68; forms Methodist Class in Tokyo, 62; house on Dōjinsha campus, 57; Japanese language ability, 58; moves from Dōjinsha to Surugadai, 65; opinion of changed Japanese

attitude toward Christianity in 1877, 66; particular strengths, 51; picture, xxii; President of Toronto Conference, 67; warned about Eby, 64-65
Cochran, Mrs., 65, 93; poor health, 67; teaching at Dōjinsha Girls' School, 69
Cochran, Maude, 118
Cochran, Susie, 118
Cohen, Paul A., xviii
College of Engineering (Tokyo), 81
Confederation (1867), and the missionary challenge of Western Canada, 19
Conference on Pacific Affairs (Washington), 203
Confucianists, 166, 193
Congregational Churches in Canada, 20
Committee of Reference and Counsel of the Foreign Mission Board Conference, 157
Conspiracy Case (Korea, 1911), 187, 209-10, 213; trial (1912), 169
Cornwall Legh, Nellie, 163
Courtice, S. R., 124
Crane, J. C., 168
Crummy, Ebenezer, 95, 129
Cunningham, M. J., 121
Cunningham, W. B., 205
Curzon of Keddleston, 195-96, 204
Cushing, Miss, 95

Dalhousie University, 22, 33
Darwinian Ideas, and E. S. Morse, 88; at Kaisei Gakkō, 88; *Origin of Species*, 60
Dohi, Akio, 86
Dōjinsha School, 40, 48, 51, 52, 54-58, 60-61, 65-66, 68-69; Cochran's religious services at, 57-58, 60-61; girls' school, 69; group, 74; size in 1874, 54; S. R. Brown's description of Bible Class at, 55; teachers, 90
Dōjinsha Bungaku Zasshi, 69
Dōshisha College (School), 21, 65, 126, 130

Dowly, Dr., 59
Drummond, Richard H., xvi
Dunlop, J. G., 95

East Asian Crisis (1930s), 218
East Asian Immigration, problem of, 182
Eaton family, 28
Ebara, Soroku, 60, 71-75, 77, 81, 86, 98-99, 128-29, 212, 220; background, 48, 72-73; central figure in Numazu group, 73; connection to Kofu group, 77; role in Numazu compared to that of Nakamura in Dōjinsha group, 74-75
Ebina Danjō, 10, 100, 162
Eby, Charles S., 31, 48, 63-64, 66-67, 71, 76, 80, 87-93, 95-102, 113, 116; advocates central Apologetical Institute of Christian Philosophy, 93, 99; and *Chrysanthemum*, 89; and Sutherland, 64-65, 76; background, 76; barely controllable enthusiasms, 88; building a Central Hall, 99; calls for a national Christian university for Japan, 93; debts, 76; dissolves Self-Support Band, 95; Evangelistic Superintendent, 96, 99; evangelistic zeal compared to George Leslie Mackay, 82-83, 86; letter in *Christian Guardian*, 96; picture, xxii; proposes formation of Self-Support Band, 94, 100, 102; public lectures, 91
Eby, Mrs., teaching English in Kofu, 77
Edinburgh Conference (1910), Continuation Committee and three-year evangelical campaign, 12, 155
Education Ministry (Mombushō), 63, 136; instruction (1899), 128-29
Eliot, Sir Charles, 107, 112, 188
Elliot, Rev. I., 59
Emmanuel College, 218
Emperor cult, 150

Endicott, James (Jr.), xv, 26
Endicott, James (Sr.), 26, 130-32, 155, 184; visit to Japan (1918), 154
English Church Mission (Korea), 112
English Presbyterian Mission in Taiwan, 31, 34, 22, 84, 101, 141, 143-44, 174-75, 208, 211
Epworth League, 27
Evangelical Alliance, 53, 106, 155
Ewing, J. A., 91
External Affairs, Department of, 108, 201, 206
Extraterritoriality, 129; missionary views of, 91; termination of, 6

Fairbank, John King, xvii; academic school, xviii
Faulds, Henry, 40, 90-91
Federation of Christian Missions, 156
Fenellosa, Ernest P., 88-89
Fenwick, Malcolm C., 32, 105; and Korean Itinerant Mission, 32
Ferguson, Duncan, 208
First World War, 143, 161, 163, 176, 179, 181, 184, 190; accelerated decline of missionary movement, 87; impact on missionary salaries, 110
Flavelle, Joseph, 25
Foote, William Rufus, 33, 167, 170, 199, 218; and Colonel Mizumachi, 200-203; picture, xxviii
Foreign Missions Committee, in London, 175
Foreign Missions committees, organization and function, 23-24
Forman, J. N., 96
Fraser, E. J. O., 208
Fraser, Mary, 107
Fraser, J. B., 81
Fukoku-Kyōhei, 36
Fukuzawa, Yukichi, 40, 54, 56, 59, 88, 90, 92; attack on missionaries, 90; Hiraiwa's opinion of, 90
Fulton, Andrew, xv

Gakumonjo, 39, 41, 42, 43, 51-52; and E. W. Clark, 42; and Nakamura, 42; curriculum, 42

INDEX267

Gale, James Scarth, 111-13, 167; background, 32; tribute to W. J. McKenzie, 33
Gauld, William, 82, 209
Gauntlett, William, 110
"Gendai Nippon Kyōkai Shiron," 84
"German Machine," 189
Gifu, 148, 163; Kunmoin Blind School in, 135; Principal Kosakai and boys, picture, xxvii
Goforth, Johnathan, xiv
Gokyō, 99
Government Higher Normal School, 61
Great Britain (England), 53, 87, 129, 219
Great Korea People's Congress, 197
Grierson, Dr. Robert, 19, 33, 167, 186-87, 191, 202
Griffis, W. E., xiv, xix, 38, 46, 48, 53-55, 88
Griffis, Margaret Clark, 55
Guizot, Francis, 77
Gulick, Sidney L., 202
Gushue-Taylor, Dr. G., 143
Gutzlaff, Charles, 33

Haeckel, *Wonders of the Universe*, 60
Hall, Dr. William James, xiv, 32
Hamamatsu, 95, 148
Hamheung, 104
Hamilton, Bishop H. J., 19, 22, 153; picture, xxv, xxvii
Hamilton, Mrs. H. J., picture, xxv
Hamilton Public Girls' School, 30
Hara, Kei, 185, 193, 197
Harbin, 187, 197
Hardie, Dr. Robert, 32
Harding, President, 203
Hargrave, I., picture, xxi
Harkness, Robert, 32
Harmsworth, Cecil, 193
Harris, Bishop M. C., and Uchimura Kanzo, 8
Hart, L. and N., picture, xxi
Hartford Theological Seminary, 11
Harvard University, xvii
Hasegawa, Field Marshal, 196
Hatakeyama, Yoshinari, 55
Heaslett, Samuel, 112
Henty, Audrey M., 149

High Treason Incident (1911), 184
Higher Commercial School (Nagoya), 114
Hiraiwa, Chikayoshi, 60
Hiraiwa, Kumei, 60
Hiraiwa, Yoshiyasu, 49, 88, 100, 103, 121, 127, 152, 162, 220; and E. W. Clark, 60-61; and Nakamura, 61-63; and Shizuoka Church, 49; and Ushigome Church, 67; and Yamaji Aizen, 49; at Kaisei Gakkō, 60-61, 65; background, 60; connection with Kondō Kisoku, 77; on scientific scepticism, 89; on Ueno Park meetings, 93; opinion of Fukuzawa Yukichi, 90; picture, xxi; visit with Eby to Nambu, 77
History of the Korean People, 112
History of the United States, 77
Hitomi, Fujitarō, 42
Hoiryung, 137, 187, 191
Holmes, C. P., 148-49, 153; "Message for Japan Today," 149
Holtom, D. C., 154
Hongo Church, 10, 100, 162
Hoonchoon, 169-70
Horvath, General D. L., 197
Hosoi, Seishō, 59, 63
Howes, John, xix
Hunchun, district, 205; Incidents, 197-99
Hunter, Jane, xviii
Huxley, 60
hyganban, 167
Hyatt, Irwin T., xviii

Iglehart, Charles W., xvi
Imai, John (Toshimichi), 150-51
Imperial Rescript on Education, 123
Ingersoll, Robert, "The Christian Religion," 89
Inoue, Kaoru, 62, 92
International Christian University (Tokyo), 93
Itō, Hirobumi, 92, 179, 187
Itō, Yuri, 60
Iwakura Embassy, 28, 53

Jack, Milton, 142
Jaisohn, Philip, 203, 206

"Jamieson Affair," 81
Jamieson, John, 81
Jamieson, Mrs., 81
Janes, Leroy, xix
Japan, 169, 177-79, 182, 215; aggression in metropolitan China, 219; Ambassador of in London, 195, 204; anti-Christian mood in, 87; appetite for further conquests in Manchura, 205-206; Army, 199-201, 207, 217; atrocities against Koreans by, 187; breaking down traditional barriers to Christianity, 179; colonialism, 16, 206; Consul-General of, in New York, 202; in Ottawa, 198-99; cultural imperialism of in Korea, 179; cultural values of and education in Korea, 138; divine story and imperial line, 150; doomed without Christianity, 151; education in, 136, 145; material progress of, 149; mobilization of national spirit and Christian movement, 220; modernization of, xix, 3-6; nationalism, 148-51; need for teachers in Government Colleges, 96; new religions, 154; parliamentary democracy in, 183-84, 218-19; perceptions of Westerners, 146; theories of civilization in, 87
Japan Advertiser, 113
Japan Chronicle, 113, 198
Japan Evangelist, 113
Japan Federation of Christian Churches, 156
Japan Methodist Church, xv-xvi, 6, 20-21, 60-61, 63, 72, 99, 107, 130, 152, 155, 157, 161-62; damage to property in Kantō Earthquake, 165; growth, 165
Japan Farmer's Union, 11
Japan Mission Yearbook, 113
Japan Socialist Party, 11
Japan Times, 113
Japan Weekly Mail, 91-92
Japanese Christian leadership, 9, 116, 221; in charge of Korea

Church, 220; response to challenge of scientific scepticism, 89
Japanese Christian movement, 9; government pressure on to rid itself of Western missionaries, 219
Japanese Christian missionary movement in Korea, 158
Japanese Commission to the Centennial Exhibition in Philadelphia, 62
Japanese National Council of Churches, 219
Japanese Protestantism, nature of, 84-86
Jerusalem World Missionary Conference (1928), 161
Joint Committee of Christian Education, 139
Jones, Hazel, xix
Junior, K. F., 81

Kagawa, Toyohiko, 11-12
Kaibara Ekken, 118
Kainei (Hoiryung)-Kirin Railway, 218
Kaisei Gakkō, 39, 46, 52, 54-55, 58, 60-61, 65, 67, 77; Christian influence at, 55, 60-61, 64-65; Darwinian ideas at, 88
Kamakura, 108
Kanamori, Paul (Kanamori Michitomo), 147-48
Kanda Naibū, 61, 89
Kantō (Chientao), see Chientao
Kantō Earthquake (1923), 100, 108, 165
Kaptsulan Plain, Taiwan, 173
Karuizawa, 108-109
Katsu, Kaishū, 44, 56
Katayama, Sen, 11
Katayama, Tetsu, 11
Kawamura, Isami, 60
Kawasaki, 159
Keiō Gijuku, 40, 54, 56, 68, 88-89, 133
Kelly, Herbert, and Uchimura Kanzō, 8; criticism of foreign community in Japan, 111
Keenleyside, H. L., 217
Kimura, 156

King, W. L. Mackenzie, 107, 182
Kirkwood, K. P., 216
Knight, Bishop of London, 161
Kobayashi, Mitsuyasu, 77, 126
Kobayashi, Yashichi, 164, 166
Kobe, 106, 113, 130, 133, 135, 178; *Chronicle*, 207
Kofu, 95, 122-24, 145; decision to open mission work at, 77; picture of Old Japan Methodist Church at, xxvi
Koishikawa Band, 35-36, 40, 50-52, 60, 62-63, 65, 69-71, 221; and central role of Nakamura in its formation, 69; and Shizuoka Band members compared to early converts in Taiwan, 81; as a family affair, 69; opposition to conversion compared to Kumamoto and Shizuoka Bands, 69
Kojima, General, 193
Kokusiu Hozon Shugi, 127
Komiyama, Seiso, 77
Kondō Kisoku, 76-77
Kondō Makatō, 54
Korea, 70, 105, 109-12, 115, 136, 153, 155, 158, 166, 168, 175, 177-79, 186, 190, 214-15; annexation by Japan, 14, 137, 169, 187; attitude of missionaries in, towards Japanese government, 188; Christian movement identified with Korean nationalism, 169, 173, 218; culture of and Christian movement, 138; education in, 137, 145; initial reaction of Canadian missionaries to Japanese colonial rule, 179; Japanese colonial rule in, 14-15; Japanese Residency-General in, 186-87; lack of religious opposition to Christianity in, 166; language problem in, 103-104; mission schools in, 136-38; missionary optimism about future of Christianity in, 148; perceptions of Westerners in, 146; Provisional Government of, 196; Shamanism in, 166

Korean Communists, 208
Korean Christians, and mission schools, 116; converts, 84; missionaries and the protection of, 202
Korean Independence Movement, 189, 203, 213; partisans, 207, 218
Korean Presbyterian Church, xvi, 13, 168
Korean Repository, 112
Korean Revolution, 221; revolutionaries, 199
"Kosai," 185
Koshusha, 54
Kōtoku, Shūsui, xix, 10
Kozaki, Hiromichi, 8, 89, 91
Kozū Sensaburō, 59, 62, 90
Kumamoto Band, xix, 65, 85-86, 92; opposition to conversion compared to Koishikawa and Shizuoka Bands, 69
Kunmoin, 135
Kuranaga, Takashi, xvi
Kwansei Gakuin, 103, 106, 130-34, 139, 145, 162, 217
Kyoto, 65, 117
Kyūshū Imperial University, 10

Lampson, Miles, 198, 204
Langdon, Frank, 158
Lansing-Ishii Agreements, 181
Large, T. A., 30, 107, 126
Large, Mrs. T. A., and Kate, picture, xxi
Latourette, K. S., xvii
Lay, Arthur Hyde, 107
Laymen's Commission on Christian Missions (1931), 12
Lea, Arthur, 148-50, 152, 154; and penal rehabilitation in Gifu, 163
Leacock, Stephen, 3, 216
League of Nations, Covenant of, 85
Lepers, work among, 163
Liberation Theology, 83
Livingstone, David, xiv, 32, 83
London *Times*, 114, 200
Loomis, Henry, 39
Lungchingtsun, 191, 192, 199-200,

205-206, 212, 218; picture,
        xxviii
Lutz, Jesse G., xviii, 6

Macdonald, Caroline, xiv, 12, 111;
        and rehabilitation of prisoners,
        12, 163
Macdonald, Sir Claude, 107
MacDonald, D. A., 137, 187
Macdonald, Sir John A., 216
Mackay, George Leslie, xiv-xv, 16, 31,
        33, 35, 71-72, 80-83, 141, 173,
        176, 209; and headhunters, 82;
        background, 34; dental work,
        81; evangelistic drive compared
        to Eby, 82-83, 101; picture, xxiv
Mackay, G. W., 141-42, 176, 210-11
MacKay, R. P., 25-26, 139, 142, 176,
        189, 191, 212
Mackay Memorial Hostpial, 143-44
MacLeod, Duncan, 143, 175, 211-12
Maclay, 57
McPhail, Sir Andrew, 3, 216
Makino, Ekichiro, 57
Manchuria, 161, 169, 180, 187, 192,
        197, 202, 207, 214; Crisis of
        1931, 1
March 1, 1919 Movement (Korea),
        27, 142, 189, 212
Marco Polo Bridge Incident, 217, 219
Martin, Dr. S. H., 191, 193, 206-207;
        and Japanese atrocities in
        Chientao, 200; picture, xxviii
Martin, Mrs. S. H., picture, xxviii
Martin, W. A. P., 53, 55
Massey family, 28
Matsudaira family, 67
Matsui, Ginko, 61
Matsumoto, 95
Matsuzawa, Hiroaki, 4
Marxism, and Christianity, 9-10
Maxwell, Dr. J. L., 144
May 4, 1919 demonstrations, 190
McClure, Robert, xv
McDonald, Davidson, xiv-xv, 3,
        34-36, 38-40, 41-42, 46-47,
        50-51, 58, 71-72, 75, 81, 83,
        87-88, 90, 96, 98, 103-104,
        106-107, 109, 221; and Ebara
        Soroku, 48; and Self-Support

Band, 95; and Shizuhatasha,
        42-45, 50; background, 29-30;
        in Tsukiji, 40, 49; Japanese lan-
        guage ability, 58; medical work
        in Shizuoka, 47-48, 50-51; on
        pay of Japanese evangelists, 64;
        opinion of Buddhism, 46-47,
        148; opinion of Shintō, 46;
        withdrawal from Shizuoka,
        48-49
McDonald, Mrs. Davidson, teaching
        in Shizuoka, 43
McKenzie, A. P., 103
McKenzie, F. A., 203
McKenzie, D. R., 95, 96, 108, 130-31,
        134, 155-56, 184
McKenzie, William J., xiv; back-
        ground, 33; Gale's tribute to,
        33; impact of death upon Mar-
        itime Division of the Canadian
        Presbyterian Church, 33; pic-
        ture, xxii
McRae, Duncan M., 33, 167, 202; pic-
        ture, xxviii
Meacham, George, 71-76, 86, 98, 104,
        106, 127; background, 74; view
        of Ebara, 75
Meighen, Arthur, 204
Meiji Constitution, 95
Meiji Emperor, 183
Meiji Government, 73, 92, 117; and
        centralization of Western
        studies in Tokyo, 42; and clo-
        sure of Gakumonjo and
        Numazu Military Academy, 42;
        attitude toward Western civili-
        zation, 36, 37; Charter Oath,
        83; Justice Department; policy
        of Westernization, 36; political
        leadership, 179
Meiji modernization, 36
Meiji oligarchy, 4
Meiji period, attitudes toward women
        in, 123; female education in,
        117
Meiji Restoration, 39, 41, 60, 84
Meiroku Zasshi, 69
Meirokusha, 36
Menzies, Arthur, 108, 135
Methodist Church of Canada, see
        Canadian Methodist Church

Methodist Episcopal Church of Canada, 19, 21

Methodist Episcopal (North) Mission in Japan, xv, 8, 20-21, 57, 67, 99, 130

Methodist Episcopal (South) Mission in Japan, xv, 20-21, 99, 130, 132, 135, 157

Methodist Episcopal (North) Mission in Korea, xiv, 33, 117

Metropolitan Church (Toronto), 29

"Mikadoism," 150, 154

Mill, J. S., 36, 68, 77; *On Liberty*, 38, 53-54

Minagaki, 57

Misener, Ethel, 134

Mission schools, 5-6, 116, 119, 125, 128-29, 144

Missionary Societies, 27

Missionary Society of the Church of England in Canada (MSCC), 31

Missions Secretary, organizational function, 24-25

Mita, Tokyo, 40

Mitsukuri, Rinshō, 61

Miyagawa, Minoru, picture, xxi

Mizumachi, Colonel, 200-201, 213; charges against missionaries, 205; letter, 206

Moken Juku, 77

Mombushō (Education Ministry), 128-29, 136

Montgomery, Bishop H. H., opinion of Christian movement in Japan, 153-54

Moody, Campbell, 82, 101, 174

Moon, Chairin, 218

Morgan, K., 121; picture, xxi

Mori Arinori, 59

Morse, Edward S., and introduction of Darwinian ideas in Japan, 88

Motoda, J. S., 8

Mott, John R., 8, 155-56, 189

Moulton, Martha, 74

Mount Hanoaka Oath, 85-86

Mount Hermon Conference, 96

Mount Potai, 198

Mukden, 161, 191; Incident, 217

Muller, Max, 195

Muno-Hide Earthquake (1891), 135

Nagano, 22, 29, 106, 154, 159; Prefecture, 105, 108

Nagasaki, Western studies in, 77

Nagoya, 29, 31, 114, 163

Nakamura, Keiū (Masanao), 4, 34, 40, 42, 48, 50-53, 68-71, 74-76, 81, 86; and Christianity as an extension of Confucianism, 38; and Christianity as religion of civilization, 43; and Cochran, 4, 40, 42, 48, 50-58; and E. W. Clark, 42-43, 51-52; and Hiraiwa, 61-62, 67; and name of Japan Methodist Church, 63; and Tokyo Normal School for Girls, 117; and Ushigome Church, 67; baptism, in England, 53; by Cochran, 58-59, 61; reception of news in Canada, 61; central role in formation of Koishikawa Band, 69; Christianity and Western civilization, 51; Christianity and Confucianism, 52; drifts away from Canadian influence to Unitarianism, 90; influence on students at Dojinsha, 52; Methodist Class leader, 62

Nakamura Tetsu, 59

Nambu, 71, 76-77

National Christian Council, 9

Neill, Stephen, xvii

netsuke, 112

Nevius Method, 148, 166, 204

New Brunswick, Presbyterians and Wesleyan Methodists in, 18

New Connexion Methodist church, 19

New England Puritanism, xvi

Newfoundland, 19, 143

Newton, J. C. C., 130

New York, 190, 203; *Times*, 190

Nihon Kiriisutokyōdan (Japan United Church), xvi, 219-20

Nihon Seikōkai (Japan Holy Catholic Church), xv-xvi, 6-7, 29; dissociation from Church of England after 1937, 219

Niigata Prefecture, 106, 160

Niijima Jō, 65

Nikolaevsk Incident (May 1920), 198
Ninomiya Sontoku, 112
Nishi Amane, 41
Nihinomiya, 103, 130
Nitobe, Inazō, 125, 150-51
Nogi, General, 208
Nojiri, Lake, 108-109
Nomura, Michiko, 119
Norman, Dan, xv, 104-106, 108, 134, 154, 159, 161; interest in rural work, 161
Norman family: E. Herbert, 105, 108, 135, 217; Grace, 105; Gwen R. P., xx; Howard, xx, 104-105; Lucy, 134
North American Review, 89
North Hamkyung Province, 169
Notehelfer, F. G., xix
Nova Scotia, 33, 110; missionaries from, 3; Presbyterians and Wesleyan Methodists in, 18; Presbyterian pioneers in northern Korea, 216-17
Numazu, 42, 44, 71-76, 104; and Tokugawa education effort after 1868 in Shizuoka Prefecture, 71; church in, 76; educational activity in, 71
Numazu Chūgakkō, 73
Numazu Group, 72; connection with mission work in Yamanashi Prefecture, 73; connection with Shizuoka Band, 75
Numazu Heigakkō Fuzoku Shōgakkō, 72; and Ebara Soroku, 72; Asagawa Hiromi at, 60
Numazu Military Academy (Numazu Heigakkō), 41-42, 73

Odlum, E., 95
Ōhama Tetsuya, 86
Oishi, Seinisuke, 9-10, 184
Ōkubo, Ichio, 56
Ōkuma, Shigenobu, 154, 158
Omori, Shunji (Shunko), 77
Onna Daigaku, 118
Ontario, 73, 104; Agricultural College, 140; Education Department of, 134; missionaries from, xiv, 2, 7, 18; Presby-
terians and Wesleyan Methodists in, 18; school primers, 42, 50; Temperance and Prohibitionary League, 25
Ōta, Kijiro, 61, 67
Ōta, Yuzō, xix
Outerbridge, H. W., 217
Oxford College, Tamsui, 82, 141
Ozaki, Yukio, 68

Pacific War, 13, 53, 93, 217, 219
Paik, George, 189
Palethorpe, Emma, 199
Pan-Anglican Conference at Lambeth (1907), 8
Paris Peace Conference, 189
Parkes, Sir Harry, 91, 107
Pearson, Lester, 108
Peterson, Louise, 31
Peking, Treaty of, 34
Poole School (Osaka), 31
Powles, Cyril H., xx, 217
Powles, P. S. C., 106; picture, xxvii
Presbyterian Church in Canada, *see* Canadian Presbyterian Church
Presbyterian Church (North), *see* American Presbyterian Mission (North) in Korea
Presbyterian Church (South), *see* American Presbyterian Mission (South) in Korea
Presbyterian Synod of Formosa, 175
Price, Thomas, xvii
Prince Edward County, Ontario, xv, 29
Princeton, 96; Theological Seminary, 34
private schools, 125, 130
P'yongyang, 137, 140; as a Christian stronghold, 13; Great Revival in, 167; Presbyterian theological seminary in, 137; Union Christian College in, 140

Quebec, 73; Presbyterians and Wesleyan Methodists in, 18
Queen's University, 95

Rabe, Valentin H., xviii
Red Cross, 9
Reformed Church in America, 157

Reed, James, xviii
Reischauer, E. O., 118
representative government, 77
republicanism, 126
Rhee, Syngman, 196, 203
Riddell, Hannah, 163
Righteous Armies, 187, 207
Rikugō Zasshi, 89, 113
Robinson, John Cooper, 29, 31, 150
Rokumeikan, 118
Roman Catholics, 46, 111; French-Canadian missionaries, 1
Ross, A. R., 191
Rowell, N. W., 25, 189
Royal Asiatic Society, Korea Branch, 111
Royal Hospital, 32
Royal Navy, 167
Royds, W. M., 191
Russo-Japanese War (1904-05), 113, 150, 1677, 172, 179, 184; Japanese Christian opposition to, 9
Rutgers College, 42, 55
Ryerson, Egerton, 112

Saigō, Tsugumichi, his wife and daughter at Nakamura's baptism, 59
St. Andrew's Church, Shiba, 68
St. John's Church, Nagoya, picture, xxvi
St. Mary's Church, Matsumoto, 31
Sakhalin, 161
Saitō, Makoto, 118
Salvation Army, 219
Sapporo Agricultural College, 37-38
Sapporo Band, 85-86
Satō, Major-General, 200-201
Satoh, Henry (Satō Shigemichi), 44-45, 75, 127
Satsuma, 33; Rebellions of 1877, 75
Saunby, J. W., 95, 126, 181-82
"Sayonara," 183-84
Scheiner, Irwin, xix, 3-4, 38, 84
Schofield, Frank, 140, 193-96, 207, 212; picture, xxviii
Schofield, John, 194
Schwantes, Robert S., xviii
Scott, Elspeth Keith Robertson, 112

Scott, William, xx, 187, 192-93, 199, 218
Scottish Presbyterian Mission in Japan, 40, 91
Sekiguchi, Ryūkichi, 121
Self-Support Band, 31, 126; and Eby, 94; and McDonald, 95; and Sutherland, 94
Seoul, 32-33, 107, 111, 138, 140, 191
Severance, Loomis H., 139
Severance Hospital (Severance Union Medical College), 32, 139-40, 193
Shakai Minshutō, 11
Shanghai, 196-97
Shaw, A. C., 7, 54, 56, 68, 112; and Karuizawa, 108; chaplain to the British Legation, 107; conversion of Keiō Gijuku students, 68; experience at Keiō Gijuku compared to Cochran's at Dojinsha, 68; death, 107; teaching at Keiō Gijuku, 40
Shaw, Loretta, 31, 151, 159, 185-86
Shaw, R. D. M., 103, 112
Shepperson, George, xvii
Shibusawa, Eiichi, 158
Shihan Gakkō, 72-73; description of, 73; and Ebara Soroku, 72-73; burnt down, 75
Shimada, 47
Shimazu, S., 199
Shimonoseki, Treaty of, 140
Shin Nihon No Seinen, 140
Shinkai, Eitarō, 77
Shintō, 9, 46-47, 148, 150, 154, 157, 166
Shirakami, 202
Shitaya Church, and Meacham, 75
Shizuhatasha (Shizuhatanoya), 42-45, 72
Shizuoka, xv, 3, 38, 42, 45, 50-51, 56, 70-71, 95, 109, 122-23, 145, 159, 221; and ex-Tokugawa samurai resident in, 41; authorities in, 39, 42; Buddhist and Shintō opposition to Christianity in, 46-47; Castle, 42; Cochran visit to, 39; decision to establish Canadian Methodist

girls' school in, 121; medical work in, 47

Shizuoka Band, 36, 40, 49, 127; and Koishikawa Band members compared to early converts in Taiwan, 81; connection to Numazu group, 75; opposition to conversion compared to Koishikawa and Kumamoto Bands, 69

Shizuoka Church, 43, 49, 85; and English-langauge teaching at, 49; and Hiraiwa, 49; and self-support, 97

Shizuoka Eiwa Jo Gakkō, 122, 124-25; size compared to Tōyō Eiwa Jo Gakkō and Yamanashi Eiwa, 122-23

Shizuoka Prefecture, 4, 41, 75; impact of Western ideas and Christianity on, 71; *Sabakuha* in, 71

Shorai No Nihon, 92

Siberia, 167, 197

Silaian Incident (1915), 209-11

Sino-Japanese War (1894-1895), 128

Slessor, Mary, xiv

Smiles, Samuel, *Self-Help*, 53

Smith, J., first WA missionary in Japan, 31

Social Gospel, 147

Society for the Propagation of the Gospel in Foreign Parts (SPG), 40, 68, 153-54

soja, 167

sonnō aikoku, 128

Soper, Dr. Julian, 67

Sorai, 33

Spencer, Herbert, ideas, 68, 92

Spencer, Eliza, *see* Mrs. T. A. Large, 118

State Normal School, Albany, New York, 62

Sugiyama, Magaroku, 43-44, 56, 86

Sugiyama, Motojiro, 11

Sumiya, Mikio, 10, 85

Sungjin, 187; Japanese response to independence demonstration in, 191

Sutherland, Alexander, 26, 64-66, 76, 87; and Albert Carman, 25; and

formation of WMS-CM, 29-30; and Self-Support Band, 94-98; background, 25; doubts about Eby's Central Hall proposal, 99-100; leadership challenged by N. W. Rowell and Joseph Flavelle, 25; opposition to union of Canadian Methodist mission with Methodist Episcopal missions, 20-21; suspicion of Eby, 76, 88

Sutherland, D. G., 74

Suzuki, Bunji, 10-11, 162

Syles, E. W., 55

Taiping Rebellion, 83

Tainan, 82, 143; missionaries and surrender of (1895), 208

Taipeh, 143, 175, 209

Taiwan, xiv, 1-2, 15, 70, 83, 109-11, 140, 144, 148, 155, 166, 169, 172-73, 179, 215; aborigines in, 173, 209; ancestral tablets in, 174; climate, 82; Confucianism in, 174; education in, 142, 145; Government-General of, 140-43, 175, 210-11; Governor-General of, 208; intellectual rejection of Christianity in, 71; Japanese colonialism in, 15, 212; compared to colonialism in Korea, 15, 209; Japanese policy of assimilation, 212; language problem, 104; Manchu rule in, 174, 208; modernization and missionary response, 16, 140-41; perceptions of Westerners, 140; proposed parliament in, 212

Takahashi, Motoguchi, 189

Takashima Taneko, 119

Takata, 106, 160

Tamsui, 34, 82, 141-43, 175; Middle School, 145

Tanaka, Giichi, 198

Tanno, Naonobu, 59

Taylor, J. Hudson, xiv, 94

Temperance Movement, 25

Tench, G. R., 134

Tendōkyoists, 193

Tendō Sakugen, 55
Tennō-Sei (the Emperor system), 9
Terada, Kisaku, 77
Terauchi, Masatake, 136, 187
The Cloud Dream of the Nine, 112
Thomas, Winburn T., xvi
Three Religions Conference (1913), 9, 157
Tientsin, Treaty of, 34
Tientsin *Times*, 207
Tōjō, Sezō, 59
Tokugawa, advisers, 56; Army, 72; *bakufu*, 60; ex-Tokugawa samurai, 73; family, 56; government, 53; Shogun, 4, 39, 41, 47, 72, 84
Tokugawa Ieyasu, 60
Tokugawa Yoshinobu, 41
Tokutomi Sohō, 92
Tokyo, 3, 39, 45, 57, 73, 108, 113, 123,145, 155, 178; concentration of Canadian Methodist missionaries in, 87; government, 218; student population in, 161
Tokyo Imperial University, 10, 63, 88-89, 91, 93, 99-100, 161-62
Tokyo and Yokohama Missionary Conference (1884), 93
Tokyo Normal School for Girls, 117
Tokyo *Seinenkai* (YMCA), 89
Tokyo Woman's Christian College, 121, 124, 139, 157
Toronto, 110, 155, 215; Higher Middle School, 30
Toronto *Globe*, 198-99
Toyama, 95, 149
Toyama, Kohei, 98
Tōyō Eiwa Gakkō, 73, 75, 107, 126, 145; course of study, 127
Tōyō Eiwa Gakkō Kaisha, theological department, 126
Tōyō Eiwa Jo Gakkō, 30, 117-21, 124, 128-29; nature of school life in 1910s, 119-20; picture, xxiii
Treaty Powers, 37
treaty revision, 87, 129
Trent, Miss E. M., 30
Triple Intervention, 92-93
Trollope, Bishop Mark Napier, 112, 153, 195-96

Tsuchiya, Hikoroku, 43, 63-64, 74-75, 220; picture, xxi
Tsuda Juku Daigaku, 117
Tsuda, Sen, 117
Tsuda, Ume, 117
Tsukada, K., picture, xxvii
Tsukiji, 39-40, 57; Canadian Methodist decision to buy property there, 65-67
Tsukuki, Seiichi, 43-45
Tumen River, 13, 173, 198

Uchimura, Kanzō, xix; and Herbert Kelly, 8; and M. C. Harris, 8
Uemura, Masahisa, 9, 91, 100, 148
Ueno Park Meetings, 88, 93; Hiraiwa on, 93
Underwood family, and Chōsen Christian College, 139
Unequal Treaties, 118
Unitarianism, 90
United Church of Canada, xv, xx, 2, 18, 20, 23, 26, 175; archives, xx; formation of, 20; Japan Mission of, xx; missionary society of, 20
United Lutheran Church of the U.S.A., 135
United Presbyterian Church of Scotland, *see* Scottish Presbyterians
United States, 53, 89, 118, 153, 156, 182-83; and relations with Japan, xviii-xix; in Asia, xvii
University of Toronto, 13, 31, 106, 112, 134; and Korean missions, 31-32; Medical Students YMCA, 32; Trinity College, 19, 22, 29, 31; Victoria College, 22, 73, 106, 108, 110, 134; Wycliffe College, 19, 22, 29, 31; YMCAS, 31
Urakami crypto-Christians, 38
Ushigome Church, 65, 67

Veazey, Miss M. E., 152
Veeder, E. P., 56
Verbeck, Guido, xvi
Versailles Peace Conference, and racial equality question, 183
Vietnam War, xvii
Vladivostock, 105, 197

Wada, Masaka, 65
Wakatsuki, Reijirō, 212
Waller, John G., xv, 22, 29, 31, 105, 160, 185
Waller, Gordon, 105
Waller, Wilfred, 105
Walker, H. E., 149
Walsh, H. H., 19
Walton, W. H. Murray, 161
Warren, Canon Max, xvii
Waseda University, 133
Watase, Injirō, 73
Webster, Senator Lorne, 134
Wesleyan Methodist Church, 28-29, 63, 73
Wesleyan Methodists of Eastern British America, Conference of, 19
Western children, 133-34
Western missionaries, and criticism of Japanese actions in Korea (1919), 158
"White Angel of Tokyo," (Caroline Macdonald), 163
White, Bishop of Honan, xv
Whittington, Robert, 126
Wilder, R. P., 96
Wilkinson, A. T., 159; and Japanese immigration to Canada, 182
Wilson, President Woodrow, and Wilsonianism, 179
Wintermute, Agnes (Mrs. H. H. Coates), 122
Women's Christian Temperance Union (WCTU), 9
Wonsan, 32-33, 105, 167; Beach, 109
Wood, Dr., 59
Woodsworth, H. F., 132-33
World Missionary Conference at Edinburgh (1910), see Edinburgh Conference

World Sunday School Association, Conference in Tokyo (1920), 8, 158
Wright, W. B., 68
Wycliffe College Missionary Society (WA), 29

Yamaji Aizan (Yakichi), 49, 85-86, 97, 99, 119, 127
Yamanaka, Emi, 43-44, 64, 98; picture, xxi
Yamanashi Eiwa Jo Gakkō, 122-24
Yamanashi Prefecture, 11, 73, 76-77, 122-23
Yamatō Damashii, 151
Yamazaki, Tamenori, 65
yangban, 167
Yasutomi, Kiyohiko, 57, 59, 60
yatoi, xix
Yates, W. E., 23
"Yellow Peril," 183
Yi Tong-Hwi, 196
Yōgakkō School (Kumamoto), xix
Yokohama, 29, 38-39, 57, 73, 108, 178
Yokahama Band, 55, 84-86
Yokoi, Shōnan, 65
Yokoi, Tokio, 65, 85
Yonsei University, 139
Yoshino, Sakuzō, 162; conception of democracy and Christianity, 10
Young, Miss, MSCC missionary in Nagoya, 31
Young, A. Morgan, 113
Young, Robert, 113
YMCA, 9, 12, 32, 94, 110, 163
Yūaikai, 10
Yūki, Bunisan, 73, 77; picture, xxi
YWCA, 9, 119

CPSIA information can be obtained at www.ICGtesting.com
Printed in the USA
BVOW11s0359280514

354624BV00011B/247/P